"Peterson offers readers a marvelous survey of the union-with-Christ theme by exploring the concept in every major portion of Scripture. Having carefully placed this important theological subject within the overall biblical story, Peterson helps readers understand the rich meaning and wide-ranging implications of this important theme for the church and the Christian life. It is a privilege to commend this carefully organized and well-written volume. Joyful, uplifting, and doxological."

David S. Dockery, President, Trinity International University

"This book is a wonderful gift to God's people as it recovers the significant biblical doctrine of union with Christ. To be saved *is* to be united with Christ, and Peterson's treatment of this truth is exegetically and systematically exemplary."

Bruce Riley Ashford, Provost and Associate Professor of Theology and Culture, Southeastern Baptist Theological Seminary

"This is a welcome addition to recent literature on the theme of union with Christ. Peterson pursues the theme through the whole of Scripture, reflects on the theological connections and implications of our union with Christ, and draws pastoral applications for the sake of the church. The result is an accessible, penetrating, and full-orbed contribution that will be of theological and spiritual benefit to all its readers."

Constantine R. Campbell, Associate Professor of New Testament, Trinity Evangelical Divinity School

"From the surprising Old Testament foundation of *Salvation Applied by the Spirit*, to the powerful concluding application to our lives today, Robert Peterson applies a lifetime of mature and loving scholarship to the 'simultaneously wonderful and bewildering' realities of our union with Christ by the work of the Spirit."

Bryan Chapell, President Emeritus, Covenant Theological Seminary; Senior Pastor, Grace Presbyterian Church, Peoria, Illinois

"Peterson presents the work of the Spirit in uniting us to Christ—first by exegeting central Bible passages on our union with Christ, and second by relating this teaching to other biblical doctrines, such as the nature of the Spirit himself, the church, the sacraments, and the Christian life. Understanding our union with Christ is a major need of Christians today. Peterson's account is accurate and profound. It can be a great blessing to our minds, hearts, and lives."

John M. Frame, J. D. Trimble Chair of Systematic Theology and Philosophy, Reformed Theological Seminary, Orlando

"Peterson does an excellent job explaining union with Christ biblically, theologically, and practically. His treatment of union with Christ in the whole biblical story is especially helpful. I recommend this volume to theologians, pastors, and serious lay persons wanting a clear and challenging treatment of life in Christ."

Paul R. House, Professor of Divinity, Beeson Divinity School; author, *Old Testament Theology*

"This is a thorough, comprehensive discussion of the biblical teaching on the work of the Holy Spirit in effecting union with Christ, together with an exploration of the theological issues connected with these immense matters. Teachers of theology, ministers, students, and many others will consult Peterson's impressive work repeatedly. He has made a significant contribution to the church."

Robert Letham, Director of Research and Senior Lecturer in Systematic and Historical Theology, Wales Evangelical School of Theology; author, *The Holy Trinity* and *Union with Christ*

"In this valuable contribution to the growing body of literature on the theme of union with Christ, Robert Peterson skillfully navigates the relevant biblical materials. His focus on the work of the Holy Spirit is illuminating and salutary."

William B. Evans, Eunice Witherspoon Bell Younts and Willie Camp Younts Professor of Bible and Religion, Erskine College; author, *What Is the Incarnation?*

"Robert Peterson's panoramic biblical theology of union with Christ is a gift to Christ's bride. It rightfully and worshipfully locates the heart of salvation in the church's union with her Savior, calling us to joyful recognition and appreciation of the astounding reality that we are really and truly joined to Jesus Christ by the Holy Spirit. Skillfully surveying the Scriptures, Peterson demonstrates what is most basic to a faithful historic, Protestant understanding of the gospel: union with the Savior who is the living reality of the good news."

Marcus Peter Johnson, Assistant Professor of Theology, Moody Bible Institute; author, *One with Christ*

"Warmly written, carefully conceived, and pastorally applied, *Salvation Applied by the Spirit* ably unpacks how what Jesus has done for us is applied to us through our union with Christ. It is an outstanding contribution to a magnificent theme, even the most thorough exegetical and theological treatment on union with Christ to date."

Christopher W. Morgan, Dean and Professor of Theology, California Baptist University

SALVATION

APPLIED BY THE

SPIRIT

Other Crossway Books by Robert A. Peterson

The Deity of Christ (coeditor)
Fallen: A Theology of Sin (coeditor)
The Glory of God (coeditor)
Heaven (coeditor)
The Kingdom of God (coeditor)
Salvation Accomplished by the Son: The Work of Christ
Suffering and the Goodness of God (coeditor)
Why We Belong: Evangelical Unity and Denominational Diversity (coeditor)

SALVATION
APPLIED BY THE
SPIRIT

Union with Christ

ROBERT A. PETERSON

WHEATON, ILLINOIS

Salvation Applied by the Spirit: Union with Christ

Copyright © 2015 by Robert A. Peterson

Published by Crossway
        1300 Crescent Street
        Wheaton, Illinois 60187

Cover design: Smartt Guys Design
Cover image: The Bridgeman Art Library

First printing 2015

Printed in the United States of America

Hardcover ISBN: 978-1-4335-3257-3
PDF ISBN: 978-1-4335-3258-0
Mobipocket ISBN: 978-1-4335-3259-7
ePub ISBN: 978-1-4335-3260-3

Library of Congress Cataloging-in-Publication Data
Peterson, Robert A., 1948–
   Salvation applied by the Spirit : union with Christ /
Robert A. Peterson.
      pages cm
   Includes bibliographical references and index.
   ISBN 978-1-4335-3257-3 (hc)
   1. Mystical union. 2. Salvation—Biblical teaching.
3. Bible—Theology. I. Title.
BT767.7.P48   2015
234—dc23   2014009494

Crossway is a publishing ministry of Good News Publishers.

SH   26 25 24 23 22 21 20 19 18 17 16 15
15 14 13 12 11 10 9 8 7 6 5 4 3 2 1

I warmly dedicate this book to my wife, Mary Pat,
with whom I have shared the closest human analogy
to union with Christ for forty-one wonderful years.

Contents

Acknowledgments

I am grateful to those who have helped me on this project:

Mary Pat Peterson, for her love, faithful support, and prayers.

The administration of Covenant Theological Seminary, for kindly granting me a sabbatical.

My friends at Crossway, including Justin Taylor and Jill Carter, for their fellowship and considerable help.

The flock of Dave and Diane Bruegger of Twin Oaks Presbyterian Church, for their prayers.

Keith Johnson, Jim Larsen, Brad Matthews, Stephen Morefield, Jake Neufeld, and Mike Williams, for commenting on the manuscript.

Nick and Ellen Pappas, for use of their "farmhouse" in Bismarck, Missouri, where writing is easy.

Mike Honeycutt, my former colleague, for team-teaching a course with me on union with Christ.

James C. Pakala, library director, and Steve Jamieson, reference and systems librarian of the J. Oliver Buswell Library at Covenant Theological Seminary, for prompt and professional help.

Special thanks are due:

Kyle Keating, for research and substantial drafts of chapters on union in the Old Testament, Synoptic Gospels, and Acts.

Jeremy McNeill, for research help, including compiling a notebook of readings.

Christopher Morgan, for serving as theological reader and making valuable comments on the whole manuscript that led to many improvements.

Thom Notaro, for expertly shepherding the manuscript through the editorial process.

Elliott Pinegar, for skillfully and tirelessly editing the entire manuscript, and for constructing the bibliography.

Introduction

How can a person who lived nearly two thousand years ago radically change a human life here and now? How can Jesus of Nazareth *radically* affect us, as persons, to the depths of our being? How can He reach out over the great span of time that divides us from Him and change us so profoundly that we can become "new creatures" in Him?

Does the Jesus of the past become, in fact, the Jesus of the present? The Apostle Paul says that He does. And this is the difference between His influence and that of any other influential person. He touches us here and now, not merely by the ripples of the historical currents He once set in motion, but by entering into union with us personally. Union with Christ—this is the sum and substance of the Christian person's status, the definition of his relationship to Jesus, the large reality in which all the nuances of his new being are embraced.[1]

These words by Lewis Smedes are as relevant today as when he penned them in 1970. The Holy Spirit's work of uniting believers to Christ is how God applies Jesus's death and resurrection to them.

Some theological context from Ephesians 1 is in order. There Paul repeatedly directs praise to the Trinity for salvation. Specifically, he praises the Father for planning salvation before creation (vv. 4–5). This is amazing, but of course our experience of salvation comes much later. Paul also praises the Son for performing the work needed to rescue sinners in the first century—redemption through his violent death (v. 7). This too is amazing, but once again, we did not experience salvation in the first century for we were not alive then. Paul's account of the amazing saving work of God continues with

---

[1] Lewis B. Smedes, *All Things Made New: A Theology of Man's Union with Christ* (Grand Rapids: Eerdmans, 1970; repr., Eugene, OR: Wipf and Stock, 1998), 7.

the Father's sealing believers "in him," that is, Christ, with the Holy Spirit (v. 13). This is when human beings experience salvation: when they believe in Christ and are sealed with the Spirit "for the day of redemption," when Jesus will come again (4:30).

We do not experience God's amazing salvation—planned by the Father in eternity past and accomplished by Jesus in the first century—until the Holy Spirit applies that salvation to our lives. We do not know God until the Spirit breaks into our life stories. We know God's forgiveness and receive the gift of eternal life only when the Spirit touches our lives with God's grace. This application of salvation, this breaking into our life story, this bringing of forgiveness and eternal life occurs only when we are joined to Christ in faith union. This book treats the glorious truth of union with Christ.[2]

Some Good Books

Before beginning my own journey, I want to give credit where it is due. For I have been helped by others in my study. After a drought, the past six years have brought a welcome rainfall of good books on union with Christ. My sparse comments do not do justice to these books, but perhaps a few words are better than none. Previously we were served by Lewis Smedes's *All Things Made New*, quoted above, which takes a helpful redemptive-historical approach. William Evans penned *Imputation and Impartation*, a valuable historical study showing how Calvin's considerable doctrine of union with Christ was lost and how it was recovered by only some of his theological heirs.[3]

Dutch pastor Hans Burger contributed *Being in Christ: A Biblical and Systematic Investigation from a Reformed Perspective*.[4] In 632 pages he considers the views of two historical figures, John Owen and Herman Bavinck; two biblical authors, John and Paul; and two moderns, Ingolf Dalferth and Oliver O'Donovan. Robert Letham's *Union with Christ: In Scripture, History, and Theology* hits the high points of union and creation, incarnation, Pentecost, and resurrection, especially from the discipline of historical theology.[5]

J. Todd Billings offered *Union with Christ: Reframing Theology and Min-*

---

[2] There is a broad sense of union with Christ that includes election ("He chose us in him," Eph. 1:4), Christ's saving work ("In him we have redemption through his blood," v. 6), and final salvation ("to unite all things in him," v. 10). While not neglecting this broad sense, I will focus on the narrow sense encompassing the application of salvation.
[3] William B. Evans, *Imputation and Impartation: Union with Christ in American Reformed Theology*, Studies in Christian History and Thought (Eugene, OR: Wipf and Stock, 2009).
[4] Hans Burger, *Being in Christ: A Biblical and Systematic Investigation from a Reformed Perspective* (Eugene, OR: Wipf and Stock, 2009).
[5] Robert Letham, *Union with Christ: In Scripture, History, and Theology* (Phillipsburg, NJ: P&R, 2011).

istry for the Church.[6] He focused on Calvin and systematics (union in light of depravity and the incomprehensibility of God) while helpfully gearing his writing toward ministry. James D. Gifford Jr. penned *Perichoretic Salvation: The Believer's Union with Christ as a Third Type of Perichoresis*, in which he argues for three types of perichoresis (mutual indwelling): those between the Trinitarian persons, between the natures in the person of Christ, and between believers and Christ.[7]

Constantine Campbell, in his outstanding *Paul and Union with Christ: An Exegetical and Theological Study*, works well with a brief history of the study of union with Christ, Greek expressions for union, the exegesis of Pauline texts and images, and Pauline theology.[8] My greatest debt is to him. Marcus Johnson wrote *One with Christ: An Evangelical Theology of Salvation* with a salutary emphasis on union with Christ—not merely with his benefits—a solid treatment of union and the church and sacraments, and more.[9] Regretfully, I was not able to obtain in time a copy of what promises to be another important work, Grant Macaskill's *Union with Christ in the New Testament.*[10]

A Road Map

This volume is the second in what, DV, will be a three-part series. The first book was *Salvation Accomplished by the Son: The Work of Christ.*[11] That volume presents Jesus's nine saving events, centering on his death and resurrection, and six scriptural pictures that interpret those events. The projected third volume, *Salvation Planned by the Father: Election in Christ*, would treat the mysterious doctrine of predestination. This one, *Salvation Applied by the Spirit: Union with Christ*, deals with the application of salvation to believers' lives, or union with Christ.

A road map of this volume will help readers keep on course. The book has two main parts, in which union with Christ will be treated in Scripture and theology, respectively. There is a definite order. The Bible's treatment of union must precede an attempt to understand its teachings.

Part One, "Union with Christ in Scripture," begins with the "foundations"

---

[6] J. Todd Billings, *Union with Christ: Reframing Theology and Ministry for the Church* (Grand Rapids: Baker Academic, 2011).
[7] James D. Gifford Jr., *Perichoretic Salvation: The Believer's Union with Christ as a Third Type of Perichoresis* (Eugene, OR: Wipf and Stock, 2011).
[8] Constantine R. Campbell, *Paul and Union with Christ: An Exegetical and Theological Study* (Grand Rapids: Zondervan, 2012).
[9] Marcus Peter Johnson, *One with Christ: An Evangelical Theology of Salvation* (Wheaton, IL: Crossway, 2013).
[10] Grant Macaskill, *Union with Christ in the New Testament* (Oxford: Oxford University Press, 2013).
[11] Robert A. Peterson, *Salvation Accomplished by the Son: The Work of Christ* (Wheaton, IL: Crossway, 2012).

for union in the Old Testament, Synoptic Gospels, and Acts.[12] I speak of foundations because these sections of Scripture do not actually teach union with Christ but set the stage for that teaching in the rest of the New Testament.[13] Readers not interested in these details may want to go directly to the next chapters, which do treat union. They consider union with Christ in the Gospel of John, a powerful but sometimes neglected source. There follow chapters on every Pauline epistle treating union (all except Titus). Paul is such a major force in this study that two chapters are given to summarizing findings from the ten chapters dealing with his letters.[14]

Doubtless, Paul is the major biblical witness to union with Christ. But he is not the only one, and to study the whole counsel of God on the topic, we must also consult the General Epistles and Revelation. Thus there is a chapter devoted to Hebrews 3:14, one focusing on five passages in 1–2 Peter, a meaty chapter on the considerable treatment of union in 1 John, and one on three texts in Revelation. That completes the investigation of union in the Bible upon which our study of theology is based.

Part Two, "Union with Christ in Theology," begins with a chapter looking at union with Christ in light of the biblical storyline, an overlooked topic. It traces high points of union from eternity past through creation, the fall, the incarnation, Christ's work, and the new creation. Next are three chapters on union and the Holy Spirit. The first treats the Spirit's personality and deity. The second tells of his works in creation, Scripture, the world, the apostles, and Jesus himself. The third and principal one, for our purposes, presents the Spirit's most important work: union with Christ.

Then follows "The Christ to Whom We Are United," lest we forget the Christ of union with Christ. The book is rounded out with chapters on union and the church, baptism and the Lord's Supper, and the Christian life.

A Wonderful and Bewildering Project

I have never been so blessed and overwhelmed by a writing project. Union with Christ is simultaneously wonderful and bewildering. Why is it wonderful? Marcus Johnson, author of one of the books on union mentioned above, answers loudly and clearly:

---

[12] I acknowledge considerable help from Kyle Keating, my teaching assistant, on these chapters.
[13] The possible exception to this statement, as we shall see, is the account of Paul's conversion in Acts 9.
[14] There are ten chapters because the Thessalonian letters and Pastoral Epistles are each grouped together in two chapters.

> The primary, central, and fundamental reality of salvation is our union
> with Jesus Christ, because of which all the benefits of the Savior flow to
> us, and through which union all these benefits are to be understood. . . .
> The most basic of all saving truths [is] the union God the Father forges
> between the believer and his Son, Jesus Christ, through the power of the
> Holy Spirit. To put it plainly, *to be saved is to be united to the Savior.*[15]

If union is so wonderful, why is it at the same time so bewildering? Richard Gaffin answers:

> Certainly, in its full dimensions this mystery is beyond the believer's com-
> prehension. Involved here, as much as in anything pertaining to salvation
> and the gospel, is the hallmark of all true theological understanding, that
> knowledge of Christ's love "that surpasses knowledge," the knowledge of
> what is beyond all human knowing (Eph. 3:18–19; cf. 1 Cor. 2:9).[16]

I invite readers to accompany me on a tour of the delightful and overwhelming topic of union with Christ in Scripture and theology.

---

[15] Johnson, *One with Christ*, 29, emphasis original.
[16] Richard B. Gaffin Jr., "Union with Christ: Some Biblical and Theological Reflections," in *Always Reforming: Explorations in Systematic Theology*, ed. A. T. B. McGowan (Downers Grove, IL: IVP Academic, 2006), 273.

PART ONE

UNION WITH CHRIST IN SCRIPTURE

Chapter 1

Foundations in the Old Testament

The Old Testament provides the foundation for every New Testament teaching, including union with Christ, because it tells so much of the biblical story. Both Testaments tell one story of God's creation, the fall, and his redemptive work in the world of saving a people for himself and ultimately recreating the cosmos. It follows, then, that the climactic movement of this redemptive story (the work of Christ) and its subsequent application (union with Christ) find their meaning in the context of God's unfolding work of redemption begun in Genesis.[1]

Finding Christ in the Old Testament

Much has been made in recent years of "finding" Christ in the Old Testament. But what does that mean? The answer corresponds to the method used to find him. Using allegorical interpretation, some find Christ in the most unlikely places. However, we must tie our reading of the text to the concerns of the original author and audience. The original Old Testament authors and audiences predated Jesus by centuries. Thus, we must avoid the error of reading the Old Testament anachronistically, as though its writers had Romans open alongside the Torah.

Today we have the added benefit of reading the Old Testament in light of the New Testament. However, while our awareness of the Son's arrival on

---

[1] I am grateful for the help of teaching assistant Kyle Keating in the writing of this chapter.

the scene should inform our interpretation of the Old Testament, it must not overwhelm the immediate circumstances in which the text was given. We should not read the Old Testament expecting Moses or Isaiah to articulate details of union with Christ. So what are we looking for? We are not looking for a clear explanation of union with Christ, an idea that would not come for centuries, but anticipations of that union. The New Testament is replete with Old Testament language and themes, as the Gospel of Matthew demonstrates.[2] If the New Testament relies on the Old as the basis for its theological principles, then it makes sense that union with Christ does not emerge from a void but rather fills out concepts introduced in the Old Testament. Ultimately, if we are to avoid reading the Old Testament anachronistically, we must look for union with Christ foreshadowed in its stories and structures.

Union with Christ Foreshadowed

What qualifies as an Old Testament foreshadowing of union with Christ? It is no simple question. The primary conceptual criteria we will use are the concepts of identification, incorporation, and participation, all of which speak of a relationship between God and his people.[3] Identification refers to God's identifying with his people through his presence and in this way giving them an identity. Incorporation refers to God's creating a people for himself. Participation refers to God's people sharing in the story and even the life of God by virtue of their own experiences in faithfully following him. The Old Testament foreshadows union with Christ through word and symbol. It shows God's commitment to be in personal covenantal relationship with his people—a relationship that climaxes in union with Christ. We will see how the Old Testament foreshadows union through these three main concepts fleshed out in texts:

- identification: God's covenantal presence with his people
- incorporation: membership in God's covenantal people
- participation: sharing in the covenantal story

Identification: God's Covenantal Presence with His People

From the very beginning God identifies with his people. He makes them in his image (Gen. 1:27), and the first question he asks guilt-ridden Adam after

---

[2] For many insights, see Charles L. Quarles, *A Theology of Matthew: Jesus Revealed as Deliverer, King, and Incarnate Creator*, Explorations in Biblical Theology (Phillipsburg, NJ: P&R, 2013).
[3] These concepts are drawn from Constantine R. Campbell, *Paul and Union with Christ: An Exegetical and Theological Study* (Grand Rapids: Zondervan, 2012), especially 413–17.

the fall, "Where are you?" (Gen. 3:9), shows God's ongoing desire to be present with his people despite their sin. God identifies himself with a particular family in choosing Abraham and establishing his covenant with him and his descendants. Throughout the Old Testament story God identifies with his people by being present with them. This theme becomes explicit as the story moves to God's establishing Israel as his special people.

Exodus 25:8–9

After God delivers the Israelites from slavery in Egypt, he establishes them as a "kingdom of priests and a holy nation" (Ex. 19:6). He gives them his law and then this command: "Let them make me a sanctuary, that I may dwell in their midst" (25:8). God commands the people to build him a sanctuary, the tabernacle, a tent where God's presence may dwell in their midst. God goes on to prescribe the specifications of the tabernacle. The attention to detail is noteworthy; after all, this is supposed to be God's royal palace, and the various curtains and barriers are meant to protect God's sinful people from his searing holiness.[4] The purpose of the tabernacle is to be God's dwelling place in the midst of his people. It is a tangible demonstration of God's desire to identify with his people by being present with them.

Exodus 33

But why is God's presence, and therefore his identification, so important for God's people? After the incident of the golden calf, God tells Moses that the people may go on to the Promised Land, but without God's presence: "Go up to a land flowing with milk and honey; but I will not go up among you, lest I consume you on the way, for you are a stiff-necked people" (Ex. 33:3). How do God's people react? "When the people heard this disastrous word, they mourned, and no one put on his ornaments" (v. 4). Then Moses intercedes before the Lord on behalf of the people: "If your presence will not go with me, do not bring us up from here. For how shall it be known that I have found favor in your sight, I and your people? Is it not in your going with us, so that we are distinct, I and your people, from every other people on the face of the earth?" (vv. 15–16).

Note the basis of Moses's intercession: the people need God's presence because it is his very presence that makes them who they are. Their identity

---

[4] For the idea of the tabernacle as God's royal palace, see Jay Sklar, *Leviticus*, Tyndale Old Testament Commentaries (Downers Grove, IL: IVP Academic, 2014), 37.

as God's distinct people is based on the presence of the Lord with them. The primary way that God identifies with his people, uniting himself to them, is by his commitment to be present with them.

Leviticus 26:11–13

Perhaps the most explicit articulation of the concept we have been illustrating appears in Leviticus 26:11–13:

> I will make my dwelling among you, and my soul shall not abhor you. And I will walk among you and will be your God, and you shall be my people. I am the LORD your God, who brought you out of the land of Egypt, that you should not be their slaves. And I have broken the bars of your yoke and made you walk erect.

The oft-ignored book of Leviticus pinpoints the essential problem for God's desire to be present with his people: their sinfulness. How can a perfect, holy God unite himself and be present with a sinful people? How can a holy God "walk among" them and declare, "I will be your God, and you shall be my people"? Leviticus offers a number of answers.

First, it is in God's character to be holy and just as well as gracious and loving. God is holy, but he also forgives his people's transgression and through the sacrificial system makes a way for them to receive forgiveness and cleansing from sin.

Second, God is committed to his covenant relationships. God promises as part of the covenant to be "among" his people, to "walk among" them, and to "be [their] God." All three images—dwelling, walking, and being their God— speak of relationship, especially God's being Israel's God and Israel's being his people. Thus, even in the Pentateuch there is a clear sense that God desires to be united to his people in covenant relationship, a relationship characterized by God's identifying self-presence with them.

Third, Leviticus establishes that God's presence with his people is a form of union. Paul quotes this passage to make the point that God's people should not unite themselves to unclean things because they are the temple of God: "What agreement has the temple of God with idols? For we are the temple of the living God; as God said, 'I will make my dwelling among them and walk among them, and I will be their God, and they shall be my people'" (2 Cor. 6:16). Paul applies the concept of union with Christ to the Corinthians to tell them not to join in religious union with unbelievers, and the underlying logic is that God has united himself with his people by his presence with them.

Isaiah 7:10–14

The Lord spoke to Ahaz, "Ask a sign of the Lord your God; let it be deep as Sheol or high as heaven." But Ahaz said, "I will not ask, and I will not put the Lord to the test." And he said, "Hear then, O house of David! Is it too little for you to weary men, that you weary my God also? Therefore the Lord himself will give you a sign. Behold, the virgin shall conceive and bear a son, and shall call his name Immanuel."

Fast-forwarding in the biblical story, Isaiah 7 gives a glimpse as to how this concept of God's presence will play out in the future. Isaiah prophesies to King Ahaz, who has looked for deliverance from sources outside the Lord, and tells him that the ultimate deliverance for Israel will come from the "Lord himself" (v. 14), who will provide a son from the house of David as a sign. But a sign of what? God's presence: he shall be called "Immanuel" or "God with us." Matthew 1:22–23 says that these verses point to the arrival of Jesus as Israel's Messiah. The Old Testament, then, foreshadows the apex of the ongoing theme of identification-by-presence in pointing to the coming Messiah called "Immanuel."

Ezekiel 37:24–28

My servant David shall be king over them, and they shall all have one shepherd. They shall walk in my rules and be careful to obey my statutes. They shall dwell in the land that I gave to my servant Jacob, where your fathers lived. They and their children and their children's children shall dwell there forever, and David my servant shall be their prince forever. I will make a covenant of peace with them. It shall be an everlasting covenant with them. And I will set them in their land and multiply them, and will set my sanctuary in their midst forevermore. My dwelling place shall be with them, and I will be their God, and they shall be my people. Then the nations will know that I am the Lord who sanctifies Israel, when my sanctuary is in their midst forevermore.

After the passage of the "two sticks," in which God promises to reunite Judah and Israel (Ezek. 37:15–23), we have more magnificent promises. David, one of several Old Testament covenant mediators, prefigures the greater David, the Messiah, who will be Israel's shepherd-king forever in the land. Unlike in their previous history, God's people will truly obey him. He will make an everlasting covenant of peace with them and cause them to multiply. He, the Sanctifier, will put his sanctuary in the midst of them and their descendants forever. In fulfillment of covenant promises, God will dwell with them, he will be their God, and they will be his people. When all this happens, the nations will know that he is the Lord.

I interpret this as a prophecy of spiritual Israel, the people of God, obeying him and his Christ, the King, the true Mediator, in the new earth forever. God will give them peace, sanctify them, and dwell among them in complete fulfillment of his previous covenant promises. Therefore, God's presence with his people is eschatological as well, pointing forward to a future when God's presence with his people is established eternally.

Many other passages could be cited,[5] but the point has been made. God's commitment to unite himself to his people by his identifying presence is fulfilled ultimately in his identification with them by becoming one of them, sending his Son in the likeness of human flesh (Phil. 2:7). In Christ's incarnation God dwells (tabernacles) among them (John 1:14) and reaffirms his commitment to be with them always, to the end of the age (Matt. 28:20). And when Christ sends the Spirit at Pentecost to be with New Testament believers and to unite them to himself, he gives them this identity—they are "in Christ" as God's people.

Incorporation: Membership in God's Covenantal People

The Old Testament foreshadows union not only through God's identification with his people but also through his joining them together into the body of his people. When God makes his covenant with people in the Old Testament, he does so corporately, not merely individually. Often when we conceive of union, we think in individualistic terms: I am personally united to Christ. While this is true, it can overlook the reality that God relates to his people not only as individuals but also as a whole. In the Old Testament the dual emphasis of individual and corporate relationships with God is embodied in the structure of God's covenant with his people.

Covenantal Structures

When God makes a covenant with his people, he does so primarily through a specific individual who represents the whole corporate people. Thus, when

---

[5] Here are three more examples: Ex. 13:21–22; Num. 14:14; Josh. 1:9.

God makes a covenant with Adam (and later Noah), Adam (and then Noah) represents all of humanity. Later, when God makes a covenant with Abraham, Abraham represents not only himself but also his entire family, including his descendants.

Subsequent covenants made with Moses and David follow suit, as Moses and David represent God's people, the nation of Israel. My colleague Jack Collins sketches a helpful diagram to describe the structure of God's covenants with his people. In figure 1, God makes a covenant with an individual (covenant mediator) who is the representative of the larger body of the covenant people. This arrangement is sometimes described as federal headship, where the federal head (covenant mediator) represents a group of people in a federation or covenant.

Figure 1. The structure of covenant relationship

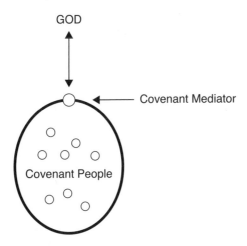

How does this covenant structure pertain to union with Christ? The New Testament portrays Christ as a covenant Mediator: "There is one God, and there is one mediator between God and men, the man Christ Jesus" (1 Tim. 2:5). The identification of Jesus as the Messiah from the house of David names him as a covenant Mediator in the line of other Old Testament covenant mediators, such as Adam, Noah, Abraham, Moses, and David. Paul affirms the relationship between Old Testament covenant mediators and Christ in Romans 5 when he explains how Adam and Christ are individuals who represent a corporate whole. If part of union with Christ is being joined to his body, the church, then God's covenantal relationship in the Old Testament sheds light on what it means to be incorporated into God's people and therefore connected to God himself.

Covenant Mediators

Jesus is the "mediator of a new covenant" (Heb. 9:15), but this unique Mediator is preceded by Old Testament covenant mediators, including Adam, Noah, Abraham, Moses, and David.

Adam. The first man represents humanity in the covenant of creation (or covenant of works). He and Eve are stewards of the earth on behalf of God their Lord; under his dominion they exercise dominion over the other creatures (Gen. 1:26–28). Adam, the first covenant mediator, plunges the human race into condemnation and death (Rom. 5:12–19; 1 Cor. 15:22). His fall also subjects the creation to "futility" and "bondage to corruption" (Rom. 8:20–21). Paul juxtaposes Adam, the first covenant mediator, with Christ, the Mediator of the new covenant. As Adam has brought guilt and corruption to his race, so Christ brings justification and eternal life to those who "receive the abundance of grace and the free gift of righteousness" (5:17).

Noah. Noah appears in the biblical story as a sort of second Adam. Even as the first man is the father of all living, so Noah is the father of the seven other souls spared by God in the great flood. To Noah and his sons God repeats the Edenic command to "be fruitful and multiply and fill the earth" (Gen. 9:1; cf. 9:7). As God made the covenant of creation with Adam, so he makes a covenant with Noah, his sons, and the nonhuman creatures spared in the flood. To them God promises, "I establish my covenant with you, that never again shall all flesh be cut off by the waters of the flood, and never again shall there be a flood to destroy the earth" (v. 11). God places the rainbow in the sky as the "sign of the covenant" (v. 12). Noah thus takes up the mantle of covenant mediator to represent all of humanity in its relationship with God. Noah's role as covenant mediator to a restored world foreshadows Christ's role as the covenant Mediator through and for whom the entire cosmos will be remade.

Abraham. While Adam and Noah represent all of humanity in their covenants with God, Abraham represents a more specific group: God's people. God calls Abraham:

> Go from your country and your kindred and your father's house to the
> land that I will show you. And I will make of you a great nation, and I will

bless you and make your name great, so that you will be a blessing. I will bless those who bless you, and him who dishonors you I will curse, and in you all the families of the earth shall be blessed. (Gen. 12:1–3)

God specifically chooses Abraham's family to be a means of blessing the whole earth. To do so, God makes a covenant with Abraham, promising to make him a great nation and bless him in order that he might be a blessing. How will Abraham's people be a blessing to the world? Ultimately through one of Abraham's descendants, Jesus himself (Matt. 1:1).

God counts Abraham righteous for his faith (Gen. 15:6) and promises to be God to him and his offspring forever (17:7–8). As God made land promises to Adam and Noah, so God gives Abraham and his offspring "all the land of Canaan, for an everlasting possession" (v. 8). Ultimately, Abraham looks forward to the new earth (Heb. 11:10, 16). Paul says that God's covenant with Abraham was based on grace, was received in faith, and dealt with his offspring, "Christ" (Gal. 3:16). The Abrahamic covenant is the basis of the new covenant, and New Testament believers are "Abraham's offspring, heirs according to the promise" of eternal life (v. 29). Christ, the Mediator of the new covenant, is far greater than the great Old Testament covenant mediator Abraham (Heb. 9:15; 12:24), even as God is greater than human beings (John 8:58).

Moses. Moses, the servant of the Lord and the man to whom God speaks face to face, is mediator of the old covenant, which God makes with redeemed Israel at Mount Sinai. As God promised Abraham that he would be a great nation, so God's covenant with Moses establishes Israel as God's chosen people. God speaks to Moses after their exodus from Egypt:

You yourselves have seen what I did to the Egyptians, and how I bore you on eagles' wings and brought you to myself. Now therefore, if you will indeed obey my voice and keep my covenant, you shall be my treasured possession among all peoples, for all the earth is mine; and you shall be to me a kingdom of priests and a holy nation. These are the words that you shall speak to the people of Israel. (Ex. 19:4–6)

God makes a covenant with Moses, who as covenant mediator represents the entire nation of Israel. In this covenant, God calls Israel his "treasured possession" (v. 5) who will be a "kingdom of priests and a holy nation" (v. 6). The people of God are to be the reconstituted humanity, fulfilling the purpose for which all human beings were created: loving and worshiping God.

Part of the covenant is expectation that God's people will obey him. Accordingly, they commit themselves, saying, "All that the LORD has spoken we will do" (24:7). Israel will fail to live up to this high calling. Time and again they will require their mediator to intervene for them until a greater Mediator, Jesus, comes and fulfills all the commands of the law (cf. Matt. 5:17).

Moses was the "intermediary" through whom the law was put in place (Gal. 3:19). The covenant mediated by Moses "came 430 years afterward," that is, after the one mediated by Abraham, and thus "does not annul" it (v. 17). Moses was a great Old Testament covenant mediator. But although there is thus continuity between the Abrahamic, Mosaic, and new covenants, Christ, as a son "over God's house," is far superior to Moses, a servant "in all God's house" (Heb. 3:2–6). The work of Christ, the Mediator and guarantor of the new covenant, annuls the covenant made with Moses, making it obsolete (7:18–19, 22; 8:6, 13). Indeed, Christ's work of redemption is so great that it not only avails for new covenant believers but also redeems Old Testament saints (9:15)!

David. David is the final Old Testament covenant mediator we will consider. God makes a covenant with him, God's choice to be king of the nation of Israel:

> I will raise up your offspring after you, who shall come from your body, and I will establish his kingdom. He shall build a house for my name, and I will establish the throne of his kingdom forever. I will be to him a father, and he shall be to me a son. . . . My steadfast love will not depart from him. . . . And your house and your kingdom shall be made sure forever before me. Your throne shall be established forever. (2 Sam. 7:12–16)

God promises David that his line will reign over God's kingdom forever. Indeed, David's son Solomon shall be as a son to God. Of course, the ultimate Davidic King is as a son to God because he *is* the Son of God himself. The Messiah, Jesus, was David's descendant, but he was also David's Lord, a point with which Jesus confounds the Jewish leaders (Matt. 1:1; 22:41–46). Jesus is the greater David, the covenant Mediator who grants his people rest from their enemies—sin, Satan, and death—and represents his people as God's own Son.[6]

The suffering servant. While David is the last significant covenant mediator

---

[6] God also calls the nation of Israel his "son." The prophet Hosea speaks the word of the Lord, saying, "When Israel was a child, I loved him, and out of Egypt I called my son" (Hos. 11:1). See Robert A. Peterson, *Adopted by God: From Wayward Sinners to Cherished Children* (Phillipsburg, NJ: P&R, 2001). The New Testament picks up on this verse as a messianic prophecy referring to Jesus's sojourn in Egypt to flee the wrath of Herod (Matt. 2:15). At various times Israel, the Davidic king, and the Messiah are all considered God's son, implying that the king who is to be as a son to God represents the nation of Israel, which is also considered to be God's son.

in the Old Testament, the prophets, specifically Isaiah, foreshadow a coming covenant Mediator who will be both a Davidic King (Isa. 9:6–7) and—surprisingly—a suffering servant. This servant is to be a light to all nations, functioning as one who will represent not only God's Israel but all the peoples of the earth (Isa. 49:6). Thus the covenant Mediator who is to fulfill this role of "servant" will be a representative not just of ethnic Israel (like Abraham) but of all peoples (like Adam).

However, this servant will come initially not as a reigning King. Instead he will be

> despised and rejected by men;
> 　　a man of sorrows, and acquainted with grief . . . .
> . . . stricken,
> 　　smitten by God, and afflicted. (53:3–4)

Why does he suffer? The following verses provide the answer:

> He was pierced for our transgressions;
> 　　he was crushed for our iniquities;
> upon him was the chastisement that brought us peace,
> 　　and with his wounds we are healed. . . .
> and the LORD has laid on him
> 　　the iniquity of us all. (vv. 5–6)

In his humiliation the servant functions as a covenant Mediator, taking the punishment his people deserve for their sin, so that "many might be accounted righteous" (v. 11). Who is this suffering servant, this covenant Mediator who makes atonement for his people's sins? The apostle Peter tells us: "Christ also suffered for you. . . . He himself bore our sins in his body on the tree, that we might die to sin and live to righteousness. By his wounds you have been healed" (1 Pet. 2:21, 24). Peter quotes Isaiah 53, telling us that it speaks of Christ himself, who suffered on the cross that we might be spiritually healed. The servant songs in Isaiah foreshadow the work of Christ as the covenant Mediator who will represent his people by dying in their place.

Participation: Sharing in the Covenantal Story

We not only are united to Christ as members of his body, incorporated in him as the ultimate covenant Mediator, but we also participate in him. Paul says that by God's grace through faith believers participate in Jesus's story. We died with Christ, were raised with him (Col. 2:20; 3:1), and sat down with him in heaven (Eph. 2:6). The Old Testament does not speak in these terms. But a similar concept of participating in God's story occurs throughout the Old Testament when God includes his people in his covenantal story. While this idea of participation becomes more explicit in the New Testament, the Old Testament invites us to see God's people as those who participate in the narrative God writes by being in relationship with him through covenants.

This principle of participation pertains to the concepts we already studied. When God's covenantal presence with his people identifies them, they experience his presence and thereby participate in his story. So, for example, when God promises to dwell among his people, walk among them, and be their God (Lev. 26:11–12), by grace through faith they know God and enjoy his presence as his people. And when God makes a covenant with Abraham and his seed, thereby incorporating them into his people, Abraham, Isaac, and Jacob know God and love him as they walk in faith and obedience.

I repeat: these examples are not identical to Christians' dying and rising with Christ (Rom. 6:3–11). But they are a part of the storyline that culminates in God's sending his Son to be Savior of the world, who in turn sends the Spirit at Pentecost to unite his people to Christ in salvation. In a sense, then, the Old Testament saints experience God's presence and belonging to his people as a foretaste of union with Christ enjoyed by New Testament saints.

And there is more. The Old Testament also contains passages in which God promises to put his Spirit within his people. We will consider two of them.

Ezekiel 36:24–28

I will take you from the nations and gather you from all the countries and bring you into your own land. I will sprinkle clean water on you, and you shall be clean from all your uncleannesses, and from all your idols I will cleanse you. And I will give you a new heart, and a new spirit I will put within you. And I will remove the heart of stone from your flesh and give you a heart of flesh. And I will put my Spirit within you, and cause you to walk in my statutes and be careful to obey my rules. You shall dwell in the land that I gave to your fathers, and you shall be my people, and I will be your God.

God promises to bring scattered Israel back to its land. Why? To vindicate his holy reputation and demonstrate to surrounding nations that he is the Lord (vv. 22–23, 36). He will do more than regather Israel; he will also purify the people from their sins (vv. 25, 29, 33). He will accomplish this by granting them a new heart and spirit. Ezekiel's words approximate the New Testament doctrine of regeneration: "I will remove the heart of stone from your flesh and give you a heart of flesh" (v. 26). This will result in renewed obedience to the Lord (v. 27). Our chief interest lies here: "I will put my Spirit within you, and cause you to walk in my statutes and be careful to obey my rules" (v. 27). This is important Old Testament background for God's corporate indwelling of his people, a New Testament theme connected to union with Christ.[7]

Ezekiel 37:11–14

> Son of man, these bones are the whole house of Israel. Behold, they say, "Our bones are dried up, and our hope is lost; we are indeed cut off." Therefore prophesy, and say to them, Thus says the Lord GOD: Behold, I will open your graves and raise you from your graves, O my people. And I will bring you into the land of Israel. And you shall know that I am the LORD, when I open your graves, and raise you from your graves, O my people. And I will put my Spirit within you, and you shall live, and I will place you in your own land. Then you shall know that I am the LORD.

Ezekiel 37 continues the theme begun in the previous chapter. To answer how these things will come about, the prophet replies: by God's supernatural life-giving power. Ezekiel sees a valley of dry bones and in obedience to God prophesies to them. At the prophet's word the bones rattle and come together and are covered with sinews and flesh. Again at Ezekiel's word, breath comes into the corpses and they come alive and stand up, constituting a great army (vv. 1–10). This pictures God's re-creating his scattered people and bringing them back to their land (vv. 12, 14). Once more Ezekiel's words prefigure New Testament teaching: "I will put my Spirit within you, and you shall live, and I will place you in your own land" (v. 14). God will vivify dead (scattered) Israel by putting his Spirit within them. At Pentecost God vivifies his New Testament saints by putting his Holy Spirit within them.

---

[7] David J. Reimer is correct, "The physical return was only the beginning of the fulfillment of these prophecies," *ESV Study Bible*, note on Ezek. 36:22–32. Their complete fulfillment occurs in the new covenant, of which Ezekiel's fellow prophet Jeremiah also spoke (Jer. 31:31–34).

Conclusion

It would be anachronistic to say that the Old Testament teaches union with Christ. Instead, it foreshadows union with Christ. In this chapter, we have seen three main ways this is so.

First, God identifies with his people in the Old Testament through his covenant presence. By doing so, he bestows on them an identity—he is their God, and they are his people. This identification foreshadows the way in which union with Christ in the new covenant is God's covenant presence par excellence. It also foreshadows the identity of New Testament saints as those "in Christ."

Second, God incorporates a chosen nation into a covenant people. This covenant people relates to God through a covenant mediator. The Old Testament gives us covenant mediators, including Adam, Noah, Abraham, Moses, and David. However, the covenant Mediator par excellence comes in the form of one who is both Davidic King and suffering servant, Jesus Christ. By his mediation in his death he makes atonement for his people's sins and in his resurrection makes them alive to God. He will come a second time, not to suffer but to reign as the son of David par excellence.

Third, God's people participate in the covenantal story, foreshadowing the way in which the church in the New Testament will participate in Christ's death and resurrection. This will happen when Old Testament prophecies concerning the Holy Spirit are fulfilled in Jesus and his ministry, including Pentecost.

Ultimately, the Old Testament lays the foundation to understand the New Testament teaching of union with Christ. Our understanding of union will be enriched by understanding the story, imagery, and concepts upon which that union is built.

Chapter 2

Foundations in the Synoptic Gospels

The three Gospels that begin the New Testament introduce us to Jesus of Nazareth. They all testify that Jesus is the Christ of God, the Messiah who will save Israel and be a light to the nations (cf. Luke 2:32). Matthew, Mark, and Luke are called the Synoptic Gospels because they contain similar content, suggesting that they share some of the same sources. The three differ from the Gospel of John, which has many unique stories and themes not found in the Synoptics.

If the Old Testament foreshadows union with Christ, then the Synoptic Gospels are a reasonable place to begin looking for union with Christ in the New Testament. After all, they tell the story of Jesus. However, compared with the Gospel of John and the Pauline Epistles, there are few references to union with Christ in the Synoptics. Why? I will suggest a few answers. First, the Gospels focus more on telling Jesus's story than on trying to explain its implications (as didactic teaching). That is, the genre of the Gospels does not lend itself to the type of explication one might find in a Pauline epistle. Where doctrines make an appearance (for example, Christ's work as sacrifice), they often do so indirectly as part of the story rather than as doctrine being taught.

Second, the redemptive-historical context of the Synoptic Gospels means that the majority of their narratives precede the death and resurrection of Christ. If union with Christ is a doctrine rooted in Christ's death and resurrection, then it would be unusual to expect a full explanation of union before those events occurred.

However, both of these explanations also hold true for the Gospel of John, which has many more references to union than the Synoptics. What can account for this difference? As we have seen, the Synoptics share much of the same source material, while John appears to be drawn primarily from independent sources. All John's texts that clearly refer to union with Christ are unique to him and appear to be drawn from his unique sources. Thus, it should not surprise us that the Synoptics do not express union in John's patterns.

Additionally, the thematic divergence of the Synoptic Gospels from John's Gospel suggests a different focus. While John focuses on the relationship between Jesus and the Father, as well as between Jesus and his people, the Synoptics spend less time here, choosing to focus on other themes, such as the kingdom or Jesus's fulfillment of Old Testament prophecies.

So what do the Synoptics say about union with Christ? They point to the actual establishing of that which believers are united to. When we say believers are united to Christ, the implicit question is, who is this Christ? The Synoptics answer this question, presenting both Jesus's identity and mission. The Synoptics, then, establish the theological foundation for union with Christ. In addition, they establish the redemptive-historical foundation for union. They show us the redeeming work of Christ, which we then partake of through union with him. We see union established through the same three concepts studied in the previous chapter:[1]

- identification in Jesus as Immanuel and Bridegroom
- incorporation through Jesus as covenant Mediator par excellence
- participation in the story of Jesus

Identification in Jesus as Immanuel and Bridegroom

Jesus as Immanuel

The Synoptics allude to union with Christ in terms of identification when they present Jesus as Immanuel. In our Old Testament chapter we saw that God identifies with his Old Testament people most frequently through his covenantal

---

[1] I gratefully acknowledge the work of Kyle Keating, my teaching assistant, in the research and writing of this chapter.

presence with them.[2] We find this theme of identification through God's presence in the Gospel of Matthew as well. Matthew cites Isaiah 7:14 and applies it to Jesus's birth. Joseph is perplexed when he learns Mary is pregnant and contemplates divorcing her quietly. But then an angel brings a welcome message:

> As he considered these things, behold, an angel of the Lord appeared to him in a dream, saying, "Joseph, son of David, do not fear to take Mary as your wife, for that which is conceived in her is from the Holy Spirit. She will bear a son, and you shall call his name Jesus, for he will save his people from their sins." All this took place to fulfill what the Lord had spoken by the prophet:

> "Behold, the virgin shall conceive and bear a son,
>   and they shall call his name Immanuel"

> (which means, God with us). (Matt. 1:20–23)

Because *Immanuel* means "God with us," Matthew presents Jesus as God's presence with his people. In two other places Matthew underlines this same theme. One of those places is the Gospel's last words from Jesus's mouth, "Go therefore and make disciples of all nations, baptizing them in the name of the Father and of the Son and of the Holy Spirit, teaching them to observe all that I have commanded you. And behold, I am with you always, to the end of the age" (28:19–20). Charles Quarles draws an important implication: "Matthew 1:23 and 28:20 serve to bracket the entire gospel. The promise that 'God [is] with us' at the beginning of the gospel is ultimately fulfilled in Jesus' assurance, 'I am with you,' at the end of the gospel."[3]

These two promises of Jesus's presence among his people enclose a third: "Where two or three are gathered in my name, there am I among them" (18:20). Again Quarles explains, "Thus, 18:20 is an element of a triad affirming God's presence with his people in the person of Jesus."[4] God identifies with his people by visiting them in the person of Jesus, thus anticipating union with Christ and his indwelling Spirit.

Jesus as Bridegroom

Another account from Matthew and Mark uses the symbol of marriage to indicate the manner in which Jesus identifies with his people:

---

[2] See chapter 1, "Foundations in the Old Testament."
[3] Charles L. Quarles, *A Theology of Matthew: Jesus Revealed as Deliverer, King, and Incarnate Creator*, Explorations in Biblical Theology (Phillipsburg, NJ: P&R, 2013), 153.
[4] Ibid., 154.

The disciples of John came to him [Jesus], saying, "Why do we and the Pharisees fast, but your disciples do not fast?" And Jesus said to them, "Can the wedding guests mourn as long as the bridegroom is with them? The days will come when the bridegroom is taken away from them, and then they will fast." (Matt. 9:14–15; cf. Mark 2:18–20)

Jesus uses wedding imagery to show the implications of his presence among them. D. A. Carson summarizes, "Jesus' answer was implicitly Christological: he himself is the messianic bridegroom."[5] He is the Bridegroom arriving at the wedding, and the only proper response is celebration, not mourning. But if Jesus is the Bridegroom, then who is the bride? This imagery appears in the Old Testament, where the Bridegroom is Yahweh and the bride is his people Israel (cf. Isa. 62:5; Hos. 2:19–20). Similarly, Jesus appeals to himself as the Bridegroom and his people, the church, as his bride. Paul picks up the same marital imagery, as we shall see (in 1 Cor. 6:15–20; 2 Cor. 11:1–5; Eph. 5:25–27).[6] While the outworking of this imagery is left to Paul, its foundation is laid by Jesus's words. He is the Bridegroom, and the church is his bride. He identifies with his people as the groom identifies himself with his bride on their wedding day.

Incorporation through Jesus as Covenant Mediator par Excellence

The Synoptic Gospels depict Jesus as the covenant Mediator par excellence— the ultimate representative of God's people. After the previous chapter's discussion of covenant mediators in incorporation in the Old Testament, the Synoptics present Jesus as the new and greater Israel.

During the transfiguration, when Peter suggests that he, James, and John make three tents for their guests—Moses, Elijah, and Jesus—God interrupts: "As he [Peter] was saying these things, a cloud came and overshadowed them, and they were afraid as they entered the cloud. And a voice came out of the cloud, saying, 'This is my Son, my Chosen One; listen to him!'" (Luke 9:34–35). The voice is that of the Father explaining the identity of Jesus. He is God's own Son, the "Chosen One." Moses and Elijah, representing the Law and Prophets, "spoke of his departure which he was about to accomplish at Jerusalem" (v. 31).[7] Walter Liefeld clarifies, "Jesus is, therefore, pictured as the

---

[5] D. A. Carson, *Matthew*, The Expositor's Bible Commentary (Grand Rapids: Zondervan, 1984), 227.
[6] See "A Summary of Union with Christ in Paul's Letters (2)," 216–21.
[7] The word translated "departure" is *exodos*, which speaks of Jesus's death and carries symbolic meaning recalling the great redemptive event of the Old Testament that foreshadowed *the* great redemptive event of Jesus.

one who at this point in redemptive history is fulfilling the prophecies and types of the OT."[8]

The words "God's Son" portray Jesus in a manner similar to Old Testament Israel's being God's son.[9] Jesus as representative of Israel is Messiah. The second title, "my Chosen One," confirms this conclusion. Just as Israel was God's chosen people, so Jesus is God's Chosen One, the Messiah, who will represent Israel as the only perfectly faithful Israelite. Darrell Bock is pithy in saying, "When one puts the two titles together, Jesus is identified as the Messiah-Servant."[10]

But why does it matter that Jesus is the Messiah, the true Israel? Because as the Messiah, he is the covenant Mediator par excellence. He is the ultimate covenant Mediator who stands as the representative of God's people for eternity. By means of a genealogy at the beginning of his Gospel, Matthew links Jesus to David and Abraham (Matt. 1:1–17). Both David and Abraham were key Old Testament covenant mediators. Matthew's genealogy shows Jesus to be a covenant Mediator of the same kind as Abraham and David, yet he is greater than they. Quarles captures the message of Matthew 1:1: "Jesus Christ, the son of David, the son of Abraham":

> Jesus is the new David, our King. He is the fulfillment of God's covenant with David. . . . Jesus is the new Abraham, our Founder. He fulfills God's covenant with Abraham by creating a new chosen people composed of both Jews and Gentiles who will be holy as God is holy and who will serve as a light to the nations.[11]

Not only is Jesus a covenant Mediator, but he is the Mediator of the new covenant prophesied by Old Testament prophets (as in Jer. 31:31–34). During the Last Supper, Jesus breaks the bread, saying, "This is my body, which is given for you. Do this in remembrance of me." And likewise he gives the cup after the meal, saying, "This cup that is poured out for you is the new covenant in my blood" (Luke 22:19–20). Jesus inaugurates the new covenant of which he is Mediator with his death and resurrection, sealed and celebrated in the Lord's Supper.

All three Synoptics establish Jesus's messianic credentials. There is no

---

[8] Walter L. Liefeld, "Theological Motifs in the Transfiguration Narrative," in *New Dimensions in New Testament Study*, ed. Richard N. Longenecker and Merrill C. Tenney (Grand Rapids: Zondervan, 1974), 178.

[9] Cf. Hos. 11:1. See note 6 in the previous chapter.

[10] Darrell L. Bock, *Luke 1:1–9:50*, Baker Exegetical Commentary on the New Testament (Grand Rapids: Baker Academic, 1994), 874.

[11] Quarles, *A Theology of Matthew*, 192–93.

doubt by the end of each of them that Jesus is the Messiah, following the pre-vious covenant mediators (Adam, Noah, Abraham, Moses, and David), but greater than all of them put together. Implicit in this identification of Jesus as Messiah is the reality that as covenant Mediator, he represents God's people. The Synoptics provide a foundation for union with Christ when they establish Jesus as *the* covenant Mediator to whom God's people are joined and by whom they are represented.

Participation in the Story of Jesus

The Synoptic Gospels paint a vivid description of the story of Jesus from his incarnation to his resurrection. The language of participation vis-à-vis union with Christ means we share in his story. That is, we participate in the events that shape the story of Jesus's life on earth. Therefore, as the Synoptics depict the story of Jesus, they show us the story that we take part in as well.

Participation in the Redemptive-Historical Story

The Synoptics tell the story of Jesus in terms of what he accomplished in his-tory. If participation entails sharing in the work he has accomplished, as Paul insists, what *is* that work? The Synoptics begin by presenting Jesus's virginal conception and incarnation (Matt. 1:18–25; Luke 1:26–38; 2:6–7). The eternal Son of God became a human being in Jesus of Nazareth. Christian tradition has understood from its earliest days that Jesus's incarnation is unique but nevertheless a kind of union between the human and the divine.

Theologians use the term *hypostatic* (or personal) union to describe the relationship between the divine and human natures of Christ. The divine Son took to himself a human nature. He is henceforth one person with two na-tures, one divine and one human. The two natures are united in his person, and thus their union is a personal one. The union God's people have with Christ is not identical to the unique hypostatic union. But the hypostatic union paves the way for seeing how deity can condescend to humanity and establish a union between the two. The unique incarnation of the Son of God is the basis for our union with Christ.

The Synoptics introduce the incarnation but focus on Jesus's death and resurrection. It is to these events that Paul so often says Christians are united, as we will see in later chapters. Matthew, Mark, and Luke tell the story that Paul's epistles say believers participate in.

Participation as Discipleship

Discipleship in the Synoptic Gospels can be summarized as the calling to follow after Jesus, imitating him in his love for God and others. The Synoptics all include this famous passage on discipleship: "[Jesus] said to all, 'If anyone would come after me, let him deny himself and take up his cross daily and follow me. For whoever would save his life will lose it, but whoever loses his life for my sake will save it'" (Luke 9:23–24; cf. Matt. 16:24–25; Mark 8:34–35). The call to discipleship is a call to follow Jesus, to participate in his story by following him. As Hans Bayer notes, the participation of discipleship is linked to union insofar as "sharing in union with Christ" is a result of the "same cause [as imitating him]: Jesus enables and facilitates the accomplishment of what he teaches, calls for, and exemplifies."[12] Union is the very means of discipleship—union in a unique sense for the twelve disciples as they lived alongside Jesus, but also union for all believers in the sense of connection to Jesus by the Spirit, by which he empowers us to live out his call to discipleship.

Conclusion

This brief survey reveals that union with Christ as a doctrine is not present in the Synoptics. Instead we find a picture of union presented in a redemptive-historical sense. The Synoptics reveal the identity of the person to whom Christians are united in salvation. The first three Gospels narrate the events Paul will later tell believers they partake in. The Synoptics portray Jesus as Immanuel and symbolically introduce him as the Bridegroom, illustrating his identification with his people by his presence with them. They describe Jesus as the covenant Mediator par excellence, who will incorporate believers into a new covenant community. Finally, they tell the story of Jesus and call believers to follow after him, participating in his story as disciples. By the end of the Gospels, the foundational events for union with Christ have been established. The next step in God's unfolding the foundation for union with Christ is for that union to be enacted in the life of the church as seen in the book of Acts.

---

[12] Hans F. Bayer, *A Theology of Mark: The Dynamic between Christology and Authentic Discipleship*, Explorations in Biblical Theology (Phillipsburg, NJ: P&R, 2012), 91.

Chapter 3

Foundations in Acts

Paul is rightly esteemed as *the* biblical theologian of union with Christ. Nevertheless, other New Testament writers do speak on this subject, as we shall see. And as with all biblical themes, union does not begin with Paul. We have laid foundations for union in the Old Testament and the Synoptic Gospels, and we now turn to Acts.[1]

Despite the focus on salvation in both Luke's Gospel and Acts, the emphasis tends to be on the "what" of salvation as opposed to the "how." As F. F. Bruce points out, "How Jesus has procured . . . salvation for believers is rarely spelled out in Acts."[2] Given Bruce's conclusion, the question remains, can we discern any doctrine of salvation in the book of Acts? And if we consider that the New Testament is telling one single story, a second question emerges: Can the descriptions of salvation in Acts be reconciled with the doctrine of union with Christ in the writings of John and Paul?

Recognizing Union with Christ

To properly assess these questions, we must first consider how to identify union with Christ in Acts. Acts is narrative- and speech-driven and not straight didactic teaching (like the Epistles). Therefore, it is to misunderstand the intent of the text to ask if it "teaches" a given doctrine. Undoubtedly, all Scripture is meant to teach God's people, but we must take into consideration

---

[1] This chapter is drawn from and relies heavily upon the work of my teaching assistant Kyle Keating and his unpublished paper "Union with Christ in the Book of Acts."

[2] F. F. Bruce, *Commentary on the Book of the Acts*, The New International Commentary on the New Testament (Grand Rapids: Eerdmans, 1954), 65.

the genre of Acts in evaluating whether Luke explains the doctrine of union with Christ.

Second, we must consider vocabulary's role in the articulation of doctrines. While there is conceptual agreement and often overlap in vocabulary, we must not assume that every appearance of the words "in Christ" necessarily invokes the whole range of meaning of the doctrine of union with Christ. Vice versa, the absence of typical union-with-Christ language (as seen in John or Paul) does not necessarily mean the absence of the concept of union with Christ.

Third, we must consider the relationship between the book of Acts and the rest of the New Testament, especially the Epistles. The absence of Pauline doctrinal formulation in Acts does not necessarily mean that Luke's narrative contradicts that doctrine. Rather, the descriptive nature of Acts (as a sort of biography of the early church) means that any hints of a concept of union will likely reflect anticipations of the doctrine that are to be fleshed out in the more didactic teaching of the Epistles. Thus, we should not expect Luke in a summary of a Pauline sermon to engage the concept of union with the intricacy and nuance of Paul in his letters.

To decide if union with Christ is present in the book of Acts, we will consider the same three concepts as in the previous two chapters: identification, incorporation, and participation.

- identification in the ministry of the Holy Spirit and Paul's conversion
- incorporation in the rite of baptism
- participation in the repetition of Jesus's story and Luke's use of Isaiah's "suffering servant"

Identification in the Ministry of the Holy Spirit and Paul's Conversion

The concept of identification as a subset of union with Christ appears in two key aspects of the book of Acts: the ministry of the Holy Spirit and the conversion of Paul.

Identification in the Ministry of the Holy Spirit

From a redemptive-historical perspective, the Pentecost event lays the foundation of the whole book of Acts. Pentecost is when the ministry of Jesus is passed down to the church as the promised Holy Spirit falls upon the crowds.

Luke, in his Gospel (part one of his two-volume Luke-Acts), focuses his discussion of the Holy Spirit on Jesus's birth, though the Spirit appears in two other key places also. In one setting, Luke highlights Jesus's foreshadowing of Pentecost (Luke 11:13). In the other, Jesus's assurance of the Spirit's guiding the disciples in what to say when confronted foreshadows the apostles' experiences in Acts when they are faced with opposition (12:11–12).

Jesus's words to the apostles in John's Gospel also prepare us for the Spirit's arrival at Pentecost. Jesus says that it is good for him to go so that the Comforter (the Spirit) might come (16:7). He will take what is Jesus's and declare it to the disciples (v. 15). After Pentecost the Spirit will mediate between Christ and the apostles, taking what is Christ's (revelation) and giving it to them. Peter conveys this in his Pentecost sermon: "This Jesus God raised up, and of that we are all witnesses. Being therefore exalted at the right hand of God, and having received from the Father the promise of the Holy Spirit, he has poured out this that you yourselves are seeing and hearing" (Acts 2:32–33).

Jesus pours out his Spirit upon his people at Pentecost, fulfilling the Old Testament prediction of the new covenant promise, "I will put my Spirit within you" (Ezek. 36:27). Jesus's giving of the Spirit echoes the language of John 16:15, where the Spirit testifies to the Son. Jesus continues to identify with his disciples through the presence of his Spirit within them. While Luke does not explain all the specifics of Pentecost, the rest of the New Testament gives insight into the significance of the Spirit's arrival for the salvation of believers. Robert Letham explains one aspect of Pentecost: "The Spirit would come to indwell believers and unite them to Christ."[3]

Therefore, in redemptive-historical terms Pentecost marks the public announcement of the indwelling of the Spirit and the beginning of his ministry of uniting people to Christ.[4] While his ministry in Acts is not described in those terms, the remainder of the New Testament functions to explain what is going on "behind the scenes" in Acts—the Spirit's uniting believers to Jesus. Thus, Pentecost functions as the redemptive-historical prerequisite for the Spirit's ministry; it is the moment when God identifies with his people by indwelling them with his Spirit. And the Spirit engages in a ministry unpacked in the rest of the New Testament as union with Christ.

Luke provides the redemptive-historical foundation for union while demonstrating what such a union produces in the lives and witness of believers.

[3] Robert Letham, *Union with Christ: In Scripture, History, and Theology* (Phillipsburg, NJ: P&R, 2011), 48.
[4] Even as the work of Christ was applied to Old Testament saints before Jesus's death and resurrection, so the work of the Spirit was applied before Pentecost.

God's identification with his people through the indwelling of the Spirit establishes the foundation for the Spirit's uniting work. What the rest of Acts supplies is a picture of the Spirit doing his work of uniting people to Christ by saving them (as in Acts 11:15) and placing them in a new relationship with the risen Lord Jesus. It is evident, then, that understanding the work of the Spirit in Luke-Acts does not contradict a doctrine of union with Christ, even if it does not explain it as such.

Identification in the Conversion of Paul

Many commentators have identified significant connections between Paul's conversion (especially as recounted in Acts 9) and the theology of his letters, including union with Christ.[5] Paul's autobiography plays an explicit role in his theological thinking.[6] However, beyond explicit references to his conversion, there are several other places where one can draw a fairly straight line from his theological conclusions in an epistle back to his conversion account.

In Acts 9, Saul of Tarsus travels to Damascus to persecute Christians beyond the borders of Judea. En route, he is struck blind as he encounters the living God. "Who are you, Lord?" Saul asks. It is none other than Jesus himself. The dialogue in verses 4–5 is critical to connecting Saul's conversion experience and his doctrine of union with Christ: "Falling to the ground he [Saul] heard a voice saying to him, 'Saul, Saul, why are you persecuting me?' And he said, 'Who are you, Lord?' And he said, 'I am Jesus, whom you are persecuting.'"

The key here is Jesus's self-identification. First, he identifies himself as the God of the theophany.[7] This implies that Jesus is claiming the authority and even identity of God. Second, Jesus identifies himself with the infant church. In one sense, Jesus's claim that Saul is persecuting him seems odd—did Jesus not ascend? One could suggest that Jesus is referring to his emotional connection with the church. However, such an interpretation does not bear the weight of Jesus's question, "Why are you persecuting *me*?" This is no mere analogy. Jesus takes issue with Saul not because it is "as though" Saul is persecuting Jesus, but because he actually is persecuting him. David Peterson is perceptive when he says, "The risen Lord viewed the persecution of his dis-

[5] See Seyoon Kim, *The Origin of Paul's Gospel* (Grand Rapids: Eerdmans, 1981), which builds upon J. Gresham Machen, *The Origin of Paul's Religion* (New York: Macmillan, 1921).
[6] For examples, see Rom. 11:1–6; Phil. 3:1–11; 1 Tim. 1:12–16.
[7] Note here how the theophany of Acts 9 contains many characteristics of Old Testament theophanies associated with Yahweh (e.g., Ex. 3:1–6; 1 Samuel 3), as well as some of the language of prophetic commission (e.g., Jer. 1:9–10).

ciples as an attack on himself, clearly identifying himself with the church. . . . Those who are united to Christ by faith suffer as he did, and he identifies with them in their struggle."[8] Thus the question becomes, what is the nature of Jesus's identification with the church?

Seyoon Kim argues that this verse provides the foundation for the concept of the church as the body of Christ: "The remarkable conversation . . . must have led Paul to recognize the unity of Christ with his people: to persecute the followers of Jesus is to persecute him."[9] If this is the case, then it is not difficult to see how Paul's conversation with Jesus on the road to Damascus shaped his theology of union with Christ. As Campbell says, "The original catalyst for the development of Paul's theology of union with Christ may be seen as Jesus's words to Paul on the Damascus Road."[10] It is too much to say that in Acts 9 Luke teaches union with Christ. But it is not too much to say that Luke's recounting of Paul's conversion paints a picture of Jesus's self-identification with his people that Paul explains and expands using the concept of union.

Incorporation in the Rite of Baptism

The incorporation aspect of union with Christ appears in the book of Acts primarily in the context of baptism in the name of Jesus. As the sacrament of incorporation, baptism plays a critical role in any doctrine of union with Christ. In Acts, baptism functions as the mark of entrance into the people of God, a mark that extends to all types of people, Jew and Gentile alike.

At the end of his Pentecost sermon, Peter enjoins his hearers, "Repent and be baptized every one of you in the name of Jesus Christ for the forgiveness of your sins, and you will receive the gift of the Holy Spirit" (2:38). We are surprised at Peter's omission of the element of faith. If non-Christians asked what they must do to be saved, "Repent and believe" would likely be our succinct response. Verse 41 ("Those who received his word") indicates that Peter includes faith by implication in the commands to repent and be baptized. But Peter purposefully summarizes the gospel response as repentance and baptism. Repentance entails the crowd's recognition that they have rejected Jesus (v. 23), while baptism includes faith and functions as a change in alle-

---

[8] David G. Peterson, *The Acts of the Apostles*, The Pillar New Testament Commentary (Grand Rapids: Eerdmans, 2009), 304.

[9] Kim, *Origin of Paul's Gospel*, 253. He also notes that this type of identification is unique in the New Testament, where the closest parallel is 1 Cor. 8:12.

[10] Constantine R. Campbell, *Paul and Union with Christ: An Exegetical and Theological Study* (Grand Rapids: Zondervan, 2012), 420.

giance. Whereas the Jewish crowds once were enemies of Jesus, they now are baptized into him. Thus, baptism becomes the mark of covenant membership in the new covenant—the sign of incorporation into Jesus and therefore into his people.

Acts lacks the typical Pauline "in Christ" language. The closest we see to a parallel is in Luke's discussion of ministry "in the name of Jesus." At least twelve times throughout Acts, Luke uses this phrase to refer to the ministry of the apostles, especially in healing and baptism.[11] Craig Keener discusses the import of the phrase: "Baptism 'in Jesus's name' probably simply specifies Christian baptism as distinct from various Jewish immersion rituals. . . . People being baptized 'in his name' designated whose followers they would be."[12]

We cannot deduce from this that Luke intended to express an idea of union with Christ. However, Keener connects the Old Testament significance of an activity done "in the name of God" (meaning "by the authority of" or "on account of") and baptism in Jesus's name. He further points out that in Acts 2, being baptized in Jesus's name is the physical index of "calling on the name of the Lord (v. 21)."[13] Thus, in Acts baptism is the physical manifestation of repentance and faith as well as incorporation into the church. "Baptism in Jesus's name" is not so much a formulation of union with Christ as a statement of ownership in baptism. Baptism in Acts declares, "This is Jesus's baptism, and those who are baptized in Jesus's name are his followers." Though the link between baptism and the person of Jesus is unexplored in Acts, the connection between the two sets the stage for further clarification in the rest of the New Testament.

Luke does not explain the inner working of baptism. Rather, he shows the significance of baptism in the church's life. His treatment of baptism is primarily descriptive, not theological. He shows us what baptism looks like and how it is practiced in the life of the early church, but does not explain all its theological implications, including its connection to union with Christ.

Participation in the Repetition of Jesus's Story and Luke's Use of Isaiah's "Suffering Servant"

The participation aspect of union with Christ appears in two main places in Acts: in the repetition of Jesus's story in the church's life and in Luke's use of Isaiah's "suffering servant" passages.

---

[11] Acts 2:38; 3:6, 16; 4:18; 5:40; 8:16; 9:27; 10:48; 16:18; 19:5; 21:13; 26:9.
[12] Craig S. Keener, *Acts: An Exegetical Commentary* (Grand Rapids: Baker Academic, 2012), 983.
[13] Ibid.

Participation in the Repetition of Jesus's Story in the Life of the Church

In considering the growth and mission of the early church in Acts, we must take into account the context of the two-volume Luke-Acts as a whole. Dennis Johnson notes that one of the interpretive keys of Acts is Luke's Gospel.[14] Luke and Acts contain a number of parallels that draw important connections between the story of Jesus and that of the early church. The most meaningful connection as we consider union with Christ in Acts is the manner in which the story of the early church is in many ways a repetition of the story of Jesus told in the Gospel of Luke.

There are structural markers suggesting that the Jesus-church parallel is part of Luke's literary intent. M. D. Goulder notes parallels between Jesus and the church at the start of Luke's two volumes: (a) anointing by the Spirit, (b) a sermon explaining the anointing, (c) effective ministry in the power of the Spirit, and (d) resulting opposition/persecution by Judaism's leadership.[15]

Others have seen structural parallels between the ministry of Jesus and the main characters of Acts. David Moessner suggests that at various points Jesus is paralleled by Peter, Stephen, and Paul in Acts.[16] The parallels include Stephen's dying words, which echo Christ's passion, and Paul's final journey, in which he is "resolved" to return to Jerusalem for a third time, just as Jesus was. We can see how the apostles participate in the story of Christ by repeating aspects of it in their own lives.

What does this participation contribute to a concept of union with Christ? It suggests that the church participates in the story of Jesus in its discipleship and mission. That is, the recapitulation of Jesus's story in the early church's life points to the story of the church as a kind of union with Christ via fellowship with him. This participation is not an exact parallel—it does not diminish the exclusive nature of Christ's work—but it provides a picture of what it means to be united to Christ.[17] To put it another way, to be united to Christ is to share in his death and resurrection, his suffering and his glory. This is not explicitly stated in Acts as it is in the Epistles, but it is enacted in Acts as the church grows and engages in mission.

---

[14] Dennis E. Johnson, *The Message of Acts in the History of Redemption* (Phillipsburg, NJ: P&R, 1997), 7.

[15] M. D. Goulder, *Type and History in Acts* (London: SPCK, 1964), 54–55. I am indebted to Dennis Johnson's observation of this connection in *Message of Acts*, 61n20, as well as in personal correspondence.

[16] David P. Moessner, "'The Christ Must Suffer': New Light on the Jesus–Peter, Stephen, Paul Parallels in Luke-Acts," *Novum Testamentum* 28 (1986): 220–56.

[17] For example, we cannot be said to be participants in the atoning aspects of Christ's suffering. It is only Christ's suffering by virtue of his being fully God and fully man that can atone for people's sin. We participate with Christ in our discipleship, but our participation does not make atonement for sin.

Participation in Luke's Use of Isaiah's Suffering Servant Passages

Another parallel in Luke-Acts pointing toward union with Christ is Luke's use of Isaiah's servant songs in both volumes. In Luke, the servant songs are alluded to with reference to Jesus, while in Acts they are quoted with reference to the apostles as God's messengers.[18]

First, Simeon in Luke greets the infant Jesus as a "light for revelation to the Gentiles" (Luke 2:32), alluding to Isaiah 49:6.[19] In Acts 13:47, Paul and Barnabas appeal to the same passage as a command for themselves as messengers of the gospel:

The Lord has commanded us, saying,

"I have made you a light for the Gentiles,
    that you may bring salvation to the ends of the earth."

In Luke, Jesus is the light for the Gentiles, but in Acts the apostles become the extension of that light to the Gentiles. Thus, the mission of the church is wrapped up in its relationship to the Son.

Second, the programmatic verse of Acts alludes to the servant songs to suggest further connections between Jesus and his people. Whereas Simeon's quotation of Isaiah 49:6 omits the final phrase—"that my salvation may reach to the end of the earth"—Luke picks up the line in Acts 1 when Jesus commissions his disciples, "You will receive power when the Holy Spirit has come upon you, and you will be my witnesses in Jerusalem and in all Judea and Samaria, and *to the end of the earth*" (v. 8). Dennis Johnson explains, "The most explicit allusion to the servant songs is the expression, 'to the last part of the earth' . . . which is verbally identical to the Septuagint's [Greek translation's] reading of Isa 49:6."[20] Thus, Luke's use of this quotation in Acts 1:8 extends the mission of Jesus through his church in Acts. In Luke's Gospel Jesus is the light to the Gentiles; in Acts the church takes that light to the ends of the earth.

Luke suggests that both Jesus *and* his people fulfill Isaiah's picture of the suffering servant. The church fulfills the picture insofar as it continues to participate in Jesus's story by embodying his mission in its ministry. As above, we must affirm the uniqueness of the way in which Jesus is the suf-

---

[18] Again I am indebted to Dennis Johnson for this connection.

[19] The phrase "light for the nations" in Isa. 49:6 hearkens back to Gen. 12:3 and Yahweh's promise to bless the nations through Abraham.

[20] Dennis E. Johnson, "Jesus against the Idols: The Use of Isaianic Servant Songs in the Missiology of Acts," *Westminster Theological Journal* 52 (1990): 346.

fering servant—only *his* suffering atones for sin. However, as God's people suffer in the pursuit of his calling, they participate in his story, a participation that Paul will later suggest means more than "following in the footsteps of Jesus" but also sharing in his sufferings that we might also share in his glory (Rom. 8:17).

Conclusion

In Acts, union with Christ is not explicitly stated, nor are the inner workings of salvation explored. Instead, Acts seeks to document the spread of the kingdom of God (from Jerusalem to Judea, to Samaria, to the end of the earth) through the gospel of Jesus. As people repent and believe in Jesus, they are baptized and given the Holy Spirit, actions that were part of the warp and woof of the early church.

When we consider union with Christ in Acts, then, it is fitting to say that Acts provides the redemptive-historical foundation for union (Pentecost), demonstrates the reality of union enacted in the life of the church (in baptism, through the Spirit, and in participation in Jesus's story), and hints at the further formation of a concept of union through identification (especially in Paul's conversion). But Acts does not explicitly define the doctrine. Rather, Acts shows us what union with Christ looks like when acted out in the life of God's people, giving us glimpses of the implications of union without explicitly recognizing it. In Acts, union is the backdrop, the subtext, for all the events that occur—a subtext that becomes explicit in the rest of the New Testament. To ask if Acts teaches a doctrine of union with Christ is to ask the wrong question. When we consider the main themes of Acts in light of its genre (a narrative of the early church), purpose (to describe the church's growth), and context (within Luke-Acts and the rest of the New Testament), we find union not so much explicitly taught as enacted on the missional stage.

This has implications for how we read Acts and apply it to the life of the church today. If Acts is a picture of union with Christ embodied in the life of the early church, then we have in Acts a set of clues as to what the life of the church today ought to be like as we live in union with him.[21] For example, we should consider suffering, especially persecution, a form of participation in Christ, a way in which we are united with him. Thus, suffering is not to

---

[21] That is, with the necessary adjustments made with reference to redemptive-historical and cultural differences.

be shunned (nor excessively sought after) but understood as part of what it means to be a Christian.

Luke's account of the early church in Acts, then, rather than glaringly omitting union with Christ, actually supports it by embodying and demonstrating that union in the context of the people of God as they are united to Christ and indwelt by his Spirit.

Chapter 4

Union with Christ
in John's Gospel

It is customary to regard union with Christ as a Pauline doctrine, and indeed Paul has much to say about it. But so does John. The two apostles' idioms and emphases are different, but their teachings overlap considerably.[1] To gain an understanding of union with Christ, both John's and Paul's writings must be shown attention. Here we will study five passages in the Fourth Gospel that treat union with the Son of God:

- Jesus the Bread of Life in John 6:32–35, 48–58
- mutual indwelling of the Father and the Son in John 10:37–38
- mutual indwelling of the Father and the Son, and the Father and the Son and believers, in John 14:8–11, 20, 23
- Jesus the Vine, believers the branches in John 15:1–17
- mutual indwelling of the Father and the Son, and the Son and believers, in John 17:20–26

Jesus the Bread of Life in John 6:32–35, 48–58

John 6 places union with Christ in the context of the incarnation and God's plan of salvation. Jesus's Bread of Life sermon is one of the major discourses

---

[1] Cf. C. H. Dodd, "We cannot safely assume that the Johannine usage depends directly upon the Pauline, or may be directly explained from it." Dodd, *The Interpretation of the Fourth Gospel* (Cambridge, UK: Cambridge University Press, 1953), 193.

in the Gospel of John. Jesus combines a sign—multiplying loaves and fishes—and a sermon to portray himself as the bread from heaven.

A big crowd follows Jesus "because they saw the signs that he was doing on the sick" (v. 2). After testing Philip by asking him how he would feed such a large crowd, Jesus responds to Andrew's news that a boy has "five barley loaves and two fish" (v. 9). Jesus instructs the disciples to have the people sit down on the ample grass. There are five thousand men, and when women and children are added, the crowd totals about twenty thousand!

Jesus thanks God for the loaves, and his disciples distribute them to the people. "So also the fish, as much as they wanted" (v. 11). When all are full, he tells the disciples to collect the leftovers. They fill twelve baskets with pieces of leftover bread! The people proclaim Jesus "the Prophet" (of Deut. 18:15, 18), but he flees to prevent them from forcibly proclaiming him king.

Manna from Heaven

This noteworthy event[2] reminds attentive readers of God's feeding the Israelites with manna in Exodus 16. The next day the people follow Jesus, who has gone (by walking on the water!) to the other side of the Sea of Galilee. Jesus rebukes them for being concerned only for their stomachs; they take no interest in spiritual matters: "Do not work for the food that perishes, but for the food that endures to eternal life, which the Son of Man will give to you" (John 6:27).

The people ask Jesus for a sign, reminding him that God fed their fathers with manna in the wilderness: "He gave them bread from heaven to eat" (v. 31, citing Neh. 9:15; Pss. 78:24–25; 105:40). Jesus, after feeding the multitude with bread and after the people's reference to the manna, draws attention to himself: "Truly, truly, I say to you, it was not Moses who gave you the bread from heaven, but my Father gives you the true bread from heaven. For the bread of God is he who comes down from heaven and gives life to the world" (John 6:32–33).

Jesus points to a prominent theme in the Fourth Gospel—his superseding Old Testament figures, institutions, and events, here God's giving Israel manna through Moses. Moreover, this same God, Jesus's Father, provides "true bread from heaven. . . . he who comes down from heaven and gives life to the world" (vv. 32–33). Manna was God's means of temporarily satisfying

---

[2] Recorded in all four Gospels; see Matt. 14:13–21; Mark 6:30–44; and Luke 9:10–17.

Israel's physical hunger. But the incarnate Son, the Word made flesh, satisfies the world's spiritual hunger.

Once more, as often in John's Gospel, Jesus's hearers misunderstand. They do not realize that Jesus refers to himself as the "bread of God" (v. 33), and they mistake his words as referring to the special physical bread they request (v. 34). In order for them not to miss his point, Jesus spells it out: "I am the bread of life; whoever comes to me shall not hunger, and whoever believes in me shall never thirst" (v. 35). Jesus in his incarnation is the true source of eternal life for all who believe. As water satisfies thirst and bread satisfies hunger, so the incarnate Son of God satisfies every believer spiritually. Jesus then holds the crowd accountable for its unbelief.

A Panorama of the Father's and Son's Roles in Salvation

The idea of Jesus as the bread from heaven departs from center stage in verses 36–47. In fact, this section only mentions that idea in the mouths of opponents. Instead, this section presents a framework for understanding Jesus as the Bread of Life. It presents a panorama of the Father's and Son's roles in salvation:

1. The Father gives people to the Son (vv. 37, 39).
2. The Father draws people to the Son and teaches them (vv. 44–45; cf. 65).
3. People come to—believe in—the Son (vv. 37, 40, 44–45, 47; cf. 65).
4. They gain eternal life (vv. 40, 47; cf. 54, 58).
5. The Son will not cast them out, will not lose them (vv. 37, 39).
6. The Son will raise them on the last day (vv. 39–40, 44; cf. 54).

The Father's giving people to the Son is one of John's pictures of election. It governs the Son's saving mission as presented in John 17.[3] In John 6 the Father's giving people to the Son results in their believing in Jesus and in his raising them on the last day (vv. 37, 39).

The Father draws people to the Son. This overlaps Paul's teaching of effectual calling, whereby God uses the universal gospel call to effectively summon his people to himself (Rom. 8:29–30; 9:24). In John 6 the Father's drawing enables people to come to, that is, believe in (v. 35), the Son. Jesus changes

---

[3] The Son gives eternal life only to those given him by the Father, reveals the Father to them, prays only for them, and desires them to see his glory in heaven (John 17:2, 6, 9, 24, and 26). See Robert A. Peterson, *Election and Free Will*, Explorations in Biblical Theology (Phillipsburg, NJ: P&R, 2007).

idioms but teaches much the same thing when he says that those whom the Father teaches, those who learn from him, come to the Son (v. 45).

People come to Jesus (vv. 37, 44–45, 65). The parallelism in verse 35 shows that coming to Jesus means believing in him: "I am the bread of life; whoever *comes* to me shall not hunger, and whoever *believes* in me shall never thirst." Elsewhere in the passage, believing in Jesus is used as a synonym for coming to him (vv. 40, 47).

Those who believe in Jesus, who come to him, gain eternal life (vv. 40, 47). The former verse points to the future resurrection (to life). In the latter verse, eternal life is the believers' present possession, as is usual in John.

The Son pledges to keep those who believe in him (vv. 37, 39). He will never reject those whom the Father gave to him and who therefore come to him (v. 37). It is the Father's will that the Son preserve the elect for resurrection (v. 39).

The Son completes the panorama of salvation by promising to raise believers on the last day (vv. 39–40, 44). This resurrection is portrayed as final salvation and thus is the "resurrection of life" (5:29).

Viewing this panorama yields three main takeaways. First, there are different saving actions ascribed to the Father and to the Son. There is a division of labor among the Trinitarian persons.[4] The Father does the work of election and calling; he gives people to the Son and draws them to him. The Son does the work of preservation and resurrection.

Second, there is wonderful harmony between the Father and the Son. Although they play different roles in salvation, they work together. The Father gives people to the Son and draws them to him. And when they believe, the Son keeps and raises them. The Trinitarian persons do not work against each other but work in an accord that leads directly to the next takeaway.

Third, there is continuity in the identity of the people of God. Those whom the Father gives to the Son and draws to him are the same people who come to the Son and gain eternal life, and whom the Son keeps and raises to life on the last day.[5] From the beginning of salvation in God's election to the end in resurrection, the saints are secure in the love and plan of the Father and Son.

Jesus, the Bread of Life

Within the framework of verses 36–47 Jesus resumes his Bread of Life Discourse:

---

[4] As is customary, John locates the Holy Spirit's work in believers chiefly after Jesus's ascension.
[5] Cf. Rom. 8:29–30.

> I am the bread of life. Your fathers ate the manna in the wilderness, and
> they died. This is the bread that comes down from heaven, so that one may
> eat of it and not die. I am the living bread that came down from heaven.
> If anyone eats of this bread, he will live forever. And the bread that I will
> give for the life of the world is my flesh. (vv. 48–51)

Jesus repeats, "I am the bread of life" (v. 48; cf. v. 35). He is the fulfillment the
manna prefigured. The fathers were sustained in the wilderness by the bread
from heaven, but they still died; it sufficed for physical but not spiritual life. By
contrast, Jesus is the true Bread of Life, true in John's sense of the fulfillment
of Old Testament prefiguring. The manna in the wilderness was a type of the
"bread that comes down from heaven," that is, the Son of God becoming a
human being. Anyone who "eats" this bread will not die but live forever.

The terms "eat" and "feed" with reference to Jesus dominate the passage,
occurring eight times (in vv. 49–58). Carson explains their meaning: to appropriate "Jesus by faith, as in the preceding verses."[6] Jesus's reference to his flesh
($\sigma\acute{\alpha}\rho\xi$/*sarx*, the same word as in 1:14) fits this conclusion: "The bread that I will
give for the life of the world is my flesh" (v. 51). Jesus gives his flesh in his sacrifice on the cross. To eat the living bread, then, is to believe in his atoning death.

Once more the hearers stumble at Jesus's message: "How can this man give
us his flesh to eat?" (v. 52). In response Jesus does not soften his message but
makes it more offensive to Jewish ears, since the law prohibits eating blood:

> Truly, truly, I say to you, unless you eat the flesh of the Son of Man and
> drink his blood, you have no life in you. Whoever feeds on my flesh and
> drinks my blood has eternal life, and I will raise him up on the last day. For
> my flesh is true food and my blood is true drink. Whoever feeds on my
> flesh and drinks my blood abides in me and I in him. As the living Father
> sent me, and I live because of the Father, so whoever feeds on me, he also
> will live because of me. This is the bread that came down from heaven,
> not like the bread the fathers ate and died. Whoever feeds on this bread
> will live forever. (vv. 53–58)

Jesus's words are stark: failing to eat his flesh and drink his blood disquali-
fies people from eternal life; eating them gives eternal life now and resurrection life at the end of the age. His flesh and blood are true spiritual food and
drink. Manna prolonged physical life, but the living bread conveys eternal

---

[6] D. A. Carson, *The Gospel according to John*, The Pillar New Testament Commentary (Grand Rapids: Eerdmans, 1991), 295.

life. Although Christians read these verses and commonly think of the Lord's Supper, their primary referent is Jesus's sacrificial death. The blood in a sacrificial context symbolizes violent death, whether of Old Testament sacrificial animals or of Jesus, the "Lamb of God, who takes away the sin of the world" (1:29). He repeats similar words at the end of the passage to underscore the importance of feeding on him to live forever (v. 58).

This passage inserts an additional point—Jesus calls himself the "Son of Man" (6:53). In the context of repeated mention of his flesh and blood, this title underscores his humanness. But if we take into account the occurrences of "Son of Man" before and after our passage, the title points to one who is more than a mere human being. Verse 27 says that the Father has set his seal on the Son of Man, and verse 62 speaks of his ascension, implying his previous descent in the incarnation. Andreas Köstenberger summarizes John's use of this title: "The expression . . . is fused in Johannine theology to denote both Jesus's heavenly origin and destination (descent/ascent; 1:51; 3:13; 6:62; cf. Dan. 7:13) and his "lifting up" (substitutionary sacrifice) on the cross (3:14; 8:28; 12:34; cf. 6:53; 12:23; 13:31)."[7] It denotes both Jesus's deity and his humanity.

Union with Christ

Much of the Bread of Life Discourse has implications for union with Christ because of the language of "eating" or "feeding on" him for eternal life. We "ingest" him, so to speak, by faith so that he becomes a part of us, even as food we eat becomes a part of us. Similarly, Jesus's words at the Last Supper imply union with him, although it will not be until after his resurrection that his disciples understand his message. This language of partaking, used throughout John 6, implies a faith union.

But verse 56 makes union explicit: "Whoever feeds on my flesh and drinks my blood abides in me and I in him." Here is the first appearance in the Fourth Gospel of language of mutual abiding or indwelling, which will reappear six times. John speaks often of the Father and Son indwelling one another, sharing the divine life, mutually existing in one another: 10:38; 14:10–11, 20; 17:21–23. This is a great mystery within the mystery of the Holy Trinity, a mystery of mysteries, if you will. Theologians call it *perichoresis* (Greek), *circumincession*, or *co-inherence*.[8]

---

[7] Andreas J. Köstenberger, *John*, Baker Exegetical Commentary on the New Testament (Grand Rapids: Baker Academic, 2004), 86.

[8] "Circumincessio: *circumincession* or *coinherence*; used as a synonym of the Greek *perichoresis* . . . or *emperichoresis*. . . . *Circumincessio* refers primarily to the coinherence of the persons of the Trinity in the divine essence and

Astonishingly, Jesus sometimes uses the language of mutual indwelling with reference to him (or him and the Father) *and believers*—14:20; 17:21–23; and here in 6:56! Certainly there are differences between the way the persons of the Trinity mutually indwell one another and the way they and believers do this. But the whole point of the three verses just mentioned is that there are similarities too! The differences include the fact that the persons of the Trinity are divine and able (mysteriously) ontologically to indwell one another, so that there is one God eternally existing in three modes or persons. And this mutual indwelling is eternal.

The persons of the Trinity do not share their deity with us, and our fellowship with them had a beginning (since we had a beginning), but there are similarities between the Trinity's mutual indwelling and ours with the divine persons. These include the divine persons' fellowship with us due to their deity and grace (1 John 1:3), and ours with them! The initiative and glory are all theirs, but the resultant fellowship is also ours.

Jesus touches on this when he says, "As the living Father sent me, and I live because of the Father, so whoever feeds on me, he also will live because of me" (John 6:57). Only God has life in himself, and so he is called the "living Father." When Jesus says, "I live because of the Father," he is speaking not of his eternal existence but of his existence as the God-*man* in the incarnation. Those who feed on Christ by faith "also live because of" him. That is, the eternal life resident in the Father and communicated to the incarnate Son is shared with believers! Raymond Brown's words are apt: "In its brevity, vs. 57 is a most forceful declaration of the tremendous claim that Jesus gives *man a share in God's own life*."[9] Of course, Jesus skips some steps and does not mention his death and resurrection, although the former is implied in the reference to feeding on him (his "flesh"), and his cross always implies his empty tomb.

Jesus's Incarnation and Mutual Abiding

I need to emphasize the significance of Jesus's incarnation for union with him. The passage says six times that Jesus, the Bread of Life, came "from heaven" (vv. 32, 33, 38, 50, 51, 58) and four times that the Father "sent" him

in each other, but it can also indicate the coinherence of Christ's divine and human natures in their communion or personal union." Richard A. Muller, *Dictionary of Latin and Greek Theological Terms* (Grand Rapids: Baker, 1985), 67.

[9] Raymond E. Brown, *The Gospel according to John: I–XII*, Anchor Bible (Garden City, NY: Doubleday, 1966), 292, emphasis original.

(vv. 38, 39, 44, 57). The incarnation is indispensable not only to the atonement and resurrection of the Son of God. It is indispensable also for fallen human beings to be united to him. Had he not become one of us, we would never be joined to him. Revisit Jesus's words: "Whoever feeds on my flesh and drinks my blood abides in me, and I in him" (v. 56). For this feeding and drinking to occur, God had to become a man. It is axiomatic: no incarnation, no union with Christ.

The theme of abiding is taken up in John 15 and 1 John. To abide in Christ is to be in Christ. But "to abide" is more. It adds a dimension of fellowship; it is warmer than merely being. Jesus, then, speaks of his and believers' having fellowship with one another: "Whoever feeds on my flesh and drinks my blood abides in me and I in him" (v. 56). This is mutual abiding. Because of our union with Christ in his death and resurrection, we have fellowship with him, and he with us. John develops this theme in chapter 15.

Mutual Indwelling of the Father and the Son in John 10:37–38

Jesus continues to run afoul of the Jewish authorities. After they try to bait him into claiming to be the Messiah, he tells them that they are not part of the people of God and for that reason do not believe in him or his works (vv. 24–26). By contrast, Jesus's own believe in him, are known by him, and obey him. He gives them eternal life as a gift and emphatically declares that they will never perish (vv. 27–28). He says that no one can seize them from his or the Father's hands (vv. 28–29). He explains that he and the Father are one in keeping the sheep safe, in performing the divine work of preserving God's people (v. 30).

Jesus Is Accused of Blasphemy

At this the Jews again pick up stones (cf. 8:59) with the intention of stoning him. In reply Jesus points to the good works he has performed in their midst, works given to him by the Father (cf. 17:4): "For which of them are you going to stone me?" (10:32). His hearers are indignant: "It is not for a good work that we are going to stone you but for blasphemy, because you, being a man, make yourself God" (v. 33).

They cannot deny that Jesus has healed a lame man and given sight to a blind man (5:1–9; 9:1–7). So, though he mentions his deeds, they steer the conversation in another direction and focus on his words. They target his saying, "I and the Father are one." He is in their estimation a mere human being, and yet he dares to exercise divine prerogatives—claiming to bestow eternal life and preserve God's people. And he has the audacity to claim unity with God in a way that implies deity![10]

Jesus's hearers react to his bold words by accusing him of blaspheming the only true God and by intending to stone him. Jesus defends himself using a Jewish argument from the greater to the lesser (or from the harder to imagine to the easier): "Is it not written in your Law, 'I said you are gods'? If he called them gods to whom the word of God came—and Scripture cannot be broken—do you say of him whom the Father consecrated and sent into the world, 'You are blaspheming,' because I said, 'I am the Son of God'?" (10:34–36). Jesus points to Psalm 82:6, where the Lord chastises human rulers (or judges) for unjust judgment in favoring the wicked rich and neglecting the poor and weak (vv. 2–4):

> I said, "You are gods,
>   sons of the Most High, all of you;
> nevertheless, like men you shall die,
>   and fall like any prince." (vv. 6–7)

Jesus Plays by His Opponents' Rules

So Jesus employs the argument from the harder to the easier. If God did the more difficult thing and called human rulers who stand in his place "gods," why do Jesus's hearers complain when he does the easier thing—calls himself the Son of God? The argument itself does not prove Jesus's deity. But his words used within the argument do that very thing, for he speaks of himself as being set apart by the Father and sent into the world (John 10:36). This speaks of his preexistence, his having lived a divine life before his incarnation. Jesus plays by his opponents' rules and responds to their accusation of blasphemy by arguing in Jewish fashion from a psalm. He calls Psalm 82:6 the "Law" because, as all of Holy Scripture, it bears its divine author's authority and thus is legally binding for settling theological arguments such as this one—it "cannot be broken" (John 10:35).

Jesus continues: "If I am not doing the works of my Father, then do not believe me; but if I do them, even though you do not believe me, believe the works, that you may know and understand that the Father is in me and I am

---

[10] Doubtless they have not recovered from his putting his healing of the lame man on par with God's works and calling God his Father in such a way as to claim equality with him (5:17–18).

in the Father" (John 10:37–38). Jesus turns the conversation back to his deeds, which the Jews cannot deny. He presents his hearers with a dilemma. Either they must prove that his deeds are not from God—but this is impossible because everyone knows who alone can heal the lame and the blind—or, if his deeds are from God, his hearers should put their faith in those deeds, even if they stumble at Jesus's words.

Jesus Teaches the Mutual Indwelling of the Father and Him

Jesus's words bear repeating: "Even though you do not believe me, believe the works, that you may know and understand that the Father is in me and I am in the Father" (v. 38). The hearers' response is predictable: "Again they sought to arrest him, but he escaped from their hands" (v. 39).[11] It is no wonder they want to arrest him, for his claims are stupendous. He declares that the one whom they regard as their God is "in" him and that he is "in" their God! Here for the first time in the Fourth Gospel Jesus speaks of the mutual indwelling of the Father and him. He wants his hearers to observe his signs and sermons (cf. 14:10; 17:4–8. In both texts God's *work* includes Jesus's *words*.) and conclude that he and the Father are "in" one another. Carson explains, "There is between the Father and the Son what theologians call a 'mutual co-inherence': each is 'in' the other."[12] The Father indwells the Son, and the Son indwells the Father.[13]

This mutual indwelling (perichoresis or circumincession) is an important corollary of the fact that God is a Trinity of divine persons. There is only one God; polytheism is never seriously entertained in either Testament. This one God exists eternally in three persons—Father, Son, and Holy Spirit. And these three are not merely successive modes of existence of the one being of God (as modalistic Monarchianism or modalism itself maintains). Rather they simultaneously exist as three persons in God. From all eternity there has always been the Father, the Son, and the Holy Spirit, one God. Perichoresis or circumincession is a corollary of these truths. It maintains that the three Trinitarian persons are not each one-third of the Deity but that each is fully

---

[11] That Jesus's hearers desire to harm him is a substantial theme in John's Gospel; cf. 5:18; 7:1, 30, 44; 8:20, 37, 40, 59; 10:31, 39; 11:53.

[12] Carson, *Gospel according to John*, 400.

[13] Of course, the Holy Spirit co-inheres Father and Son, as they co-inhere him. But John primarily locates the Holy Spirit after Pentecost (cf. 7:39). Köstenberger says, "In every case where the Spirit is clearly in view [in the first half of John's Gospel, where such references are few], the reference relates to the Spirit's role in Jesus' ministry (1:32–33; 3:34; 6:63; 7:39)." Andreas J. Köstenberger, *A Theology of John's Gospel and Letters*, Biblical Theology of the New Testament (Grand Rapids: Zondervan, 2009), 542. The references in the second half of John's Gospel are numerous and relate primarily to the Spirit's ministry to believers after Pentecost.

God. The Father is all of God; the Son is all of God; the Spirit is all of God. Yet there are not three Gods but one. The entirety of the divine essence resides in Father, Son, and Holy Spirit. Or to say it another way, the three persons mutually indwell one another. The Father indwells the Son and the Holy Spirit. The Son indwells the Father and the Spirit. And the Spirit indwells the Father and the Son. Although the persons are distinguishable—and we must distinguish them and not put the Father or the Spirit on the cross, for example—they are inseparable. And another way to confess this inseparability is to affirm mutual indwelling.

Therefore, because the Father indwells the Son and vice versa, Jesus is not guilty of blasphemy. When he speaks, the Father speaks. When he acts, the Father acts. This mysterious truth of mutual indwelling sheds light on many sayings in John's Gospel that would otherwise remain opaque, as we will see. Moreover, this mutual indwelling, to which 10:38 attests, is the basis for the mutual indwelling of the Father and Son (and Spirit) *and* believers in chapters 14 and 17. Beasley-Murray is succinct: the unity of Jesus and the Father is "now defined in terms of mutual indwelling. . . . The expression conveys the thought of completest unity, a relation *sui generis*; nevertheless we learn later that it forms the basis of a union between God and man through the Son by virtue of the redemptive event."[14] It is to this grand topic that we now turn.

Mutual Indwelling of the Father and the Son, and the Father and the Son and Believers, in John 14:8–11, 20, 23

Jesus comforts the disciples by encouraging their faith in him. He tells them of his departure to prepare places for them in the Father's heavenly house and promises to return for them (vv. 1–3). Furthermore, he tells them that they know the way to the Father's house in heaven (v. 4). Thomas protests that they know neither where Jesus is going nor the way to get there (v. 5). To this Jesus says famously: "I am the way, and the truth, and the life. No one comes to the Father except through me" (v. 6).

Philip Asks for a Theophany

Jesus is the only road ("way") to the Father's heavenly home; he is the only Savior of the world. He explains that if his disciples knew him, they would

---

[14] George R. Beasley-Murray, *John*, Word Biblical Commentary (Waco, TX: Word, 1987), 177–78.

know the Father; in fact, says Jesus, "From now on you do know him and have seen him" (v. 7). At this Philip asks for a theophany, an appearance of God: "Show us the Father, and it is enough for us" (v. 8). Discouraged, Jesus replies:

> Have I been with you so long, and you still do not know me, Philip? Whoever has seen me has seen the Father. How can you say, "Show us the Father"? Do you not believe that I am in the Father and the Father is in me? The words that I say to you I do not speak on my own authority, but the Father who dwells in me does his works. Believe me that I am in the Father and the Father is in me, or else believe on account of the works themselves. (14:9–11)

Jesus is chagrined that, after all their time together, Philip (who speaks for the disciples) does not understand that to see the Son is to see the Father. Is this because the Son is the revealer of God, a familiar theme in John? The answer is yes, but there is a deeper reason, one that qualifies the Son to make the Father known. Jesus puts this answer in the form of a question: "Do you not believe that I am in the Father and the Father is in me?" (v. 10).

Once more Jesus speaks of the mutual indwelling of the Father and the Son. Here he reverses the order he gave in 10:38:

> . . . that you may know and understand that the Father is in me and I am in the Father. (10:38)

> Do you not believe that I am in the Father and the Father is in me? (14:10)

The disciples do not need a theophany of the invisible Father—they see the incarnate Son. Since he and the Father mutually co-inhere, to see the Son is to see the Father. It is only the Son's incarnation that enables him to be seen—and make no mistake: in seeing him they see the invisible God made visible (Col. 1:15; Heb. 1:3).

Because the Father indwells the Son, Jesus can say, "The words that I say to you I do not speak on my own authority, but the Father who dwells in me does his works" (John 14:10). The Father indwelling the Son performs his "works," which include the words and deeds of Jesus. Next Jesus calls for faith from his disciples: "Believe me that I am in the Father and the Father is in me, or else believe on account of the works themselves" (v. 11). Even though the disciples do not yet understand perichoresis, the signs point them in the right direction: "The miracles are non-verbal Christological signposts" that point to God's saving work in Jesus's ministry.[15]

The Disciples Will Enjoy Mutual Indwelling with the Son

Jesus promises to ask the Father to send the Spirit of truth to his followers. Moreover, the Spirit will dwell with the disciples and be in them (vv. 16–17). Jesus tells them of his departure but promises to come to them in the resurrection (v. 18). They, not the world, will see the resurrected Son; because of his resurrection, they too will experience resurrection life—regeneration now and resurrection from the grave to life at the end of the age (v. 19). Jesus's next words involve an important addition to our study of the mutual indwelling of the Father and Son: "In that day you will know that I am in my Father, and you in me, and I in you" (v. 20).

Here for the first time *believers* are caught up in the divine co-inherence. After Jesus is raised, his followers will understand that he indwells the Father, that is, that Jesus is divine. They will come to understand also a wonderful corollary—they are "in" Christ and he is "in" them. The language of perichoresis, used exclusively of the persons of the Godhead up until now, is extended to include the disciples, who will enjoy a form of mutual indwelling with the Son. I say a "form" of mutual indwelling because on one level the Trinitarian persons' sharing of the divine life is theirs alone. On another level, however, believers enter into fellowship with the Son (and the Father and the Spirit), and they do so now by faith in the risen Lord Jesus. The disciples will be "in" the Son, that is, united to him spiritually—in union with the living Christ. And he will join the Spirit of truth indwelling them (vv. 17, 20). C. K. Barrett's words are apt: "The resurrection of Jesus and his presence with his own points [sic] unmistakably to the continuity of the divine life which flows from the Father, through the Son, and in the church."[16]

Here is Johannine language of union with Christ. Of course, the disciples do not understand all of this in the upper room. After their Lord is raised, however, they will both experience it and understand it in part.

The Father and the Son Will Make Their Home with Christians

Jesus continues to speak of the same wonderful reality—this time expressed as the Father's and the Son's dwelling with believers—by using a different

---

[15] Carson, *Gospel according to John*, 495.
[16] C. K. Barrett, *The Gospel according to St. John*, 2nd ed. (Philadelphia: Westminster, 1978), 465.

figure of speech. In 14:1–3 he spoke of his preceding the disciples to heaven to prepare rooms for them in the Father's heavenly house. Now he returns to the image of a home but this time uses it of his and the Father's coming to the disciples to make their home with them on earth: "If anyone loves me, he will keep my word, and my Father will love him, and we will come to him and make our home with him" (v. 23). Brown correctly states, "Here it ['dwelling place'] is used for the indwelling of the Father and the Son with the believer."[17] And Köstenberger is right: "This is the only place in the NT where the Father and the Son are both said to indwell believers."[18]

It is important to see the differences between the uses of "home" imagery in 14:1–6 and verse 23. In the former passage Jesus goes ahead of the disciples to heaven to prepare a place for them in God's house. In the latter passage, the Father and the Son come to make their home with believers on earth. Carson captures the significance for our study:

> *My Father will love him, and we will come to him and make our home . . . with him.* Thus, while Jesus leaves his disciples in order to prepare in his Father's house "dwelling-places" (cf. v. 2) for his followers, he simultaneously joins with the Father . . . making a "dwelling-place" in the believer. Presumably this manifestation of the Father and the Son in the life of the believer is through the Spirit, although the text does not explicitly say so. Other New Testament passages testify to the dwelling of the Son in the Christian (e.g., Eph. 3:17); this is the only place where the Father and Son are linked in this task. . . . This is an anticipation, an inauguration, of the final, consummating experience of God.[19]

When Jesus departs, he will not leave his disciples as orphans. He will send them the Spirit, whom they will know, who will indwell them and be in them (vv. 16–18). In addition, he will not leave them "homeless." Instead, the Father and the Son will come to "make their home" with believers. Jesus, then, employs this "homey" figure to reinforce his teaching on union. When Jesus ascends to the Father, the two of them will indwell God's people so that believers will experience the "immediate presence of the Deity."[20] It will be

---

[17] Raymond E. Brown, *The Gospel according to John: XIII–XXI*, Anchor Bible (Garden City, NY: Doubleday, 1970), 648.
[18] Köstenberger, *John*, 441. Believers are said to be "in" the Father and the Son in John 17:21.
[19] Carson, *Gospel according to John*, 504, emphasis original.
[20] Leon Morris, *The Gospel according to John*, The New International Commentary on the New Testament (Grand Rapids: Eerdmans, 1971), 654.

Paul's part to emphasize the Spirit's indwelling of God's people corporately and individually.

Jesus the Vine, Believers the Branches in John 15:1–17

In Jesus's Vine and Branches Discourse we find the largest concentration of "abiding" language in Scripture; the word "abide(s)" appears no fewer than eleven times in these verses. And many of the uses pertain to the mutual abiding of believers and Christ. To understand this language we must investigate Jesus's use of vine and branches imagery.

Jesus, the True Vine

Building on the Old Testament picture of Israel as the vineyard of the Lord (found, e.g., in Isa. 5:1–7), Jesus, as is customary in John, presents himself as the fulfillment of Israel: "I am the true vine, and my Father is the vinedresser" (John 15:1). Jesus is the true Vine, the completion of Old Testament Israel; whereas Israel the vine always failed, he succeeds.[21] The picture of the Father as vinedresser speaks of him as the director of the Son's mission and implies harmony between the Father and Son in executing this mission.

Jesus portrays two kinds of branches "in" him. The first bears no fruit, so the Father removes it from the vine. The second kind of branch bears fruit, so the Father prunes it to make it more fruitful. Does the language of being "in" Jesus the Vine unfailingly indicate union with him, so that the fruitless branch is in union and then becomes detached? There are two good reasons for answering in the negative. First, throughout Scripture, although God's people exhibit degrees of fruitfulness (cf. Matt. 13:23), to be *fruitless* indicates an absence of divine life (cf. Matt. 7:16–19). Fruitlessness is indicative of a false profession of faith. Persons partaking of divine life produce fruit.

The second reason that "every branch in me that does not bear fruit" indicates an unsaved person is the immediate context. A key is given in verse 8: "By this my Father is glorified, that you bear much fruit and so prove to be my disciples." Fruit bearing is proof of discipleship, and lack of fruit betrays that one was never really connected to the vine in a life-giving way. The unfruitful branch Jesus has most in mind is Judas, who, inspired by Satan, has already departed to betray his master (13:27–30). Judas fooled his fellow disciples (13:29) but not Jesus (6:64, 70–71).

---

[21] Beasley-Murray, *John*, 272.

If the fruitless branch's being "in" the Vine (15:2) does not indicate true union with him, what does it indicate? The answer is that it shows close contact with Jesus, and though this pertains to all future apostates, it especially pertains to him who was so trusted as to be entrusted with the moneybag but proved untrustworthy (12:6; 13:2, 21, 26–30)!

Mutual Abiding of Jesus and the Disciples

Jesus's purifying word has cleansed the eleven; now he tells them to abide in him and he will abide in them (15:4). Even as a branch severed from a vine cannot produce fruit, so it is with Jesus's disciples, as he says, "apart from me you can do nothing" (v. 5). False, that is, fruitless, branches are cast into hellfire: "If anyone does not abide in me he is thrown away like a branch and withers; and the branches are gathered, thrown into the fire, and burned" (v. 6).

The most important question for our project is the meaning of abiding in Jesus. What does it mean? It is helpful to see the uses of "abide" set out in a list:

- "*Abide* in me, and I in you." (v. 4)
- "As the branch cannot bear fruit by itself, unless it *abides* in the vine, neither can you, unless you *abide* in me." (v. 4)
- "Whoever *abides* in me and I in him, he it is that bears much fruit." (v. 5)
- "If anyone does not *abide* in me . . ." (v. 6)
- "If you *abide* in me, and my words *abide* in you, ask whatever you wish, and it will be done for you." (v. 7)
- "As the Father has loved me, so have I loved you. *Abide* in my love." (v. 9)
- "If you keep my commandments, you will *abide* in my love, just as I have kept my Father's commandments and *abide* in his love." (v. 10)
- "You did not choose me, but I chose you and appointed you that you should go and bear fruit and that your fruit should *abide*." (v. 16)

In verse 9, Jesus implies what it means to abide in him—it means to abide in his love. That is, it means to continue in fellowship with him, to love (and obey) him, even as he does the Father (v. 10). Beasley-Murray is correct: abiding "connotes continuing to live in association or in union with him. . . . To 'remain' in Jesus is also to remain in his *love*, just as Jesus throughout this life remained in the Father's love."[22]

Jesus does not mention the mutual indwelling of the Father and Son in this passage. Rather, he focuses on his and believers' mutual abiding in love:

---

[22] Ibid., emphasis original.

"Abide in me, and I in you" (v. 4). Mutual abiding overlaps the idea of mutual indwelling. Again, to abide in Christ is to "be" in him, but it is more—to love him. Likewise, for him to abide in us is for him to continue to love us. Abiding, then, is a covenantal concept that speaks of the Son's continuing to love his people and their continuing to love him. As with many pictures of union with Christ, this one is corporate and individual: "I am the vine; you are the branches. Whoever abides in me and I in him . . ." (v. 5).

What Is the Fruit?

Jesus gives many wonderful ramifications of this mutual abiding; he fleshes out what fruit bearing entails, as I summarized twenty-five years ago:

> The fruit of which he speaks is obedience to his commands (v. 10) and love for other believers (vv. 12–14). Moreover, Jesus himself is the disciples' model of both of these: he obeys his Father's commands (v. 10), and he gives the greatest example of love in laying down his life for them (vv. 12–13). Still another fruit is the great joy that comes from continuing in a warm personal relationship with Jesus (v. 11).[23]

Though the repeated emphasis of John 15 is on the disciples' responsibility and obedience as covenant keepers, divine sovereignty is not omitted. "You did not choose me, but I chose you and appointed you that you should go and bear fruit and that your fruit should abide, so that whatever you ask the Father in my name, he may give it to you" (v. 16). Their covenant Lord Jesus chose and ordained them to fruit bearing. And he ordained that their fruit should "abide." He adds another result of bearing fruit—answered prayer.

Hans Burger sums up the message of the vine and the branches this way: "Jesus is the true vine. Apart from him, his disciples can do nothing (15:5), but remaining in him they will bear much fruit. He is the source of life and only in a communion of reciprocal inhabitation will his disciples find life and be fruitful."[24] Now this "communion of reciprocal inhabitation" amazingly grows out of the "communion of reciprocal inhabitation" of the divine Father and the divine Son. In all of Scripture this is most powerfully communicated in John 17, to which we now turn.

---

[23] Robert A. Peterson, *Getting to Know John's Gospel: A Fresh Look at Its Main Ideas* (Phillipsburg, NJ: P&R, 1989), 11.
[24] Hans Burger, *Being in Christ: A Biblical and Systematic Investigation in a Reformed Perspective* (Eugene, OR: Wipf and Stock, 2009), 363.

Mutual Indwelling of the Father and the Son, and the Son and Believers, in John 17:20–26

In John 17, an amazing chapter, the Son of God envisions himself as having already completed his mission and returned to the Father in heaven. I regard the traditional division as correct: Jesus prays for himself (vv. 1–5), his disciples (vv. 6–19), and the world (vv. 20–26). Although the unity of the Trinity is the measure of the disciples' unity in verse 11, our focus is on the verses in which Jesus prays for the world.

Jesus prays for the unity of future believers, "that they may all be one, just as you, Father, are in me, and I in you, that they also may be in us, so that the world may believe that you have sent me" (v. 21). Here the mutual indwelling of the Father and Son is the basis for the unity of those who will believe in Jesus through the apostles' witness. Furthermore, Jesus prays "that they also may be in us."

Believers Are in the Father and the Son

This is the only time John speaks of believers' being in the Father and the Son; every other time believers are said to be in the Son.[25] John thus encourages systematizing his teachings. In fact, though John never says we are in the Holy Spirit (and this is in keeping with his post-Pentecostal positioning of the Spirit), systematically we may conclude that we are in the Holy Trinity. This is an inescapable conclusion, given the unity of the Godhead. We distinguish the divine persons but never separate them.[26] Here believers are caught up in the mutual indwelling of the Godhead! We maintain the Creator/creature distinction and insist that the members of the Trinity indwell one another and us in ways we do not indwell the Trinity. Still, it is mysterious and marvelous to try to understand that believers are "in" the Trinity. In a creaturely, grace-caused way, through Christ we participate in the divine love and life the Trinitarian persons have always shared.

Jesus specifies the reason for his praying for unity among believers inspired by mutual indwelling of the Father and Son: "that the world may believe that you have sent me" (v. 21). In the epitome of Jesus's teaching on the subject in John's Gospel, we learn that perichoresis is missional. The remarkable unity among God's people is for the purpose of lost persons' believing in the Son's incarnation (and saving ministry).

---

[25] As previously noted, in John 14:23 the Father and Son are said to indwell believers. See pp. 62–63.

[26] Even the separation evidenced in Jesus's cry of dereliction in Matt. 27:46 is relational and not ontological.

The Co-inherence of the Father and Son and the
Son's Co-inherence with Believers

Jesus continues to talk to the Father: "The glory that you have given me I have given to them, that they may be one even as we are one, I in them and you in me, that they may become perfectly one, so that the world may know that you sent me and loved them even as you loved me" (vv. 22–23). The divine glory the Father gave to the incarnate Son is the basis for believers' being unified even as the Father and Son are unified (v. 22). Jesus adds, "I in them and you in me" (v. 23). He combines the Father's indwelling the Son with his own indwelling believers. The co-inherence of the Father and Son is put alongside the Son's indwelling of believers. Once more, though John never says so, we may systematize and conclude that the Trinity indwells believers.[27]

We must repeat: the divine co-inherence is unique and cannot be duplicated with mere creatures. Still, the measure that Jesus gives for Christians' unity is the unity between Father and Son. And that unity involves the Father's indwelling the Son and the Son's indwelling Christians. Leon Morris is succinct: "Indwelling is the secret of it all. Christ indwells believers and the Father indwells Him."[28] Once more the Savior points in a missional direction: "that the world may know that you sent me and loved them even as you loved me" (v. 23). Christian unity is one of God's means of drawing unsaved people to the love of the Father in the Son.

At the end of his prayer Jesus returns to the theme of love: "I made known to them your name, and I will continue to make it known, that the love with which you have loved me may be in them, and I in them" (v. 26). Jesus rehearses his words earlier in the prayer—he revealed the Father to his disciples (cf. vv. 6–8). Now he adds that he will keep on revealing the Father to them. His purpose? That the love the Father has for the Son may be in the disciples, and Christ may be in them. It is fitting that the last three words of this great prayer speak of the Son's indwelling the people of God as fulfillment of the ministry given him by the Father.

Conclusion

The Gospel of John has much to say about union with Christ. John never speaks of believers' dying with Christ or being buried and raised with him, as

---

[27] Cf. Jesus's command in Matt. 28:19 to baptize "in the name of the Father and of the Son and of the Holy Spirit," that is, baptize them into union with the three Trinitarian persons.
[28] Morris, *Gospel according to John*, 735.

does Paul. And he does not speak as does Paul of God's blessing us "in Christ" or "in him." Instead, in the Fourth Gospel Jesus speaks largely in the first person in his discourses of the Bread of Life, the Good Shepherd, and the vine and the branches, and in his High Priestly Prayer to teach complementary truths. I will treat the following themes:

- The Father and the Son indwell one another.
- The Father and the Son will indwell believers.
- The Father and the Son and believers will indwell one another.

The Father and the Son Indwell One Another

John declares that the Father is in the Son and indwells him, the Son is in the Father, and the Father and the Son are in one another. In sum: the Father and the Son mutually indwell one another.

The Father is in the Son. Addressing the Father, Jesus, before his death and resurrection, prays concerning believers, "I in them and *you in me*" (17:23). And the Father indwells the Son. Being in the Son is equivalent to indwelling the Son, as the following parallelism reveals. Jesus says to Philip, "Do you not believe that I am in the Father and *the Father is in me*? The words that I say to you I do not speak on my own authority, but *the Father who dwells in me* does his works" (14:10).

Additionally, the Son is in the Father. Jesus prepares the disciples for his exit and the Spirit's entrance—"In that day you will know that *I am in my Father*" (14:20).

In point of fact, the Father and Son are in one another:

The Father is in me and I am in the Father. (10:38)

Do you not believe that I am in the Father and the Father is in me? (14:10)

Believe me that I am in the Father and the Father is in me. (14:11)

. . . just as you, Father, are in me, and I in you. (17:21)

We conclude, then, that the Father and the Son are in one another or indwell one another. Because of this perichoresis (mutual divine indwelling), amazingly, seeing Jesus means seeing the invisible Father (14:9). None of the passages above include the Holy Spirit in the mutual indwelling. This fits John's pattern of relegating the Spirit's ministries largely to after Pentecost.

Therefore, admitting this silence in John, we apply systematic theology to his teaching and include the Holy Spirit. All three Trinitarian persons are in one another. They share the divine life; each of them is wholly God and is in the other two divine persons.

The Father and the Son Will Indwell Believers

John affirms that the Son will be in believers and the Father and the Son will come to make their home with believers. In sum: the Father and the Son will indwell believers.

The Son will be in believers. Jesus promises that when he sends the Spirit of truth, "You will know that I am in my Father, and you in me, and *I in you*" (14:20). Not only will Christ indwell believers; he will also make them aware of his presence. In his priestly prayer to the Father Jesus twice says he will be in believers. Jesus gave the disciples glory so that they may be unified, "even as we are one, *I in them* and you in me" (17:22–23). A few verses later he says that he made the Father known to the disciples and will continue to do so, that the Father's love for the Son "may be in them, and *I in them*" (v. 26).

Moreover, both the Father and the Son will indwell Christians. Jesus communicates this vital truth via a warm image. Anyone who loves and obeys Jesus will receive special blessings and be especially loved by the Father. Jesus declares, "We [he and the Father] will come to him and make our home with him" (14:23). The Father and the Son will make their dwelling place with believers. Of course, fuller New Testament revelation teaches us to include the Spirit in the divine indwelling; in fact, Paul chiefly assigns this role to the Spirit. Carson cites Augustine on this verse as arguing for "the indwelling of the Triune God in the believer."[29]

The Father and the Son and Believers Will Indwell One Another

John teaches that believers will be in the Father and the Son, Jesus and believers will be in one another, and Jesus and his disciples mutually will abide in one another. In sum: the Father and the Son and believers will mutually indwell one another.

Believers will be in the Father and the Son. Jesus prays for the unity of future believers and uses the unity of the Father and the Son as his measure— "just as *you, Father, are in me, and I in you,* that they also may be in us" (17:21).

---

[29] Carson, *Gospel according to John*, 504. He cites Augustine's *In Johan. Tract.* lxxxvi, 4.

John frequently says that Jesus and believers will be in one another or abide in one another. Jesus predicts, "In that day you will know that I am in my Father, and *you in me, and I in you*" (14:20). Jesus and his true disciples will mutually abide in one another:

> My flesh is true food, and my blood is true drink. Whoever feeds on my flesh and drinks my blood *abides in me, and I in him*. (6:55–56)

> *Abide in me, and I in you*. As the branch cannot bear fruit by itself, unless it abides in the vine, neither can you, unless you abide in me. I am the vine; you are the branches. *Whoever abides in me and I in him*, he it is that bears much fruit, for apart from me you can do nothing. (15:4–5)

Because of the Father's love for the Son and their love for the world, and because of the Son's incarnation, death, and resurrection, believers will be in the Father and the Son. Amazing as it sounds, believers will mutually indwell the Trinitarian persons as an act of grace insofar as creatures can partake of the divine life. David Crump's words are pointed: "Mutually indwelling the life of God is the heart and soul of John's understanding of salvation. . . . Every believer's inclusion within the exchange of divine life and love between the Father and Son is the essence, the heart and the soul, of his message about eternal life."[30]

John includes the Holy Spirit in the mission of God. Jesus will ask the Father to send the Spirit to indwell and be with believers, and they will know him (John 14:17). Although John does not correlate the Spirit's work and union with Christ, as does Paul, John provides the raw materials for systematic theology to do so.

Application

The question cries to be asked: So what? What difference does this Johannine theology make? First of all, believers should be filled with wonder and worship at these truths and the realities they convey. What human being would conceive of them? Here is much food for thought and the adoration of a God who would love us like this!

Second, we must "eat" and "drink" the Son of God, who is our true "food" (John 6:55–57). That is, we must rely on him for spiritual sustenance as we

---

[30] David Crump, "Re-examining the Johannine Trinity: Perichoresis or Deification?," *Scottish Journal of Theology* 59 (2006): 410.

rely on our daily bread for physical life. The incarnate Son gives us eternal life now and will raise us from the dead unto eternal life at the end of the age.

Third, because of the co-inherence of the divine persons, we must focus on the Son to learn of the invisible Father (14:8–11). Our study of union with Christ must lead us not away from his person but deeper into his person. We derive many benefits, but they are only from union with *Christ*.[31] He must remain our focus. If we want to learn of God's character, words, and ways, we must study christology, because he said, "Whoever has seen me has seen the Father. . . . I am in the Father and the Father is in me" (vv. 9–10).

Fourth, we are branches who have the privilege and responsibility of "abiding" in the Vine, the Son of God. This means that we abide in his love, the love with which the Father loved him (15:9). We continue in a personal relationship with Jesus; because we know that he loves us, we love him in return. We love him who first loved us; we enjoy rich fellowship with him as we walk with him in obedience. Answered prayers and joy follow.

Fifth, after hearing of our mutual indwelling with the Father and Son in Jesus's prayer in John 17:22–23, we must be motivated to live out the unity for which Jesus prays. It is shameful for us to allow doctrine, prejudice, or anything else to keep us from welcoming other Christians as Christ welcomed us (Rom. 15:7). Instead, we must be doctrinally sound believers, which includes living out the Bible's doctrines of love for and fellowship with other believers.

Sixth, we too are caught up in the mission of God (John 17:20–23). We are to pray that God might make our lives count in bringing the good news to those who need it.

---

[31] This is an outstanding contribution of Marcus Peter Johnson, *One with Christ: An Evangelical Theology of Salvation* (Wheaton, IL: Crossway, 2013).

Chapter 5

Union with Christ in Romans

"One of the most significant elements of Paul's Christology is his teaching about being 'in Christ.' Union with Christ or participation with Christ is surely one of the fundamental themes of his theology."[1] Thomas Schreiner is correct: union with Christ is a key theme of Pauline theology. Furthermore, Paul is the main teacher in all Scripture of this important theme. Paul's teaching is so extensive that it will be divided into ten chapters. We begin with Romans.

Romans 1:1–6

> Paul, a servant of Christ Jesus, called to be an apostle, set apart for the gospel of God, which he promised beforehand through his prophets in the holy Scriptures, concerning his Son, who was descended from David according to the flesh and was declared to be the Son of God in power according to the Spirit of holiness by his resurrection from the dead, Jesus Christ our Lord, through whom we have received grace and apostleship to bring about the obedience of faith for the sake of his name among all the nations, including you who are called to belong to Jesus Christ.

Paul includes the believers at Rome among those for whom he received "grace and apostleship" to bring about the "obedience of faith" for the sake

---

[1] Thomas R. Schreiner, *New Testament Theology: Magnifying God in Christ* (Grand Rapids: Baker Academic, 2008), 314.

of Christ's name. The focus of Paul's ministry is "all the nations." Thus, when he next writes "including you," he implies that the church in Rome comprises predominately Gentiles. Paul describes his readers as "among whom you yourselves also are called of Jesus Christ" (v. 6, literal translation). Douglas Moo translates it, as does the ESV, "called to belong to Jesus Christ" and explains in a note that this translation means "taking the genitive Ἰησοῦ Χριστοῦ with predicate force."[2]

This is, then, a reference to believers' belonging to Jesus Christ. Belonging is an entailment of union with Christ. Because we have been spiritually joined to Christ by faith, we are his. This theme of belonging occurs nine times in Paul's epistles. In eight references—Romans 1:6; 7:4; 8:9; 14:8; 1 Corinthians 3:21–23; 15:23; 2 Corinthians 10:7; and Galatians 5:24—Christians are said to belong to Christ. In one—1 Corinthians 12:15–16—the use of this theme in the body metaphor implies that Christians belong to each other.

This first reference to union does double duty. It introduces the theme of belonging to Christ and also occurs in a greeting of one of Paul's epistles. Romans, the first of Paul's letters canonically, includes union with Christ in both initial and final greetings. This usage recurs in Romans 16:3–13, 22; 1 Corinthians 1:2; 16:19, 24; Ephesians 1:1; 6:21; Philippians 1:1; 4:21; Colossians 1:2; 4:7, 17; 1 Thessalonians 1:1; 5:18; 2 Thessalonians 1:1; 2 Timothy 1:1; and Philemon 23. Union is in Paul's mind when he begins and finishes his epistles.

Romans 3:23–24

All have sinned and fall short of the glory of God, and are justified by his grace as a gift, through the redemption that is in Christ Jesus.

Some comments concerning the study of Paul's use of the prepositional phrase "in Christ" are in order. Linguists do not agree on the exact meaning of "in Christ" language and have made many suggestions. Its meaning remains elusive because it shows great range and flexibility. This creates problems for studying union with Christ in Paul, because the "in Christ" formula and its variants ("in the Lord," "in him," and "in whom") play such a significant role in that study. I regard Constantine Campbell's methodology, analysis, and conclusions to be exemplary. He is aware of the issues and problems, engages in a thorough inductive study of the evidence in Paul, and reaches balanced

---

[2] Douglas J. Moo, *The Epistle to the Romans*, The New International Commentary on the New Testament (Grand Rapids: Eerdmans, 1996), 54n81.

and nuanced conclusions. I gratefully build on his work. He regards the usage of the preposition ἐν (*en*, "in") as "flexible," the role of its context to be of "utmost importance," the spatial sense to be primary, the notion of "sphere" as key in figurative uses, and the phrase ἐν Χριστῷ [*en Christō*, "in Christ"] as denoting "personal relatedness."[3]

This is the first of many passages where Paul affixes the words "in Christ Jesus" to a synonym for salvation or uses "in him we have [some benefit of grace]" as a synonym for salvation. Various aspects of salvation come readily to the apostle's mind when he thinks of union with Christ. Here salvation is called "redemption," which "depicts lost persons in various states of bondage and presents Christ as Redeemer, who through his death . . . claims people as his own and sets them free."[4] Believers' redemption is not apart from Christ; it is "in Christ," that is, in association with him.[5]

Romans 5:5

> Hope does put us to shame, because God's love has been poured into our hearts through the Holy Spirit who has been given to us.

God assures us of salvation by making gospel promises to us, by working in our lives, and by the Holy Spirit's witnessing within. Here the Father comforts us by pouring his love "into our hearts through the Holy Spirit who has been given to us."

This is the first of many passages that teach that believers are indwelt by God—Father, Son, and, most often, Holy Spirit. We are indwelt by the Spirit, are given the Spirit (as here in Rom. 5:5), have the Spirit, receive the Spirit, and have the Spirit sent into our hearts. Six times Paul attributes indwelling to the Son. Christ is in us, lives in us, and dwells in our hearts. And two times Paul attributes indwelling to the Father. Believers are a dwelling place for God and are a temple for God, who dwells among them.

Indwelling is a corollary to union with Christ for two reasons. First, the same Holy Spirit both unites us to Christ and indwells us. The Spirit creates continuity between initial union with Christ and indwelling. Second, union involves God's presence in and with his people. Not only are we brought into a positive relation to God; he also comes to live in us. He takes up residence

---

[3] Constantine R. Campbell, *Paul and Union with Christ: An Exegetical and Theological Study* (Grand Rapids: Zondervan, 2012), 73.
[4] Robert A. Peterson, *Salvation Accomplished by the Son: The Work of Christ* (Wheaton, IL: Crossway, 2012), 353.
[5] So Campbell, *Paul and Union with Christ*, 94.

in our lives and bodies. He indwells his people individually and corporately. In fact, indwelling *is* the dynamic and ongoing aspect of union with Christ. The Spirit joins us to the living Christ once and for all, but not only so. He continues to join us to Christ and his eternal life, and that vital, continuing aspect of union is indwelling.

Romans 5:12–19

Therefore, just as sin came into the world through one man, and death through sin, and so death spread to all men because all sinned—for sin indeed was in the world before the law was given, but sin is not counted where there is no law. Yet death reigned from Adam to Moses, even over those whose sinning was not like the transgression of Adam, who was a type of the one who was to come.

But the free gift is not like the trespass. For if many died through one man's trespass, much more have the grace of God and the free gift by the grace of that one man Jesus Christ abounded for many. And the free gift is not like the result of that one man's sin. For the judgment following one trespass brought condemnation, but the free gift following many trespasses brought justification. For if, because of one man's trespass, death reigned through that one man, much more will those who receive the abundance of grace and the free gift of righteousness reign in life through the one man Jesus Christ. Therefore, as one trespass led to condemnation for all men, so one act of righteousness leads to justification and life for all men. For as by the one man's disobedience the many were made sinners, so by the one man's obedience the many will be made righteous.

A few preliminaries are in order. First, though this passage does not specifically address union with Christ, it is a major source for understanding Christ as new covenant Mediator. Second, this is the *textus classicus* for the doctrine of original sin. I agree with that assessment but note that Romans says much about actual sins before it deals with original sin. After announcing his theme—the revelation of God's saving righteousness in the gospel (1:16–17)—Paul launches into another topic—the revelation of God's wrath against sinners (v. 18). He pursues this topic until returning to the main theme in 3:21. In between he stresses humanity's need for the gospel due to its actual sins. Thus Paul says a lot about actual sin before he treats original sin, so both are important.

Third, Romans 5:12–19 is rightly regarded as the main text on original sin.

But in its context it chiefly concerns justification, not sin. Paul surrounds his discussion of the means of justification—faith in Christ in chapter 4—with discussions of the basis of justification—Christ's work. In 3:25–26 the basis is Christ's propitiation of God's justice, and in 5:18–19 it is his "one act of righteousness" on the cross and his "obedience" unto death that counter the disobedience of the first Adam.

In 5:12 Paul begins by a comparison between the two Adams: "Therefore, just as sin came into the world through one man, and death through sin, and so death spread to all men because all sinned—." The dash shows that Paul interrupts his flow of thought. His goal is to compare Adam's devastating effects on humankind with Christ's wonderful effects on his people. But Paul does not complete the comparison. Rather, he immediately shows that only Adam's sin can explain sin's tyranny over humanity from the fall to the giving of the Mosaic law (vv. 13–14).

Paul lays the foundation for the completion of the unfinished comparison (of v. 12) when he says, "Adam, who was a type of the one who was to come" (v. 14). In some ways Adam is a type, an acted prophecy or prefiguring, of the Christ to come. Both have cataclysmic effects on others. The destinies of the whole human race are tied to the two Adams because Adam is the mediator of the covenant of creation and Christ is the Mediator of the new covenant.

There are basic similarities between Adam and Christ. But before presenting these, Paul underlines their differences. Adam's one sin brings death; Christ brings grace and eternal life (v. 15). Adam's one sin brings condemnation; Christ's grace brings justification (v. 16). Adam's one sin brings the reign of death; Christ brings a reign of life to believers (v. 17).

Having contrasted the two Adams, Paul builds upon their fundamental similarity to finish the comparison of verse 12. "Therefore, as one trespass led to condemnation for all men, so one act of righteousness leads to justification and life for all men" (v. 18). Adam's original sin warrants God's verdict of condemnation to humankind. His one sin makes all guilty before God. In other places in this passage, Paul says that the outcome of Adam's sin is physical and spiritual death (vv. 12, 14–15, 17). He means that Adam's primal sin brings condemnation, which in turn brings death to men and women.

Christ, the second Adam, also has colossal effects upon his race, his people, but unlike Adam's effects, Christ's are positive: "One act of righteousness leads to justification and life for all men" (v. 18). The second Adam stands in contrast to the first Adam. Christ's "one act of righteousness" refers to his death on the cross. His death generates the opposite of the condemnation caused by Adam's first sin, namely "justification," God's verdict of righteousness. Paul unbalances the equation when he adds to justification "and life for all men," thereby emphasizing the magnitude of Christ's accomplishment. Christ's cross brings God's declaration of righteousness, which in turn produces eternal life. He means Christ's one act of righteousness brings justification, which in turn brings life.

In verse 19 Paul essentially repeats the idea of verse 18. "As by the one man's disobedience the many were made sinners, so by the one man's obedience the many will be made righteous." Adam's disobedience, his original sin, caused his race to become sinners. By contrast, Christ's obedience will cause his race (all who believe in him, v. 17) to become righteous in God's sight. Paul's emphasis is on Christ's "becoming obedient to the point of death, even death on a cross" (Phil. 2:8). Here is a diagram of the great consequences of the two Adams upon their respective races:

Adam's disobedience → Many were made sinners.
Christ's obedience → Many will be made righteous.

To summarize: Paul presents Christ as the second and last Adam, the Mediator of the new covenant, whose "one act of righteousness," his "obedience" unto death on the cross, is the ground for God's declaring righteous (justifying) sinners who trust Christ for salvation and eternal life. So while this passage does not deal with an actual faith union with Christ, it lays a foundation for that doctrine in presenting the momentous accomplishment of Christ, the second Adam and Mediator of the new covenant, juxtaposed to the momentous deed of the first Adam and mediator of the covenant of creation. James Dunn traces the apostle's train of thought:

At this point the features of Adam Christology are most sharply drawn, with Christ's work described precisely as an antithesis to Adam's— the deed which accords with God's will set against the trespass which marked humanity's wrong turning, the act defined as obedience precisely because it is the reversal of Adam's disobedience. The inaugurating act of the new epoch is thus presented as a counter to and cancellation of the inaugurating act of the old, Christ's right turn undoing Adam's wrong turn.[6]

---

[6] James D. G. Dunn, *Romans 1–8*, Word Biblical Commentary (Dallas: Word, 1988), 297.

Romans 6:1–14

> What shall we say then? Are we to continue in sin that grace may abound? By no means! How can we who died to sin still live in it? Do you not know that all of us who have been baptized into Christ Jesus were baptized into his death? We were buried therefore with him by baptism into death, in order that, just as Christ was raised from the dead by the glory of the Father, we too might walk in newness of life.
>
> For if we have been united with him in a death like his, we shall certainly be united with him in a resurrection like his. We know that our old self was crucified with him in order that the body of sin might be brought to nothing, so that we would no longer be enslaved to sin. For one who has died has been set free from sin. Now if we have died with Christ, we believe that we will also live with him. We know that Christ, being raised from the dead, will never die again; death no longer has dominion over him. For the death he died he died to sin, once for all, but the life he lives he lives to God. So you also must consider yourselves dead to sin and alive to God in Christ Jesus.
>
> Let not sin therefore reign in your mortal body, to make you obey its passions. Do not present your members to sin as instruments for unrighteousness, but present yourselves to God as those who have been brought from death to life, and your members to God as instruments for righteousness. For sin will have no dominion over you, since you are not under law but under grace.

Paul previously blasted enemies who attributed antinomianism to him: "Why not do evil that good may come?—as some people slanderously charge us with saying. Their condemnation is just" (Rom. 3:8). Here he returns to this false charge. He just wrote, "Where sin increased, grace abounded all the more"—the worse our sins looks, the better God's grace in justification looks (5:20). Now his enemies accuse: "Are we to continue in sin that grace may abound?" (6:1). Paul recoils at this suggestion and responds with incredulity: "How can we who died to sin still live in it?" (v. 2).

Moo accurately summarizes Paul's argument by working backward:

Christ died to sin (vv. 8–10)
We died with Christ (vv. 3–7)
Therefore: we died to sin (v. 2)[7]

---

[7] Moo, *Epistle to the Romans*, 354n12.

But when did we die to sin? Paul explains that this occurred when we were baptized: "Do you not know that all of us who have been baptized into Christ Jesus were baptized into his death?" (v. 3). It is as if Paul said, "Don't you know that Christian baptism denotes union with Christ in his death (and resurrection)?" Our baptism is baptism into Christ; it means we participate in his story. So just as he died, in union with him we too died to sin. Christ's atonement broke the stranglehold of sin over our lives; we no longer have to do the bidding of that cruel master. Instead, we belong to another Master, who bought us in his death and resurrection, even Christ Jesus our Lord. He is the one we now obey.

"We were buried therefore with him by baptism into death, in order that, just as Christ was raised from the dead by the glory of the Father, we too might walk in newness of life" (v. 4). The apostle laments that Christians would continue to live in sin after baptism (v. 2). To do so is a fundamental misunderstanding. In baptism God promises to identify us with Christ in his death and resurrection. Baptism does not automatically effect that which it represents. But for those who believe, God delivers what he promised. We must live, then, as those who died to sin with Christ and who live to God, because we participated in Christ's death and resurrection.

The apostle teaches that Christians participate in Jesus's narrative. Here we are crucified with him (v. 6), share in his death (vv. 5, 8) and resurrection (v. 5), and "will also live with him" (v. 8). Our union with him in his death and resurrection is the basis for victorious Christian living now (vv. 4, 6–7, 11–13). Indeed, Paul urges, "Do not present your members to sin as instruments for unrighteousness, but present yourselves to God as those who have been brought from death to life, and your members to God as instruments for righteousness" (v. 13). Our participation in Christ's story is also the basis for our final salvation—the resurrection of the body (vv. 5, 8). I agree with Dunn concerning verses 5 and 8:

> More likely Paul has in mind the full outworking of that epoch-introducing event [Christ's resurrection] in the resurrection of the dead . . . a resurrection just like his.[8]

"We shall also live with him." It is almost impossible to take the future here as merely logical (it follows from the fact that we died with Christ

---

[8] Dunn, *Romans 1–8*, 318.

that we have also risen with him); it must refer to a still future sharing in Christ's resurrected life.[9]

Verse 11 is one of many places where Paul adds the words "in Christ" to an adjective to speak of it in relation to Christ: "You also must consider yourselves dead to sin and alive to God in Christ Jesus." The foundation of this statement is found in Christ's death and resurrection: "Christ, being raised from the dead, will never die again; death no longer has dominion over him. For the death he died he died to sin, once for all, but the life he lives he lives to God" (vv. 9–10). When we are joined to him by grace through faith, we move, just as Christ our Vicar did, from the realm of sin and death to the realm of life and God. Campbell has taught me that Paul frequently uses "in Christ" language to "express the locative notion of being within the realm or sphere of Christ."[10] I take "in" here to indicate realm or sphere and the whole expression to mean being alive to Christ by virtue of union with him in his death and resurrection. Paul speaks of two spheres: being "dead to sin" and being "alive to God." He describes the second sphere as "in Christ."

Romans 6:23

The wages of sin is death, but the free gift of God is eternal life in Christ Jesus our Lord.

Again Paul speaks of salvation—here as "eternal life"—"in Christ Jesus our Lord." Everlasting spiritual life is found only through the Mediator's person and work.

Romans 7:4

You also have died to the law through the body of Christ, so that you may belong to another, to him who has been raised from the dead, in order that we may bear fruit for God.

The apostle says that Christians take part in Jesus's narrative. Here we "have died to the law through the body of Christ." Paul means that our co-crucifixion with Christ has freed us from the tyranny (and condemnation) of the law that characterizes this age. When he died, we died, and we now are

---

[9] Ibid., 322.
[10] Campbell, *Paul and Union with Christ*, 115–16. I follow him and identify many such uses of "in Christ" language in Paul's epistles.

not enslaved to the law but belong to the risen one. In his death and resurrection he has inaugurated a new era, and by our participating in his story, we too are "released from the law, having died to that which held us captive, so that we serve in the new way of the Spirit and not in the old way of the written code" (v. 6).

Paul speaks of believers as "belong[ing] to another, to him who has been raised from the dead" (v. 4), that is, Christ. Here, as elsewhere in Paul, union includes belonging to Christ.

Romans 8:1–2

> There is therefore now no condemnation for those who are in Christ Jesus. For the law of the Spirit of life has set you free in Christ Jesus from the law of sin and death.

I understand "those who are in Christ Jesus" (v. 1) to mean those in the sphere of Christ Jesus. Paul contrasts that sphere with the one "of sin and death." People who are in Christ's realm are justified and will not be condemned at the last judgment. They are in Christ's domain and will be declared righteous in the judgment.

The use of "in Christ Jesus" in verse 2 is complicated by the difficulty of determining which words in the verse the phrase modifies. Owing to this ambiguity I follow the Greek word order, put the phrase with "the law of the Spirit of life," and understand it to speak of sphere. The dominion of the Holy Spirit—who brings life in the realm of Christ Jesus—has liberated Christians from the dominion of sin and death. Both uses of "in Christ Jesus" in these two verses relate believers to him. Though they use local language to speak figuratively of realm, they imply a personal relationship with him.

Romans 8:9–11

> You, however, are not in the flesh but in the Spirit, if in fact the Spirit of God dwells in you. Anyone who does not have the Spirit of Christ does not belong to him. But if Christ is in you, although the body is dead because of sin, the Spirit is life because of righteousness. If the Spirit of him who raised Jesus from the dead dwells in you, he who raised Christ Jesus from the dead will also give life to your mortal bodies through his Spirit who dwells in you.

This is a powerful passage on indwelling. Four times it speaks of believers' being indwelt by the Spirit, and once by Christ himself—"if Christ is in you." Paul connects indwelling with our being in the realm of the Spirit, not of the flesh (v. 9), with our having eternal life now (v. 10), and with our future resurrection from the dead (v. 11).

Furthermore, Paul teaches that having the Holy Spirit is an indispensable condition, a *sine qua non*, of belonging to Christ. Therefore, it follows that "anyone who does not have the Spirit of Christ does not belong to him."

Romans 8:14–17

All who are led by the Spirit of God are sons of God. For you did not receive the spirit of slavery to fall back into fear, but you have received the Spirit of adoption as sons, by whom we cry, "Abba! Father!" The Spirit himself bears witness with our spirit that we are children of God, and if children, then heirs—heirs of God and fellow heirs with Christ, provided we suffer with him in order that we may also be glorified with him.

Paul celebrates our adoption by God. "The Spirit of adoption" has enabled us to call God "Father" in truth. As a result, we are no longer slaves of sin but children of God. The Spirit assures us within of our sonship. And with placement into God's family comes inheritance: "If children, then heirs—heirs of God and fellow heirs with Christ" (v. 17). But all this is true only for genuine sons, those who bear a family resemblance to the Father and the Son. For this reason Paul adds a proviso: "provided we suffer with him in order that we may also be glorified with him." He means that only those who are joined to Christ in his death and resurrection are the true sons of God. Union in his saving events means salvation in all of its aspects: from sin's penalty (justification), power (progressive sanctification), and presence (final sanctification). But union with him in his death also means suffering with him now, just as union with him in his resurrection means being glorified with him later.

Romans 8:38–39

I am sure that neither death nor life, nor angels nor rulers, nor things present nor things to come, nor powers, nor height nor depth, nor anything else in all creation, will be able to separate us from the love of God in Christ Jesus our Lord.

These verses appear at the end of a passage that, as strongly as any in Scripture, affirms God's preservation of his people. Those whom God has saved he will keep unto the end. Paul argues for preservation based on God's plan (vv. 28–30), his very deity (vv. 31–32), his justice (vv. 33–34), and his love (vv. 35–39). I follow Campbell, who follows BDAG,[11] in understanding this use of "in Christ" to signify that "by which something is recognized," and the idea here to be the "love of God that is seen in Christ Jesus our Lord." Nothing can separate believers from God's love, which is "direct and personal and is recognized through Christ."[12]

Romans 9:1

I am speaking the truth in Christ—I am not lying; my conscience bears me witness in the Holy Spirit.

Here is one of many places where Paul speaks of believers' actions being performed "in Christ." What does it mean that Paul speaks the "truth in Christ"? The key seems to be the parallelism with the expression "my conscience bears me witness in the Holy Spirit." "Both phrases are used in connection to the utterance of testimony . . . which suggests that they could profitably be understood the same way." Campbell follows BDAG in understanding both uses under the category "marker of close association," and more particularly, "under the control of."[13] Thus Paul means he is not lying but telling the truth under Christ's control or influence; his conscience under the Spirit's control or influence confirms this fact. Paul speaks, then, in relation to Christ and dependent on him, and as such, he speaks only the truth.

Romans 12:4–5

As in one body we have many members, and the members do not all have the same function, so we, though many, are one body in Christ, and individually members one of another.

Shortly after beginning the mainly practical section of Romans (chaps. 12–16) in 12:1–2 (built on the mainly doctrinal chaps. 1–11), Paul urges his

[11] Walter Bauer, Frederick W. Danker, William F. Arndt, and F. Wilbur Gingrich, *Greek-English Lexicon of the New Testament and Other Early Christian Literature*, 3rd ed. (Chicago: University of Chicago Press, 2000); hereafter, BDAG in this or a 2nd (1979) edition.
[12] Campbell, *Paul and Union with Christ*, 131.
[13] Ibid., 96.

readers to humility (12:3). For the basis of his appeal he points to our bodies: "As in one body we have many members, and the members do not all have the same function . . ." (v. 4). Our bodies are characterized by diversity of members and functions. He completes his appeal by comparing our bodies to the church: "so we, though many, are one body in Christ, and individually members one of another" (v. 5).

Even as a human body, although having many members with various functions, is still one body, so it is with Christ's church. But Paul does not mention "the church." Instead, he introduces his favorite picture of the church—the body of Christ. Helpfully, though the apostle does not usually use the words "in Christ" with the metaphor of the church as Christ's body, here, when he first mentions the concept, he does. Believers "are one body in Christ" (v. 5). He means they are in Christ's domain and consequently have a new identity—they are "in Christ," members of his spiritual body, the church. He thus signals that the body of Christ is a picture of the church in union with Christ.

Herman Ridderbos rightly maintains that the idea of the body of Christ speaks of incorporation into Christ.[14] Just as our bodily members are each a part of us, so believers belong to Christ. And to each other! This metaphor is ideal for teaching not only the relationship of believers, the members, to Christ, their Head, but also that of believers to one another. So Paul writes, "We, though many, are one body in Christ, and individually members one of another." Next he encourages various members of Christ's body with different gifts to serve the Lord appropriately: "If prophecy, in proportion to our faith; if service, in our serving; the one who teaches, in his teaching; the one who exhorts, in his exhortation; the one who contributes, in generosity; the one who leads, with zeal; the one who does acts of mercy, with cheerfulness" (vv. 6–8).

Romans 13:14

Put on the Lord Jesus Christ, and make no provision for the flesh, to gratify its desires.

After exhortations to "love each other" and so fulfill the law, to "put on the armor of light" in light of the eschatological times, and to avoid a sinful lifestyle (vv. 8–13), Paul makes a summary ethical statement: "Put on the Lord Jesus Christ" (v. 14). The apostle uses the imagery of getting dressed, of put-

---

[14] See Herman Ridderbos, *Paul: An Outline of His Theology*, trans. John Richard de Witt (Grand Rapids: Eerdmans, 1975), 362.

ting on clothing, to urge his readers to live for Christ and as he lived. In verse 12 Paul has encouraged the Romans to put on a moral suit of armor. Now he commands them to put on Christ himself.

We are made one with Christ at conversion, "but our relationship to Christ, the new man, while established at conversion, needs constantly to be appropriated and lived out." Paul speaks here not of initial union with Christ but of believers' need "consciously to embrace Christ in such a way that his character is manifested in all that we do and say."[15]

This is a positive point. The negative counterpoint follows: "Make no provision for the flesh, to gratify its desires" (v. 14). "Flesh" here has the negative meaning of the principle within us that turns us outwardly to the world system opposed to God and inwardly to our selfish desires. We are to "make no provision for the flesh" and its lusts; that is, we are not to indulge our evil desires.

Romans 14:7–9

> None of us lives to himself, and none of us dies to himself. For if we live, we live to the Lord, and if we die, we die to the Lord. So then, whether we live or whether we die, we are the Lord's. For to this end Christ died and lived again, that he might be Lord both of the dead and of the living.

Paul exhorts Jewish and Gentile believers in Rome to accept each other and live in harmony in the observance of religious days. We live and die not for ourselves, but for him who lived and died for us to be our Lord. Equally important to his ruling over us is the fact that we belong to him. This belonging is a feature of union with Christ.

Romans 14:14

> I know and am persuaded in the Lord Jesus that nothing is unclean in itself, but it is unclean for anyone who thinks it unclean.

Paul addresses divisions in the Roman church along Jewish and Gentile ethnic lines. He acknowledges the abolishment of the Old Testament dietary code; no longer are there unclean foods. He introduces this principle with the words "I know and am persuaded in the Lord Jesus." Paul is swayed by the Lord Jesus, God's agent leading Paul to his conclusion.

---

[15] Moo, *Epistle to the Romans*, 825–26.

Romans 15:17–19

In Christ Jesus, then, I have reason to be proud of my work for God. For I will not venture to speak of anything except what Christ has accomplished through me to bring the Gentiles to obedience—by word and deed, by the power of signs and wonders, by the power of the Spirit of God—so that from Jerusalem and all the way around to Illyricum I have fulfilled the ministry of the gospel of Christ.

Here again Paul speaks of believers' actions done "in Christ," this time his own action of boasting of his "work for God." The next two verses reveal what that work is—preaching the gospel successfully to Gentiles across the Roman Empire. It seems that "in Christ" functions adverbially to modify "I have reason to be proud." Thus Paul's boasting is appropriate because he boasts in this manner—"in Christ."[16]

Romans 16:3–13

Greet Prisca and Aquila, my fellow workers in Christ Jesus, who risked their necks for my life, to whom not only I give thanks but all the churches of the Gentiles give thanks as well. Greet also the church in their house. Greet my beloved Epaenetus, who was the first convert to Christ in Asia. Greet Mary, who has worked hard for you. Greet Andronicus and Junia, my kinsmen and my fellow prisoners. They are well known to the apostles, and they were in Christ before me. Greet Ampliatus, my beloved in the Lord. Greet Urbanus, our fellow worker in Christ, and my beloved Stachys. Greet Apelles, who is approved in Christ. Greet those who belong to the family of Aristobulus. Greet my kinsman Herodion. Greet those in the Lord who belong to the family of Narcissus. Greet those workers in the Lord, Tryphaena and Tryphosa. Greet the beloved Persis, who has worked hard in the Lord. Greet Rufus, chosen in the Lord; also his mother, who has been a mother to me as well.

This is the prime example of Paul's practice of including references to union with Christ in the opening and closing greetings of his epistles, showing how pervasive union is in his thought. These verses contain ten occurrences of "in Christ Jesus" or the like ("in Christ," "in the Lord"). Paul instructs the Romans to welcome Phoebe "in the Lord in a way worthy of the saints"

---

[16] So Campbell, *Paul and Union with Christ*, 96–97. He taught me to recognize many times "in Christ" is used as an adverb of manner in Paul.

(v. 2). "In the Lord" expresses manner, as the words immediately following confirm—"in a way worthy of the saints."

In seven instances here Paul uses "in Christ" "as a label to indicate that people are Christian. . . . In Christ might be regarded as roughly equivalent to the modern label 'Christian.'"[17]

- "Prisca and Aquila, my fellow workers in Christ Jesus" (v. 3)
- "Andronicus and Junia . . . in Christ before me" (v. 7)
- "Ampliatus, my beloved in the Lord" (v. 8)
- "Urbanus, our fellow worker in Christ" (v. 9)
- "those in the Lord" (v. 11)
- "those workers in the Lord, Tryphaena and Tryphosa" (v. 12)
- "Rufus, chosen in the Lord" (v. 13)

Prisca and Aquila, then, are Paul's *Christian* fellow workers, Andronicus and Junia were *Christians* before Paul, and so forth.

When Paul refers to Apelles as "approved in Christ" (v. 10), he describes him as possessing the characteristic of being approved, that is, as worthy of approval.[18] When the apostle refers to "beloved Persis, who has worked hard in the Lord" (v. 12), he uses "in Christ" language to depict cause. Persis labored because of the Lord, showing the kind of work he was doing—the Lord's work.[19]

Romans 16:22

I, Tertius, who wrote this letter in the Lord, greet you. [my translation]

The words "in the Lord" go either with "wrote this letter" or with "greet you." Many commentators and translations adopt the latter alternative, as does the ESV: "I Tertius, who wrote this letter, greet you in the Lord." Nevertheless, I favor the former because of word order. I assume that where the Greek is ambiguous, Greek writers use word order to communicate their intentions. If that is correct in this instance, then the translation is, "I, Tertius, who wrote this letter in the Lord, greet you." Because Tertius is Paul's scribe and not the author of Romans, the meaning probably is that the "letter concerns the Lord, whose person and work form its substance."[20] Tertius, then, greets the Romans as Paul's amanuensis of this letter having to do with Christ.

---

[17] Ibid., 120. Campbell instructed me to classify this frequent Pauline usage as a periphrasis for believers.
[18] Ibid., 101–2.
[19] Ibid., 155–56. Once more, I learned from Campbell to recognize this category (cause) in Paul's uses of "in Christ."
[20] Ibid., 156–57. Campbell cites BDAG's category of "specification or substance" as appropriate.

Chapter 6

Union with Christ
in 1 Corinthians

1 Corinthians 1:1–2

> Paul, called by the will of God to be an apostle of Christ Jesus, and our brother Sosthenes,
>
> To the church of God that is in Corinth, to those sanctified in Christ Jesus, called to be saints together with all those who in every place call upon the name of our Lord Jesus Christ, both their Lord and ours.

The addressees of Paul's first epistle to the Corinthians are the "church of God that is in Corinth." The apostle then qualifies that expression with an appositive, "to those sanctified in Christ Jesus." Here is another place where Paul speaks of salvation "in Christ," this time salvation in terms of sanctification. The believers in Corinth were set apart as holy—constituted the saints of God in connection to Christ, specifically through his mediation.[1] As Mediator, he sanctifies his people initially and definitively (as here), progressively, and finally and entirely.

1 Corinthians 1:4–8

> I give thanks to my God always for you because of the grace of God that was given you in Christ Jesus, that in every way you were enriched in him

---

[1] Constantine R. Campbell, *Paul and Union with Christ: An Exegetical and Theological Study* (Grand Rapids: Zondervan, 2012), 329, rightly notes a tendency toward the instrumental function of "in Christ" language in references I have included under "salvation in Christ." Instrumental is another common use of this language in Paul.

in all speech and all knowledge—even as the testimony about Christ was confirmed among you—so that you are not lacking in any gift, as you wait for the revealing of our Lord Jesus Christ, who will sustain you to the end, guiltless in the day of our Lord Jesus Christ.

Paul thanks God for the grace he gave the Corinthian Christians. God gave this grace "in Christ Jesus" (v. 4). This makes perfect sense, for God "has blessed us *in Christ* with every spiritual blessing in the heavenly places" (Eph. 1:3). All of God's blessings are given "in Christ." As a result, the apostle says, "In every way you were enriched in him in all speech and all knowledge . . . so that you are not lacking in any gift" (vv. 5, 7). The Corinthians received many spiritual gifts "in Christ." The "in Christ" language in these two verses is used instrumentally. Christ is the Mediator through whom God's gifts come to his people.

1 Corinthians 1:30–31

Because of him you are in Christ Jesus, who became to us wisdom from God, righteousness and sanctification and redemption, so that, as it is written, "Let the one who boasts, boast in the Lord."

Here is a very concise summary of grace and salvation: "because of him you are in Christ Jesus." As befits the preceding context, it is "because of him"—God the Father—that the Corinthians, and all other believers, are in saving union with the Son. This is a key passage on union with Christ. It is unusual for the apostle to say directly, "You are in Christ Jesus," as he does here. And the meaning he intends for "in Christ Jesus" is also unusual. Though "in Christ" language in general expresses a personal relation to Christ, Campbell shows that it often has other nuances attached to it, indicating realm, agency, association, or more. But in this case he accurately says that the language communicates "some kind of union with Christ."[2] That is, its nuance is union with Christ.

I quote the wise words of Roy Ciampa and Brian Rosner:

Paul summarizes the blessings of salvation in . . . succinct fashion . . . . To be saved is to be *in Christ*. Pregnant with meaning, not surprisingly, this phrase has been variously interpreted. If Deissmann stressed the mystical and experiential sense of the phrase, a religious energy in the soul of

---
[2] Ibid., 132.

the believer, Weiss and Schweitzer understood the eschatological status of being-in-Christ as the mode of existence of God's new creation. . . . Charting a middle course, Davies, Wikenhauser, and Tannehill argue that the emphases on state and status both have some validity, for Christian experience derives from the objective standing of being in Christ. . . . As the following four terms in v. 30 suggest, to be in Christ is to enjoy both a secure and objective status before God and a new mode of eschatological existence in solidarity with other believers.[3]

It is important to note that believers possess everything in union with Christ not merely privately but collectively. They are joined to Christ the Head as members of his body. Union with Christ is a personal soteriological principle, but it is also a communal soteriological principle. When I am joined to Christ, I am joined to all others who are joined to him.

Christ gives many benefits to those who are united to him by grace. Paul mentions four benefits, but they are not coordinate; rather, the latter three unpack the first. Christ "became to us wisdom from God," that is, "righteousness and sanctification and redemption" (v. 30). This wisdom clashes with the wisdom that the Corinthians prized—cultured rhetorical persuasion. Against this Paul has lauded the "folly" of God's wisdom, centered in preaching about Christ crucified. By God's grace the message of Jesus's crucifixion with its "weakness" and "folly" was shown to be actually a message of power and wisdom. C. K. Barrett's words are apt: "True wisdom is not to be found in eloquence, or in gnostic speculation about the being of God; it is found in God's plan for the redemption of the world, which, for all its own wisdom, had fallen away from God, a plan that was put into operation through the cross."[4]

This same Christ, now risen and glorified, gives a salvation expressed in different pictures. The wisdom he became for our advantage includes righteousness, holiness, and redemption. Though these characterize the risen Christ, the thrust of Paul's message is that he imparts them to those united to him by faith. He gives righteousness, a forensic term that speaks of our acquittal before the bar of God's judgment, now and in the last judgment. He gives holiness, a moral term that speaks of God's having constituted us saints once and for all, of our gradual growth in purity, and our final presentation before God as spotless. He gives redemption, a term from the slave market

---

[3] Roy E. Ciampa and Brian S. Rosner, *The First Letter to the Corinthians*, The Pillar New Testament Commentary (Grand Rapids: Eerdmans, 2010), 108.

[4] C. K. Barrett, *A Commentary on the First Epistle to the Corinthians* (Peabody, MA: Hendrickson, 1968), 60.

that speaks of our deliverance from the bondage of sin by the payment of a ransom price, the blood or violent death of the Son of God. The wisdom that Christ became for us, then, is both theological and ethical. It has to do with God's truth in the gospel applied to life. In this verse Paul thereby previews much that he attempts to accomplish in this epistle.

The apostle follows with a purpose clause: "so that, as it is written, 'Let the one who boasts, boast in the Lord'" (v. 31). Paul returns to the theme of verses 26–29, where he explained why God called to salvation few "wise," "power-ful," or "of noble birth" (v. 26) and instead chose the "foolish," "weak," "low and despised"—"even things that are not" (vv. 27–28). Why did God act so contrary to the world's wisdom? Paul answers loudly and clearly: "so that no human being might boast in the presence of God" (v. 29). Now Paul writes, citing Jeremiah 9:23–24, "Let the one who boasts, boast in the Lord" (1 Cor. 1:31). As in Jeremiah's day, human beings are to boast not in wisdom, strength, or wealth, but in knowing the Lord. They are to boast "in the Lord"; that is, he is to be the content of their boasting.[5] Paul thus begins 1 Corinthians 1:30–31 by declaring that union with Christ is "because of him," namely God, and ends by directing all boasting to the Lord Jesus. The apostle thereby shows that because salvation is all due to God alone, he alone deserves praise for his great grace given us "in Christ Jesus." "Thus human boasting is eliminated by God himself in favor of boasting in Christ's redemptive work, wherein alone one has favor with God," as Gordon Fee summarizes.[6]

1 Corinthians 3:1

> I, brothers, could not address you as spiritual people, but as people of the flesh, as infants in Christ.

Paul expresses disappointment in the Corinthian congregation. Whereas they should show spiritual maturity, they show little. Rather, too frequently in their attitudes, words, and behavior they resemble unsaved people, "people of the flesh." Another way of describing their spiritual immaturity is to label them "infants in Christ." Similar to some other occurrences of "in Christ" language, this use is a periphrasis for believers. Its meaning is close to our use of "Christians." The apostle means that he cannot address the Corinthians as mature Christians but essentially deems them "baby Christians."

---

[5] Campbell, *Paul and Union with Christ*, agrees (157). I follow him in identifying this use in Paul's letters.
[6] Gordon D. Fee, *The First Epistle to the Corinthians*, The New International Commentary on the New Testament (Grand Rapids: Eerdmans, 1987), 87.

1 Corinthians 3:16–17

> Do you not know that you are God's temple and that God's Spirit dwells in you? If anyone destroys God's temple, God will destroy him. For God's temple is holy, and you are that temple.

In speaking of the Corinthian congregation, Paul shifts metaphors. First he calls them a "field," and then a "building" (v. 9). Paul Barnett points to the indispensable Old Testament background: "Under the old covenant the temple of God was that sanctuary of Yahweh, the God of Israel. . . . Under the new covenant, however, the temple of God is the congregation of holy ones, those set apart to God in Jesus Christ and made so by God's indwelling presence, the Holy Spirit."[7]

Paul hints at union with Christ when he states that the only foundation is "that which is laid, which is Jesus Christ" (v. 11). Campbell is correct: "Here we glimpse the concept of incorporation into Christ: God's people are 'built' on Christ, and he must—by the very nature of the metaphor—be integrated with God's people, as the foundation of a building is essentially integrated with the structure of which it is a part."[8]

Now Paul explains what kind of building this is—a temple. The Corinthian believers communally are a sanctuary in which God's Spirit dwells (v. 16). As such they are a holy temple, a holy people, and anyone who defiles them destroys God's temple and will answer to him (v. 17). Two Pauline themes here pertain to union with Christ—that of a building/temple and that of indwelling of the Spirit. Campbell sets both themes against their Old Testament background:

> The Corinthians are here described as God's temple, the corollary of which is that God's Spirit dwells in them. . . . Furthermore, as God's temple is holy, so too are the Corinthians since they are his temple. . . . Rather than being built of stone, this temple consists of people; and rather than God's Spirit dwelling in a physical structure, which could be accessed by people to varying degrees, he dwells within a people. . . . They are apparently attributed with the sanctions once enjoyed by the original temple: God's punishment of those who would ruin it and his holiness.[9]

---

[7] Paul Barnett, *The Second Epistle to the Corinthians*, The New International Commentary on the New Testament (Grand Rapids: Eerdmans, 1997), 349.
[8] Campbell, *Paul and Union with Christ*, 295.
[9] Ibid., 290.

1 Corinthians 3:21–23

> Let no one boast in men. For all things are yours, whether Paul or Apollos
> or Cephas or the world or life or death or the present or the future—all
> are yours, and you are Christ's, and Christ is God's.

Paul, seeking to restore unity to the Corinthian congregation, urges them
not to "boast in men." Because of God's grace to us through his Son, we are
heirs of all things. Therefore, "all things are yours," including Christian leaders around whom the Corinthians were dividing into factions (vv. 21–22).
Most importantly, "You are Christ's, and Christ is God's" (v. 23). We belong
to Christ, and he to God; it is no wonder all belongs to us. To divide into factions is to show foolish selfishness and not to act as the heirs of all. In short,
it is to forget our identity "in Christ." Belonging to God is a consequence of
being joined to Christ.

1 Corinthians 4:15–17

> Though you have countless guides in Christ, you do not have many fa-
> thers. For I became your father in Christ Jesus through the gospel. I urge
> you, then, be imitators of me. That is why I sent you Timothy, my beloved
> and faithful child in the Lord, to remind you of my ways in Christ, as I
> teach them everywhere in every church.

Here we find four occurrences of "in Christ" language in the space of three
verses! Paul answers his critics and seeks to correct and edify the Corinthians
at the same time. He admonishes them, his "beloved children" (v. 14). In contrast to the many guides they have had, including Apollos and Cephas (Peter),
they have only one spiritual father—Paul himself. "Guides in Christ" reflects
"in Christ" language used as a periphrasis for believers. Thus the meaning is
"Christian guides."

Over against the many Christian guides, the apostle is their "father in
Christ Jesus." "In Christ Jesus" is used here to describe Paul's action ("father-
ing") rather than Paul himself. Paul's becoming their "father in Christ Jesus,
through the gospel" indicates "close personal relationship." Under Christ's
influence Paul fathers the Corinthians by leading them to a saving knowledge
of Christ.[10]

Paul urges them to follow his example, which has been communicated to

---

[10] Ibid., 143–44.

them by Timothy, whom Paul describes as his "beloved and faithful child in the Lord" (v. 17). "In the Lord" specifies the nature of the relationship between "father" Paul and his "child" Timothy. Here again "in Christ" is used as a periphrasis for believers. Timothy is Paul's Christian son.

Furthermore, it is Timothy's job to remind the Corinthian church of Paul's "ways in Christ." Timothy is to teach the believers how Paul lives and what he teaches (both "ways"—of life and of teaching—are referred to in v. 17). Specifically, Paul's Christian son is to teach the Corinthians Paul's ways "in Christ," his manner of living and teaching.

1 Corinthians 6:15–20

> Do you not know that your bodies are members of Christ? Shall I then take the members of Christ and make them members of a prostitute? Never! Or do you not know that he who is joined to a prostitute becomes one body with her? For, as it is written, "The two will become one flesh." But he who is joined to the Lord becomes one spirit with him. Flee from sexual immorality. Every other sin a person commits is outside the body, but the sexually immoral person sins against his own body. Or do you not know that your body is a temple of the Holy Spirit within you, whom you have from God? You are not your own, for you were bought with a price. So glorify God in your body.

Paul here paints three pictures of union with Christ: marriage, temple, and body. The apostle presents his most intimate picture of union with Christ—marriage union between husband and wife—in three passages. And this is the most intimate of those passages, for it focuses on the human body and sexual union. The historical context is crucial. In 1 Corinthians Paul treats the classic Gentile sins of idolatry and sexual immorality—here the latter. Apparently, some men in the Corinthian congregation were using theological arguments to defend their right to visit temple prostitutes. They claimed that as people of the Spirit they were free as to the use of their bodies; their sexual activity had no effect on the spiritual realm, where they lived. Although the matter is debated, it seems most likely that the prostitution referred to here is temple prostitution, wherein "many of the temple precincts hosted dinners after which prostitutes were on offer. . . . In the Greco-Roman world prostitution at pagan cultic events was not uncommon."[11]

---

[11] Ciampa and Rosner, *First Letter to the Corinthians*, 248–49. See their full discussion on 246–51.

The apostle will have none of this. He contends against it chiefly with three appeals to the idea of union. First and most basically, Paul argues that from creation God ordained that "the two," Adam and Eve, "will become one flesh" (v. 16, citing Gen. 2:24). The first pair set the pattern for human life. God wills for men and women to marry and within the marriage covenant to enjoy exclusive sexual intercourse. And most men leave their parents and hold fast to a wife. This one-flesh relationship is the most intimate in human life.

Second (though actually appearing first in the text), contrary to that exclusivity and intimacy, another manifestation of unity warrants Paul's attention: "Or do you not know that he who is joined to a prostitute becomes one body with her?" (1 Cor. 6:16). For Corinthian men (or anyone else) to engage in sexual relations with prostitutes violates the oneness and permanence God ordains for marriage. Paul emphasizes a high view of the body and bodily behavior to a church that needs to heed his message. Sexual intercourse with prostitutes, then, is not inconsequential, as some Corinthian men claimed. The powerful emotional, psychological, and (in this context chiefly) physical unity of sex is reserved for those who have covenanted lifetime fidelity to one another.

Third, sexual union with a prostitute desecrates not only the Creator's ordinance for marriage; it also desecrates one's spiritual marriage to Christ. Ciampa and Rosner juxtapose the mutually exclusive alternatives (in 6:16–17): either one cleaves to a prostitute or one cleaves to the Lord. "Thus the Genesis test is used not only to prove the seriousness of sexual union with a prostitute, but to introduce the notion of the believer's nuptial union with Christ.[12]

Paul's argument is seen most powerfully as he piles these three appeals to union on top of one another: "Do you not know that he who is joined to a prostitute becomes one body with her? For, as it is written, 'The two will become one flesh.' But he who is joined to the Lord becomes one spirit with him" (vv. 16–17). Although Paul does not here use the words *marriage, bride,* or *groom,* he presents the relationship between Christ and believers as a spiritual marriage. This is seen most clearly in his words "He who is joined to the Lord becomes one spirit with him," which closely parallel "He who is joined to a prostitute becomes one body with her." Both speak of being "joined" and becoming "one" with the partner to whom someone is united. Here the similarities end, for in the first case one is joined to *a prostitute* and becomes one *body* with her, while in the other case one is joined to *the Lord Jesus* and becomes one *spirit* with him.

Fee helpfully points out that Paul probably refers to the Holy Spirit:

---

[12] Ibid., 259–60.

In a parallel sentence, with "Lord" substituted for "prostitute" and "spirit" for "body," the illicit union is now contrasted to the believer's union with Christ. . . . In light of vv. 19–20, Paul is probably referring to the work of the Spirit, whereby through the "one Spirit" the believer's "spirit" has been joined indissolubly with Christ. The believer is united to the Lord and thereby has become one S/spirit with him. . . . Paul's point is that the physical union of a believer with a prostitute is not possible because the believer's body already belongs to the Lord, through whose resurrection one's body has become a "member" of Christ by his Spirit.[13]

Paul's second picture of union is that of a temple. In 1 Corinthians 3:16–17 he presented the church corporately as God's dwelling place, his temple. Now he presents believers' bodies individually as temples of the Holy Spirit. I say this because the context here treats sexual immorality and believers' using their bodies individually for the Lord instead of for sinful pleasure. "Do you not know that your body is a temple of the Holy Spirit within you, whom you have from God? You are not your own, for you were bought with a price. So glorify God in your body" (6:19–20). Paul uses plural pronouns, as he did in 3:16–17, but here it is because he views the congregation as made up of individual bodies.

The apostle gives another reason to use our bodies as instruments that bring honor to God: our bodies are temples of the Holy Spirit. God gave us the Spirit, and we have him within us. We should, therefore, have nothing to do with prostitution, for it defiles God's temple. Christ redeemed us with his blood and claimed us for his own. As a result, we belong to him. Once more, as in 3:16–17, it is the presence of God that makes a building a temple. In this case the Holy Spirit resides in the individual bodies of believers, making them holy. Paul urges the Corinthians to treat them as such.

The apostle's third picture of union is that of members of a body. Although the image of the body of Christ is not as evident in this passage as are those of marriage and temple/indwelling, it is nonetheless implied. It is implied in Paul's first words in this section, "Do you not know that your bodies are members of Christ? Shall I then take the members of Christ and make them members of a prostitute? Never!" (6:15). When twice in this verse the apostle says our bodies are members of Christ, he appeals to the image of the church as Christ's body. He shocks readers, as Ciampa and Rosner illustrate: "Shall I then tear from Christ his limbs and organs and make them the limbs

---

[13] Fee, *First Epistle to the Corinthians*, 260.

and organs of a prostitute?"[14] When Paul recoils at believers' making Christ's members "members of a prostitute" (v. 15), it shows that the metaphor of believers as the body of Christ is more than a metaphor. There is a spiritual reality behind it. We are truly and spiritually joined to Christ. By virtue of our union with Christ, becoming one with a prostitute involves Christ in sin! It joins his members to the prostitute's!

1 Corinthians 7:22

He who was called in the Lord as a bondservant is a freedman of the Lord. Likewise he who was free when called is a bondservant of Christ.

In a passage in which Paul urges the Corinthian believers to remain in the economic, familial, or religious situation in which they found themselves when coming to Christ, he ironically describes Christian slaves as the Lord's freedmen and Christian freemen as Christ's slaves. The former slave is described as "called in the Lord as a bondservant." "In the Lord" here probably is a periphrasis for "Christian" and hence signifies "called as a Christian bondservant." Paul reminds his readers of the cost of their redemption (v. 23), alluding to Christ's sacrifice on the cross, and summarizes his counsel: "In whatever condition each was called, there let him remain with God" (v. 24).

1 Corinthians 7:39

A wife is bound to her husband as long as he lives. But if her husband dies, she is free to be married to whom she wishes, only in the Lord.

Paul gives freedom for a widow to marry "whom she wishes." But he makes a qualification—she is to do so "only in the Lord." Once again we encounter "in Christ" language used as a periphrasis for believers. The Christian widow is free to marry, but only another Christian. Her new husband must be "in the Lord," that is, a Christian man.

1 Corinthians 9:1–2

Am I not free? Am I not an apostle? Have I not seen Jesus our Lord? Are not you my workmanship in the Lord? If to others I am not an apostle, at least I am to you, for you are the seal of my apostleship in the Lord.

---

[14] Ciampa and Rosner, *First Letter to the Corinthians*, 258.

As often in the Corinthian letters, in 1 Corinthians 9 Paul defends himself against the attacks of his accusers. In fact, in the verse immediately following the two quoted above he writes, "This is my defense to those who would examine me" (v. 3). Paul uses rhetorical questions to set forth the qualifications of his apostleship, which his enemies doubt. The first three questions affirm he is free, is an apostle, and has seen the risen Christ. The fourth question asserts that the existence of the Corinthian church is evidence of his apostolic ministry. In fact, he declares, "If to others I am not an apostle, at least I am to you, for you are the seal of my apostleship" (v. 2).

"In Christ" language occurs twice, both times appearing as "in the Lord." When Paul asks rhetorically, "Are not you my workmanship in the Lord?" he employs "in the Lord" to describe his labor in the gospel. That is, the Corinthian believers are the fruit of his work.[15] The second occurrence of "in Christ" language appears in Paul's statement, "You are the seal of my apostleship in the Lord" (v. 2). In defending his apostleship he produces as evidence the fact that the Corinthians are Christians. "In the Lord" is used causally: *because* they are believers the Corinthians attest to Paul's apostleship.

1 Corinthians 10:16–22

The cup of blessing that we bless, is it not a participation in the blood of Christ? The bread that we break, is it not a participation in the body of Christ? Because there is one bread, we who are many are one body, for we all partake of the one bread. Consider the people of Israel: are not those who eat the sacrifices participants in the altar? What do I imply then? That food offered to idols is anything, or that an idol is anything? No, I imply that what pagans sacrifice they offer to demons and not to God. I do not want you to be participants with demons. You cannot drink the cup of the Lord and the cup of demons. You cannot partake of the table of the Lord and the table of demons. Shall we provoke the Lord to jealousy? Are we stronger than he?

In the larger and narrower contexts Paul seeks to dissuade the Corinthian Christians from participating unwittingly in pagan worship. Some of them think foolishly that they can eat meals at idol temples with impunity. They claim such behavior has no bearing on the Christian life. Their reasoning seems to be that because idols have no reality, eating meals sacrificed to

---

[15] I here follow Campbell, *Paul and Union with Christ*, 158.

them is harmless. Although Paul agrees that idols have no reality, he rejects their line of reasoning. On the contrary, believers should have nothing to do with idols or their temples. Why? Because "what pagans sacrifice they offer to demons and not to God. I do not want you to be participants with demons" (v. 20).

This notion of participation with the supernatural realm is reinforced by Paul's references to Old Testament sacrifices: "Consider the people of Israel: are not those who eat the sacrifices participants in the altar?" (v. 18). With a rhetorical question Paul points to the Jewish worship practices of his day, which were based on Old Testament teaching. Partaking of the food offered in the sacrifice meant partaking in the religious act of the sacrifice, namely, participating in the worship of Israel's God. It meant partaking, in faith, of the benefits of the sacrifice.

In the immediate context, therefore, Paul speaks of participating with demons in pagan religious meals and participating with the God of Israel in Jewish sacrifices. The emphasis is on the supernatural effects of partaking. Hence when he speaks of Christians' partaking of the Lord's Supper, he means that in so doing they participate in the body and blood of Christ. That is, they partake of the benefits of Christ's once-for-all sacrifice on the cross. "The cup of blessing that we bless, is it not a participation in the blood of Christ? The bread that we break, is it not a participation in the body of Christ?" (v. 16). As Ciampa and Rosner observe, with the aid of a rhetorical question the apostle teaches that believing partakers of the Lord's Supper enjoy "true communion with God and participation in the life he [Christ] has won for us through the cross."[16]

This interpretation is confirmed by verse 21: "You cannot drink the cup of the Lord and the cup of demons. You cannot partake of the table of the Lord and the table of demons." Paul's concern is not merely with appearances; participants have fellowship with demons in pagan sacrifices and with Christ in the Supper. Once more Ciampa and Rosner come to our aid:

> Paul's argument, with its emphasis on participation in the blood and body
> of Christ, seeks to stress where God is (or gods are) invoked as the host or
> patron (or hosts/patrons) of the meal, the fellowship is not merely with
> the men and women gathered around the table, but with the deity as well.
> Through our fellowship with Christ we participate in the benefits of his

---

[16] Ciampa and Rosner, *First Letter to the Corinthians*, 469.

sacrifice, which serves to establish or renew our covenantal relationship with God.[17]

As Romans 6:1–11 and Colossians 2:11–12 speak of union with Christ as the most important meaning of Christian baptism, so here Paul teaches that believing participants in the Lord's Supper receive the benefits of union with Christ. They enjoy true fellowship with him and partake of the blessings of his atoning sacrifice. And as 1 Corinthians 10:16 speaks of vertical fellowship with Christ in the Supper, the next verse speaks of horizontal fellowship with other believers in the Supper: "Because there is one bread, we who are many are one body, for we all partake of the one bread" (v. 17). And this is the reason Paul inverts the bread and the cup in verse 16—to provide for an easy transition from vertical to horizontal union in the next verse.

In addition, in verse 17 Paul appeals to the image of the church as Christ's body: "Because there is one bread, we who are many are one body, for we all partake of the one bread." As the many members of the Corinthian congregation partake of the one common loaf of bread in the Lord's Supper, they are "one body." The many become one body of Christ, one church, in the partaking of the bread. Their union with Christ, experienced in the Supper, establishes and exhibits their union with one another as the body of Christ.

1 Corinthians 11:11–12

> In the Lord woman is not independent of man nor man of woman; for as woman was made from man, so man is now born of woman. And all things are from God.

In discussing women's covering their heads in worship, Paul appeals to a creation ordinance to assert the interdependence of men and women. So, though it is tempting to regard "in the Lord" as locative, pointing to Christ's domain, the creational context (referring to Genesis 2) suggests that an instrumental understanding is better. Mutual dependence between men and women is true not merely for believers; it is a function of creation. Hence it is the Lord's work to establish such mutual dependence. And this conclusion is confirmed by verse 12, which further explains verse 11: "As woman was made from man, so man is now born of woman" (1 Cor. 11:12). Just as God took

---

[17] Ibid., 474.

Eve from Adam's side at her creation, so all human beings, including males, come out of their mother's womb.

1 Corinthians 11:23–26

I received from the Lord what I also delivered to you, that the Lord Jesus on the night when he was betrayed took bread, and when he had given thanks, he broke it, and said, "This is my body which is for you. Do this in remembrance of me." In the same way also he took the cup, after supper, saying, "This cup is the new covenant in my blood. Do this, as often as you drink it, in remembrance of me." For as often as you eat this bread and drink the cup, you proclaim the Lord's death until he comes.

Paul indicates that other apostles transmitted to him authoritative tradition concerning the Lord's Supper. This tradition presents Jesus's taking the role of a household head or patron who blesses and passes out the food. Paul rehearses Jesus's saying, "This is my body which is for you," and, "This cup is the new covenant in my blood" (vv. 24–25), and his following these sayings with commands to partake. Of course, Jesus said these things at the final dinner he shared with his disciples before his death, a first-century Passover meal. Although the disciples did not understand the meaning at the time, the symbolism powerfully communicates union with Christ. Consider: Jesus identifies the bread with his body and the wine with his blood and tells the disciples to eat and drink, respectively. They are to "ingest" him metaphorically so that he becomes a part of them. Such symbolism speaks of union between the partakers and that which is partaken, even the body and blood of the Son of God.

This understanding is corroborated by the fact, as Ciampa and Rosner correctly state, that the words from 10:16–17 "are expected to inform our understanding of the present text."[18] Drinking and eating this meal in faith is a "participation in the blood of Christ" and "participation in the body of Christ."

1 Corinthians 12:12–27

Just as the body is one and has many members, and all the members of the body, though many, are one body, so it is with Christ. For in one Spirit we

---

[18] Ibid., 552.

were all baptized into one body—Jews or Greeks, slaves or free—and all were made to drink of one Spirit.

For the body does not consist of one member but of many. If the foot should say, "Because I am not a hand, I do not belong to the body," that would not make it any less a part of the body. And if the ear should say, "Because I am not an eye, I do not belong to the body," that would not make it any less a part of the body. If the whole body were an eye, where would be the sense of hearing? If the whole body were an ear, where would be the sense of smell? But as it is, God arranged the members in the body, each one of them, as he chose. If all were a single member, where would the body be? As it is, there are many parts, yet one body.

The eye cannot say to the hand, "I have no need of you," nor again the head to the feet, "I have no need of you." On the contrary, the parts of the body that seem to be weaker are indispensable, and on those parts of the body that we think less honorable we bestow the greater honor, and our unpresentable parts are treated with greater modesty, which our more presentable parts do not require. But God has so composed the body, giving greater honor to the part that lacked it, that there may be no division in the body, but that the members may have the same care for one another. If one member suffers, all suffer together; if one member is honored, all rejoice together.

Now you are the body of Christ and individually members of it.

This is Paul's chief "body life" passage, one that uses the image of the body of Christ to emphasize the horizontal dimension of union with Christ. Once again (cf. Rom. 12:4) Paul compares the human body, which is unified despite its many members, to the church: "Just as the body is one and has many members, and all the members of the body, though many, are one body, so it is with Christ" (1 Cor. 12:12). Paul uses images of baptism and drinking of a liquid to communicate that it is the Spirit who unites us to Christ (v. 13). Christ baptized us "in one Spirit . . . into one body . . . and all were made to drink of one Spirit."[19] Assuming that the two statements of verse 13 are to be read in light of each other, Ciampa and Rosner equate the "drinking or drenching with the Spirit" and "the baptism by or of the Spirit here or elsewhere."[20] The Holy Spirit joins us spiritually to Christ and thereby to other believers.

The apostle treats various aspects of horizontal union with Christ in verses

---

[19] For discussion of different interpretations of various aspects of 1 Cor. 12:13, see ibid., 589–96.
[20] Ibid., 592.

14–27. First, he discusses the interdependence of the various members in verses 14–26: "The body does not consist of one member but of many" (v. 14). Those who consider themselves inferior to their fellows are mistaken (vv. 15–20). Each member is important to the functioning of the body (vv. 15–17). And this is precisely as God has ordered things: "God arranged the members in the body, each one of them, as he chose" (v. 18). His plan was to have many members doing their part in one body (vv. 19–20). As it is with the human body, so it is with the church, the body of Christ.

Furthermore, those who consider themselves superior to others are also mistaken (vv. 21–26). No part of the body can claim it does not need the other parts (v. 21). In fact, parts of our bodies we take for granted or cover in modesty are indispensable (vv. 22–24). And this is by divine design: "God has so composed the body, giving greater honor to the part that lacked it" (v. 24). His purpose is doing so? "That there may be no division in the body, but that the members may have the same care for one another" (v. 25). Paul is now certainly speaking of the church, for he continues, "If one member suffers, all suffer together; if one member is honored, all rejoice together" (v. 26). D. E. Garland comments: "The church is not to be like its surrounding society, which always honors those who are already honored. It is to be counter-cultural and bestow the greatest honor on those who seem to be negligible."[21]

Union with Christ begins in the vertical dimension of people being spiritually united to the Son of God individually and corporately. Paul rounds out his greatest treatment of the corporate, horizontal dimension of union with Christ: "Now you are the body of Christ and individually members of it" (v. 27).

This passage also pertains to Paul's theme of belonging to Christ. As we have seen, Paul's references to body members that say, "I do not belong to the body" because they are not other parts of the body (vv. 15–16) pertain to believers as members of Christ's body. Hence, in belonging to Christ we belong to other believers. Union with Christ results in our belonging to Christ. And since union is communal as well as individual, when I am joined to Christ by faith union and belong to him, I am joined to all other believers and belong to them as well.

1 Corinthians 15:16–19

If the dead are not raised, not even Christ has been raised. And if Christ has not been raised, your faith is futile and you are still in your sins. Then

---

[21] D. E. Garland, *1 Corinthians*, Baker Exegetical Commentary on the New Testament (Grand Rapids: Baker Academic, 2003), 596. Cited in Ciampa and Rosner, *First Letter to the Corinthians*, 607.

those also who have fallen asleep in Christ have perished. If in Christ we have hope in this life only, we are of all people most to be pitied.

In a passage that played a major part in my conversion to Christ as a twenty-one-year-old, Paul frankly explores what would obtain if there were no resurrection of the dead and therefore Christ were not raised (vv. 12–19): the apostles' preaching and the faith of those who heard them would be "in vain" and "futile" (vv. 14, 17), the apostles would have misrepresented God (v. 15), believers would be "still in their sins" and would not be forgiven by God (v. 17), and those who died under Christ's reign would have gone to hell (v. 18); and if believers' hope in Christ pertained only to this life, it would be a false hope and they would deserve much pity (v. 19).

Verses 18 and 19 each contain "in Christ" language. If Jesus were still in the tomb, "then those also who have fallen asleep in Christ [would] have perished" (v. 18). This is the common use of "in Christ" to denote his sphere of influence or reign. Paul's message is that if Christ were not risen, believers who died under his rule would be in hell. His use of the verb "to sleep" for death, however, anticipates his conclusion in verse 20: "But in fact Christ has been raised from the dead." Death, therefore, does not separate Christ's people from his rule. Because Christ died for sinners and arose, believers experience death as "sleep"; death cannot hold them but is only temporary as they await their resurrection within Christ's domain.

Paul also writes, "If in Christ we have hope in this life only, we are of all people most to be pitied" (v. 19). This is one of a half dozen places where Paul uses "in Christ" as the object of Christian faith or hope: Christians hope in Christ in this life.[22] Paul's point is that if that is the full extent of their faith, they are foolish and pathetic.

1 Corinthians 15:21–23

As by a man came death, by a man has come also the resurrection of the dead. For as in Adam all die, so also in Christ shall all be made alive. But each in his own order: Christ the firstfruits, then at his coming those who belong to Christ.

Paul compares and contrasts two human beings. As Adam brought death into the world of humanity through his primal sin, so Christ, the second

---

[22] Campbell, *Paul and Union with Christ*, 111–12. Once more he helps me locate this common usage in Paul.

Adam, brings life through his resurrection from the dead. He was raised first and will raise his people when he comes again. Paul here describes Christians as "those who belong to Christ" (v. 23).

Paul's use of "in Christ" in verse 22 is to be read over against his use of "in Adam" in the same verse. As such, "in Christ" reflects the basic locative sense of the expression, used figuratively to denote realm. All those in Adam's domain die; all those in Christ's domain will be made alive at his return.

Ciampa and Rosner capture the spirit of Paul's "in Adam"/"in Christ" parallel in this passage:

> Paul is presenting the most concise form of the story of redemption imaginable: the archetypal problem of sin finds its eschatological resolution through the climactic breakthrough of the resurrection accomplished by Christ. . . . *For as in Adam all die, so in Christ all will be made alive.* . . . To be *in Adam* is to be part of the group which finds in Adam its representative and leader, which finds its identity and destiny in Adam and what he has brought about for his people. To be *in Christ* is to be part of the group which finds in Christ its representative and leader, which finds its identity and destiny in Christ and what he has brought about for his people. . . . The expressions *in Adam* and *in Christ* reinforce the idea of corporate solidarity. . . . The following verse makes it clear that by "being made alive" Paul has in mind the resurrection since those who belong to him will be made alive (= resurrected) "when he comes."[23]

1 Corinthians 15:30–33

> Why are we in danger every hour? I protest, brothers, by my pride in you, which I have in Christ Jesus our Lord, I die every day! What do I gain if, humanly speaking, I fought with beasts at Ephesus? If the dead are not raised, "Let us eat and drink, for tomorrow we die." Do not be deceived: "Bad company ruins good morals."

Paul continues his argument for the resurrection of the dead—specifically, for the resurrection of Christ. He points to the danger he faces for the gospel, including fighting "beasts at Ephesus" (v. 32). This is metaphorical language for "bloodthirsty human antagonists who would eagerly tear him to pieces."[24] If Christ were not alive, such risk taking would be the height of folly. If Christ

---

[23] Ciampa and Rosner, *First Letter to the Corinthians*, 763–64.
[24] Garland, *1 Corinthians*, 121, quoted in Ciampa and Rosner, *First Letter to the Corinthians*, 789.

is still dead, then let us pursue pleasure with all our might (v. 32)! In the midst
of this Paul writes, "I protest, brothers, by my pride in you, which I have in
Christ Jesus our Lord, I die every day!" (v. 31). As in Romans 15:17, Paul here
employs "in Christ Jesus" to denote Christians' actions done "in Christ." Here
"in Christ Jesus" modifies Paul's action of boasting of the Corinthian church;
he boasts in this manner "in Christ Jesus."

1 Corinthians 15:58

> Be steadfast, immovable, always abounding in the work of the Lord,
> knowing that in the Lord your labor is not in vain.

This is one of many places where the apostle expresses Christians' actions
"in the Lord," meaning "for Christ." The "labor" referred to here is Christian
labor, service done for Christ.[25] Because Jesus is alive from the dead, Paul
exhorts the Corinthians to be unwavering and steady. They can stand fast regardless of circumstances, having this anchor—the crucified one is the living
one! As a result, they can be fruitful in the Lord's work, knowing that it will
not be in vain. Speaking of Christian labor, Barrett is pithy—"Since it is done
in the Lord it can no more perish than he."[26]

1 Corinthians 16:19, 24

> The churches of Asia send you greetings. Aquila and Prisca, together with
> the church in their house, send you hearty greetings in the Lord. . . . My
> love be with you all in Christ Jesus. Amen.

As Paul does in half of his greetings to churches, so here he uses "in the
Lord" language at the close of this letter to the Corinthians. When he brings
them "hearty greetings in the Lord" from Aquila, Priscilla, and their house
church, he expresses the Christian manner of extending greetings. It is "a
Christian greeting."

In his very last words in the epistle, Paul gives all of them his love "in Christ
Jesus" (v. 24). Campbell argues—successfully, in my opinion—that "in Christ"
"is descriptive of *you*—the Corinthians. This reading is strengthened by Anthony Thiselton's suggestion that the subtext of this verse is that Paul loves
them *all*, not any particular faction or party within the Corinthian church."[27]

---

[25] Campbell, *Paul and Union with Christ*, agrees (158–59).
[26] Barrett, *Commentary on the First Epistle to the Corinthians*, 385, emphasis original.
[27] Campbell, *Paul and Union with Christ*, 123, emphasis original. He cites Anthony C. Thiselton, *The First Epistle to the Corinthians*, New International Greek Testament Commentary (Grand Rapids: Eerdmans, 2000), 1353.

Chapter 7

Union with Christ in 2 Corinthians

---

2 Corinthians 1:3–7

> Blessed be the God and Father of our Lord Jesus Christ, the Father of mercies and God of all comfort, who comforts us in all our affliction, so that we may be able to comfort those who are in any affliction, with the comfort with which we ourselves are comforted by God. For as we share abundantly in Christ's sufferings, so through Christ we share abundantly in comfort too. If we are afflicted, it is for your comfort and salvation; and if we are comforted, it is for your comfort, which you experience when you patiently endure the same sufferings that we suffer. Our hope for you is unshaken, for we know that as you share in our sufferings, you will also share in our comfort.

Paul begins by praising God, the Father of the Lord Jesus. Significantly, the apostle describes him as the "Father of mercies and God of all comfort" (v. 3). These words form the basis for Paul's teaching that follows. The merciful and comforting Father comforts believers in their suffering to prepare them to comfort others in their suffering. God's comfort is what comforted believers pass on to others (v. 4).

So far, the only mention of Christ has been as God's Son. Now things change. Paul views Christians' afflictions christologically: "As we share abundantly in Christ's sufferings, so through Christ we share abundantly in comfort too" (v. 5). It is important to declare what this verse does *not* mean. Of course, believers do not participate in Christ's redemptive suffering; that remains utterly unique. Also, the combination of present sufferings and future comfort, while not excluded, is not primarily in view. Rather, Paul has in mind the combination of present afflictions and present comfort.

That is, union with Christ in his death and resurrection involves not only present suffering and future glory, but also present suffering and present "glory," experienced as the Father's aid and encouragement. And this aid and encouragement are to be shared: "If we are afflicted, it is for your comfort and salvation; and if we are comforted, it is for your comfort, which you experience when you patiently endure the same sufferings that we suffer" (v. 6). As surely as the Lord Jesus died and arose, we can be confident of believers' sharing in his affliction and comfort now: "Our hope for you is unshaken, for we know that as you share in our sufferings, you will also share in our comfort" (v. 7).

Philip E. Hughes eloquently summarizes:

> For the Christian, however, as Paul explains elsewhere, there is such a thing as the fellowship of Christ's sufferings (Phil. 3:10 . . .), that is, a sharing or participation with Christ in suffering. . . . But Christ, let it be remembered, is no longer suffering in humiliation, for He is now exalted in glory. If we are called to fellowship in the sufferings of the Christ of humiliation, it is the Christ of glory who mediates an abundance of comfort to us—one and the same Christ.[1]

Though the emphasis is on present suffering and comfort, the passage is not devoid of the hope of future comfort, for it draws attention to "God who raises the dead" (2 Cor. 1:9).

2 Corinthians 1:17–22

> Was I vacillating when I wanted to do this? Do I make my plans according to the flesh, ready to say "Yes, yes" and "No, no" at the same time? As surely as God is faithful, our word to you has not been Yes and No. For the Son of God, Jesus Christ, whom we proclaimed among you, Silvanus and Timothy and I, was not Yes and No, but in him it is always Yes. For all the promises of God find their Yes in him. That is why it is through him that we utter our Amen to God for his glory. And it is God who establishes us

---

[1] Philip E. Hughes, *The Second Epistle to the Corinthians*, The New International Commentary on the New Testament (Grand Rapids: Eerdmans, 1962), 13–14.

with you in Christ, and has anointed us, and who has also put his seal on us and given us his Spirit in our hearts as a guarantee.

Accused by enemies of vacillating in both ministry and message when he did not return to Corinth as planned, Paul defends himself on both counts. He explains that he changed his plans to visit Corinth "to spare" them (v. 23). More importantly, he maintains that his message has always remained stable and has not changed (v. 19). This is because it is centered on Christ and the gospel: "The Son of God, Jesus Christ, whom we proclaimed among you, Silvanus and Timothy and I, was not Yes and No, but *in him* it is always Yes. For all the promises of God find their Yes *in him*" (vv. 19–20). These two uses of "in him" are instrumental. God makes his promises and fulfills them through the person and work of his Son, Jesus Christ. Because of the stability Christ brings to the gospel, it is "through him that we utter our Amen to God for his glory" (v. 20).

Paul is not a vacillator; on the contrary, he and all Christians have a tremendous stabilizing force in their lives: "It is God who establishes us with you in Christ, and has anointed us, and who has also put his seal on us and given us his Spirit in our hearts as a guarantee" (vv. 21–22). The Holy Trinity makes believers stable. The Father stabilizes us through the ministries of the Holy Spirit. Four times Paul speaks of the Spirit. The Father anoints us with the Spirit, seals us with the Spirit, gives us his Spirit in our hearts, and gives us the Spirit as a down payment or guarantee of our final inheritance (vv. 21–22). God's giving us the Spirit in our hearts is another way of talking about indwelling, a correlative to union with Christ.

Paul writes, "It is God who establishes us with you in Christ" (v. 21). Here is a third "in Christ" reference in these six verses. In this case, "The verse . . . expresses the status of believers, who are confirmed as being in some way defined by, or belonging to, Christ."[2]

2 Corinthians 2:12–13

When I came to Troas to preach the gospel of Christ, even though a door was opened for me in the Lord, my spirit was not at rest because I did not find my brother Titus there. So I took leave of them and went on to Macedonia.

---

[2] Constantine R. Campbell, *Paul and Union with Christ: An Exegetical and Theological Study* (Grand Rapids: Zondervan, 2012), 204–5.

Paul explains his movements to his readers. Upon arrival in Troas, where he expected to spend time ministering the gospel, he was disappointed not to find Titus. And out of deep concern for Titus, Paul left Troas for Macedonia. Paul expresses his conviction that God had provided opportunity to minister in Troas in this way, "even though a door was opened for me in the Lord" (v. 12). Paul uses "in the Lord" to communicate instrument: it was by the Lord Jesus that a door was opened, an opportunity afforded, for ministry.

2 Corinthians 2:14

Thanks be to God, who in Christ always leads us in triumphal procession, and through us spreads the fragrance of the knowledge of him everywhere.

Paul was discouraged, but he did not despair. Why? His confidence lay in "God, who in Christ always leads us in triumphal procession." The apostle uses the image of a Roman triumphal parade to describe his gospel ministry. Though all the details are not clear to us, it is clear that God "in Christ" directs Paul's triumphal procession. Paul engages in his ministry as an apostle because of Christ, with the result that those who believe are saved, while those who reject the gospel perish (vv. 15–16).

2 Corinthians 2:17

We are not, like so many, peddlers of God's word, but as men of sincerity, as commissioned by God, in the sight of God we speak in Christ.

Paul engages in polemics, contrasting his sincerity as an apostle with the scheming for profit of the false apostles who oppose his ministry. They, he intimates, are "peddlers of God's word." By contrast, he and the other true apostles "speak in Christ." Because he opposes the faulty motivation of the false teachers, "in Christ" probably gives his proper motivation—he speaks because of Christ.

2 Corinthians 3:14–15

Their minds were hardened. For to this day, when they read the old covenant, that same veil remains unlifted, because only through Christ is it taken away. Yes, to this day whenever Moses is read a veil lies over their hearts.

Paul speaks of the hardening of Jewish hearts when they read the Old Testament. He says "only through Christ is it taken away" (v. 14). The prepositional phrase (ἐν Χριστῷ/*en Christō*) is correctly rendered "through Christ" to express agency; only Christ sets aside the veil of misunderstanding the Scriptures.

2 Corinthians 4:7–14

> We have this treasure in jars of clay, to show that the surpassing power belongs to God and not to us. We are afflicted in every way, but not crushed; perplexed, but not driven to despair; persecuted, but not forsaken; struck down, but not destroyed; always carrying in the body the death of Jesus, so that the life of Jesus may also be manifested in our bodies. For we who live are always being given over to death for Jesus' sake, so that the life of Jesus also may be manifested in our mortal flesh. So death is at work in us, but life in you.
>
> Since we have the same spirit of faith according to what has been written, "I believed, and so I spoke," we also believe, and so also we speak, knowing that he who raised the Lord Jesus will raise us also with Jesus and bring us with you into his presence.

The gospel is a "treasure" for God's glory, committed to us who are beset with human weaknesses. God is victorious in spite of and through human weakness, embodying the principle of the crucifixion of the Son of God. Paul refers to the Lord's crucifixion ("death of Jesus") and resurrection ("life of Jesus"). Union with Christ defines our existence as believers. Thus we always carry "in the body the death of Jesus, so that the life of Jesus may also be manifested in our bodies" (v. 10). Paul Barnett explains:

> The "dying of Jesus" that takes place "in [Paul's] body" is the affliction, bewilderment, persecution, and humiliation mentioned in vv. 8–9. The "life of Jesus," on the other hand, is the deliverance represented by the four "but nots" of those verses. The former (the "dying of Jesus") were endured precisely in order that rescue from them ("life of Jesus") might be experienced. There is a divine purpose for apostolic suffering, namely, that Paul might testify to God's deliverance (1:11; 4:12–15). Paul sees God's mercy in these present difficulties as of a piece with the eschatological deliverance of resurrection (cf. v. 14).[3]

[3] Paul Barnett, *The Second Epistle to the Corinthians*, The New International Commentary on the New Testament (Grand Rapids: Eerdmans, 1997), 235–36.

Verse 11 virtually recapitulates verse 10: "For we who live are always being given over to death for Jesus' sake, so that the life of Jesus also may be manifested in our mortal flesh." The next two verses explain Paul's intent to suffer and endure so the Corinthians may know now and at the end of the age the same resurrection life of Christ that Paul does. And verse 14 teaches that the apostles minister with the confidence that "he who raised the Lord Jesus will raise us also with Jesus and bring us with you into his presence." Death does not destroy our union with Christ. Instead, we die in the Lord and are raised "with Jesus" (v. 14). Thus, by virtue of union with Christ, God saves us, keeps us, and brings us safely home.

2 Corinthians 5:16–21

> From now on, therefore, we regard no one according to the flesh. Even though we once regarded Christ according to the flesh, we regard him thus no longer. Therefore, if anyone is in Christ, he is a new creation. The old has passed away; behold, the new has come. All this is from God, who through Christ reconciled us to himself and gave us the ministry of reconciliation; that is, in Christ God was reconciling the world to himself, not counting their trespasses against them, and entrusting to us the message of reconciliation. Therefore, we are ambassadors for Christ, God making his appeal through us. We implore you on behalf of Christ, be reconciled to God. For our sake he made him to be sin who knew no sin, so that in him we might become the righteousness of God.

Paul speaks of believers' change of status. "If anyone is in Christ, he is a new creation" (v. 17). "In Christ" characterizes the new domain in which Christians find themselves; this is Christ's domain, his realm. Being under his realm means being part of God's new creation. The apostle continues to describe this state of affairs: "The old has passed away; behold, the new has come" (v. 17).

Paul brings together "in Christ" and reconciliation (v. 17). He seems to make "in Christ" in verse 19 parallel to "through Christ" in verse 18:

God . . . through Christ reconciled us to himself . . . (v. 18)

That is, in Christ God was reconciling the world to himself. (v. 19)

"In Christ," then, is used instrumentally (in v. 19)—God was making peace between the world and himself through Christ's person and work.

Paul also combines "in him" and justification: "For our sake he made him to be sin who knew no sin, so that in him we might become the righteousness of God" (v. 21). Although all uses of "in Christ" language communicate a relationship between Christ and believers, most uses do not directly indicate union with Christ. But it appears this one does. After regarding "sphere" and "instrument" as good options, Campbell explains his preference for a third option—union with Christ:

> The phrase could indicate union with Christ: believers are made righteous by sharing in the righteousness of Christ. The strength of this reading comes from the apparent symmetry in the verse in which Christ becomes sin for us and believers become righteousness in him. Since Christ—who knew no sin—was made "sin," thus sharing in the plight of the sinful, so sinners are made righteous by sharing in his right standing. . . . The internal logic of the verse itself must finally be conclusive: ἐν αὐτῷ ["in him"] indicates union with Christ.[4]

2 Corinthians 6:14–18

Do not be unequally yoked with unbelievers. For what partnership has righteousness with lawlessness? Or what fellowship has light with darkness? What accord has Christ with Belial? Or what portion does a believer share with an unbeliever? What agreement has the temple of God with idols? For we are the temple of the living God; as God said,

> "I will make my dwelling among them and walk among them,
>   and I will be their God,
>   and they shall be my people.
> Therefore go out from their midst,
>   and be separate from them, says the Lord,
> and touch no unclean thing;
>   then I will welcome you,
> and I will be a father to you,
>   and you shall be sons and daughters to me,
> says the Lord Almighty."

Paul argues vigorously for separation from unbelief. The Corinthians must break with the cultic worship of idols. Six times, with much vocabulary

---

[4] Campbell, *Paul and Union with Christ*, 185–87.

variation, he says believers must not participate in idolatry with unbelievers. He explains why such separation is necessary: "For we are the temple of the living God" (v. 16). Once again the apostle uses temple imagery to identify God's people. And once again it is the presence of God that constitutes the temple. Believers are to eschew idolatry, Paul urges, "For we are the temple of the living God; as God said, 'I will make my dwelling among them'" (v. 16, citing Lev. 26:12).

The apostle teaches that "the living God" lives in the temple, which is made up of his people. To which person of the Godhead does Paul refer? It is God the Father who indwells his people! We conclude this from the language of 2 Corinthians 6:17–18, where God promises those who separate from unbelief, "I will welcome you, and I will be a father to you, and you shall be sons and daughters to me, says the Lord Almighty."

2 Corinthians 10:7

> Look at what is before your eyes. If anyone is confident that he is Christ's, let him remind himself that just as he is Christ's, so also are we.

Because of enemies' attacks, Paul must resort to defending his ministry. Three times in the space of one verse he refers to belonging to Christ: "If anyone is confident that he is Christ's, let him remind himself that just as he is Christ's, so also are we." Paul affirms that the apostles belong to Jesus just as do all other true believers. Such belonging is a product of union with Christ; God's joining us to him means we belong to him.

2 Corinthians 10:17–18

> "Let the one who boasts, boast in the Lord." For it is not the one who commends himself who is approved, but the one whom the Lord commends.

Unlike his opponents, who boast without good reason and beyond measure, Paul does not boast beyond limit; he boasts of what the Lord has accomplished through him (vv. 13–16). Here Paul uses Jeremiah 9:23–24—"Let the one who boasts, boast in the Lord"—in the same way as in 1 Corinthians 1:31. That is, Paul emphasizes that the Lord Jesus is to be the content of our boasting. At the end of the day, Paul is happy to leave commendation to the Lord, who does so by working in and through his people's lives, as he does

Paul's: "For it is not the one who commends himself who is approved, but the one whom the Lord commends" (2 Cor. 10:18).

2 Corinthians 11:1–4

> I wish you would bear with me in a little foolishness. Do bear with me! For I feel a divine jealousy for you, since I betrothed you to one husband, to present you as a pure virgin to Christ. But I am afraid that as the serpent deceived Eve by his cunning, your thoughts will be led astray from a sincere and pure devotion to Christ. For if someone comes and proclaims another Jesus than the one we proclaimed, or if you receive a different spirit from the one you received, or if you accept a different gospel from the one you accepted, you put up with it readily enough.

As is not uncommon in 2 Corinthians, Paul is forced to defend himself and his apostolic ministry against detractors who extol themselves and attack him. Thus with irony he asks the Corinthians to put up with a "little foolishness" on his part. The apostle's speech is ironic because the Corinthians "put up with it readily enough" when his opponents, "these super-apostles," preach a Jesus or a gospel different from the one the apostle Paul preached (vv. 4–5).

Paul speaks as their father who "betrothed" them to "one husband," even Christ. In ancient Near Eastern culture, "a father pledges a daughter in marriage to a prospective husband, taking responsibility for her virginal fidelity to her betrothed in the period between the betrothal and the marriage."[5] So, acting paternally, Paul wants to preserve the Corinthians in purity for Jesus on the day of his return. Union with Christ is here presented beautifully via the image of marriage. Believers, the bride, are wed to Jesus, their Groom.

A searching application flows from union viewed as marriage between Christians and Christ. Paul is concerned, lest "as the serpent deceived Eve by his cunning, your thoughts will be led astray from a sincere and pure devotion to Christ" (v. 3). Professed believers must be faithful to Jesus, their betrothed spouse. They must eschew marital unfaithfulness. There must be no "intellectual deception" leading to "spiritual apostasy," no "adulterous flirting with a false gospel."[6] We must be on guard and not permit ourselves to be seduced by spiritual imposters into committing spiritual infidelity. Instead, we are to cling spiritually to our Divine Husband alone until his second coming.

---

[5] Barnett, *Second Epistle to the Corinthians*, 499.
[6] Murray J. Harris, *The Second Epistle to the Corinthians*, New International Greek Testament Commentary (Grand Rapids: Eerdmans, 2005), 739.

2 Corinthians 12:1–2

I must go on boasting. Though there is nothing to be gained by it, I will go on to visions and revelations of the Lord. I know a man in Christ who fourteen years ago was caught up to the third heaven—whether in the body or out of the body I do not know, God knows.

Paul speaks with mild sarcasm as he continues his "boasting," this time of "visions and revelations of the Lord." Paul knows a "man in Christ" who was taken to the third heaven fourteen years earlier. "In Christ" functions as a periphrasis for believers here, and "man in Christ" is equivalent to "Christian man."

2 Corinthians 12:19

Have you been thinking all along that we have been defending ourselves to you? It is in the sight of God that we have been speaking in Christ, and all for your upbuilding, beloved.

Paul was forced by his foes' attacks to defend himself to the Corinthian church. He explains that he reluctantly did so for their benefit, their edification. Furthermore, he did so transparently: "in the sight of God . . . we have been speaking in Christ." As in 2 Corinthians 2:17, "in Christ" is used here with reference to Paul's speaking. And again, as in its use in 2:17, here it shows cause. He speaks not primarily in self-defense but because of Christ. Christ is his primary motive for communicating to the Corinthians.

2 Corinthians 13:2–6

I warned those who sinned before and all the others, and I warn them now while absent, as I did when present on my second visit, that if I come again I will not spare them—since you seek proof that Christ is speaking in me. He is not weak in dealing with you, but is powerful among you. For he was crucified in weakness, but lives by the power of God. For we also are weak in him, but in dealing with you we will live with him by the power of God.

Examine yourselves, to see whether you are in the faith. Test yourselves. Or do you not realize this about yourselves, that Jesus Christ is in you?—unless indeed you fail to meet the test! I hope you will find out that we have not failed the test.

In an ironic passage Paul calls the Corinthians to test themselves to see whether they are believers. It is ironic because Paul *does* think they are Christians, even as he knows he and his fellow apostles are as well. Being a Christian is described as having "Jesus Christ in" someone. When the Corinthians examine themselves and find that Christ is in them, they must conclude that Paul is a genuine apostle, which is what his enemies have denied. Barnett explains, "Their verdict about themselves will likewise be their verdict about him. That is, however they fare in their self-examination is how he also fares, because they owe their existence in Christ to him."[7]

Even as Christ died in weakness and arose by God's power, so Paul is weak "in him" and "will live with him by" God's power (v. 4). Paul not only follows Christ as a ministry model; he also participates in Christ's weakness and power. Therefore, "in him" here speaks of union with Christ in his death and resurrection.[8]

Furthermore, by drawing a parallel between "in dealing with you we will live *with* him by the power of God" and, in the previous line, Christ's living by God's power, Paul employs "with [Christ]" to indicate sharing in Christ's resurrection life.[9] Paul exults to participate in Christ's story with regard to the past and also with regard to the future, as here.

---

[7] Barnett, *Second Epistle to the Corinthians*, 607.
[8] Campbell, *Paul and Union with Christ*, 184.
[9] Ibid., 224–25.

Chapter 8

Union with Christ
in Galatians

Galatians 1:18–24

> After three years I went up to Jerusalem to visit Cephas and remained
> with him fifteen days. But I saw none of the other apostles except James
> the Lord's brother. (In what I am writing to you, before God, I do not lie!)
> Then I went into the regions of Syria and Cilicia. And I was still unknown
> in person to the churches of Judea that are in Christ. They only were hear-
> ing it said, "He who used to persecute us is now preaching the faith he
> once tried to destroy." And they glorified God because of me.

Paul received his gospel by special revelation from Jesus Christ. After his
conversion he did not confer with anyone else but went away to Arabia. Three
years later he went to see Peter in Jerusalem, where he also saw Jesus's brother
James. Paul then went into Syria and Cilicia but not Judea. In his words, "I was
still unknown in person to the churches of Judea that are in Christ" (v. 22). "In
Christ" is used as a periphrasis for believers, a usage we have seen a number
of times. The sense, then, is the "Christian churches in Judea." These churches
had not yet met Paul, but they praised God that the former persecutor was
now a proponent of the gospel.

Galatians 2:4–5

> Because of false brothers secretly brought in—who slipped in to spy out
> our freedom that we have in Christ Jesus, so that they might bring us into

slavery—to them we did not yield in submission even for a moment, so that the truth of the gospel might be preserved for you.

Paul strenuously resisted the efforts of Judaizers to pressure Gentile Christians into keeping the law, including accepting circumcision, in order to become Christians. He helped Titus resist this pressure. He calls the Judaizers "false brothers" and feels that the gospel is at stake. Persons, whether Jewish or Gentile, are saved by believing in Christ alone. Paul highly values the "freedom that we have in Christ Jesus," which in this context is a near synonym for salvation. The apostle contrasts "freedom . . . in Christ Jesus" with "slavery," which the "false brothers" wanted to impose on Titus and Paul himself. "In Christ" is used metaphorically as a locative to contrast Christ's realm with the bondage of the Judaizers. Union with Christ brings freedom, and that freedom cannot be compromised without compromising the gospel itself.

Galatians 2:15–21

We ourselves are Jews by birth and not Gentile sinners; yet we know that a person is not justified by works of the law but through faith in Jesus Christ, so we also have believed in Christ Jesus, in order to be justified by faith in Christ and not by works of the law, because by works of the law no one will be justified.

But if, in our endeavor to be justified in Christ, we too were found to be sinners, is Christ then a servant of sin? Certainly not! For if I rebuild what I tore down, I prove myself to be a transgressor. For through the law I died to the law, so that I might live to God. I have been crucified with Christ. It is no longer I who live, but Christ who lives in me. And the life I now live in the flesh I live by faith in the Son of God, who loved me and gave himself for me. I do not nullify the grace of God, for if righteousness were through the law, then Christ died for no purpose.

In context Paul speaks against any attempt to be justified "by works of the law" (three times in v. 16!). Salvation is only by faith in Christ. "In Christ Jesus" (εἰς Χριστὸν Ἰησοῦν/eis Christon 'Iēsoun) functions to mark the goal of faith; "Christ is the personal object toward whom trust is extended."[1]

Verse 17 is one of only two places (along with Rom. 3:24) where Paul links "in Christ" with justification. He rejects the charge of Judaizers, that Jewish

---

[1] Constantine R. Campbell, *Paul and Union with Christ: An Exegetical and Theological Study* (Grand Rapids: Zondervan, 2012), 206.

believers become "sinners" (which is what Judaizers considered Gentiles to be, because they did not follow the law) by associating with Gentiles. He contrasts Christ's being a "servant of sin" (a concept he rejects, of course) with believers' being "justified in Christ." Campbell explains:

> By raising the question of whether Christ is a promoter of sin, Paul implies Christ has *acted* in the event of justifying sinners. . . . The best sense is made of the question of whether Christ promotes sin by regarding him as actively involved in the event of justification. Consequently, the preferred reading of ἐν Χριστῷ [*en Christō*—"in" or "by Christ"] here is to ascribe the notion of agency. Christ brings about justification.[2]

Because Paul has been spiritually joined to Christ in his death—because he died with Christ—the apostle no longer lives, but "Christ . . . lives in" him (v. 20). Paul is not denying his personality, but rather affirming that the old Paul, who he was in Adam, has died with Christ. The new age has dawned in Christ's resurrection, and all believers now enjoy the life of the age to come.[3] Here again Paul asserts that he is indwelt by Christ. This passage wonderfully correlates co-crucifixion with Christ and his indwelling of believers. Jesus not only died and arose outside of us; he also comes to make his home with us and makes us his own people.

F. F. Bruce captures the idea of verse 20 in its context:

> A change of lordship, from law to Christ, has taken place, but that is not all, says Paul: "I have been crucified with Christ." Those who place their faith in Christ are united to him by that faith—united so closely that his experience now becomes theirs: they share his death to the old order ("under law"; cf. 4:4) and his resurrection to new life.[4]

Galatians 3:13–14

Christ redeemed us from the curse of the law by becoming a curse for us—for it is written, "Cursed is everyone who is hanged on a tree"—so that in Christ Jesus the blessing of Abraham might come to the Gentiles, so that we might receive the promised Spirit through faith.

---

[2] Ibid., 114–15.
[3] I have received help from Thomas R. Schreiner, *Galatians*, Zondervan Exegetical Commentary on the New Testament (Grand Rapids: Zondervan, 2010), 172.
[4] F. F. Bruce, *The Epistle to the Galatians*, New International Greek Testament Commentary (Grand Rapids: Eerdmans, 1982), 144.

In a context that speaks of the blessing God promised to Abraham and the curse lawbreakers deserve—punishment—Paul makes a powerful statement of penal substitution. Christ took the curse, the penalty, that we lawbreakers deserved; in his crucifixion he became a curse for us. Why? To redeem "us from the curse of the law" (v. 13). The result? We receive the blessing God promised to Abraham (vv. 8–9). In fact, even Gentiles who believe in Jesus receive the blessing of Abraham "in Christ Jesus" (v. 14). Probably "in Christ Jesus" is used instrumentally; it is through the saving accomplishment of Christ that God blesses the Gentiles.

Moreover, through faith in Christ we receive the Holy Spirit, promised in the Old Testament (v. 14). Indwelling is here referred to as receiving the Spirit.

Galatians 3:25–29

Now that faith has come, we are no longer under a guardian, for in Christ Jesus you are all sons of God, through faith. For as many of you as were baptized into Christ have put on Christ. There is neither Jew nor Greek, there is neither slave nor free, there is no male and female, for you are all one in Christ Jesus. And if you are Christ's, then you are Abraham's offspring, heirs according to promise.

Now that the new covenant has come in Christ, we are no longer under the law as a jailer or pedagogue. Anticipating 4:1–7, Paul says, "In Christ Jesus you are all sons of God, through faith" (v. 26). There is some ambiguity as to where the words "in Christ Jesus" belong in the translation. The NIV puts those words with "faith," hence, "You are all sons of God through faith in Christ Jesus." The ESV renders it, "In Christ Jesus you are all sons of God, through faith." As mentioned earlier, where the Greek is potentially ambiguous, I assume that a Greek writer uses word order to clear up the ambiguity. In this instance, the NIV follows the Greek word order. Thus Paul uses "in Christ Jesus" to present Christ as the object of saving faith.

We have been adopted into God's family by grace through faith in Christ the Redeemer. Adoption is a subset of union with Christ, as Paul explains, "As many of you as were baptized into Christ have put on Christ" (v. 27). Being "baptized into Christ" denotes incorporation into Christ, as the image of putting on clothes suggests.[5] The apostle combines baptism and the image of putting on Christ as clothing. Baptism/conversion involves figuratively putting

---

[5] Campbell, *Paul and Union with Christ*, 207–8.

on Christ as one puts on clothes. "The believer is identified with Christ. . . . Hence the image of clothing makes clear the union between Christ and the believer who is in Christ," according to Hans Burger.[6]

Paul does not command believers, "Put on the Lord Jesus Christ," as in Romans 13:14. Rather, he says that they already "have put on Christ" (v. 27). Nevertheless, Paul's teaching in this text carries ethical import. Richard Longenecker correctly asserts that "put on, clothe" used with a person means "to take on the characteristics, virtues, and/or intentions of the one referred to, and so to become like that person."[7] Bruce comments, "To be 'baptized into Christ' is to be incorporated into him by baptism, and hence to be 'in Christ.'"[8] Bruce says also that "it is difficult to suppose that the readers would not have understood it as a statement about their initiatory baptism in water" or that Paul, having learned the inadequacy of circumcision, would ascribe an efficacy *ex opere operato* to baptism.[9]

Faith in Christ and Christian baptism are great levelers and unifiers. "There is neither Jew nor Greek, there is neither slave nor free, there is no male and female, for you are all one in Christ Jesus" (v. 28). "In Christ Jesus" is used, as often, to show sphere or realm. The Galatian believers are unified in the sphere of Christ Jesus, which cuts across spheres of ethnicity, socio-economics, and gender.

Galatians 4:6

> Because you are sons, God has sent the Spirit of his Son into our hearts, crying, "Abba! Father!"

In a famous adoption passage, Paul rejoices that believers are no longer slaves of sin, but sons and heirs of God (v. 7). All of this is made possible because the Father sent his Son to accomplish his work of redemption (vv. 4–5). Paul singles out one of many wonderful results: "God has sent the Spirit of his Son into our hearts, crying, 'Abba! Father!'" (v. 6). The Father sent into the hearts of believers the Spirit of his Son. Here the Trinity appears in a single clause! The Father sent the Holy Spirit even as he previously sent his Son. The Holy Spirit is affectionately called the "Spirit of his [the Father's] Son." The Fa-

---

[6] Hans Burger, *Being in Christ: A Biblical and Systematic Investigation in a Reformed Perspective* (Eugene, OR: Wipf and Stock, 2009), 243.

[7] Richard N. Longenecker, *Galatians*, Word Biblical Commentary (Nashville: Thomas Nelson, 1990), 156.

[8] Bruce, *Epistle to the Galatians*, 185.

[9] Ibid.

ther sent the Spirit into our hearts, that is, to dwell in and with us always. The Spirit bears witness to the One who sent him. In our hearts he cries, "Abba! Father!" The Spirit witnesses within believers that they belong to God, that they are his children (cf. Rom. 8:16).

Galatians 5:4–6

You are severed from Christ, you who would be justified by the law; you have fallen away from grace. For through the Spirit, by faith, we ourselves eagerly wait for the hope of righteousness. For in Christ Jesus neither circumcision nor uncircumcision counts for anything, but only faith working through love.

Paul condemns those who would seek justification by the law. On the contrary, justification is by grace through faith. The apostle here contrasts two realms—that of the bondage of trusting in circumcision and law keeping, and that of the freedom (cf. v. 1) of trusting in Christ by the Spirit. "In Christ Jesus," in his domain, "neither circumcision nor uncircumcision counts for anything, but only faith working through love" (v. 6).

Galatians 5:10

I have confidence in the Lord that you will take no other view, and the one who is troubling you will bear the penalty, whoever he is.

Paul uses the words "in the Lord" with "I have confidence" to communicate the reason for his confidence. The prepositional phrase expresses cause—because of the Lord, Paul is confident that the Galatians will come around to his view.

Galatians 5:22–25

The fruit of the Spirit is love, joy, peace, patience, kindness, goodness, faithfulness, gentleness, self-control; against such things there is no law. And those who belong to Christ Jesus have crucified the flesh with its passions and desires. If we live by the Spirit, let us also keep in step with the Spirit.

Paul virtually defines belonging to Christ as co-crucifixion with him to sinful "passions and desires" (v. 24).[10] The apostle refers to believers as "those

---

[10] Cf. 6:14: "But far be it from me to boast except in the cross of our Lord Jesus Christ, by which the world has been crucified to me, and I to the world."

who belong to Christ." Longenecker correctly asserts that those "who belong to Christ Jesus" are "those in Christ Jesus."[11]

This passage contrasts the deeds of the flesh and the fruit of the Spirit. Verse 24 is the only place where the passage mentions union with Christ. Christ's people participate in his narrative. Here they died with him to their "flesh." Paul means that our sinful impulses were put to death with the Son of God and no longer have the right to dominate us. Sinfully we may yield to their power, but this is unnecessary. Christ died to break their stranglehold over our lives. When we let them control us, we forget who we are—those who belong to Christ and have died with him to our "flesh."

Again Longenecker is on target:

> The self-giving of Christ through death on a cross is the central soteriological theme of Galatians (cf. 1:4; 3:1, 13; 6:12, 14). . . . Identification with Christ in his crucifixion means a new type of existence for the believer, for now "Christ lives in me" (2:20). . . . Identification with Christ in his crucifixion has implications for issues having to do with libertinism (so here at v. 24). For Paul, to claim identification with Christ in his crucifixion means that one cannot espouse a lifestyle that expresses either a legalistic or libertine orientation. For in being with Christ both the demands of the law and the impulses of the flesh have been crucified as well (cf. Rom. 7:1–6; Col. 2:13–15).[12]

---

[11] See Longenecker, *Galatians*, 264.
[12] Ibid.

Chapter 9

Union with Christ
in Ephesians

Ephesians 1:1

Paul, an apostle of Christ Jesus by the will of God,
> To the saints who are in Ephesus, and are faithful in Christ Jesus.

Paul again includes union with Christ in a salutation of a letter—this time, Ephesians. He writes with apostolic authority to the "saints who are in Ephesus, and are faithful in Christ Jesus." Frank Thielman expresses the view of a number of commentators:

> The adjective πιστοί (*pistoi*) probably does not mean "faithful ones" in the sense of "loyal" or "trustworthy" people . . . , although that is the most common meaning of the adjective . . . . Since he will soon describe his readers as those who "have believed" (πιστεύσαντες [*pisteusantes*]) the gospel (1:13), it is more likely that he addresses them here as "believers" in the sense that they have trusted the gospel message when they heard it.[1]

I thus favor the translation "and are believers in Christ Jesus" and regard the prepositional phrase "in Christ Jesus" as expressing the object of faith.

---

[1] Frank Thielman, *Ephesians*, Baker Exegetical Commentary on the New Testament (Grand Rapids: Baker Academic, 2010), 34. The following commentators agree: Andrew T. Lincoln, *Ephesians*, Word Biblical Commentary (Dallas: Word, 1990), 6; Peter T. O'Brien, *The Letter to the Ephesians*, The Pillar New Testament Commentary (Grand Rapids: Eerdmans, 1999), 87; Harold W. Hoehner, *Ephesians: An Exegetical Commentary* (Grand Rapids: Baker, 2002), 142; Ernest Best, *Ephesians*, International Critical Commentary (Edinburgh, UK: T&T Clark, 1998), 101.

Ephesians 1:3–6

> Blessed be the God and Father of our Lord Jesus Christ, who has blessed
> us in Christ with every spiritual blessing in the heavenly places, even as
> he chose us in him before the foundation of the world, that we should be
> holy and blameless before him. In love he predestined us for adoption
> as sons through Jesus Christ, according to the purpose of his will, to the
> praise of his glorious grace, with which he has blessed us in the Beloved.

When Paul tells of how greatly God has blessed us, he uses comprehensive language for salvation: "every spiritual blessing in the heavenly places." And we are not surprised to find that when God bestowed on us this rich heavenly blessing, he did so "in Christ" (v. 3). This is one of many texts in which Paul uses "in Christ" to communicate God's giving gifts to believers, in this case, "every spiritual blessing in the heavenly places" (v. 3). Further investigation favors the nuance of instrument and the rendering "through Christ." The Father has gifted all Christians with every heavenly blessing through the person and work of his Son.

Paul goes on to say that the Father "chose us in him before the foundation of the world, that we should be holy and blameless before him" (v. 4). "In him" (Christ) modifies God's choosing his people for final holiness. Because it is parallel with "in love he predestined us for adoption as sons through Jesus Christ" (vv. 4–5), which uses "through Jesus Christ" instrumentally, the use of "in him" in verse 3 would also seem to be instrumental. The Father chose us through Christ for holiness and in love predestined us through Christ for adoption.

The ultimate purpose of God's electing his people for final sanctification and predestinating them for final adoption is that all might redound to the "praise of his glorious grace, with which he has blessed us in the Beloved" (v. 6). Though it is hard to choose between instrument and realm as the nuance of "in the Beloved" (a reference to Christ), I opt for the former. Because God the Father has blessed us abundantly with his sovereign grace in his beloved Son, he deserves the unending praise of his people.

Ephesians 1:7–10

> In him we have redemption through his blood, the forgiveness of our
> trespasses, according to the riches of his grace, which he lavished upon
> us, in all wisdom and insight making known to us the mystery of his will,

according to his purpose, which he set forth in Christ as a plan for the fullness of time, to unite all things in him, things in heaven and things on earth.

Once more the apostle combines a word indicating salvation with union with Christ. "In him we have redemption" (v. 7). Redemption means deliverance of slaves by the payment of a price—in this case, Christ's "blood," his violent death. It results in release for the slaves and "forgiveness of our trespasses," which had held us in bondage. "In him" probably has the nuance of a locative used figuratively; we belong to Christ's realm and are no longer in a realm of spiritual bondage, having been redeemed by his death.

Paul expands his purview temporally and cosmically when he says that God made "known to us the mystery of his will, according to his purpose, which he set forth in Christ as a plan for the fullness of time, to unite all things in him" (vv. 9–10). This use of "in Christ" in conjunction with God's setting forth his plan to unite all in Christ is one of a handful of times Paul uses "in Christ" to show union with Christ directly. "The meaning, then, is that God has planned the revelation of his will in conjunction and in unity with Christ."[2]

The last use of "in him" is also locative, used figuratively to speak of Christ as the focal point or goal.[3] God's plan is to bring together "all things" in heaven and earth in Christ as the goal. Peter O'Brien says it well:

Christ is the one *in whom* God chooses to sum up the cosmos, the one in whom he restores harmony to the universe. He is the focal point, not simply the means, the instrument, or the functionary through whom all this occurs. . . . The emphasis is now on a universe that is centered and reunited . . . in Christ as focal point.[4]

Ephesians 1:11–13

In him we have obtained an inheritance, having been predestined according to the purpose of him who works all things according to the counsel of his will, so that we who were the first to hope in Christ might be to the praise of his glory. In him you also, when you heard the word of truth,

---

[2] Constantine R. Campbell, *Paul and Union with Christ: An Exegetical and Theological Study* (Grand Rapids: Zondervan, 2012), 189.
[3] Ibid., 145–46.
[4] O'Brien, *Letter to the Ephesians*, 111–12, emphasis original.

the gospel of your salvation, and believed in him, were sealed with the promised Holy Spirit.

"In him we have obtained an inheritance" is another expression of salvation in union with Christ. "In him" is a locative used figuratively to show domain or realm and thus narrow the goal. In the previous verse the goal was to bring "all things" (i.e., the universe) together in Christ. Here Paul narrows the focus to believers. Believers' inheritance is the whole world in the new earth! "All things are yours, whether Paul or Apollos or Cephas or the world or life or death or the present or the future—all are yours" (1 Cor. 3:21–22).

When the apostle says "we" (Jews) were "the first to hope in Christ" (Eph. 1:12), he uses "in Christ" to express the truth that Christ is the object of Christian hope. The same is true for the second use of "in him" in Ephesians 1:13: "You . . . believed in him." Christ is the object of saving faith.

The first use of "in him" in verse 13 is the figurative use of the locative to show realm. The Father seals believers with the Holy Spirit in Christ's domain. God makes us part of Christ's realm permanently.

Ephesians 1:15–16

For this reason, because I have heard of your faith in the Lord Jesus and your love toward all the saints, I do not cease to give thanks for you.

Paul keeps praying for the Ephesians, spurred on by their faith in Christ and love for other believers. When he writes of their "faith in the Lord Jesus," "in" indicates the object of faith—the Lord Jesus Christ.

Ephesians 1:22–23

He put all things under his feet and gave him as head over all things to the church, which is his body, the fullness of him who fills all in all.

Paul prays that the Ephesians would have a deeper understanding of three things: their future hope of final salvation, how valuable God's people (his inheritance) are to him, and his great power toward believers (vv. 16–19). Paul describes this awesome power in two ways. First, it is God's resurrection power that raised Christ and exalted him to God's right hand (vv. 19–20). Second, it is the power Christ wields at God's right hand, the place of greatest authority in the universe (vv. 21–23).

This power of Christ is in turn viewed from three vantage points. Viewed from above, he is over all things, the whole creation, including angels, good and bad. Viewed from below, God "put all things under his feet" (v. 22). Here, in light of Psalm 8:6, which Paul is quoting, Christ is viewed as the second Adam, whose exaltation restores the original dominion given to Adam and Eve at creation, a dominion that fallen human beings have forfeited.

Viewed from above once again, God "gave him as head over all things to the church" (Eph. 1:22). This teaching (and that of Col. 1:18–19) represents an advance over that in Romans 12 and 1 Corinthians 12 on Christ's relation to the church, for now the "relationship which the church, as the body of Christ, bears to Christ as head of the body is treated," as O'Brien notes.[5] The Father appointed the Son as Head of the church, which is his body. Christ has supreme authority over the church. And he exerts this authority as the one who is Head over "all things," not only the church. But he exerts that universal authority for the sake of the church.

Admittedly, the phrase "[God] gave him as head over all things to the church, which is his body, *the fullness of him who fills all in all*" (Eph. 1:22–23), is very difficult. I point readers to O'Brien's fair discussion of views and cite his conclusion:

> The final clause in v. 23 makes the additional point that the church is Christ's *fulness*. In Colossians the term "fulness" was applied to Christ; here in Ephesians its referent is the church. As head over all things Christ exercises his sovereign rule by "filling" the universe. But only the church is his body, and he rules it, that is, fills it in a special way with his Spirit, grace, and gifts: it is his fulness.[6]

Ephesians 2:4–10

> God, being rich in mercy, because of the great love with which he loved us, even when we were dead in our trespasses, made us alive together with Christ—by grace you have been saved—and raised us up with him and seated us with him in the heavenly places in Christ Jesus, so that in the coming ages he might show the immeasurable riches of his grace in kindness toward us in Christ Jesus. For by grace you have been saved through faith. And this is not your own doing; it is the gift of God, not a result of works, so that no one may boast. For we are his workmanship,

---

[5] Ibid., 148.
[6] Ibid., 152.

created in Christ Jesus for good works, which God prepared beforehand, that we should walk in them.

The apostle teaches that believers were united to Christ in his resurrection and session, his sitting at God's right hand after his ascension. This implies that they are joined to Christ in his ascension as well. Twice in the context Paul teaches that we were spiritually dead, devoid of the life of God (vv. 1, 5). We needed to be made alive, and that is exactly what God did: he "made us alive together with Christ" (v. 5), regenerating us by spiritually uniting us to the risen Christ. His life thus became ours, and we became alive spiritually. O'Brien underscores these truths: "Paul's readers have come to life with Christ, who was dead and rose again; their new life, then, is a sharing in the new life which we received when he rose from the dead. It is only in union with him that death is vanquished and new life, an integral part of God's new creation, received."[7]

Paul regards God's making the spiritually dead alive as the epitome of grace; that is why he injects an aside at the end of verse 5: "by grace you have been saved." Grace is God's helping those who cannot help themselves; it is his saving those who are hopelessly lost.

Paul repeats, God "raised us up with him," and then adds, "and seated us with him in the heavenly places in Christ Jesus" (v. 6). "In Christ Jesus" is used in a locative sense, not to speak of Christ's realm, but concretely; we are seated in heaven *with Christ*.[8] One could argue that the verb "seated with" already expresses this idea, but we should remember that repetition is a normal function of language.

Here we share in Christ's victory over the "prince of the power of the air" and his demons. Our union with Christ is so vital and unbreakable that it is as if we ascended with him and sat down in heaven with him! This is well brought out by Thielman:

> The most unusual element about all three verbs ["made alive together with," "raised up with," and "seated with"] is their past tense: here the Christian's life, resurrection, and royal position with Christ are events that have already happened.
>
> Here salvation is something that is emphatically present for believers. They have already been made alive with Christ, already raised with him,

---

[7] Ibid., 167.
[8] Campbell, *Paul and Union with Christ*, 84–86.

and even already seated with him in heavenly places. Their resurrection has, in some sense, already taken place (cf. Col. 3:1).[9]

God lavished his love on us when we were spiritually dead. He joined us to the risen/ascended/seated Christ so that we share in his victory over the powers. What is God's purpose for doing these things? "So that in the coming ages he might show the immeasurable riches of his grace in kindness toward us in Christ Jesus" (Eph. 2:7). "In Christ Jesus" is used here to show the recognition or revelation of something—in this instance, God's kindness.[10] We truly know Christ now, but we have not seen anything yet! "What God has done for those in Christ is a reality, but only in the coming ages will it be fully seen for what it is," O'Brien reminds us.[11]

The apostle uses the language of creation to speak of the new creation. "We are his workmanship, created in Christ Jesus for good works, which God prepared beforehand, that we should walk in them" (v. 10). The new creation, though only to be fully manifested when Christ returns, began with power when he was raised from the dead. For believers to experience salvation now is for them to be recreated "in Christ Jesus." This familiar phrase is used instrumentally: the Father planned the new creation, and it is put into effect "through Christ Jesus," namely, by him and his saving work.

Ephesians 2:11–16

> Remember that at one time you Gentiles in the flesh, called "the uncircumcision" by what is called the circumcision, which is made in the flesh by hands—remember that you were at that time separated from Christ, alienated from the commonwealth of Israel and strangers to the covenants of promise, having no hope and without God in the world. But now in Christ Jesus you who once were far off have been brought near by the blood of Christ. For he himself is our peace, who has made us both one and has broken down in his flesh the dividing wall of hostility by abolishing the law of commandments expressed in ordinances, that he might create in himself one new man in place of the two, so making peace, and might reconcile us both to God in one body through the cross, thereby killing the hostility.

---

[9] Thielman, *Ephesians*, 134–35.
[10] As Campbell, *Paul and Union with Christ*, 86, notes, citing BDAG.
[11] O'Brien, *Letter to the Ephesians*, 173.

Paul gives his most expansive description of lost persons' need for union with Christ. That need is underscored in the case of Gentile unbelievers. Paul writes, "You were at that time separated from Christ" (v. 12). The need for union with Christ is that we are separated from him. He possesses eternal life and forgiveness. As long as we are separated from him, we are also separated from his saving benefits. This situation is accentuated in the case of Gentiles because they are also "alienated from the commonwealth of Israel and strangers to the covenants of promise" (v. 12). Consequently, Gentile unbelievers, as representative of all unbelievers, have "no hope and [are] without God in the world" (v. 12).

But thanks be to God's marvelous grace that Paul could say to readers who were in such dire straits, "In Christ Jesus you who once were far off have been brought near by the blood of Christ" (v. 13). It is not difficult to discern the nuance of "in Christ Jesus" here. It is a locative used metaphorically to indicate the realm of Christ, which stands in stark contrast to the realm of separation from him described so vividly in verse 12. The Father has transferred us to the domain of his Son, wherein we have been brought near to God. As a result, Jew and Gentile "both have access in one Spirit to the Father" (v. 18).

Christ is the reconciler, the peacemaker, who unites believing Jews and Gentiles into one people of God. He makes peace through his death on the cross, thereby abolishing the Jewish law (in a sense), which divided Jews from Gentiles (vv. 14–15). His goal was to "create in himself one new man in place of the two, so making peace" (v. 15). Christ the reconciler is also the second Adam who by his death and resurrection inaugurates the new creation. He thereby joins individual believers to himself in salvation and also joins them to all other believers. Christ creates "in himself" one new man in place of the two, Jew and Gentile. Campbell correctly maintains that Paul employs the words "in himself" (in v. 15) to express "incorporation into Christ." Indeed, it is he who "has brought them [Jew and Gentile] together by joining them both to him."[12] The subsequent words corroborate this interpretation, because Paul teaches that Christ reconciles "both to God in one body through the cross" (v. 16). God makes peace between Jews and Gentiles by combining them into the one body of Christ.

Ephesians 2:18–22

Through him we both have access in one Spirit to the Father. So then you are no longer strangers and aliens, but you are fellow citizens with the

---

[12] Campbell, *Paul and Union with Christ*, 178.

saints and members of the household of God, built on the foundation of the apostles and prophets, Christ Jesus himself being the cornerstone, in whom the whole structure, being joined together, grows into a holy temple in the Lord. In him you also are being built together into a dwelling place for God by the Spirit.

Amazingly, God has granted salvation to Gentiles! They along with believing Jews constitute the church. Jew and Gentile "both have access in one Spirit to the Father" (v. 18). Gentiles are no longer excluded from God's people; they are citizens and members of God's household (v. 19). Here for the fourth time Paul identifies the church with a spiritual temple.[13]

In terms of redemptive history, Christ is the cornerstone, implying the idea of incorporation into him, as in 1 Corinthians 3:11, 16–17; the New Testament apostles and prophets are the foundation; and the whole is "a holy temple in the Lord" (Eph. 2:21). This passage is no exception to the rule that God's presence makes a building a temple, a "dwelling place for God by the Spirit" (v. 22).

This time Paul makes explicit the idea of incorporation into Christ. He does so in three ways. He says it is Christ "in whom" the building grows into a temple, "in him" it is being built into God's dwelling place, and this holy temple is "in the Lord" (vv. 21–22). Thielman correctly states, "The phrase ἐν κυρίῳ [en kyriō, "in the Lord"] refers not to God the Father but to 'the Lord Jesus Christ.'"[14] It is noteworthy that all three uses of "in Christ language" ("in whom," "in the Lord" [both in v. 21], and "in him" [v. 22]), in keeping with the building metaphor, speak of incorporation into Christ.[15]

Furthermore, worship of the Holy Trinity takes place in this temple, for believing Jews and Gentiles "through him [Christ] . . . both have access in one Spirit to the Father" (v. 18). And God makes this "holy temple in the Lord . . . a dwelling place for God [the Father] by the Spirit" (vv. 21–22).

Campbell adds two important points: "The temple metaphor is dynamic since God's people are *being built* together for his dwelling . . . [and] the metaphor is organic, in that God's people *grow* into a holy temple in the Lord (2:21)."[16] To communicate his theological vision Paul mixes metaphors. He depicts a building as growing into a temple before our eyes. And this dynamic action is ongoing—believers "are being built together" progressively by the Spirit.

[13] See 1 Cor. 3:16–17; 6:19–20; 2 Cor. 6:16.
[14] Thielman, *Ephesians*, 184.
[15] Following Campbell, *Paul and Union with Christ*, 151, 194.
[16] Ibid., 293, emphasis original.

Paul adds the idea of indwelling. The Holy Spirit is working to build believers, both Jewish and Gentile, "into a dwelling place for God by the Spirit" (v. 22). Though Paul usually ascribes indwelling to the Spirit and five times to Christ, this is one of only two times he ascribes it to God the Father (the other is 2 Cor. 6:16). The Trinity indwells the people of God individually and communally.

Ephesians 3:6

This mystery is that the Gentiles are fellow heirs, members of the same body, and partakers of the promise in Christ Jesus through the gospel.

Gentile believers in Christ "are fellow heirs" with their Jewish fellow believers, "members of the same body" of Christ (the church) with them, and "partakers of the promise in Christ Jesus through the gospel." The Gentiles' new status is in view, and that status is "in Christ Jesus," in the realm over which he rules. They enter this new status and realm by God's grace through faith in Christ as offered "through the gospel."

Ephesians 3:11–12

This was according to the eternal purpose that he has realized in Christ Jesus our Lord, in whom we have boldness and access with confidence through our faith in him.

Paul writes to encourage his readers (v. 13). He tells them that it was God's "eternal purpose" to unite both Jewish and Gentile believers in Christ through the preaching of Paul and others (v. 11). God did this so that he could display his great wisdom to the angels (v. 10). This plan was accomplished "in Christ Jesus our Lord." This prepositional phrase is used to show instrument, telling how God accomplished his plan. He did so in the person and saving work of "Christ Jesus our Lord." Furthermore, he is the one "in whom we have boldness and access with confidence through our faith in him" (v. 12). Probably "in whom" shows the cause or reason for believers' coming before God with bold confidence in faith—it is only because of Christ's identity and accomplishment.

Ephesians 3:14–19

For this reason I bow my knees before the Father, from whom every family in heaven and on earth is named, that according to the riches of his glory he may grant you to be strengthened with power through his Spirit in your inner being, so that Christ may dwell in your hearts through faith—that you, being rooted and grounded in love, may have strength to comprehend with all the saints what is the breadth and length and height and depth, and to know the love of Christ that surpasses knowledge, that you may be filled with all the fullness of God.

The apostle prays that God the Father would strengthen the Ephesian Christians by the inner working of the Holy Spirit. To what end? "So that Christ may dwell in your hearts through faith" (v. 17). But don't the Ephesians, and all believers, already have Christ in their hearts? Yes, Thielman explains, Christ is present; but "what they apparently lack is the inner strength and encouragement they should draw from these truths. . . . Union with Christ by faith brings personal, inner strength that allows the believer to live in a world dominated by rebellion against God."[17]

The following words are among the most exalted in all Scripture: "that you, being rooted and grounded in love, may have strength to comprehend with all the saints what is the breadth and length and height and depth, and to know the love of Christ that surpasses knowledge, that you may be filled with all the fullness of God" (vv. 17–19). The encouragement believers are to draw from an increasing awareness that Christ lives in them is a greater appreciation of God's love.

This works on at least three levels. First, Christ's love is the foundation of the Christian life; we are "rooted and grounded in love" (v. 17). Second, this foundation in turn enables us better to comprehend the awesome limitlessness of God's love for us in Christ, which is beyond measure (v. 18). Third, as a result of this, we are to be filled with all the fullness of God (v. 19), that is, we are to grow to be the mature believers God intends. Here the church is to aspire to this fullness; according to 1:23, it has already attained it. The resolution is found in the common Pauline notion of the "already" and the "not yet." Already "in Christ" we believers have the divine fullness; not yet have we attained the lifestyle in keeping with this exalted status. Thielman summarizes:

Paul prays that God, by his Spirit, would give his readers inner strength so that they could believe that Christ dwells in their hearts. This in turn will enable them to comprehend the vast extent of Christ's love. This inner

---

[17] Thielman, *Ephesians*, 320–31.

renewal, Paul prays, will take them further along the path of becoming the people that God intended "all the saints" to be.[18]

Ephesians 3:20–21

Now to him who is able to do far more abundantly than all that we ask or think, according to the power at work within us, to him be glory in the church and in Christ Jesus throughout all generations, forever and ever. Amen.

After extolling the love of Christ, Paul—as is his custom—bursts into doxology. He praises God for his wonderful working beyond our expectations, "according to the power at work within us" (v. 20). In praise he gives God "glory in the church and in Christ Jesus" (v. 21). Paul uses "in Christ" language in the sense of revealing or making something known, in this case the glory of God.[19] He prays for this to be done "throughout all generations, forever and ever," to which he adds, "Amen" (v. 21).

Ephesians 4:4–6, 11–12, 15–16

There is one body and one Spirit—just as you were called to the one hope that belongs to your call—one Lord, one faith, one baptism, one God and Father of all, who is over all and through all and in all. . . . He gave the apostles, the prophets, the evangelists, the shepherds and teachers, to equip the saints for the work of ministry, for building up the body of Christ. . . . Speaking the truth in love, we are to grow up in every way into him who is the head, into Christ, from whom the whole body, joined and held together by every joint with which it is equipped, when each part is working properly, makes the body grow so that it builds itself up in love.

Three times in these verses Paul speaks of the church as the body of Christ. Although the very concept of the body of Christ implies union between him and his members, only the third time does Paul mention union with Christ. Shortly after beginning the hortatory part of his epistle in 4:1, Paul presents the seven objective unities of the Christian church. These are the basis for the subjective unity he pleads for in verse 3 and are one of the results that

---

[18] Ibid., 238.
[19] Campbell, *Paul and Union with Christ*, 136–37.

will obtain (in vv. 13, 16) if the church's leaders and people play their parts. Included in the unities are one God the Father, one Lord (Jesus), one Spirit, one hope (of eternal life), one faith (in Christ), one (Christian) baptism, and one church. Yet Paul does not say "one church," but "one body," and he puts it first on the list (v. 4). It is instructive that the apostle is able to communicate clearly the idea of "one church" with the words "one body." Doubtless, they refer to the church as the body of Christ.

The second occurrence follows Paul's teaching that the ascended Christ gave gifts to his church: gifted men tasked to train the saints to perform the church's ministry so as to achieve results, the first of which is "building up the body of Christ" (v. 12). The first result, therefore, is edification; the other three results follow (unity, maturity, and doctrinal stability), but our focus is on edification, which we note is placed first—even as "one body" was in verse 4. Church leaders are to equip believers to do the work of the ministry to build up the body of Christ. This is an organic and dynamic reference to the church as Christ's body. The body needs to grow not only in the sense of adding members but also in unity, maturity, and theological stability.

The third occurrence includes union with Christ as Head of his body and the one who stimulates growth and maturity. Paul writes, "Speaking the truth in love, we are to grow up in every way into him who is the Head, into Christ, from whom the whole body, joined and held together by every joint with which it is equipped, when each part is working properly, makes the body grow so that it builds itself up in love" (vv. 15–16). Christ is the Head of the body; each believer is a "part" that must do its job for the proper functioning of the body. The result is growth of the body and edification in love.

Campbell treats two odd expressions that stretch the metaphor beyond its anatomical limits:

> First, the body is described as *growing into Him who is the Head* but also as growing *from Him*. Both expressions are odd when applied to the *body* metaphor, since the images of a body growing *into* its head or growing *out from* its head are equally strange. . . . Growing *into* the head likely refers to being conformed to Christ, becoming more like him, and "growing into" the unity between believers and Christ. Growing *from* him depicts Christ as the source of the body; he is its origin and provides the stimulus for growth. Thus, while the notions of growing into and out from the head might be odd expansions of the body metaphor, they nevertheless

enhance the organic nature of the body of Christ. The head is dynamically and organically infused with his body.[20]

Note that both Christ and his body are active in causing the body to grow. Christ provides the stimulus for growth. But it is also true that "when each part is working properly, [Christ] makes the body grow so that it builds itself up in love" (vv. 15–16). The Head and parts of the body work together to produce growth. "The union believers share with Christ is organic, involving growth that flows from Christ but also into Christ. . . . Moreover, the dynamic growth of the body is promoted by Christ *and* involves the contribution of all its members."[21]

Ephesians 4:17

This I say and testify in the Lord, that you must no longer walk as the Gentiles do, in the futility of their minds.

This sentence introduces a section in which Paul exhorts his readers to live a new life in Christ: "You must no longer walk as the Gentiles do." He wants them to make a clean break from their pre-Christian lifestyle of ignorance, hardness of heart, sensuality, and impurity (vv. 18–19). He prefaces this exhortation with the solemn words, "This I say and testify in the Lord" (v. 17). "In the Lord" is used of believers' actions to express manner. Campbell applies this truth: "Paul does not merely wish to say what he says; he says it as a word of testimony and of witness. As such, he is concerned to underscore the integrity and veracity of his statement. . . . Paul's testimony conforms to the Lord and is therefore genuine and authoritative."[22]

Ephesians 4:20–22

That is not the way you learned Christ!—assuming that you have heard about him and were taught in him, as the truth is in Jesus, to put off your old self, which belongs to your former manner of life and is corrupt through deceitful desires.

Paul writes these words immediately following his exhortation in verses 17–19. The usage of "in him" in verse 21 depends on two other choices. If the

---

[20] Ibid., 281, emphasis original.
[21] Ibid., 282, emphasis original.
[22] Ibid., 160.

translation is, "You have heard about him and were taught in him," as in the
ESV, "in him" is used as a locative to indicate Christ's sphere. If, however, the
translation is, "You have heard him and were taught by him," as in the NASB,
"by him" is used to express agency—the Ephesian believers were taught by
Christ. While both options are possible, I adopt the second.

Ephesians 4:32

> Be kind to one another, tenderhearted, forgiving one another, as God in
> Christ forgave you.

Paul exhorts the Ephesians to live a new life in Christ. As such, they are
to "put off" their "old self," be renewed in their thinking, and "put on the new
self" (vv. 22–24). Paul then proceeds to apply this "putting off" and "putting
on" principle to telling the truth, anger, working for a living, using edifying
talk, and showing kindness (vv. 25–32). As part of kindness, he writes, "forgiving one another, as God in Christ forgave you" (v. 32). The measure according to which we are to grant forgiveness is "as God in Christ forgave" us!
Paul employs "in Christ" adverbially to show cause. We are to freely forgive
others as God freely forgave us because of Christ's saving accomplishment.

Ephesians 5:7–10

> Do not become partners with them; for at one time you were darkness,
> but now you are light in the Lord. Walk as children of light (for the fruit
> of light is found in all that is good and right and true), and try to discern
> what is pleasing to the Lord.

The apostle again urges his readers not to return to the ungodly manner
of life that characterized them before conversion. He strongly contrasts "darkness" with "light," and "all that is good and right and true" with "sexual immorality and all impurity or covetousness," "filthiness," and "foolish talk" (vv.
3–4). The contrast suggests that "in the Lord" is used as a locative to denote
Christ's domain of godliness, truth, and "what is pleasing to the Lord" (v. 10).
He wants the Ephesians to live as befits citizens of Christ's realm.

Ephesians 5:22–32

> Wives, submit to your own husbands, as to the Lord. For the husband is
> the head of the wife even as Christ is the head of the church, his body, and

is himself its Savior. Now as the church submits to Christ, so also wives should submit in everything to their husbands.

Husbands, love your wives, as Christ loved the church and gave himself up for her, that he might sanctify her, having cleansed her by the washing of water with the word, so that he might present the church to himself in splendor, without spot or wrinkle or any such thing, that she might be holy and without blemish. In the same way husbands should love their wives as their own bodies. He who loves his wife loves himself. For no one ever hated his own flesh, but nourishes and cherishes it, just as Christ does the church, because we are members of his body. "Therefore a man shall leave his father and mother and hold fast to his wife, and the two shall become one flesh." This mystery is profound, and I am saying that it refers to Christ and the church.

This passage richly combines two metaphors for union with Christ—those of marriage and body—and we will treat them sequentially. If 1 Corinthians 6:16–17 is the most intimate of Pauline passages describing union as the marriage of Christ and believers, while 2 Corinthians 11:1–3 contains the strongest application, then Ephesians 5:23–32 is the most explicit; for after citing Genesis 2:24, Paul writes, "This mystery [of two uniting in marriage] is profound, and I am saying that it refers to Christ and the church" (Eph. 5:32). Remarkably, in this passage the apostle uses the metaphor of the marriage between Christ and his people as a model for proper relations between husband and wife.

Campbell draws solid conclusions from this passage. First, Christ and his bride are intimately joined in marriage, but Paul does not confuse them. Each retains a separate identity. Second, as a woman is submissive to her husband in the bonds of matrimony, so the church submits to Christ, its Head (vv. 23–24). Union with Christ does not undercut his headship over the church. And union does not entitle the church to rebel against him.

Third, Christ takes the lead in every aspect of the marriage. He woos, wins, and keeps his bride. And she enjoys his loving attention. He is his church's Savior, who loves her deeply and gives himself for her (5:23, 25). He sanctifies her to finally present her to himself sinless (5:26–27). He sustains her through provision and care (5:29).[23] All this, of course highlights Christ's abundant grace for his bride. The church is not loved for her merit. Rather, she is shown mercy by her divine-human suitor and lover.

---

[23] Ibid., 308–9.

Ephesians 5:23, 29–30

The husband is the head of the wife even as Christ is the head of the church, his body, and is himself its Savior. . . .

. . . No one ever hated his own flesh, but nourishes and cherishes it, just as Christ does the church, because we are members of his body.

In his famous passage dealing with marital relations, Paul also presents Christ as his body's Head and Savior, who loves and cares for its members. In all this he is portrayed as the model for husbands to imitate in loving their wives.

In Paul's version of a first-century household code, husbands are to lead and love their wives, and wives are to submit to their husbands. "The husband is the head of the wife even as Christ is the head of the church, his body, and is himself its Savior" (v. 23). Husbands are to strive to lead and love their wives according to Christ's example. He is both Head and Savior of his body, the church. Paul defines Christ's headship in relation to the headship of Christ the Savior. Thielman clarifies, "Paul pictures the wife's submission as the recognition of the authority of a husband who imitates the self-sacrificial, nurturing, and supporting roles that Christ fills with respect to the church."[24]

Paul goes into more detail concerning Christ's care for the church in verses 29–30: "No one ever hated his own flesh, but nourishes and cherishes it, just as Christ does the church, because we are members of his body." As it is natural and normal for men to take care of their own bodies, they are to do the same for their wives, with whom they have become one flesh. And, the apostle declares, this is what Christ does for us, the members of his body—he nourishes and cherishes us. O'Brien speaks with pastoral wisdom:

> It is the powerful example of Christ that is again invoked. For all its imperfections Christ nurtures and tenderly cares for his body, the church. He is both its Head and Savior (1:22–23; 4:15; 5:23). He gave himself up for the church in order to sanctify it (5:25, 26), and he constantly provides for its nourishment and growth (4:11–16). Let each husband, then, follow Christ's example and be wholehearted in loving and tenderly caring for his wife.[25]

Ephesians 6:1

Children, obey your parents in the Lord, for this is right.

---

[24] Thielman, *Ephesians*, 379.
[25] O'Brien, *Letter to the Ephesians*, 428.

As part of his Christian household code, Paul exhorts believing children to obey their parents "in the Lord." The apostle teaches that all children are to obey their parents, whether they are believers or not, but Christian children who live in Christian homes are especially to obey their parents, because they belong to Christ's domain. "In the Lord" is used as a locative to indicate Christ's realm or domain. Within Christ's kingdom, families are to be marked by doing what is right.

Ephesians 6:10–12

Finally, be strong in the Lord and in the strength of his might. Put on the whole armor of God, that you may be able to stand against the schemes of the devil. For we do not wrestle against flesh and blood, but against the rulers, against the authorities, against the cosmic powers over this present darkness, against the spiritual forces of evil in the heavenly places.

In this spiritual-warfare text, Paul enjoins readers to "put on the whole armor of God" in light of the fact that their battle is against "cosmic powers over this present darkness" (vv. 11, 12). Campbell notes that this recalls not only "Roman military weaponry but also descriptions of Yahweh (and/or his Messiah) in battle as found in Isaiah." He concludes:

Thus, one of the implications of [Eph.] 6:10–17 is that believers are to put on the armour that the Lord himself wears in battle, which evokes a sense of union with him in the matter of spiritual warfare. Given that this union pervades the whole pericope, it is reasonable to conclude that ἐν κυρίῳ [*en kyriō*, "in the Lord"] in 6:10 conveys union with the Lord.[26]

Therefore, when the apostle commands readers to "be strong in the Lord and in the strength of his might," he means they are to be strong due to their union with Christ and his great strength.

Ephesians 6:21–22

So that you also may know how I am and what I am doing, Tychicus the beloved brother and faithful minister in the Lord will tell you everything. I have sent him to you for this very purpose, that you may know how we are, and that he may encourage your hearts.

---

[26] Campbell, *Paul and Union with Christ*, 151–53.

Union with Christ so pervades Paul's thinking that half the time he includes references to union in the initial and final greetings of his epistles, as he does here. He tells the Ephesian church that he is sending Tychicus to them to inform them concerning Paul's circumstances and to encourage them. He describes Tychicus as a "beloved brother and faithful minister in the Lord" (v. 21). "In the Lord" functions here, as frequently in Paul, as a periphrasis for believers. The sense, then, is that Tychicus is a faithful *Christian* minister.

Chapter 10

Union with Christ
in Philippians

Philippians 1:1

> Paul and Timothy, servants of Christ Jesus,
>   To all the saints in Christ Jesus who are at Philippi, with the overseers
> and deacons.

Once again Paul refers to union in a greeting, this time an initial one. He
and Timothy write to "all the saints in Christ Jesus" at Philippi, along with the
church officers. Frequently, as here, Paul uses "in Christ Jesus" and its variants
as a periphrasis for believers. He thus writes to all the Christian saints "who
are at Philippi."

Philippians 1:14

> Most of the brothers, having become confident in the Lord by my impris-
> onment, are much more bold to speak the word without fear.

The apostle tells of the advance of the gospel despite his imprisonment.
The good news has been heard "throughout the whole imperial guard" (v. 13).
"Most of the brothers" are emboldened by Paul's chains to preach the Word
more boldly (v. 14). Paul rejoices whenever the gospel is preached, even from
wrong motives (v. 15).

The words "in the Lord" could go with "brothers" or with the verb "having become confident." As noted earlier, in cases of ambiguity, I assume that Greek writers help readers by means of word order. If that is correct, we should translate the beginning of verse 14, "Most of the brothers in the Lord." Paul uses "in the Lord" as a periphrasis for believers and means "most of the Christian brothers."

Philippians 1:25–26

Convinced of this, I know that I will remain and continue with you all, for your progress and joy in the faith, so that in me you may have ample cause to glory in Christ Jesus, because of my coming to you again.

Paul has weighed dying and being with Christ against living on to minister to the Philippians and others. He is convinced that they need him and resolves to live on for their "progress and joy in the faith" (v. 25). His goal? That they rejoice when he visits them again. Specifically, he wants them to "have ample cause to glory in Christ Jesus" because of Paul's ministry to them (v. 26). "In Christ Jesus" seems to function to show specification; Christ Jesus is the one in whom they are to glory.[1]

Philippians 1:29–30

It has been granted to you that for the sake of Christ you should not only believe in him but also suffer for his sake, engaged in the same conflict that you saw I had and now hear that I still have.

Paul tells how it is the lot of believers to believe in Christ and to suffer because of him, even as Paul does. In the expression "believe in him," Paul uses "in" (εἰς/eis) to present Christ as the goal of faith. We trust "in him" for the forgiveness of sins.

Philippians 2:1–2

If there is any encouragement in Christ, any comfort from love, any participation in the Spirit, any affection and sympathy, complete my joy by being of the same mind, having the same love, being in full accord and of one mind.

---

[1] Constantine R. Campbell, *Paul and Union with Christ: An Exegetical and Theological Study* (Grand Rapids: Zondervan, 2012), 104.

Paul uses three words to express the motivation that should drive Christians to be united with one another in heart and mind: "encouragement," "comfort," and "participation" (or "fellowship"). It seems that the first two are qualified by references to their sources: "encouragement" because of Christ; "comfort from love."[2] Paul seems to use "in Christ" to indicate the source of the encouragement that comes from knowing Jesus as Lord and Savior. "In Christ," therefore, indicates cause and means "on account of Christ" or "because of Christ."

Philippians 2:19–24

I hope in the Lord Jesus to send Timothy to you soon, so that I too may be cheered by news of you. For I have no one like him, who will be genuinely concerned for your welfare. For they all seek their own interests, not those of Jesus Christ. But you know Timothy's proven worth, how as a son with a father he has served with me in the gospel. I hope therefore to send him just as soon as I see how it will go with me, and I trust in the Lord that shortly I myself will come also.

Paul communicates his plans to send Timothy to his beloved Philippians and his desire to visit them himself as well when he is released from prison. The two desires are expressed similarly:

I hope in the Lord Jesus to send Timothy to you soon. (v. 19)

I trust in the Lord that shortly I myself will come also. (v. 24)

Both of these uses seem to fit the same category, that of expressions of faith in the Lord. Paul expresses his hopes and desires in terms of faith "in the Lord (Jesus)."

Philippians 2:29–30

Receive him in the Lord with all joy, and honor such men, for he nearly died for the work of Christ, risking his life to complete what was lacking in your service to me.

---

[2] Perhaps the third is also so qualified—"participation" from the Spirit—but a good case could also be made for translating "participation in the Spirit," as the ESV does above.

Paul highly commends Epaphroditus, a minister sent from the Philippians, who cared for Paul while in prison. This unselfish brother was disturbed when his church in Philippi heard he was very ill and almost died. Paul instructs the church, "Receive him in the Lord with all joy, and honor such men, for he nearly died for the work of Christ, risking his life to complete what was lacking in your service to me" (vv. 29–30).

Paul uses "in the Lord" to speak of believers' actions, instructing the Philippians how they are to welcome back Epaphroditus. They are to do so "in the Lord," that is, in a manner that pleases Christ.

Philippians 3:1

Finally, my brothers, rejoice in the Lord. To write the same things to you is no trouble to me and is safe for you.

Just before Paul warns his dear Philippians of dangers from Judaizers, he encourages them by telling them to "rejoice in the Lord." He probably uses "in the Lord" to show cause, reminding them of their relationship to Jesus, who loved them and gave himself for them. Because of who Christ is and what he has done for him, they are to rejoice indeed.

Philippians 3:3

We are the circumcision, who worship by the Spirit of God and glory in Christ Jesus and put no confidence in the flesh.

Paul sharply contrasts the Judaizers—"the dogs ... the evildoers ... those who mutilate the flesh" (v. 2)—and true believers in Christ. These are the true spiritual "Jews," regardless of ethnic background. They, believers in Christ, are spiritual Israel, "the circumcision." The apostle further defines the true circumcision as those who "worship by the Spirit of God and glory in Christ Jesus and put no confidence in the flesh" (v. 3). The true people of God worship by the Holy Spirit, exult in Christ, and do not trust their human pedigree or performance for acceptance in God's sight. Paul ought to know, because he trusted these things as much as anyone (vv. 4–6). But now because of Jesus, Paul counts as "rubbish" all he prized before (v. 8). When Paul says he and other Christians "glory in Christ Jesus," he uses "in Christ" language to give the ground or reason for their boasting. Believers boast because of who Jesus is and what he did for them.

Philippians 3:8–11

> For his sake I have suffered the loss of all things and count them as rubbish, in order that I may gain Christ and be found in him, not having a righteousness of my own that comes from the law, but that which comes through faith in Christ, the righteousness from God that depends on faith—that I may know him and the power of his resurrection, and may share his sufferings, becoming like him in his death, that by any means possible I may attain the resurrection from the dead.

Paul is willing to lose everything to gain Christ and "be found in him" (v. 9). This is another example of "in him" being used to show union with Christ. Campbell's explanation is noteworthy. After mentioning the locative option, indicating Christ's domain or realm, he says:

> The second option is to regard ἐν αὐτῷ ["in him"] as expressing union with Christ. Paul's point is to indicate that, while he has lost all things, he has gained Christ by becoming one with him. Indeed, this is stronger than the locative option because of the personal nature of gaining Christ; Paul does not merely refer to his 'location' within the sphere of Christ's rule, but regards his situation as one of personal connection such that he "obtains" Christ somehow and is found in him. This is reinforced by what follows.... Consequently, ἐν αὐτῷ ["in him"] is best regarded as expressing union with Christ: Paul has gained Christ, he is found in him, and he shares his righteousness.[3]

Paul discounts anything that he once thought would make him acceptable to God—either lineage or accomplishments—in order to gain "one pearl of great value" (Matt. 13:46), Christ Jesus himself. He wants Christ's righteousness credited to his spiritual bank account. This righteousness comes from grace and is received through faith in Christ. Paul's goal is to know Christ. In an initial sense he came to know Christ on the Damascus road years ago. But now, as Christ's apostle of more than twenty-five years, he wants to know Christ better, to grow in his relationship with Christ.

Growing in relationship to Christ involves, for Paul and all believers, knowing through experience the power of Christ's resurrection, even sharing his sufferings. That is, we are joined to Christ not only once for all at conversion, so that his death and resurrection save us. We are joined to Christ also

---

[3] Campbell, *Paul and Union with Christ*, 187–88.

in the Christian life. From the perspective of union with Christ, the Christian life is a life of sharing in his sufferings and relying on the power of his resurrection.

Gerald Hawthorne has his finger on Paul's pulse:

> Paul desired to come to know Christ more fully, not as a theological point to be discussed . . . but as a person to be enjoyed. He desires to experience in practice what he knew to be true in theory, i.e. that when Christ died he died, when Christ was resurrected he, too, was resurrected. He desired to sense within himself the power of the resurrected living Christ. He desired to realize in personal experience the fact that Christ's suffering had indeed put to the death his own sin.[4]

Paul's ultimate goal is to die in Christ and to be raised from the dead on the last day to eternal life. Although it is still future, and in that sense unrealized, with humility and confidence in Christ the apostle anticipates the resurrection of his body.

Philippians 3:12–14

> Not that I have already obtained this or am already perfect, but I press on to make it my own, because Christ Jesus has made me his own. Brothers, I do not consider that I have made it my own. But one thing I do: forgetting what lies behind and straining forward to what lies ahead, I press on toward the goal for the prize of the upward call of God in Christ Jesus.

Paul is accepted by God in Christ, but he also strives in the Christian life. He does not strive for acceptance by God. He already has that by grace through faith. But he struggles with his own sins as he longs for the resurrection of the body. Here is how he expresses it: "I press on toward the goal for the prize of the upward call of God in Christ Jesus" (v. 14). "In Christ Jesus" is more than likely used causally. Paul's upward call is "in Christ Jesus," that is, because of the person and saving accomplishment of Christ.

Philippians 4:1

> Therefore, my brothers, whom I love and long for, my joy and crown, stand firm thus in the Lord, my beloved.

---

[4] Gerald F. Hawthorne, *Philippians*, Word Biblical Commentary (Waco, TX: Word, 1983), 147–48.

Paul is exuberant in his expressions of love for the Philippian church. Even when he exhorts them to "stand firm," he addresses them as "my beloved." Specifically, he urges them to "stand firm thus in the Lord." Here the apostle uses "in the Lord" to describe believers' actions. It appears to be another use of the locative to indicate the realm of Christ. Paul's beloved Philippians are to remain committed to the faith under Christ's lordship.

Philippians 4:2

I entreat Euodia and I entreat Syntyche to agree in the Lord.

The Philippian congregation is healthy, as a comparison of this epistle with those to the Corinthians or Galatians shows. But the Philippian church is not perfect. There is a rift between two key woman workers, Euodia and Syntyche. Paul praises them for their service alongside him in the gospel. But before he does that, he implores them to "agree in the Lord." "In the Lord" is probably used as a locative to express Christ's sphere of influence. Because Christians live in Christ's kingdom, they are to live accordingly. Euodia and Syntyche, then, must reconcile, for that is how things work in Christ's domain.

Philippians 4:4

Rejoice in the Lord always; again I will say, rejoice.

This is a repetition of Philippians 3:1, with the addition of "always." "In the Lord" shows the cause of their rejoicing. Paul encourages the Philippians to rejoice because of who Jesus is and what he has done for them.

Philippians 4:7

The peace of God, which surpasses all understanding, will guard your hearts and your minds in Christ Jesus.

Paul tells worried believers to bring their cares to God in prayer along with thanksgiving (v. 6). He then gives a promise: God's peace, which is beyond our ability to understand, will stand guard over their hearts and minds "in Christ Jesus." Paul uses "in Christ Jesus" to show the cause or reason for the peace of God standing guard over Christians' hearts and minds. Because of Jesus's person and work, believers can enjoy God's peace even in troubling circumstances.

Philippians 4:10

I rejoiced in the Lord greatly that now at length you have revived your concern for me. You were indeed concerned for me, but you had no opportunity.

Paul expresses joy over the fact that the Philippians cared for him in a time of need. He uses "in the Lord" as he did in 3:1 and 4:4—to show reason or cause. It is because of what Jesus had done for them that the Philippians acted in the gracious manner that they did.

Philippians 4:19

My God will supply every need of yours according to his riches in glory in Christ Jesus.

The apostle expresses confidence that God will meet the Philippians' needs. Probably "in Christ Jesus" qualifies "riches in glory" and is used to mark association; God's glorious riches are so linked with Christ in Paul's mind that he easily associates the one with the other.[5]

Philippians 4:21

Greet every saint in Christ Jesus. The brothers who are with me greet you.

As he does so often, Paul includes "in Christ" language in greetings—here, final ones. Exchanging greetings, he writes, "Greet every saint in Christ Jesus." The usage here is as a periphrasis for believers. Paul means, "Greet every Christian saint."

---

[5] Campbell, *Paul and Union with Christ*, 90–91.

Chapter 11

Union with Christ
in Colossians

Colossians 1:2

> To the saints and faithful brothers in Christ at Colossae:
>   Grace to you and peace from God our Father.

Here Paul includes "in Christ" language in the initial greeting to the Colossian church. And as we have seen many times, "in Christ" is frequently used as a periphrasis for believers. Paul addresses his readers as the saints and Christian brothers at Colossae.

Colossians 1:13–14

> He has delivered us from the domain of darkness and transferred us to the kingdom of his beloved Son, in whom we have redemption, the forgiveness of sins.

Paul speaks of God the Father's saving believers from the kingdom of darkness (of sin and judgment) and putting them into another kingdom—that of "his beloved Son" (v. 13). This kingdom transfer is the key to understanding the use of "in [ἐν] whom," for it is the familiar locative used figuratively to speak of Christ's realm or domain. In the realm of God's beloved Son, Christians have redemption and forgiveness.

Colossians 1:18

He is the head of the body, the church.

These words appear in a context in which Paul presents Christ as preeminent "in everything," namely, in creation and redemption. Christ is Lord over the creation because he was the Father's agent in creation. He is Lord over the church as "head of the body." The head/body image is organic and thus implies union between Christ and his people. He is the church's Head, its source of life, as the next expression says: "He is the beginning, the firstborn from the dead" (v. 18). As the risen one he is the beginning of God's new creation, the giver of eternal life to his people. As Head he also directs the church to do his will in the world.

F. F. Bruce highlights these truths:

> Thus, in speaking of the church as the body of Christ, one thinks of it as vitalized by his abiding presence with it and his risen life in it; one thinks of it as energized by his power; one may even (without transgressing legitimate bounds) think of it as the instrument through which he carries on his work on earth.[1]

Colossians 1:24–25

Now I rejoice in my sufferings for your sake, and in my flesh I am filling up what is lacking in Christ's afflictions for the sake of his body, that is, the church, of which I became a minister according to the stewardship from God that was given to me for you, to make the word of God fully known.

In the context Paul speaks of his ministry of proclaiming the gospel (vv. 23, 25). Although there are a number of difficult issues in interpreting verse 24, my understanding, informed by the context, is as follows.[2] Underlying this text is the truth that union with Christ involves sharing now in his sufferings and the power of his resurrection. The sufferings in which Paul rejoices are those that he experiences in his body as he identifies with Christ's sufferings on the cross. Of course, Paul's sufferings are not redemptive, as Christ's were. But Christ has allotted a measure of suffering to his church as it participates in his sufferings and death.

---

[1] F. F. Bruce, *The Epistles to the Colossians, to Philemon, and to the Ephesians*, The New International Commentary on the New Testament (Grand Rapids: Eerdmans, 1984), 70.

[2] See Constantine R. Campbell, *Paul and Union with Christ: An Exegetical and Theological Study* (Grand Rapids: Zondervan, 2012), 284–86, for a discussion of views, including his, with which I agree.

In similar fashion, as he toils and struggles in ministry, Paul shares in the power of the risen Christ, "with all his energy that he powerfully works within me" (v. 29). As the apostle has explained in chapter 1, this is "all power" and God's "glorious might" that strengthens believers (v. 11). Campbell draws a reasonable conclusion concerning Paul:

> Since his sense of union with Christ in strength is revealed in 1:29, it is entirely plausible that 1:24 reveals Paul's sense of union with Christ in suffering. . . . Paul is discussing his own suffering and his desire to conform fully to Christ's afflictions. He is completing in himself what is lacking with respect to Christ's afflictions, identifying himself with the suffering of Christ, just as he also identifies with Christ's strength. All of this is for the sake of the body of Christ, the church, of which he has become a servant.[3]

As we will increasingly see, union with Christ is the key to salvation applied—past, present, and future. In this text the present dimension is in view. Christians share in Jesus's sufferings and resurrection power now. "As members of Christ's own body, his people participate in the sufferings of Christ himself," Douglas Moo explains.[4] They are called to suffer for the ministry of the gospel and are strengthened as they labor and struggle in that ministry.

Colossians 1:27–28

> To them God chose to make known how great among the Gentiles are the riches of the glory of this mystery, which is Christ in you, the hope of glory. Him we proclaim, warning everyone and teaching everyone with all wisdom, that we may present everyone mature in Christ.

Writing to Gentiles, Paul here describes in grand terms the salvation God has revealed to the saints: "the riches of the glory of this mystery" (v. 27). The mystery refers to God's great work in Christ, fully revealed only when Christ came and poured out the Spirit on the church. We tend to skip over the word "glory" because it is hard to define. Peter O'Brien corrects that practice: "The apostle wished to emphasize that this wonderful mystery partook of the char-

---

[3] Ibid., 285–86.
[4] Douglas J. Moo, *The Letters to the Colossians and to Philemon*, The Pillar New Testament Commentary (Grand Rapids: Eerdmans, 2008), 152.

acter of God himself." By "riches" Paul points to the "lavish bestowal of his blessings in Christ."[5]

What is this great mystery? "Christ in you, the hope of glory" (v. 27). The beloved Son of God, "in whom we have redemption, the forgiveness of sins," performs his saving work outside of us when he dies in our place and rises again on the third day. More than that, he deigns to live inside of Gentiles, those formerly outside of his people! In fact, Christ indwells all believers, both Jew and Gentile. In this intimate relationship, he is the source of our hope for future salvation—he is the "hope of glory." His presence within us assures us of final glorification.

It is the proclamation of this Christ, with appropriate warning and instruction, that is God's primary means to bring his people to maturity (v. 28). Paul's goal is to present every believer "mature in Christ." The verb "present" has forensic overtones (compare its use in v. 22), and thus the idea is presenting everyone mature "in Christ," that is, before Christ the Judge (and Savior!).[6] Believers work hard at living for God, but they do so, as Paul testifies, "with all his energy that he powerfully works within me" (v. 29). That is, the indwelling Christ empowers his people to toil for him and his kingdom.

Colossians 2:5–7

Though I am absent in body, yet I am with you in spirit, rejoicing to see your good order and the firmness of your faith in Christ.

Therefore, as you received Christ Jesus the Lord, so walk in him, rooted and built up in him and established in the faith, just as you were taught, abounding in thanksgiving.

Paul is not with the Colossians physically but rejoices in the good report he has received concerning their faith and lives. He speaks of hearing of the "firmness of" their "faith in Christ" (v. 5). It is easy to identify this use of "faith in Christ"; Paul presents him as the goal or object of saving faith.

Paul exhorts the Colossians to live for Christ. The verb "received" points to accepting apostolic tradition or teaching as authoritative. The words "just as you were taught" (v. 7) reinforce this idea. Here "received" involves more than accepting the truth; it involves commitment to Christ himself. Moo is

---

[5] Peter T. O'Brien, *Colossians, Philemon*, Word Biblical Commentary (Waco, TX: Word, 1982), 86.
[6] So Campbell, *Paul and Union with Christ*, 106–7. He cites a subcategory under BDAG's locative category for ἐν (BDAG, 327).

succinct: here receiving Christ "involves a commitment to the apostolic teaching about Christ and his significance."[7]

Believers are to live dedicated to Christ, even as they dedicated themselves to him when they trusted him as Lord and Savior. Paul describes this committed life with four participles: "rooted," "built up," "established," and "abounding" (v. 7). The first three express much the same idea—remaining stable in the light of the false teaching that Colossians opposes; the fourth speaks of overflowing with gratitude to God.

Twice the apostle uses "in him": the first time with "walk" and the second with "built up." Both uses of this "in Christ" language are the same. Campbell, building on BDAG, explains the nuance: "The imperative *walk in him* and the modifying participles *rooted and built up in him* are to be understood as instructing believers to live under the controlling influence of Christ, according to the teaching they have received about him."[8]

Colossians 2:9–10

In him the whole fullness of deity dwells bodily, and you have been filled in him, who is the head of all rule and authority.

The verses form a key unit to help us understand union with Christ. The first speaks of Christ's union with God; the second of our union with Christ. Campbell draws the theological implications of the correlation between the two:

It is better to understand ἐν αὐτῷ ["in him"] as expressing union with Christ. Believers are "filled" because of their union in him. The strength of this reading arises from the verses to either side of 2:10. First, 2:9 speaks of the fullness of God dwelling in Christ bodily. This does not mean that Christ's body is "filled" with God, but that through his union with God, Christ shares in the fullness of his deity. Second, 2:11 speaks of being circumcised in the circumcision of Christ . . . ; 2:12 refers to being buried with Christ . . . in baptism and being raised with him . . . ; 2:13 speaks of being made alive with him. . . . These three verses thus contain several references to the realities that believers share with Christ through their union and participation with him. Given that its context so strongly com-

---

[7] Moo, *Letters to the Colossians and to Philemon*, 177.
[8] Campbell, *Paul and Union with Christ*, 182–84, emphasis original.

mends union with Christ, ἐν αὐτῷ ["in him"] in 2:10 is likewise best understood this way.[9]

Bruce puts it succinctly: "Christians by their union with him participated in his life. If the fullness of deity resided in him, his fullness was imparted to them."[10]

Colossians 2:11–15

In him also you were circumcised with a circumcision made without hands, by putting off the body of the flesh, by the circumcision of Christ, having been buried with him in baptism, in which you were also raised with him through faith in the powerful working of God, who raised him from the dead. And you, who were dead in your trespasses and the uncircumcision of your flesh, God made alive together with him, having forgiven us all our trespasses, by canceling the record of debt that stood against us with its legal demands. This he set aside, nailing it to the cross. He disarmed the rulers and authorities and put them to open shame, by triumphing over them in him.

The heretics troubling the Colossian Christians have been teaching that the Colossians' faith in Christ is lacking; he is not enough. To the contrary, Paul explains that in Christ the "whole fullness of deity dwells bodily," and believers "have been filled in him" (v. 10). Now Paul explains how that filling has come about. Astoundingly, he tells his Gentile readers that "in him also you were circumcised"! He does not mean literal circumcision of the body. Rather, he speaks of a "circumcision made without hands, by putting off the body of the flesh, by the circumcision of Christ" (v. 11). This is a spiritual circumcision. It occurs "in him," which here indicates transference into Christ's realm. Believers have been transferred from the realm of the flesh to that of the Spirit. Though its meaning is debated, I understand the "circumcision of Christ" to refer to the one that Christ performs.[11] This is because Paul identifies that expression with a "circumcision made without hands." That is, even as the Jewish *mohel* would circumcise the flesh of males, so Christ spiritually

---

[9] Ibid., 181.

[10] Bruce, *Epistles to the Colossians, to Philemon, and to the Ephesians*, 101.

[11] Although a good case can be made for understanding the circumcision "of Christ" as an objective genitive—the circumcision performed on Christ, and hence here as a metaphor for his violent death—I favor the view that it is a subjective genitive, denoting the circumcision that Christ performs. See Moo, *Letters to the Colossians and to Philemon*, 198–200, for discussion of views and his reasons for favoring the subjective genitive interpretation.

circumcises all who put their faith in him ("through faith," v. 12). He thus puts "off the body of the flesh,"[12] conveying forgiveness, by his spiritual circumcision.

When did Christ spiritually circumcise the Colossian believers? When they were baptized: "having been buried with him in baptism, in which you were also raised with him through faith in the powerful working of God, who raised him from the dead" (v. 12). They were spiritually circumcised by Jesus when they were baptized. The meanings of Christian baptism and spiritual circumcision overlap. They both signify the cleansing of sin. Of course, neither outward act automatically accomplishes what it promises. But when God's promises are combined with faith, he gives what he promised.

As in Romans 6:1–4, here Christians are said to have been united to Christ in their baptism. Baptism signifies union with Christ in his death and resurrection. That is why Paul says: "having been *buried with him in baptism,* in which *you were also raised with him* through faith in the powerful working of God, who raised him from the dead" (Col. 2:12). O'Brien underlines the main idea: "The Colossians' burial with him in baptism shows that they were truly involved in his death, and laid in his grave."[13] That is, union with Christ involves participation in Christ's redemptive events. We participate in Jesus's story. As in Romans 6, we participate in Christ's death, burial, and resurrection so that in a sense they become *our* death, burial, and resurrection. Because we died with him, as is evidenced in our "burial with him," we are forgiven. His death counts for us. Because we were "raised with him," we have new life because of the "powerful working of God, who raised him from the dead" (Col. 2:12).

Though Paul does not explicitly draw out ethical implications here as he does in Romans 6, it is not difficult to do so, as Moo explains:

> All people (or all Christians) were "in Christ" when he died, was buried, and was raised to new life. By being identified with Christ in these key redemptive events, Christians experience in themselves the "change of eras" that God in Christ has brought to pass. No longer are we dominated by those "powers" of the old era, sin, death, and the flesh; we are now ruled by righteousness, life, grace, and the Spirit.[14]

Through union with Christ, to which baptism points, we have no excuse for not living for Christ who loved us so. His story is our story, and we must "no

---

[12] This expression fits better with the view that "of Christ" is a subjective, rather than objective, genitive.

[13] O'Brien, *Colossians, Philemon,* 118.

[14] Moo, *Letters to the Colossians and to Philemon,* 201.

longer live for [ourselves] but for him who for [our] sake died and was raised" (2 Cor. 5:15).

After presenting Christ's saving work in terms of legal substitution in Colossians 2:13–14, Paul shifts to the Christus Victor theme of the atonement: "He disarmed the rulers and authorities and put them to open shame, by triumphing over them in him" (v. 15). Paul uses the image of a Roman triumphal march to teach that God stripped the demons of their weapons and publicly embarrassed them. He did this by "triumphing over them in him." There is ambiguity concerning the translation of the last word; the NIV says, "triumphing over them by the cross," translating the pronoun αὐτῷ (*autō*) "it" and interpreting "it" to mean "the cross." Both translations are possible, and for theological purposes they end up at the same place. If the correct rendering is "him," the word surely refers to the Christ of the cross. If the correct rendering is "it," the word surely refers to the cross of the Christ. But what is the meaning of "in him" in the expression "by triumphing over them in him" or "it"? It is used to show instrument—it is through the work of Christ, as substitute and Victor, that God's triumph over the evil powers was secured.

Colossians 2:18–19

> Let no one disqualify you, insisting on asceticism and worship of angels, going on in detail about visions, puffed up without reason by his sensuous mind, and not holding fast to the Head, from whom the whole body, nourished and knit together through its joints and ligaments, grows with a growth that is from God.

Although scholars have not agreed on the precise identification of the Colossian heresy, it seems to involve a combination of Jewish and pagan folk belief. In this verse Paul speaks against a false asceticism that promotes not true holiness but rather prayers to angels to ward off evil spirits, and claims of mystical insight based on visions.[15] He warns his readers to shun these things and instead to cling to "the Head," that is, Christ himself. Once again we find the organic image of the church as Christ's body and him as its Head.

Christ is the Head, "from whom the whole body" is "nourished and knit together through its joints and ligaments" (v. 19). Here, as in Ephesians 4:15–16, the body of Christ is said to be strengthened and held together by "joints," and this text adds "ligaments." In addition, the whole body "grows with a

---

[15] I thank Clint Arnold for help from the *ESV Study Bible* on Col. 2:19.

growth that is from God" (Col. 2:19). This means the body image is dynamic, not static; the body grows and matures. Furthermore, this growth has divine and human elements. The body's growth is "from its head," that is, Christ (as in Eph. 4:15), and its growth is "from God." But it is also "nourished" by its "joints and ligaments," which apparently mean its members.[16]

Union with Christ is here portrayed as his living, growing body participating in the life of its Head. In this union God and his people cooperate in the organic and dynamic growth of Christ's body, the church.

Colossians 2:20–23

> If with Christ you died to the elemental spirits of the world, why, as if you were still alive in the world, do you submit to regulations—"Do not handle, Do not taste, Do not touch" (referring to things that all perish as they are used)—according to human precepts and teachings? These have indeed an appearance of wisdom in promoting self-made religion and asceticism and severity to the body, but they are of no value in stopping the indulgence of the flesh.

Again, it is difficult to identify exactly the Colossian heresy. It seems to combine Jewish, visionary, and ascetic elements, and here the last comes in for condemnation. Paul chides his readers for submitting to worldly regulations requiring abstinence from "food and drink" (v. 16), because they are based entirely on "human precepts and teachings" (v. 22). Indeed, these regulations make an outward show of religiosity and self-denial but do not actually promote holiness. "They are of no value in stopping the indulgence of the flesh" (v. 23).

What is the basis for Paul's appeal? Union with Christ in his death. "If with Christ you died to the elemental spirits of the world, why . . . do you submit to regulations?" True believers in Christ died with him to the "elemental spirits of the world," that is, to "those deities or spirits who were so closely associated with the elements."[17] By starting this sentence with "if," Paul wants readers to examine themselves to see if they really were joined to Jesus in his death. If they were, they are to eschew the false teachers' lures to deny their physical appetites in order to appease demons. Paul's words "Do not handle, Do not taste, Do not touch" (v. 21) mock the asceticism of the false teachers.

---

[16] I received help from Campbell, *Paul and Union with Christ*, 286–87.
[17] Moo, *Letters to the Colossians and to Philemon*, 191.

Here union with Christ in his death brings victory over evil spiritual be-ings, as Paul earlier taught: in the cross God "disarmed the rulers and authori-ties and put them to open shame, by triumphing over them in him" (v. 15). Believers in the majority world are better situated to understand Paul here than those in the minority world are. Moo's summary helps us:

> Many people in Paul's day lived in fear of these "forces" and sought ways to live in harmony with them. The sense of bondage to these powers appears to have been what made the false teachers' program especially seductive. Paul is therefore at pains to show that Christ's victory over the spiritual beings that are included in the "elemental forces" was complete and final (vv. 14–15) and that people who are in union with Christ share in that victory.[18]

Colossians 3:1–4

> If then you have been raised with Christ, seek the things that are above, where Christ is, seated at the right hand of God. Set your minds on things that are above, not on things that are on earth. For you have died, and your life is hidden with Christ in God. When Christ who is your life appears, then you also will appear with him in glory.

Paul has been speaking against the program of the false teachers and their ascetic demands (2:8–23). Here he briefly does this again: "[Set your minds] not on things that are on earth" (3:2). But his focus lies elsewhere; positively, he points his readers in another direction altogether—up. Twice he com-mands, "Seek the things that are above. . . . Set your minds on things that are above" (vv. 1–2). Why? Because "above" is "where Christ is, seated at the right hand of God." The antidote to the ruinous teaching of the false teachers is Christ (2:8–15). The antidote to the futile asceticism of the false teaching is Christ (vv. 16–23). So it comes as no surprise when the apostle points the Colossian Christians "above," where Christ is.

Specifically, Paul underscores our union with Christ in his story as moti-vation to "seek" him. When he tells his readers "you have died" (3:3), surely he means "with Christ" (having said so in 2:20). He specifically mentions union with Christ in his resurrection (3:1). In light of his readers' union with Christ in his death and resurrection, Paul says, "Your life is hidden with Christ in

---

[18] Ibid., 234.

God" (v. 3). Moo explains that Paul appeals to a Jewish apocalyptic worldview in which a "hidden"/"revealed" motif is basic.

> According to this perspective, many things relating to God and his purposes exist in the present, but because they are in heaven, they are hidden from human sight. But the apocalyptic seer is given a vision of these things, things that will one day be revealed as they come to pass and are seen by people on earth. So, Paul suggests, at the present time our heavenly identity is real, but it is hidden. . . . In the meantime our true status is veiled and, though we may not look any different than those around us, Paul's point is that we certainly need to behave differently.[19]

Contrary to the ascetic doctrine of the false teachers, Paul's readers are to pursue Christ, who is above. Does this mean they are to despise their earthly lives? Hardly, for in the rest of chapter 3 the apostle gives instructions for relating to one another in the church and to families at home. This is "earthy" teaching. It does not involve the denial of bodily appetites as a means of spirituality; rather, it involves focusing on Christ in heaven and drawing strength from union with him for everyday life on earth.

Amazingly, Paul takes our participation in Christ's narrative even further. We died with him, were buried with him, arose with him, ascended with him, and sat down in heaven with him; and in a sense we even come again with him! This is what Paul means when he writes, "When Christ who is your life appears, then you also will appear with him in glory" (v. 4). "When Christ . . . appears" refers to his return, and "you also will appear with him in glory" refers to *our* return, so to speak. We need to carefully define in what sense we have a second coming in union with Christ. Moo comes to our aid:

> When he appears in glory at the time of his return, believers will appear with him. Our identification with Christ, now real but hidden, will one day be manifest. . . . Because Christ is now "in us," we have "the hope of glory" (Col. 1:27), and it is that same union, expressed in the other direction—we "in Christ"—that will bring hope to its certain accomplishment.[20]

Our union with Christ is so comprehensive that Paul teaches we will (in a sense) come again with him; only at his return will our true spiritual identity

---

[19] Ibid., 250.
[20] Ibid., 251–52.

be revealed. Now we only approximate the new persons we will be in glory and holiness in the resurrection. Though it is little known, Paul speaks of the same truth in Romans 8:18–19: "I consider that the sufferings of this present time are not worth comparing with the glory that is to be revealed to us. For the creation waits with eager longing for the *revealing* of the sons of God." The word translated "revealing" is ἀποκάλυψις (*apokalypsis*), more literally rendered "revelation."

This word, included in the title of Scripture's last book—"The Revelation of John"—frequently refers to Jesus's return, and in Romans 8:19, it refers to our return, so to speak. How is this possible? Because of union with Christ. John speaks of the same reality: "Beloved, we are God's children now, and what we will be has not yet appeared; but we know that when he appears we shall be like him, because we shall see him as he is" (1 John 3:2).

In sum, Paul's readers' lives and futures are so bound up with the Son of God that by virtue of union with him, Paul could speak of "Christ who is your life" (Col. 3:4). In context, he is countering false teachers who claim that the Colossian Christians are lacking in something. To the contrary, the apostle insists, they have all they need in union with the Son and are therefore secure. Indeed, now their lives are "hidden with Christ in God" (v. 3). O'Brien expresses their and our joyous prospect: "We too who share his life will share his glorious epiphany."[21]

Colossians 3:15

Let the peace of Christ rule in your hearts, to which indeed you were called in one body. And be thankful.

After teaching that Christians have died with Christ and been raised with him (2:20; 3:1, 3), Paul applies these two aspects of union with Christ. Believers are to "put to death" sinful practices (vv. 5–11) and "put on" godly qualities and actions (vv. 12–17). Among them are letting Christ's peace rule in their congregation and being grateful to God (v. 15). That the apostle means communal peace and not merely peace in individual hearts is communicated by his reference to the body of Christ: "Let the peace of Christ rule in your hearts, to which indeed you were called in one body" (v. 15).

God called us individually to himself in salvation. But that individual call involves our being called into the people of God, the church. We were called

---

[21] O'Brien, *Colossians, Philemon*, 166.

to promote harmony and unity when we "were called in one body." There is interplay between the plural "hearts" and singular "body." As God's people submit to Christ's peace and promote harmony in the congregation, they fulfill a purpose for which God summoned them to the one body of Christ.

Colossians 3:18

Wives, submit to your husbands, as is fitting in the Lord.

As part of Paul's Christian household code, wives are told to be submissive to their own husbands "as is fitting in the Lord." The prepositional phrase "in the Lord" is used as a locative to express what is right within Christ's domain.

Colossians 3:20

Children, obey your parents in everything, for this pleases the Lord.

Also part of the household code, this verse gives the children's responsibility. I prefer to translate the last phrase (parallel to the end of v. 18 above) "as is pleasing in the Lord" to preserve the "in Christ" language. The usage here is the same as in Ephesians 6:1 and Colossians 3:18: Christian children are to be obedient to their parents, for this is proper within Christ's realm.

Colossians 4:7

Tychicus will tell you all about my activities. He is a beloved brother and faithful minister and fellow servant in the Lord.

In a familiar use, "in the Lord" is employed as a periphrasis for believers to approximate "Christian" as an adjective in English. Paul will send the letter to the Colossians with Tychicus, whom Paul regards as a "beloved brother and faithful minister and fellow Christian servant." Here again Paul includes "in Christ" vocabulary in his final greetings of an epistle.

Colossians 4:17

Say to Archippus, "See that you fulfill the ministry that you have received in the Lord."

Later in the final greetings the apostle brings a word to Archippus, a Colossian servant of the Lord, encouraging him to fulfill his ministry. Paul describes this ministry as one he has "received in the Lord." If "in the Lord" goes with "received," as seems likely, then this prepositional phrase conveys agency. Archippus received his ministry from the Lord Jesus.

Chapter 12

Union with Christ in
1–2 Thessalonians

1 Thessalonians

1 Thessalonians 1:1

Paul, Silvanus, and Timothy,
    To the church of the Thessalonians in God the Father and the Lord
Jesus Christ:
    Grace to you and peace.

Paul includes Silvanus and Timothy, his companions in planting the church in Thessalonica, as those responsible for this letter. He describes the church in a most unusual way. Uniquely in Paul's epistles, 1 Thessalonians 1:1 and 2 Thessalonians 1:1 describe believers as "in God the Father and the Lord Jesus Christ," where the preposition "in" goes with both Father and Son.

This uniqueness has prompted various responses. Some have ruled out the possibility that Paul is speaking of union with the Father and the Son on the grounds that this is a "non-Pauline usage as regards God"[1] or because "Paul nowhere thinks of the believer as 'in God' in the spatial sense."[2] But, in fact, it appears Paul does that very thing in two places—the first verse in each of 1 and 2 Thessalonians.

F. F. Bruce agrees:

---

[1] So, Earl J. Richard, *First and Second Thessalonians*, Sacra Pagina (Collegeville, MN: Liturgical Press, 1995), 41.
[2] Ernest Best, *A Commentary on the First and Second Epistles to the Thessalonians*, Harper's New Testament Commentaries (New York: Harper and Row, 1972), 62.

The believing community in Thessalonica, is not called the church of God, but the church "in God." This is an unusual expression in the Pauline corpus, where otherwise "in God" is used of boasting in God (Rom 2:17; 5:11) or of being hidden in God (Eph 3:9; Col 3:3). On the other hand, "in Christ," "in Christ Jesus," or "in the Lord" is a characteristic Pauline expression, especially when it has "incorporative" force, pointing to believers' participation in Christ's risen life or their membership in his body. If this is the force of the words "in . . . the Lord Jesus Christ" here, then "in God the Father" must be understood in the same way.[3]

I find Bruce's reasoning compelling, as do others, including Gene Green, Gordon Fee, and Leon Morris.[4] Moreover, Paul's bringing the Father and Son into such close association is characteristic of his Thessalonian epistles, as Morris explains: "It is Paul's usual habit to speak of being 'in Christ,' though 'in God' occurs as in Col. 3:3. But throughout these two Epistles he constantly associates the Father and the Son in the closest of fashions (cf. v. 3; 3:11–13; 5:18; II Thess. 1:1, 2, 8, 12; 2:16f.; 3:5 . . .)."[5]

The apostle's teaching in the first verse of each Thessalonian letter has important implications for his doctrine of union with Christ.[6] Green agrees: "The *church of the Thessalonians* finds its unique identity in its union or relationship with *God the Father* and the exalted *Lord Jesus Christ*."[7] In these verses Paul approaches John's teaching expressed in Jesus's prayer to the Father in John 17, "that they also may be in us" (v. 21). Paul thus has a doctrine of union with the Father and the Son. This will be explored further in my summary of Paul's theology of union with Christ (pp. 195–97) and in my attempt to systematize union at the end of this volume (pp. 380–81).

1 Thessalonians 2:14

For you, brothers, became imitators of the churches of God in Christ Jesus that are in Judea.

---

[3] F. F. Bruce, *1 & 2 Thessalonians*, Word Biblical Commentary (Waco, TX: Word, 1982), 7.

[4] See Gene L. Green, *The Letters to the Thessalonians*, The Pillar New Testament Commentary (Grand Rapids: Eerdmans 2002), 85; Gordon D. Fee, *The First and Second Epistles to the Thessalonians*, The New International Commentary on the New Testament (Grand Rapids: Eerdmans, 2009), 15; and Leon Morris, *The First and Second Epistles to the Thessalonians*, rev. ed., The New International Commentary on the New Testament (Grand Rapids: Eerdmans, 1991), 35–36.

[5] Morris, *First and Second Epistles to the Thessalonians*, 48.

[6] Unfortunately the person from whom I learned most about union with Christ in Paul—Constantine Campbell—omitted 1 Thess. 1:1 and 2 Thess. 1:1 from his outstanding *Paul and Union with Christ: An Exegetical and Theological Study* (Grand Rapids: Zondervan, 2012).

[7] Green, *Letters to the Thessalonians*, 85, emphasis original.

Paul gives thanks to God that the Thessalonians received the apostolic preaching as the word of God, which continues to work in their lives (v. 13). This is evidenced by their being willing to suffer persecution for the faith. In this way they "became imitators of the churches of God in Christ Jesus that are in Judea" (v. 14). Paul employs "in Christ Jesus" as a periphrasis for believers and means the "Christian churches of God" in Judea.

1 Thessalonians 4:1–2

> Brothers, we ask and urge you in the Lord Jesus, that as you received from us how you ought to walk and to please God, just as you are doing, that you do so more and more. For you know what instructions we gave you through the Lord Jesus.

Paul urges the Thessalonian church to grow in their Christian lives to please God. He praises them for their current level of spiritual growth and spurs them on to more. He urges them "in the Lord Jesus." Paul uses "in the Lord Jesus" to qualify "ask" and "urge." Due to the parallelism with "through the Lord Jesus" in the next verse, I suggest that "in the Lord" shows manner. Paul urges his readers in a manner fitting Jesus, his Lord, thereby adding clout and urgency to his exhortation.

1 Thessalonians 4:8

> Whoever disregards this, disregards not man but God, who gives his Holy Spirit to you.

Paul exhorts the Thessalonians in progressive sanctification, especially in the area of sexual purity (vv. 1–7): "God has not called us for impurity, but in holiness" (v. 7). To drive home his words to his hearers, he adds, "Therefore whoever disregards this, disregards not man but God, who gives his Holy Spirit to you" (v. 8). Paul as an apostle writes with the authority of God himself, and his words are not to be rejected. Rather, they are to be obeyed.

God is described as the one "who gives his Holy Spirit to you." Gary Shogren captures the force of these words: "Christians should be holy because God commands it and because his Spirit, who is holy, is within them."[8] We note that the apostle here makes an ethical appeal based on the Spirit's indwelling of God's people.

---

[8] Gary S. Shogren, *1 & 2 Thessalonians*, Zondervan Exegetical Commentary on the New Testament (Grand Rapids: Zondervan, 2012), 167.

1 Thessalonians 4:16

> The Lord himself will descend from heaven with a cry of command, with
> the voice of an archangel, and with the sound of the trumpet of God. And
> the dead in Christ will rise first.

The Thessalonians had become confused in their understanding of last
things. They did not anticipate some of their number dying before the second
coming. When that occurred, their faith was upset. Paul writes to calm their
fears. He describes Christ's return: Christ will descend and an archangel will
announce Christ's coming, accompanied by a trumpet blast. And deceased
believers will not miss out. Rather, they will be raised from the dead and will
accompany living believers to meet Jesus in the air as a welcoming committee.

When the Lord comes back, "the dead in Christ will rise first." Campbell
explains:

> Being dead in Christ refers to the status that describes all who die as
> believers in Christ. The use of ἐν Χριστῷ ["in Christ"] here does not
> describe the manner in which such deaths took place, but rather indicates
> the sphere under which the dead are situated: "even death does not break
> the union; we are still *in him*."[9]

1 Thessalonians 5:9–10

> God has not destined us for wrath, but to obtain salvation through our
> Lord Jesus Christ, who died for us so that whether we are awake or asleep
> we might live with him.

Paul wrote 1 Thessalonians in part to correct false impressions the believers had about the second coming. They were afraid deceased believers
may miss out on that blessed event. In addition, their zeal for Christ's return
combined with their intense persecution to raise questions as to whether the
day of the Lord had already come. Paul assures them that deceased believers would not miss out and that the day of the Lord had not come (4:13–18;
5:1–11). The current text appears at the end of the passage treating this second
issue—the day of the Lord. Make no mistake, the apostle insists: "God has not
destined us for wrath, but to obtain salvation through our Lord Jesus Christ"
(v. 9). God has not elected his people, including the Thessalonian believers

---

[9] Campbell, *Paul and Union with Christ*, 119, emphasis original. Campbell quotes Leon Morris, *Epistles of Paul to the Thessalonians*, 93.

(1:4–5), to experience his wrath. Rather, he chose them to "obtain salvation through our Lord Jesus Christ."

The work Jesus accomplished to rescue his own is that he "died for" them (5:10). Jesus loved his people and gave himself up for them, dying in their place. The result of his saving work is that "whether we are awake or asleep we might live" (v. 10). Christ's death saves living and deceased believers; it obtains eternal life for them. Paul's focus is eschatological, and so future resurrection life is in view. He expresses this hope succinctly as "that . . . we might live with him." The last two words speak of final union with the risen Christ, as Green explains: "The portion that the believers await, whether they are the living or the dead in Christ, is the promise of the resurrection and life in union with him."[10]

1 Thessalonians 5:12–13

> We ask you, brothers, to respect those who labor among you and are over you in the Lord and admonish you, and to esteem them very highly in love because of their work. Be at peace among yourselves.

Paul urges his Thessalonian readers to respect and honor their church leaders. He describes the leaders (using three substantival participles) as "laboring," "being over" others, and "admonishing" them. It seems "in the Lord" goes with each of the three participles to give the cause or reason believers should respect and honor them—because of the person and saving work of the Lord Jesus.

1 Thessalonians 5:16–18

> Rejoice always, pray without ceasing, give thanks in all circumstances; for this is the will of God in Christ Jesus for you.

Once more in the final instructions of an epistle, Paul includes union. He commands his readers to rejoice, pray ceaselessly, and give thanks in all situations. He specifies that the last of these is the "will of God in Christ Jesus for you." Though different possibilities obtain, it may be best to see this as a locative indicating the sphere of Christ. He is Lord (hence the commands), and Christians are to live appropriately as citizens of his domain.

---

[10] Green, *Letters to the Thessalonians*, 245.

2 Thessalonians

2 Thessalonians 1:1-2

Paul, Silvanus, and Timothy,
    To the church of the Thessalonians in God our Father and the Lord
Jesus Christ:
    Grace to you and peace from God our Father and the Lord Jesus
Christ.

This salutation is identical to that of 1 Thessalonians 1:1, except for the
substitution of "our" for "the" between "God" and "Father," and the addition
of "from God our Father and the Lord Jesus Christ" after "Grace to you and
peace." This, then, becomes the second time Paul speaks of union with the
Father and the Son in his epistles. Fee comments, "Paul has here repeated
the unique feature, found elsewhere only in 1 Thessalonians, of designating
the church as existing simultaneously in God the Father and the Lord Jesus
Christ."[11]

2 Thessalonians 1:11-12

To this end we always pray for you, that our God may make you worthy
of his calling and may fulfill every resolve for good and every work of
faith by his power, so that the name of our Lord Jesus may be glorified
in you, and you in him, according to the grace of our God and the Lord
Jesus Christ.

After teaching that Christ's return will mean relief for persecuted believers and wrath for unbelievers, Paul says that he prays for the Thessalonian
church. He prays that God would enable them to live up to the calling they
have received from him and that his power would bless them with many
works of faith. The result of God's answering Paul's prayer will be the mutual
glorification of Christ and believers: "so that the name of our Lord Jesus
may be glorified in you, and you in him" (v. 12). How is "in him" used? It
seems to be used to show instrument, since the end of the verse implies that
the agency is the "grace of our God and the Lord Jesus Christ" (v. 12). God's
power will enable Christ to be honored by the Thessalonians and them to
be honored by him.

---

[11] Fee, *First and Second Epistles to the Thessalonians*, 245.

2 Thessalonians 3:11–12

We hear that some among you walk in idleness, not busy at work, but busybodies. Now such persons we command and encourage in the Lord Jesus Christ to do their work quietly and to earn their own living.

After stressing the necessity for each person in the Thessalonian congregation to work, Paul indicates that he is not happy to hear reports of idle persons in their midst (v. 11). He admonishes those who are idle with strong language: "Now such persons we command and encourage in the Lord Jesus Christ to do their work quietly and to earn their own living" (v. 12).

The form of this exhortation is very similar to that of 1 Thessalonians 4:1: "Finally, then, brothers, we ask and urge you in the Lord Jesus." In fact, the same word is used in both texts: παρακαλέω (*parakaleō*) is translated "urge" (in 1 Thess. 4:1) and "encourage" (in 2 Thess. 3:12). Given the similarity of the texts, it makes sense to take "in the Lord Jesus" as expressing manner here (as in 1 Thess. 4:1). Paul commands and encourages idlers in a manner fitting the Lord Jesus. The apostle's admonishment carries Jesus's authority.

Chapter 13

Union with Christ in the Pastoral Epistles

1 Timothy

1 Timothy 1:12–14

> I thank him who has given me strength, Christ Jesus our Lord, because he judged me faithful, appointing me to his service, though formerly I was a blasphemer, persecutor, and insolent opponent. But I received mercy because I had acted ignorantly in unbelief, and the grace of our Lord overflowed for me with the faith and love that are in Christ Jesus.

Paul gives thanks to Christ for appointing Paul to his ministry even though he previously was a "blasphemer, persecutor, and insolent opponent." Jesus showed Paul mercy because he "had acted ignorantly in unbelief" (v. 13). Jesus abundantly poured out grace upon Paul "with the faith and love that are in Christ Jesus" (v. 14). The apostle puts "in Christ Jesus" in apposition to "faith and love." Campbell draws a sound conclusion:

> Of the categories listed in BDAG, the most appropriate for this use is that indicating state or condition. Thus ἐν Χριστῷ ["in Christ"] refers to the state or condition of πίστεως ["faith"] and ἀγάπης ["love"]; faith and love are conditioned by Christ. . . . In other words, the faith and love in view are conditioned by Christ in juxtaposition to false versions thereof.[1]

---

[1] Constantine R. Campbell, *Paul and Union with Christ: An Exegetical and Theological Study* (Grand Rapids: Zondervan, 2012), 92.

1 Timothy 3:13

Those who serve well as deacons gain a good standing for themselves and also great confidence in the faith that is in Christ Jesus.

After Paul discusses qualifications for the office of deacon, he gives motivation for people to seek that office. Two benefits will accrue to those who serve faithfully as deacons. The first is that "those who serve well as deacons gain a good standing for themselves." This means they will "be esteemed, or held in high regard . . . in the church."[2]

The second benefit is "great confidence in the faith that is in Christ Jesus." Here "in Christ Jesus" is used to indicate the object of belief; Paul speaks of faith in Christ. By God's grace, faithful service will strengthen deacons' faith in Christ.

2 Timothy

2 Timothy 1:1–2

Paul, an apostle of Christ Jesus by the will of God according to the promise of the life that is in Christ Jesus,
    To Timothy, my beloved child:
    Grace, mercy, and peace from God the Father and Christ Jesus our Lord.

In this opening greeting Paul employs "in Christ" language; he speaks of "the promise of the life that is in Christ Jesus" (v. 1). The apostle puts "in Christ Jesus" in apposition to "the promise of life." He seems to use "in Christ Jesus" to indicate a state or condition—the promise of eternal life is conditioned by Christ.[3]

2 Timothy 1:8–9

Do not be ashamed of the testimony about our Lord, nor of me his prisoner, but share in suffering for the gospel by the power of God, who saved us and called us to a holy calling, not because of our works but because of his own purpose and grace, which he gave us in Christ Jesus before the ages began.

Paul encourages his understudy Timothy to boldness in the ministry and willingness to suffer for the gospel. Paul speaks of God as the one who

---

[2] Philip H. Towner, *The Letters to Timothy and Titus*, The New International Commentary on the New Testament (Grand Rapids: Eerdmans, 2006), 268.
[3] Campbell, *Paul and Union with Christ*, 92–93.

saved and called his people to holiness. God did so not by taking into account human efforts but "because of his own purpose and grace." Paul specifies that this grace was "given us in Christ Jesus before eternal ages" (my translation). The "in Christ" language is used instrumentally, as the next verse confirms: "and which has now been manifested through the appearing of our Savior Christ Jesus, who abolished death and brought life and immortality to light through the gospel" (v. 10).

2 Timothy 1:13–14

> Follow the pattern of the sound words that you have heard from me, in the faith and love that are in Christ Jesus. By the Holy Spirit who dwells within us, guard the good deposit entrusted to you.

Paul exhorts Timothy by his own example to courage and steadfastness as he calls him to be his successor in the mission: "I am not ashamed, for I know whom I have believed, and I am convinced that he is able to guard until that Day what has been entrusted to me" (v. 12). The apostle then enjoins Timothy to follow Paul's example in preaching the gospel, the "pattern of the sound words that you have heard from me" (v. 13). He is to do this with authenticity in faith and love—specifically, the "faith and love that are in Christ Jesus" (v. 13). Paul seems to use "in Christ Jesus" to show ground or reason. The apostle means: follow my teaching in the faith and love that come from Christ Jesus.

He tells his understudy to guard what God has given him by "the Holy Spirit who dwells within us" (2 Tim. 1:14). The "good deposit" is the gospel viewed as a trust from God to believers and ministers of the Word. The agency of the Spirit is the means by which we guard the gospel in life and service. The Spirit indwells God's people and empowers them for ministry.[4]

2 Timothy 2:1

> You then, my child, be strengthened by the grace that is in Christ Jesus.

Paul seeks to encourage Timothy to persevere in the ministry. He tells him, "Be strengthened by the grace that is in Christ Jesus." The apostle qualifies "grace" by using "in Christ Jesus" as a locative indicating the sphere of Christ, the domain over which he rules. Paul thus tells Timothy to be strong in the grace that exists within Christ's domain.

---

[4] I received considerable help from Towner, *The Letters to Timothy and Titus*, 477–78.

2 Timothy 2:10

> I endure everything for the sake of the elect, that they also may obtain the salvation that is in Christ Jesus with eternal glory.

Paul writes as a prisoner, but he will endure more than prison for the sake of the gospel. Why? He does so for the sake of those whom God has chosen, "that they also may obtain the salvation that is in Christ Jesus." Someone will ask: If they are "the elect," why do they need to obtain salvation? Aren't the elect automatically saved? The answer to both questions is that election means God's choosing people for salvation. They do not obtain that salvation until they believe the gospel. Paul, the most fervent teacher of the doctrine of election in Scripture, was also a zealous missionary. He was eager for God's chosen people to hear the gospel, believe, and obtain salvation.

Again Paul speaks of salvation "in Christ Jesus." And here alone he uses the very word "salvation." Paul perseveres through hardships so that "the elect . . . may obtain the salvation that is in Christ Jesus." "In Christ Jesus" (like its occurrences in 1 Tim. 1:14 and 2 Tim. 1:1) appears in apposition to a substantive, this time "salvation." And like its use in those two places, "It is probably best to regard it as indicating a state or condition. Salvation is conditioned by Christ, such that ἐν Χριστῷ ["in Christ"] marks out 'the specifically Christian character of the salvation to be obtained.'"[5]

This salvation involves resurrection and eternal life on the new earth with God and all his saints. Paul uses a cipher for these concepts when he simply adds to "salvation that is in Christ Jesus" the words "with eternal glory."

2 Timothy 2:11–13

> The saying is trustworthy, for:
>
> > If we have died with him, we will also live with him;
> > if we endure, we will also reign with him;
> > if we deny him, he also will deny us;
> > if we are faithless, he remains faithful—
>
> for he cannot deny himself.

Paul gives his fifth faithful saying, inserting a confession or hymn from the early church: "If we have died with him, we will also live with him" (v. 11).

---

[5] Campbell, *Paul and Union with Christ*, 93–94. He quotes Donald Guthrie, *The Pastoral Epistles*, 2nd ed., Tyndale New Testament Commentaries (Leicester, UK: Inter-Varsity, 1990), 156.

Paul, recalling Romans 6:3–5, means that if we have been united to Christ in his death, we will also be united to him in his resurrection. If we have been joined spiritually to Christ by trusting him as our crucified Savior, we will be raised from the dead in union with him, our risen Lord, unto eternal life.

"If we endure, we will also reign with him" (2 Tim. 2:12). If we professed believers persevere to the end, we will be saved in the ultimate sense and reign with Christ in glory. Just as Paul exhorted Timothy to do (vv. 1–7) and he himself does (vv. 8–10), so all who claim to know Christ must endure if they would be saved. We must persevere in suffering with him if we would reign with him. Such suffering is evidence of true union with Christ in his death, which will issue into union with him in his resurrection.

"If we deny him, he also will deny us" (v. 12). Behind Paul's words are those of Jesus: "Everyone who acknowledges me before men, I also will acknowledge before my Father who is in heaven, but whoever denies me before men, I also will deny before my Father who is in heaven" (Matt. 10:32–33). Merely claiming to be Jesus's disciple is insufficient. People must publicly confess him. The result is that he will acknowledge them in the court of his Father. But rejecting Jesus also brings consequences—rejection by the Father.

Though there are similarities between Jesus's words and Paul's, there is an important difference as well. Jesus said "everyone" and "whoever" in Matthew 10:32–33 to separate true disciples from false ones. Paul says, "If we deny him, he also will deny us" (2 Tim. 2:12). The apostle's words belong to a profession of faith made in common by church members. Those who continue will reign with Christ (v. 12). "However, if some deny Christ, if through their lives they deny knowing him by their word and deed, then before the judgment seat Christ will also deny knowing them."[6] Scripture affords assurance to those who walk in faith, but it does not promise salvation to those who profess Christ but later reject him.

God is gracious! As soon as these hard words are confessed publicly, words of comfort follow: "If we are faithless, he remains faithful—for he cannot deny himself" (v. 13). Even if we fail, and at times fall, he still is our fortress. He is dependable even when we are not. Being unfaithful here is less serious than denying him in the previous line. We are all unfaithful at times, but true believers do not deny him totally and finally, as apostates do. Though the church is composed of unsteady people, its ultimate success depends on the faithfulness of God, who cannot deny himself. "Even if there are false teach-

---

[6] William D. Mounce, *Pastoral Epistles*, Word Biblical Commentary (Nashville: Thomas Nelson, 2000), 519.

ers and false believers in the church, God will not fail to preserve his people; that is, whatever happens to the church and its leadership, God will remain faithful to his covenant."[7] As for those who truly "have died with him," just as truly they "will also live with him" (v. 11).

2 Timothy 3:12

> All who desire to live a godly life in Christ Jesus will be persecuted.

This verse serves as a transition between verses in which Paul praises Timothy for following his teaching and lifestyle for Christ, including enduring persecution (vv. 10–11), and a warning that "evil people and impostors will go on from bad to worse" (v. 13). Paul does not hide the truth from his disciple: "Indeed, all who desire to live a godly life in Christ Jesus will be persecuted" (v. 12). "In Christ Jesus," seems to be employed as a locative pointing to the sphere of Christ's rule. The context favors this use because it contrasts Paul's God-honoring lifestyle with that of the false teachers he condemns. The apostle thus tells Timothy a difficult truth: believers who strive to live as befits Christ's domain will not be received well by the world system ranged against him.

2 Timothy 3:14–15

> As for you, continue in what you have learned and have firmly believed, knowing from whom you learned it and how from childhood you have been acquainted with the sacred writings, which are able to make you wise for salvation through faith in Christ Jesus.

Contrary to the false teachers, who give themselves over to evil and masquerade as servants of Christ even when they are not, Timothy is to persevere in the Christian faith he learned from his mother, Eunice, and grandmother, Lois (cf. 1:5). He is to persist in studying and living the Holy Scriptures, which bring salvation through faith in Christ Jesus. These last two words give the object of belief—faith in Christ.

---

[7] Towner, *Letters to Timothy and Titus*, 514. For more, see Robert A. Peterson, *Our Secure Salvation: Preservation and Apostasy*, Explorations in Biblical Theology (Phillipsburg, NJ: P&R, 2009).

Chapter 14

Union with Christ
in Philemon

Philemon 8–10

> Though I am bold enough in Christ to command you to do what is required, yet for love's sake I prefer to appeal to you—I, Paul, an old man and now a prisoner also for Christ Jesus—I appeal to you for my child, Onesimus, whose father I became in my imprisonment.

Although Paul, as an apostle, could order Philemon to take back his runaway slave Onesimus, he instead appeals to him as a brother in Christ. Paul says he is "bold enough in Christ to command" Philemon. Campbell correctly identifies the usage of "in Christ" as ground or cause, pointing to the contrast between two such causes: Paul's unissued command of verse 8 and the actual cause of his appeal, "his loving spiritual fatherhood of Onesimus."[1] Paul has enough confidence because of Christ's person and work to order Philemon, but he instead appeals to him in love.

Philemon 15–16

> This perhaps is why he was parted from you for a while, that you might have him back forever, no longer as a bondservant but more than a bond-

---

[1] Constantine R. Campbell, *Paul and Union with Christ: An Exegetical and Theological Study* (Grand Rapids: Zondervan, 2012), 110–11.

servant, as a beloved brother—especially to me, but how much more to you, both in the flesh and in the Lord.

Paul appeals to Philemon on behalf of his runaway slave Onesimus, whom Paul led to Christ and sent back to Philemon. The apostle urges Philemon to receive Onesimus back "no longer as a bondservant but more than a bondservant, as a beloved brother" (v. 16). Paul expects Philemon the believer to welcome back his servant Onesimus, who is now a fellow believer. Philemon is to receive Onesimus "as a beloved brother . . . both in the flesh and in the Lord."

Moo notes that this contrast is unusual and its second part comprehensive: "The contrast that Paul presents here, between Philemon's relationship to Onesimus 'in the Lord' and 'in the flesh' is striking. Nowhere else does Paul contrast 'the Lord' and 'the flesh.' Moreover, 'in the Lord' covers all possible elements of the Christian's existence."[2]

"Flesh" here has a positive meaning, pointing to our common humanity. "In the flesh" thus means "as a fellow human being." Because Paul contrasts "in the Lord" with "in the flesh," the former is plainly used as a periphrasis for believers. The apostle wants his friend to welcome back his former slave as both a human brother and a *Christian* brother.

Philemon 18–20

If he has wronged you at all, or owes you anything, charge that to my account. I, Paul, write this with my own hand: I will repay it—to say nothing of your owing me even your own self. Yes, brother, I want some benefit from you in the Lord. Refresh my heart in Christ.

Paul asks Philemon to welcome back Onesimus as a new fellow believer. Paul offers to pay any debt the slave incurred. He also reminds Philemon of his greater debt to Paul—he was converted under Paul's ministry and thus "owes" him his "own self" (v. 18–19). Twice Paul uses "in Christ" language. First, he writes, "Yes, brother, I want some benefit from you in the Lord" (v. 20). Like the use of "in Christ" in Romans 9:1, "in the Lord" here seems to mark close association—specifically, "under the control of, under the influence of, in close association with."[3] Paul asks that Philemon would give Paul joy under the influence of the Lord Jesus.

---

[2] Douglas J. Moo, *The Letters to the Colossians and to Philemon*, The Pillar New Testament Commentary (Grand Rapids: Eerdmans, 2008), 424.
[3] Campbell, *Paul and Union with Christ*, 127.

Second, Paul tells Philemon, "Refresh my heart in Christ" (Philem. 20). The use of "in Christ" here parallels its use of "in the Lord" in the previous sentence—it shows close association—specifically, under the influence of. Consequently, Paul wants his friend Philemon to refresh Paul's heart under Christ's influence.

Philemon 23

Epaphras, my fellow prisoner in Christ Jesus, sends greetings to you.

As he does more often than not, Paul uses "in Christ" language in the final greeting to an epistle, this time his epistle to Philemon. And as he frequently does, Paul employs this language—this time "in Christ Jesus"—as a periphrasis for believers. Epaphras, Paul's fellow *Christian* prisoner, sends greetings to Philemon.

Chapter 15

A Summary of Union with Christ in Paul's Letters (1)

Lewis Smedes is undoubtedly correct: "Paul's message was Christ crucified. The object of his preaching was to summon men to a decision about Jesus and His cross. But Paul was also the apostle of our union with Christ in the new age of the Spirit."[1] Indeed, Paul preaches Jesus's death and resurrection as the most important events in the history of the world. And he also preaches God's means of connecting unsaved persons with Jesus and his cross—union with Christ. Certainly, other New Testament authors write of union with Christ. This book treats union in Hebrews, 1–2 Peter, and Revelation. It acknowledges a significant doctrine of union in John's Gospel and first epistle. But, all things considered, Smedes is right: Paul is the "apostle of our union with Christ."

After devoting ten chapters to Paul's presentation of union with Christ in every letter except Titus (where it is absent), we now attempt to summarize Paul's teaching in two chapters. This chapter explores four Pauline themes of union:

- union in greetings
- "in Christ" language
- being "in" the Father and the Son
- participation in Jesus's narrative

---

[1] Lewis B. Smedes, *Union with Christ: A Biblical View of the New Life in Jesus Christ*, rev. ed. (Grand Rapids: Eerdmans, 1983), 26.

Union in Greetings

We begin by pointing to a neglected feature—the appearance of union in fully one-half of Paul's epistolary greetings at the beginning and end of his letters. Union pervades his thought.

> Paul, a servant of Christ Jesus, called to be an apostle . . . [of] Jesus Christ our Lord, through whom we have received grace and apostleship to bring about the obedience of faith for the sake of his name among all the nations, including *you who are called to belong to Jesus Christ*. (Rom. 1:1, 4–6)

> Greet Prisca and Aquila, my *fellow workers in Christ Jesus*. . . . Greet Andronicus and Junia . . . [who] were *in Christ* before me. Greet Ampliatus, *my beloved in the Lord*. Greet Urbanus, our *fellow worker in Christ*. . . . Greet Apelles, who is *approved in Christ*. . . . Greet *those in the Lord* who belong to the family of Narcissus. Greet those *workers in the Lord*, Tryphaena and Tryphosa. Greet the beloved Persis, who has *worked hard in the Lord*. Greet Rufus, *chosen in the Lord*. (16:3, 7–13)

> I Tertius, who wrote this letter, *greet you in the Lord*. (16:22)

> To the church of God that is in Corinth, to *those sanctified in Christ Jesus*, called to be saints together with all those who in every place call upon the name of our Lord Jesus Christ, both their Lord and ours. (1 Cor. 1:2)

> Aquila and Prisca, together with the church in their house, *send you hearty greetings in the Lord*. (16:19)

> My love be with you all *in Christ Jesus*. (16:24)

> To the saints who are in Ephesus, and are faithful *in Christ Jesus*. (Eph. 1:1)

> Tychicus the beloved brother and *faithful minister in the Lord* will tell you everything. (6:21)

> To all *the saints in Christ Jesus* who are at Philippi, with the overseers and deacons. (Phil. 1:1)

> Greet *every saint in Christ Jesus*. (4:21)

> To the saints and *faithful brothers in Christ* at Colossae. (Col. 1:2)

Tychicus will tell you all about my activities. He is a beloved brother and faithful minister and *fellow servant in the Lord*. (4:7)

See that you fulfill the ministry that you have received *in the Lord*. (4:17)

To the church of the Thessalonians *in God the Father and the Lord Jesus Christ*. (1 Thess. 1:1)

Rejoice always, pray without ceasing, give thanks in all circumstances; for this is *the will of God in Christ Jesus* for you. (5:16–18)

To the church of the Thessalonians *in God our Father and the Lord Jesus Christ*. (2 Thess. 1:1)

Paul, an apostle of Christ Jesus by the will of God according to the promise of *the life that is in Christ Jesus*. (2 Tim. 1:1)

Epaphras, my *fellow prisoner in Christ Jesus*, sends greetings to you. (Philem. 23)

Paul's mind is steeped in thoughts of union with Christ. If all thirteen of his epistles contained initial and final greetings, that would make twenty-six slots for greetings. Paul refers to union eighteen times (fifteen different occasions, as three occurrences overlap) in those initial and final greetings. Plainly, he thinks of union when beginning and finishing his letters. It is never far from his thoughts or prayers.

"In Christ" Language

When most people think of union with Christ, their minds immediately go to Paul's use of "in Christ" and its equivalents.[2] While the apostle's presentation of union with Christ is greater than these occurrences, "in Christ" language plays an important part in his thought. Accordingly, I will treat it among the themes and pictures that speak of union.

Again I gratefully acknowledge a debt to Constantine Campbell for his remarkable *Paul and Union with Christ: An Exegetical and Theological Study*.[3] I learned much from him and build upon his solid foundation of lexical semantics, exegesis, and theology. He considers the use of the preposition ἐν

---

[2] These include "in the Lord," "in the Lord Jesus," "in him," and "in whom."
[3] Constantine R. Campbell, *Paul and Union with Christ: An Exegetical and Theological Study* (Grand Rapids: Zondervan, 2012).

(*en*, "in") to be "flexible"; the role of its context to be most significant; the spatial sense to be primary; the idea of sphere, domain, or realm to be central in figurative uses; and the phrase "in Christ" (ἐν Χριστῷ/*en Christō*) to denote a "personal relatedness."[4]

I agree with these conclusions and draw special attention to the last one. "In Christ" language denotes "personal relatedness," a connection to the person of Christ. This is vital to our present concerns. In keeping with the flexibility of the preposition ἐν (*en*, "in"), our summary will show more than eight major nuances (shades of meaning) of usage of "in Christ" and its equivalents. Although recognizing these nuances is important to discourage a simplistic understanding of appearances of "in Christ," this could give a false impression. While I agree with Campbell's identification of various nuances in uses of "in Christ" language, I underscore his last point above—each usage of "in Christ" conveys personal relatedness in addition to any other meaning it may hold. I will label this idea of personal relatedness as a "broad sense" of "in Christ" language.

Here I introduce a distinction between "broad" and "narrow" senses of "in Christ" language. A *broad* sense primarily has another nuance besides direct union with Christ, while a *narrow* sense refers directly to union with Christ. Every use of "in Christ" communicates a connection between believers and Christ that pertains to union with Christ—union in a broad sense—even if many of these uses also have other nuances. So while we want to appreciate the trees—the nuances—we don't want to miss the forest—that "in Christ" language always speaks of union in a broad (indirect) sense.

In this section I will list the various major nuances of "in Christ" language and then focus on texts that teach union with Christ in a narrow (direct) sense. I will not attempt to include every nuance here but will only include references that have more than three occurrences. (There are many such minor nuances.) Major nuances include agency, association, cause, instrument, manner, object of faith, periphrasis for "Christian," and realm, sphere, or domain.

Agency

At least five "in Christ" texts teach agency, the idea that God accomplishes many things through Christ. Accordingly, therefore, the ESV translates 2 Corinthians 3:14: "Their [unbelieving Jews'] minds were hardened. For to

---

[4] Ibid., 73.

this day, when they read the old covenant, that same veil remains unlifted, because only *through Christ* is it taken away." In this category Christ is not merely the means (as in the category of instrument, below) but the originator of actions. Additional texts include Romans 14:14; Galatians 2:17; Ephesians 4:21; and Colossians 4:17.

Association

Five or more passages establish an association between Christ and believers, sometimes indicating close personal relationship or the idea of persons' being under Christ's influence. So Paul claims to speak under the influence of Christ when he confesses his love for fellow Jews: "I am speaking the truth *in Christ*—I am not lying; my conscience bears me witness in the Holy Spirit— that I have great sorrow and unceasing anguish in my heart" (Rom. 9:1–2). Other texts include Romans 3:24; 1 Corinthians 4:15; Colossians 2:6–7; and Philemon 20 (2x).

Cause

At least seventeen "in Christ" texts communicate cause, the idea that people do things because of Christ's person and work. Paul thus expresses the cause of his confidence in the Galatians: "I have confidence *in the Lord* that you will take no other view (Gal. 5:10). Additional texts include Romans 16:12; 2 Corinthians 2:14, 17; 12:19; Ephesians 3:12; 4:32; Philippians 2:1; 3:1, 3, 14; 4:4, 7, 10; 1 Thessalonians 5:12; 2 Timothy 1:13; and Philemon 8.

Instrument

Fifteen or more "in Christ" texts convey instrument, the idea that God accomplishes many things by means of Christ. This is similar to agency, though the former is used of the originator of actions. A good example is found in Romans 6:23: "The wages of sin is death, but the free gift of God is eternal life *in Christ Jesus our Lord.*" Other texts include 1 Corinthians 1:2, 4–5; 7:22; 11:11; 2 Corinthians 1:19–20; 2:12; 5:19; Galatians 3:14; Ephesians 1:3–4, 6; 2:10; 3:11; Colossians 2:15; 2 Thessalonians 1:12; and 2 Timothy 1:9.

Manner

At least eight texts present "in Christ" as the manner in which something is or should be done. Many times this means "in a manner pleasing to Christ."

Paul thus communicates his appreciation for Epaphroditus to the Philippians: "Receive him *in the Lord* with all joy" (Phil. 2:29). Other texts include Romans 15:17; 16:2; 1 Corinthians 4:17; 15:31; Ephesians 4:17; 1 Thessalonians 4:1; and 2 Thessalonians 3:12.

Object of Faith

Many texts use "in Christ" to present Jesus as the personal object of belief or hope. Paul does this when he writes, "If *in Christ* we have hope in this life only, we are of all people most to be pitied" (1 Cor. 15:19). Additional texts include Galatians 2:16 (3x); 3:26; Ephesians 1:1, 12–13, 15; Philippians 1:29; 2:19, 24; 3:9; Colossians 2:5; 1 Timothy 3:13; and 2 Timothy 3:15.

Periphrasis for "Christian"

Sometimes "in Christ" approximates our use of "Christian" as an adjective or noun. Paul instructs us: "A wife is bound to her husband as long as he lives. But if her husband dies, she is free to be married to whom she wishes, only *in the Lord*" (1 Cor. 7:39). Paul means that if she remarries, she must marry a *Christian* man. Other texts include Romans 16:3, 7–13; 1 Corinthians 3:1; 4:15, 17; 9:2; 16:19; 2 Corinthians 12:2; Galatians 1:22; Ephesians 6:21; Philippians 1:1, 14; 4:21; Colossians 1:2; 1 Thessalonians 2:14; and Philemon 16, 23.

Realm, Sphere, or Domain

This major category represents a locative used figuratively to indicate the realm over which Christ rules, his kingdom, often in contrast to the realm of Satan and sin. Romans 6:11 is a good example: "Consider yourselves dead to sin and alive to God *in Christ Jesus*." "In Christ Jesus" signifies the realm over which he rules in contrast to the realm of sin and death (vv. 6–9, 12–14). This usage also occurs in Romans 8:1–2; 12:5; 1 Corinthians 15:18, 22; 2 Corinthians 5:17; Galatians 2:4; 5:6; Ephesians 1:7, 11, 13; 2:13; 3:6; 5:8; 6:1; Philippians 4:1–2; Colossians 1:14; 2:11; 3:18, 20; 1 Thessalonians 4:16; 5:18; and 2 Timothy 2:1; 3:12.

Texts That Teach Union with Christ in a Narrow (Direct) Sense

We glimpsed eight main categories of meaning for "in Christ" and its synonyms. A point made previously bears reiteration. Even with the various nuances (shades of meaning) just seen, each nuance conveys a personal relationship between Christ and believers. Union-with-Christ language is more complicated than many of us have thought. But even with nuances, the idea of personal relationship—which we labeled union with Christ in a broad (indirect) sense—remains. Mark Seifrid puts it this way: "In varying ways, then, the expression 'in Christ' conveys Paul's belief that God's saving purposes are decisively effected through Christ."[5]

Nevertheless, there are at least seven texts Campbell identifies as communicating the nuance of union with Christ, and two that he missed.[6] I will refer to these as passages that speak of union with Christ in a narrow (direct) sense. They don't have other nuances (shades of meaning), but their nuance is union with Christ.

1 Corinthians 1:30–31. Paul gives a concise summary of salvation: "Because of him you are in Christ Jesus" (v. 30). It is "because of him"—God the Father in this context—that the Corinthians are united to Christ. Paul rarely says, "You are in Christ Jesus," as he does here, and this communicates union with Christ.[7] Ciampa and Rosner's words bear repeating: "To be saved is to be *in Christ*. . . . As the following four terms in v. 30 suggest, to be in Christ is to enjoy both a secure and objective status before God and a new mode of eschatological existence in solidarity with other believers."[8]

Christians possess the blessings of union with Christ not merely as private individuals but also communally. They are connected to Christ the Head as living members of his body. Paul mentions four benefits Christ gives them, the last three explaining the first. Christ "became to us wisdom from God," namely, "righteousness and sanctification and redemption" (v. 30). This wisdom clashes with that prized by the Corinthians—cultured rhetorical persuasion. Against this Paul praises the "folly" of God's wisdom, centered in preaching about Christ crucified. By God's grace the message of Jesus's crucifixion with its "weakness" and "folly" is shown to be a message of power and wisdom.

This same Christ, now risen and glorified, gives a salvation expressed in different pictures. The wisdom he became for us includes righteousness, holiness, and redemption, all of which Christ imparts to those united to him. He gives *righteousness*, a term that speaks of our acquittal by God the Judge,

---

[5] Mark A. Seifrid, "In Christ," in *Dictionary of Paul and His Letters*, ed. Gerald F. Hawthorne, Ralph P. Martin, and Daniel G. Reid (Downers Grove, IL: InterVarsity, 1993), 433.

[6] As he humbly and kindly admitted in an e-mail to me.

[7] So Campbell, *Paul and Union with Christ*, 132.

[8] Roy E. Ciampa and Brian S. Rosner, *The First Letter to the Corinthians*, The Pillar New Testament Commentary (Grand Rapids: Eerdmans, 2010), 108.

now and in the last judgment. He gives *holiness*, a term that speaks of God's making us his saints once and for all, and of our growth in purity and final presentation before God as sinless. He gives *redemption*, a term that speaks of our deliverance from sin's bondage by the payment of a ransom price, Christ's violent death. The wisdom that Christ became for us, then, has to do with gospel truth applied to life.

Paul explains the purpose of God's action in Christ: God chose "what is foolish. . . . weak . . . low and despised . . . even things that are not . . . so that no human being might boast in the presence of God" (vv. 26–29). Next he cites Jeremiah 9:23–24, "Let the one who boasts, boast in the Lord" (1 Cor. 1:31). Paul thus begins 1 Corinthians 1:30–31 by declaring union with Christ to be "because of him," namely God, and ends by directing all boasting to the Lord Jesus.

2 Corinthians 5:21. Paul brings together "in Christ" language and justification: "For our sake he made him to be sin who knew no sin, so that in him we might become the righteousness of God" (v. 21). "In him" here seems to indicate union with Christ directly, as Campbell concludes:

> Believers are made righteous by sharing in the righteousness of Christ. . . .
> Since Christ—who knew no sin—was made "sin," thus sharing in the plight of the sinful, so sinners are made righteous by sharing in his right standing. . . . The internal logic of the verse itself must finally be conclusive: ἐν αὐτῷ ["in him"] indicates union with Christ.[9]

2 Corinthians 13:3–6. Paul speaks ironically when he tells the Corinthians to test themselves to see whether they are Christians. His language is ironic because he *does* consider them to be believers. To be a Christian is to have "Jesus Christ in" you (v. 5). After the Corinthians examine themselves and find that Christ is in them, their conclusion must be that Paul is a genuine apostle, which his enemies have denied.

Even as Christ died in weakness and arose by God's power, so Paul is weak "in him" and "will live with him" by God's power (v. 4). Paul not only follows Christ as a ministry model; he also participates in his weakness and power. "In him," then, speaks here of union with Christ in his death and resurrection.[10]

Ephesians 1:7–10. After saying of believers, "In him we have redemption" (v. 7), Paul expands his purview in both time and space and declares that God

9 Campbell, *Paul and Union with Christ*, 186–87.
10 Ibid., 184.

made "known to us the mystery of his will, according to his purpose, which he set forth in Christ as a plan for the fullness of time, to unite all things in him" (vv. 9–10). Paul's words amaze. God's previously hidden plan, the "mystery of his will," fulfills his eternal purpose. And that purpose centers on Christ. The use of "in Christ" (v. 9) along with God's setting forth his plan to unite everything in Christ is one of a few times Paul employs "in Christ" to indicate union with Christ directly. Paul means "God has planned the revelation of his will in conjunction and in unity with Christ."[11]

The last use of "in him" (v. 10) is locative also and is used figuratively to portray Christ as the focal point. God plans to unite "all things" in heaven and earth in Christ as goal. As F. F. Bruce says, "It is equally 'in Christ' that he has planned to 'gather up' the fragmented and alienated universe. . . . All things, then, are to be 'summed up' in Christ and presented as a coherent totality in him."[12]

Ephesians 6:10–12. This is a spiritual-warfare text in which Paul charges readers to "put on the whole armor of God" in their battle against "cosmic powers over this present darkness" (vv. 11–12). Campbell points out that this recalls weapons used by Roman soldiers and also Isaiah's descriptions of Yahweh and Messiah in war.[13] He concludes that 6:10–17 implies Christians must put on the armor the Lord wears in battle, which suggests a sense of union with him in spiritual warfare. Since this union permeates the whole passage, a reasonable conclusion is that "in the Lord" in 6:10 expresses union with Christ.[14] Consequently, when Paul directs readers to be "strong in the Lord and in the strength of his might" (v. 10), he means they are to be strong because of their bond to the powerful Christ.

Philippians 3:8–11. Paul will lose all to obtain Christ and "be found in him" (v. 9). Here again the apostle uses "in him" to show union with Christ. Gerald Hawthorne's words describing Paul are notable: "He desires (and fully intends) to be found ἐν Χριστῷ, 'in Christ,' incorporate in him . . . and thus to stand before the Judge not presenting himself and his merits, but because he is in Christ, presenting Christ and the all-prevailing merits of Christ."[15]

Colossians 2:9–10. These verses are foundational to a doctrine of union with Christ: "In him the whole fullness of deity dwells bodily, and you have

---

[11] Ibid., 189.
[12] F. F. Bruce, *The Epistles to the Colossians, to Philemon, and to the Ephesians*, The New International Commentary on the New Testament (Grand Rapids: Eerdmans, 1984), 261.
[13] Campbell, *Paul and Union with Christ*, 153.
[14] Ibid., 151–53.
[15] Gerald F. Hawthorne, *Philippians*, Word Biblical Commentary (Waco, TX: Word, 1983), 140.

been filled in him, who is the head of all rule and authority." Verse 9 tells of Christ's union with God. Verse 10 tells of our union with Christ. Campbell correctly argues that "you have been filled in him" expresses union with Christ: "Believers are 'filled' because of their union in him. . . . The verses to either side of 2:10 . . . contain several references to the realities that believers share with Christ through their union and participation with him."[16] Given that its context so strongly commends union with Christ, we are to interpret "in him" in 2:10 in the same manner.

Paul here connects Christ, in whom all the fullness of deity is embodied, and believers. When Christians are united to him spiritually, they are united to the living God. Paul teaches that the Colossians are made complete in a living bond with this divine Christ. They lack nothing. Speaking of the proponents of the Colossian heresy, Moo draws a sound conclusion: "Against those claims Paul asserts again the exclusivity of Christ. In him, and in him alone, God has decisively and exhaustively revealed himself. All that we can know or experience of God is therefore found in our relationship with him."[17]

1 Thessalonians 1:1; 2 Thessalonians 1:1–2. For completeness I list these two texts here. But given their uniqueness, I will treat them below under the heading "Being 'in' the Father and the Son."

Conclusion

Paul's writings are replete with references to "in Christ," "in Christ Jesus," "in him," "in whom," and "in the Lord," which all have the same referent—Jesus Christ. Most of these references refer to union not in the narrow and direct sense but in a broad and indirect sense. That is, union with Christ is not their precise and only nuance; they have other nuances, or shades of meaning. But they always show connectedness to Christ.

Various nuances. These various nuances (shades of meaning) are important in drawing attention to Christ's person and work applied to individuals and churches. Their variety highlights various manifestations of the application of salvation. Salvation is always "in Christ," always in relation to him. And this relation is expressed as agency, association, cause, instrument, manner, object of faith, periphrasis for "Christian," or realm, among many other minor ways.

---

[16] Campbell, *Paul and Union with Christ*, 181.
[17] Douglas J. Moo, *The Letters to the Colossians and to Philemon*, The Pillar New Testament Commentary (Grand Rapids: Eerdmans, 2008), 195.

I have chosen these eight major nuances out of twenty or more. Paul uses "in Christ" language to show agency and instrumentality, the idea that God accomplishes salvation and other things through Christ. We may distinguish agency from the similar idea of instrumentality by ascribing to the former origination of the specified action. When Paul uses "in Christ" to portray Christ as agent, Christ himself takes the initiative. When Paul portrays Christ as instrument, God the Father takes the initiative and accomplishes good things through his Son. Both agency and instrumentality set forth Christ as the "one mediator between God and men, the man Christ Jesus" (1 Tim. 2:5).

Paul also uses "in Christ" and synonyms to depict an association between Christ and his people. At times this association sets forth persons as influenced by Christ. The apostle uses "in Christ" terminology to present Jesus as the cause of various things, including various ministries. Christians engage in diverse enterprises because of the person and work of Christ.

Sometimes "in Christ" language is used to show that the manner in which believers do many things is affected by their relationship to Christ. At times this portrays a manner pleasing to Christ. Many times Paul employs "in Christ" nomenclature to set forth Christ as the object of saving faith; Christian faith and hope are in him.

Paul uses "in Christ" so commonly that it becomes a way for him to replicate the adjective or noun "Christian" when referring to people, roles, or churches.

Most often the apostle uses "in Christ" and equivalents to depict the realm, domain, or sphere over which Christ is Lord. This is frequently set over against the realm of Satan, sin, and death. Jesus is Christus Victor in his death and resurrection, defeating our foes and giving us the victory by transferring us into his domain. God's people submit to Christ's rule, enjoy its many benefits, and stand strong against God's enemies.

Union with Christ as a nuance. As we have seen, though these expressions have many different shades of meaning (nuances), they all establish a relationship between human beings and Christ, which we have called union in a broad sense. But at a minimum nine occurrences speak of union with Christ in a narrow (direct) sense—their nuance *is* union. Christians are in union with Christ corporately and individually. Moreover, they have a secure status before God and a new manner of life in common with other believers. Because of God the Father they "are in Christ Jesus who became to [them] wisdom from God, righteousness and sanctification and redemption" (1 Cor.

1:30). The crucified Christ, who to the world is nothing but foolishness and weakness, is to believers God's wisdom and power. The crucified one is the risen one, and in union with him ours are all the blessings of salvation. The result? We do not boast in the world, or ourselves, but in him who loved us and gave himself for us (vv. 29, 31).

Justification, along with every aspect of the application of salvation, comes to us in union with Christ. Believers, therefore, are declared righteous "in him" (2 Cor. 5:21). Christ shared in the plight of sinners; by grace through faith union, believers share in him and his saving righteousness.

Union with Christ is so determinative of salvation for the apostle that he describes Christians this way: "Jesus Christ is in you" (2 Cor. 13:5). As a corollary of this principle, those who do not have Christ in them "fail to meet the test" of Christian identity (v. 5)! In addition, union with the crucified and risen Christ not only makes people Christians in the first place. As they serve God, they continue to participate in Christ's death and resurrection ("He was crucified in weakness, but lives by the power of God," v. 4). So Paul attests, "We also are weak in him, but in dealing with you we will live with him by the power of God" (v. 4).

Western Christians too easily individualize and contemporize the Christian faith. We focus on ourselves as individuals and the time in which we live. While this is not completely wrong, it is shortsighted in two ways. First, Scripture takes a larger view: God joins individuals to his Son to make up the church. Union with Christ means union with other believers. Moreover, Paul startles us by taking a much larger view: God plans "to unite *all things* in" Christ, "things in heaven and things on earth" (Eph. 1:10). Paul views union with Christ and what it accomplishes—salvation—as individual, corporate, and cosmic.

Second, though we should not neglect the present, a biblical worldview demands that we expand our horizons in light of God's past eternal plan and future eternal goal. In eternity past (v. 4) God formulated his purpose to bring all things together in his Son. This will happen only in the "fullness of time" (10), that is, when Christ returns. Christ-centeredness takes on new meaning when we realize Christ will be the center of a reunited world, for it is God's plan to unite "all things" in Christ as goal.

In a spiritual-warfare passage Paul commands believers to "put on the whole armor of God" as they war against "cosmic powers over this present darkness" (Eph. 6:11–12). While it is common to note Paul's appeal to Roman military armor and weapons, it is not as common to note his appeal to Isaiah's descriptions of Yahweh and Messiah engaged in war. When the armor is seen in this light, readers discover a picture of union with Christ. Christians are to put on the Lord's armor, "which evokes a sense of union with him in the matter of spiritual warfare."[18] Hence, when Paul writes, "Be strong *in the Lord* and in the strength of his might" (v. 10), he urges readers to be strong due to their tie to the mighty Christ.

Paul will give up everything, including ancestry and reputation, because of the "surpassing worth of knowing Christ Jesus my Lord" (Phil. 3:8). He regards his former laurels not only as loss; he now regards them as "rubbish" (v. 8). Why? To "gain Christ and be found in him, not having a righteousness of my own . . . but that which comes through faith in Christ" (vv. 8–9). Paul is willing to exchange everything for Christ, for in so doing he gains Christ and his righteousness. Campbell is convincing: to be found "in him" (v. 9) here expresses union with Christ: "Paul has gained Christ, he is found in him, and he shares his righteousness . . . because of the personal nature of gaining Christ."[19] Here justification is a subset of union with Christ. Gaining Christ, we gain all the blessings of salvation, including saving righteousness.

This profound text is basic to an understanding of union with Christ: "In him the whole fullness of deity dwells bodily, and you have been filled in him, who is the head of all rule and authority" (Col. 2:9–10). First, Paul speaks of Christ's union with God. Then the apostle speaks of our union with Christ. The two ideas are inseparable. It is only because Christ as God incarnate is one with God that we in Christ become one with God. Of course, Christ's union is by nature, and ours by grace. He is God in the flesh; we are sinners joined to God in Christ. Consequently, Paul here joins Christ, in whom all the fullness of deity lives in a body, and Christians, who are given fullness in him. The Colossians, indeed all of God's people, are made complete in a living union with this divine Christ. They find all they need in union with him.

Being "in" the Father and the Son

> Paul, Silvanus, and Timothy,
>> To the church of the Thessalonians in God the Father and the Lord Jesus Christ:
>> Grace to you and peace. (1 Thess. 1:1)

---

[18] So Campbell, *Paul and Union with Christ*, 151–53.
[19] Ibid., 187–88.

Paul, Silvanus, and Timothy,

To the church of the Thessalonians in God our Father and the Lord Jesus Christ:

Grace to you and peace from God our Father and the Lord Jesus Christ. (2 Thess. 1:1–2)

After including Silvanus and Timothy, his companions in planting the Thessalonian church, as co-senders of this letter, Paul describes that church in a unique manner. Only in these two places in his epistles does he describe believers as "in God the Father and the Lord Jesus Christ," where the preposition "in" goes with both Father and Son.[20]

This unique phenomenon has elicited varied responses. Some have rejected as "non-Pauline" the possibility that Paul writes of union with the Father and the Son.[21] It is better, however, to allow the letters themselves to define what is Pauline. It is plain to me that Paul uses "in Christ" language of both Father and Son in the first verse of each Thessalonians letter. Bruce argues that since "in . . . the Lord Jesus Christ" here denotes union with Christ, "then 'in God the Father' must be understood in the same way."[22]

Bruce's reasoning convinces me and others, including Gene Green, Gordon Fee, and Leon Morris.[23] Nevertheless, we must recognize the uniqueness of Paul's opening words in his two Thessalonian epistles. Fee, speaking of 2 Thessalonians, is accurate: "Paul has here repeated the unique feature, found elsewhere only in 1 Thessalonians, of designating the church as existing simultaneously in God the Father and the Lord Jesus Christ."[24]

The first verses of both Thessalonian letters impact our understanding of union with Christ, as Green explains: "The *church of the Thessalonians* finds its unique identity in its union or relationship with *God the Father* and the exalted *Lord Jesus Christ*."[25] In these verses Paul teaches a doctrine of union with God the Father and his Christ. With distinctive genre and idiom, Paul overlaps John's record of Jesus's prayer on behalf of believers in John 17. John's

[20] They are identical, except 2 Thess. 1:1 substitutes "our" for "the" between "God" and "Father" and adds "from God our Father and the Lord Jesus Christ" after "Grace to you and peace."
[21] So Earl J. Richard, *First and Second Thessalonians*, Sacra Pagina (Collegeville, MN: Liturgical Press, 1995), 41, and Ernest Best, *A Commentary on the First and Second Epistles to the Thessalonians*, Harper's New Testament Commentaries (New York: Harper and Row, 1972), 62.
[22] F. F. Bruce, *1 & 2 Thessalonians*, Word Biblical Commentary (Waco, TX: Word, 1982), 7.
[23] See Gene L. Green, *The Letters to the Thessalonians*, The Pillar New Testament Commentary (Grand Rapids: Eerdmans, 2002), 85; Gordon D. Fee, *The First and Second Epistles to the Thessalonians*, The New International Commentary on the New Testament (Grand Rapids: Eerdmans, 2009), 15; and Leon Morris, *The First and Second Epistles to the Thessalonians*, The New International Commentary on the New Testament, rev. ed. (Grand Rapids: Eerdmans, 1991), 35–36.
[24] Fee, *First and Second Epistles to the Thessalonians*, 245.
[25] Green, *Letters to the Thessalonians*, 85, emphasis original.

report of Jesus's words to the Father "that they also may be in us" (v. 21) is akin to Paul's epistolary address to "the church of the Thessalonians in God the Father and the Lord Jesus Christ" (1 Thess. 1:1; cf. 2 Thess. 1:1). Both express an exalted view of Christians' union with the Godhead that should both humble and amaze us. It is astounding that God should express his love for his people by joining them to the Father and Son (and Spirit)!

Participation in Jesus's Narrative

Uniquely in Scripture Paul teaches that Christians take part in Jesus's narrative. They do not participate in every aspect of his story. They do not become incarnate with him, live a sinless life with him, pour out the Spirit with him, or make intercession with him. But they do share in many of his redemptive experiences. Specifically, they die with him, are buried with him, are raised with him, ascend with him, sit down with him in heaven, and amazingly, in a sense will even come again with him.

Romans 6:1–14

Believers were crucified with Christ (v. 6), have a part in his death (vv. 5, 8) and resurrection (v. 5), and "will also live with him" (v. 8). Our spiritual connection with him in his death and resurrection is the basis for victorious Christian living now (vv. 4, 6–7, 11, 13). Union with Christ in his death breaks the power of sin over believers. Sin has no more right to lord over us (v. 6); Jesus does! And union with Christ in his resurrection enables believers to walk in newness of life (v. 4). This is why Paul enjoins, "Consider yourselves dead to sin and alive to God in Christ Jesus" (v. 11). Our participation in Christ's story is also the basis of future salvation—bodily resurrection (vv. 5, 8).

Romans 7:4–6

Believers take part in Jesus's story. Here we "have died to the law through the body of Christ" (7:4). Co-crucifixion with Christ has liberated us from the bondage of the law that characterizes this age. When he died, we died, and we now are not enslaved to the law but belong to the risen Christ. In his death and resurrection he has inaugurated a new era, and by our taking part in his story, we too are "released from the law, having died to that which held us captive, so that we serve in the new way of the Spirit and not in the old way of the written code" (v. 6).

Romans 8:15–19

Paul rejoices in our adoption by God. The "Spirit of adoption" has enabled us to call God "Father" in truth (v. 15). Consequently, we are no longer sin's slaves but God's children. The Spirit also bears witness within of our sonship (v. 16). And with adoption comes inheritance: "If children, then heirs—heirs of God and fellow heirs with Christ" (v. 17). But all this is true only for genuine sons, those bearing a family resemblance to the Father and the Son. That is why Paul adds the stipulation, "provided we suffer with him in order that we may also be glorified with him." Only those joined to Christ in his death and resurrection are true sons of God. Union in his saving events means complete salvation—now and forever. But union with him in his death also means suffering with him in the present, just as union with him in his resurrection will mean glorification with him in the future.

2 Corinthians 4:8–14

The good news is a "treasure" (v. 7) entrusted to us by God for his glory, though we are beset with human weaknesses. God is triumphant despite and even through human weakness, exemplifying the principle of Christ's crucifixion. Paul tells us of Jesus's crucifixion ("death of Jesus," v. 10) and resurrection ("life of Jesus," v. 10). Union with Christ defines our existence as Christians. Therefore, we always bear in "the body the death of Jesus, so that the life of Jesus may also be manifested in our bodies" (v. 10).

Verse 11 reiterates the previous verse. Next Paul makes known his intent to suffer and persevere so that the Corinthians may know now and at the end of the age the same resurrection life of Christ that Paul does (vv. 12–13). He and the other apostles minister with confidence, says Paul, that "he who raised the Lord Jesus will raise us also with Jesus and bring us with you into his presence" (v. 14). Death does not destroy our union with Christ. Instead, we die in the Lord and are raised "with Jesus" (v. 14). Union with Christ, then, saves us once and for all, preserves us, and will yet bring us to our resurrected life on the new earth.

Galatians 2:17–20

Because Paul has been spiritually linked to Christ in his death, he no longer lives, but "Christ . . . lives in" him (v. 20). Paul does not repress his personality but instead affirms that the old Paul, his identity in Adam, has died with Christ. Christ's resurrection has brought the new age, and Christians now enjoy the life of that age. Paul affirms that he is indwelt by Christ. This passage fittingly coordinates crucifixion with Christ and his indwelling of believers. Jesus died and arose outside of us but comes to make his home with us and makes us his own people.[26] Indeed, indwelling *is* union with Christ in an ongoing and dynamic way.

Ephesians 2:4–10

Christians were joined to Christ in his resurrection and his sitting at God's right hand. This implies that they were joined to Christ in his ascension, too. Twice Paul says we were spiritually dead, devoid of God's life (vv. 1, 5). We were unable to make ourselves alive, but God graciously "made us alive together with Christ" (v. 5). The Father regenerated us by spiritually linking us to the risen Christ.

Paul reiterates: God "raised us up with him" and, Paul says, "seated us with him in the heavenly places in Christ Jesus" (v. 6). Our bond with Christ is so dynamic and indestructible that it is as if we ascended with him and sat down in heaven with him! Frank Thielman captures the spirit of the text: "Here salvation is something that is emphatically present for believers. They have already been made alive with Christ, already raised with him, and even already seated with him in heavenly places. Their resurrection has, in some sense, already taken place (cf. Col. 3:1)."[27] And that is not all! God united us to his Son "so that in the coming ages he might show the immeasurable riches of his grace in kindness toward us in Christ Jesus" (Eph. 2:7). Bruce waxes eloquent:

> In thus lavishing his mercy on sinners, giving them a share in Christ's risen life and in his exaltation, God has a further purpose—namely, that they should serve as a demonstration of his grace to all succeeding ages. . . . Throughout time and in eternity the church, this society of pardoned rebels, is designed by God to be the masterpiece of his goodness.[28]

Philippians 3:8–11

Paul repudiates all he once counted on to make God accept him—his bloodline and accomplishments—in order to gain Christ himself. He wants the

---

[26] I acknowledge help from Thomas R. Schreiner, *Galatians*, Zondervan Exegetical Commentary on the New Testament (Grand Rapids: Zondervan, 2010), 172.

[27] Frank Thielman, *Ephesians*, Baker Exegetical Commentary on the New Testament (Grand Rapids: Baker Academic, 2010), 135.

[28] F. F. Bruce, *The Epistles to the Colossians, to Philemon, and to the Ephesians*, The New International Commentary on the New Testament (Grand Rapids: Eerdmans, 1984), 288.

righteousness of Christ applied to his spiritual bank account. This righteousness comes from grace and is received through trusting Christ (v. 9). Paul's
goal is to know Christ better.

Growing in relationship with Christ involves experiencing the power of
Christ's resurrection, which in turn means sharing in his sufferings. We are
linked to Christ once for all at conversion so that his death and resurrection
save us. We are linked to him also progressively in the Christian life (v. 10). In
fact, seen from the perspective of union with Christ, the Christian life *is* participating in Jesus's sufferings and depending on the power of his resurrection.

Paul's consummate goal is to die in Christ and be raised from the dead to
eternal life on the last day. Although it is still future and in that sense unrealized, with humility and confidence in Christ the apostle looks forward to the
resurrection of his body (vv. 10–11).

Colossians 2:11–15

Combating heretics, Paul contends that in Christ the "whole fullness of deity
dwells bodily" (v. 9), and believers "have been filled in him" (v. 10). Telling
how that filling came about, he astonishingly informs Gentile readers that "in
him also you were circumcised" (v. 11)! He does not mean literal circumcision. Instead, he speaks of a "circumcision made without hands, by putting off
the body of the flesh, by the circumcision of Christ" (v. 11). This is a spiritual
circumcision. It occurs "in him," that is, in union with Christ. Though not all
agree, I take "circumcision of Christ" to refer to the circumcision performed
by Christ,[29] for Paul identifies it with a "circumcision made without hands."
As the Jewish *mohel* circumcises the flesh of males, so Christ spiritually circumcises males and females who trust him (v. 12). Thus he puts "off the body
of the flesh," bringing forgiveness by his spiritual circumcision.

Christ spiritually circumcises the Colossian believers at baptism (v. 12).
Christian baptism and spiritual circumcision overlap in meaning. They both
signify cleansing from sin. Of course, baptism does not automatically produce
cleansing. Paul here teaches that believers are united to Christ in baptism. It
signifies union with Christ in his death and resurrection (v. 12). Via union
with Christ we take part in his death, burial, and resurrection so that they
become *our* death, burial, and resurrection. Because we died with him, as is
evidenced in our "having been buried with him," we are forgiven. His death

---

[29] See pp. 158–59 for discussion.

counts for us. Because we were "raised with him," we have new life owing to the "powerful working of God, who raised him from the dead" (v. 12).

Colossians 2:20–23

Paul scolds the Colossians for subjecting themselves to worldly regulations that require abstinence from "food and drink" (v. 16), for such are built on "human precepts and teachings" (v. 22) and make an outward show of religiosity and self-denial but do not further holiness (v. 23). The basis for Paul's appeal is union with Christ in his death. "If with Christ you died to the elemental spirits of the world, why . . . do you submit to regulations?" (v. 20). True believers in Christ died with him to the "elemental spirits of the world," that is, "those deities or spirits who were so closely associated with the elements."[30] By writing "if," Paul wants readers to examine themselves to see whether they really are united to Jesus in his death. If so, they are to reject false teachers' temptations to repress physical appetites in order to appease demons (v. 22). Here union with Christ in his death triumphs over evil spiritual beings, as Paul taught earlier (vv. 14–15).

Colossians 3:1–4

Paul opposes the false teachers' asceticism, telling readers not to dwell on "things that are on earth" (v. 2). He points them in another direction twice— "above" (vv. 1–2). He does so because "above" is "where Christ is, seated at the right hand of God." Christ is the cure to the false teachers' disastrous teaching (2:8–15) and fruitless asceticism (vv. 16–23).

Paul points to union with Christ in his narrative as motivation to "seek" him. In light of his readers' union with Christ in his death (3:3; cf. 2:20) and resurrection (3:1), Paul explains, "Your life is hidden with Christ in God" (v. 3). They are to concentrate on Christ in heaven and draw energy for everyday life on earth from their union with him.

Incredibly, Paul extends our sharing in Jesus's story. We participate not only in his death, burial, resurrection, ascension, and session. We will participate also in his return! Paul writes, "When Christ who is your life appears," referring to his second coming, "then you also will appear with him in glory" (v. 4). These last words refer to *our* "appearance," our second coming, so to speak. Paul comprehensively depicts believers' union with Christ by saying

---

[30] Moo, *Letters to the Colossians and to Philemon*, 191.

that, in a sense, we will come again with him. Now our true spiritual identity is only partially revealed. Only at Jesus's return will that identity be manifested!

1 Thessalonians 5:9-10

Paul penned 1 Thessalonians to correct false ideas about the second coming. His readers feared that deceased Christians would miss out on that joyous event. Also, their zeal for Christ's return and their experience of intense persecution raised questions about the timing of the day of the Lord. Paul assures them that deceased believers would not miss out; the day of the Lord has not come (4:13–5:11). God has not chosen his people, including the Thessalonians (1:4–5), to experience his wrath. Rather, he elected them to "obtain salvation through our Lord Jesus Christ" (5:9).

Jesus loved his people and gave himself up for them, dying in their place (v. 10). He did this "so that whether we are awake or asleep we might live" (v. 10). Christ's death obtains eternal life for living and deceased believers. Paul's focus is on future resurrection life. He expresses this hope concisely: "so that . . . we might live with him." The last two words express final union with Christ.

2 Timothy 2:11-13

In his fifth faithful saying Paul offers a hymn or confession from the early church: "If we have died with him, we will also live with him" (v. 11). Paul means that if we have been joined to Christ in his death, we will also be joined to him in his resurrection. "If we endure, we will also reign with him" (v. 12). If professed believers persevere to the end, they will be saved finally and reign with Christ in glory.

Paul writes: "If we deny him, he also will deny us" (v. 12). These words belong to church members' communal profession of faith. Those who continue will reign with Christ (v. 12). But if some professing Christians subsequently reject Christ, "if through their lives they deny knowing him by their word and deed,"[31] then Christ also will reject them. And this rejection is final and terrible. As George Knight articulates, "The denial by Christ . . . is that future final evaluation which he will make to the Father (Mt. 10:33)."[32]

In God's grace, no sooner are these difficult words confessed publicly than

---

[31] William D. Mounce, *Pastoral Epistles*, Word Biblical Commentary (Nashville: Thomas Nelson, 2000), 519.
[32] George W. Knight III, *Commentary on the Pastoral Epistles*, New International Greek Testament Commentary (Grand Rapids: Eerdmans, 1992), 406.

words of comfort are right on their heels: "If we are faithless, he remains faithful—for he cannot deny himself" (v. 13). If we fail, and at times even fall, God still is our strong tower. He is dependable even when we are not. Being unfaithful here is not as serious as denying him in the previous line. We are all unfaithful at times, but genuine believers do not deny him totally and finally, as apostates do. Although the church is composed of unsteady people, its ultimate success depends on the faithfulness of God, who cannot deny himself. As for those who truly "have died with him," just as truly they "will also live with him" (v. 11).

Conclusion

Paul teaches that when believers in Christ are united to him by faith, they participate in his story. They are united to him in everything, from his death to his second coming and beyond. This theme appears in at least twelve texts: Romans 6:1–14; 7:4–6; 8:15–19; 2 Corinthians 4:8–14; Galatians 2:17–20; Ephesians 2:4–10; Philippians 3:8–11; Colossians 2:11–15; 2:20–23; 3:1–4; 1 Thessalonians 5:9–10; and 2 Timothy 2:11–13.

Christians share in many events in Jesus's narrative, including his

- suffering (Rom. 8:17; Phil. 3:10),
- death (Rom. 6:3, 6, 8; 7:4; 2 Cor. 4:10; Gal. 2:20; Phil. 3:10; Col. 2:20; 3:3; 2 Tim. 2:11),
- burial (Rom. 6:4; Col. 2:12),
- being made alive (Eph. 2:5; Col. 2:13),
- life (1 Thess. 5:10; 2 Tim. 2:11),
- resurrection (Rom. 6:4–5, 8; 7:4; 2 Cor. 4:10–11, 14; Eph. 2:6; Col. 2:12; 3:1),
- being seated in heaven (Eph. 2:6),
- being hidden in God (Col. 3:3),
- return (Col. 3:4; cf. Rom. 8:19),
- glory (Rom. 8:17),
- reign (2 Tim. 2:12).

Paul thus teaches that believers share in everything from Jesus's suffering to his second coming and reign. This is because we share in *him*. In being joined spiritually to him, we participate in his story. His story becomes our story.

A few qualifications are in order. We do not share in his incarnation. The Son of God's becoming the Son of Man is unique. Neither do we share in his sinless life (although its effects are imputed to us in justification, 2 Cor. 5:21). We do not share in his pouring out the Holy Spirit at Pentecost; that is a unique and unrepeatable event of Christ. Neither do we share in his intercession, when he prays for us and presents his finished work in the Father's heavenly presence. These events of Christ are his alone and are not shared.

If we do not share in his sinless life, then to what does his "suffering" refer in the above list (and texts on which it is based)? It refers to our being united to Christ in his crucifixion, and as a result suffering in the Christian life. This is the same idea Paul refers to in Colossians 1:24–25, though he does not use union-with-Christ language: "Now I rejoice in my sufferings for your sake, and in my flesh I am filling up what is lacking in Christ's afflictions for the sake of his body, that is, the church, of which I became a minister."

So our union with Christ's saving events begins with his sufferings on the cross. It ends with his return and reign. As I explained previously, Colossians 3:4 ascribes to believers a second coming, so to speak.[33] I say "so to speak" because he alone is the Redeemer and we are the redeemed. Nevertheless, our union with him is so intimate, definitive, and permanent that there is a sense in which we will return and reign with him. This is because our identity and existence are bound up with him and our union with him.

In other words, our true identity as his sons or daughters is revealed only partially now. On the last day, however, it will be fully revealed. Or, to use Paul's expression: "I consider that the sufferings of this present time are not worth comparing with the glory that is to be revealed to us. For the creation waits with eager longing for *the revealing* of the sons of God" (Rom. 8:18–19). We will be "revealed," have a "revelation" (another word referring to the second coming), only when Jesus is revealed in his second coming. It is no accident that Romans 8:18 refers to the "glory . . . to be revealed to [or "in"] us." Colossians 3:4 says the same: "When Christ who is your life appears, then you also will appear with him in glory." Union with Christ in his second coming is inseparable from glorification.

What is the upshot of Paul's teaching that we participate in Christ's narrative? It powerfully communicates that Christ's redemptive deeds applied are the only antidote to the poison of sin. Altogether there are nine redemptive deeds: two essential presuppositions (Christ's incarnation and sinless life), the heart and soul of his redemptive accomplishment (his death and

---

[33] See pp. 163–64.

resurrection), and five essential results of his cross and empty tomb (his ascension, session, giving the Spirit, intercession, and return). We must get this right: the center of his saving accomplishment is his death and resurrection.[34]

Jesus's death and resurrection are the only remedy to the disease of sin. This is true in all of sin's aspects with respect to past, present, and future. Christ's cross and empty tomb *saved* us from sin's *penalty* in justification (a subset of union). "There is therefore now no condemnation for those who are in Christ Jesus" (Rom. 8:1). Condemnation is the Pauline opposite of justification. The latter is God's declaration of righteousness based on Christ's righteousness (in his life and death). Condemnation is God's declaration of judgment based on sinners' thoughts, words, and deeds. Justification and condemnation are the verdicts of the Judge on the last day. But by virtue of the already/not yet pattern, those verdicts are announced ahead of time based upon persons' relationship to Christ. Of course, the words of Romans 8:1 apply only to those who have trusted Christ's propitiation and righteousness for their standing with God (3:25–26; 5:18–19).

Christ's death and resurrection *save* us from sin's *power* in progressive sanctification (a subset of union). "We were buried therefore with him by baptism into death, in order that, just as Christ was raised from the dead by the glory of the Father, we too might walk in newness of life" (6:4).

The Savior's atonement and resurrection life *will save* us from sin's *presence* in glorification (and final sanctification, subsets of union). "Since, therefore, we have now been justified by his blood, much more *shall we be saved* by him from the wrath of God. For if while we were enemies we were reconciled to God by the death of his Son, much more, now that we are reconciled, *shall we be saved* by his life" (5:9–10).

It is important not to lose sight of the forest for the trees. Justification, progressive sanctification, and glorification are all subsets of union with Christ. When we say, then, that Christ's death and resurrection are the only answer to sin, we mean in union with Christ. Union with Christ is another way of speaking of the application of salvation, which is Christ's death and resurrection (and more!).

Participation in Jesus's saving events gives great confidence to God's people, as Moo points out, commenting on Colossians 3:3:

---

[34] For exposition of Christ's nine saving events, see Robert A. Peterson, *Salvation Accomplished by the Son: The Work of Christ* (Wheaton, IL: Crossway, 2012), 21–269.

Paul may intend another nuance in asserting that our lives are "hidden" with God. BDAG classify *kryptō* ("hide") in this verse under the meaning "hide in a safe place." This extension of meaning is quite natural, since hiding is often the way that people find safety and security when enemies are pursuing them (e.g., 1 Sam. 13:6). Several Old Testament texts suggest that "hide" can carry the connotations of safety and security. Psalm 27:5 is especially clear: "For in the day of trouble he will keep me safe in his dwelling; he will hide me in the shelter of his tabernacle and set me high upon a rock."

The phrase "in God" at the end of the verse may also point in this direction. Therefore, Paul's claim that the lives of believers are now hidden with Christ may be more than simply the "setup" for the emphasis on future revelation in v. 4. It may also remind us that the time between our initial identification with Christ and the revelation of that status on the last day is a time when God is working to keep us secure in that relationship. As Paul put it earlier: we have a "hope stored up for [us] in heaven" (Col. 1:5).[35]

---

[35] Moo, *Letters to the Colossians and to Philemon*, 250–51.

Chapter 16

A Summary of Union with Christ in Paul's Letters (2)

"In our summary probe of the center of Paul's theology, there is another factor that needs to be noted, the union of Christians with Christ. . . . It is of paramount importance for Paul, absolutely decisive for what falls within the purview of matters 'of first importance.'"[1] These words by Richard Gaffin are full of wisdom: union is enormously important for Paul, of even first importance. Accordingly, we devote a second chapter to our summary of Paul's presentation of union with Christ by pulling together his treatment of six more pictures and themes:

- body of Christ
- temple
- marriage
- new clothing
- filled to all the fullness
- indwelling

Body of Christ

Paul employs the "body of Christ" image, one of his favorite pictures of the church, many times:

---

[1] Richard B. Gaffin, Jr., *By Faith, Not by Sight: Paul and the Order of Salvation*, 2nd ed. (Phillipsburg, NJ: P&R, 2013), 40.

As in one body we have many members, and the members do not all have the same function, so we, though many, are one body in Christ, and individually members one of another. (Rom. 12:4–5)

Do you not know that your bodies are members of Christ? Shall I then take the members of Christ and make them members of a prostitute? Never! Or do you not know that he who is joined to a prostitute becomes one body with her? For, as it is written, "The two will become one flesh." (1 Cor. 6:15–16)

Just as the body is one and has many members, and all the members of the body, though many, are one body, so it is with Christ. For in one Spirit we were all baptized into one body—Jews or Greeks, slaves or free—and all were made to drink of one Spirit.

For the body does not consist of one member but of many. If the foot should say, "Because I am not a hand, I do not belong to the body," that would not make it any less a part of the body. And if the ear should say, "Because I am not an eye, I do not belong to the body," that would not make it any less a part of the body. If the whole body were an eye, where would be the sense of hearing? If the whole body were an ear, where would be the sense of smell? But as it is, God arranged the members in the body, each one of them, as he chose. If all were a single member, where would the body be? As it is, there are many parts, yet one body.

The eye cannot say to the hand, "I have no need of you," nor again the head to the feet, "I have no need of you." On the contrary, the parts of the body that seem to be weaker are indispensable, and on those parts of the body that we think less honorable we bestow the greater honor, and our unpresentable parts are treated with greater modesty, which our more presentable parts do not require. But God has so composed the body, giving greater honor to the part that lacked it, that there may be no division in the body, but that the members may have the same care for one another. If one member suffers, all suffer together; if one member is honored, all rejoice together.

Now you are the body of Christ and individually members of it. (1 Cor. 12:12–27)

There is one body and one Spirit—just as you were called to the one hope that belongs to your call—one Lord, one faith, one baptism, one God and Father of all, who is over all and through all and in all. . . . He gave the apostles, the prophets, the evangelists, the shepherds and teachers, to equip the saints for the work of ministry, for building up the body of Christ. . . . Speaking the truth in love, we are to grow up in every way into him who is the head, into Christ, from whom the whole body, joined and held together by every joint with which it is equipped, when each part is working properly, makes the body grow so that it builds itself up in love. (Eph. 4:4–6, 11–12, 15–16)

The husband is the head of the wife even as Christ is the head of the church, his body, and is himself its Savior. . . . No one ever hated his own flesh, but nourishes and cherishes it, just as Christ does the church, because we are members of his body. (Eph. 5:23, 29–30)

He is the head of the body, the church. (Col. 1:18)

Now I rejoice in my sufferings for your sake, and in my flesh I am filling up what is lacking in Christ's afflictions for the sake of his body, that is, the church. (Col. 1:24)

Let no one disqualify you, insisting on asceticism and worship of angels, going on in detail about visions, puffed up without reason by his sensuous mind, and not holding fast to the Head, from whom the whole body, nourished and knit together through its joints and ligaments, grows with a growth that is from God. (Col. 2:18–19)

Let the peace of Christ rule in your hearts, to which indeed you were called in one body. And be thankful. (Col. 3:15)

The picture of the body of Christ powerfully communicates union with Christ in many theological and practical dimensions.

Headship and Christology

Christ is the "head of the body, the church" (Col. 1:18), Paul writes, presenting Christ as preeminent "in everything," that is, creation and redemption. Christ is Lord over creation because he was the Father's agent in creation. He is Lord over the church as the "head of the body" (v. 18). The head/body image is organic and implies union between Christ and his people. He is the church's Head, its source of life, as the next expression says: "He is the beginning, the firstborn from the dead" (v. 18). As the risen one he is the beginning of God's new creation, the giver of eternal life to his people. As Head he also directs the church to do his will in the world.

Paul warns his readers to shun false religion and instead to cling to "the Head," that is, Christ himself (v. 19). O'Brien summarizes: "It signifies 'head' as 'ruler' or 'authority', rather than 'source' or one who is 'prominent, preeminent.'"[2] Christ is the Head, the supreme authority over his body, his people, the church. It is him we love and obey, even as his first loving us is a model for husbands to be loving leaders of their wives (Eph. 5:23, 25). Indeed, our Head and Savior nourishes and cherishes us (vv. 23, 29–30).

"The Body of Christ" and Its "Members"

"Christ is the head of the church, his body" (Eph. 5:23; cf. Col. 1:18). And, "You are the body of Christ and individually members of it" (1 Cor. 12:27). The very concept of the body of Christ expresses incorporation into him, as Ridderbos explains: "The qualification of the church as the body of Christ is a denotation of the special, close relationship and communion that exist between Christ and his church."[3]

The designation "body of Christ" for the church became standard for Paul. For this reason, when he sets forth the seven unities of the Christian faith in Ephesians 4:4–6, he begins, "There is one body" (v. 4). Paul does not say "one church" or even "one body of Christ" but simply "one body." The apostle communicates clearly the idea of "one church" by simply using the phrase "one body." These words had become common Christian parlance.

Similarly, when three times in 1 Corinthians 6:15 Paul says our bodies are members of Christ, he appeals to the image of the church as Christ's body, which he expects his readers to understand. When he goes on to recoil at believers' taking Christ's members and making them "members of a prostitute" (v. 15), it shows that the metaphor of believers as the body of Christ is more than a metaphor. There is a spiritual reality behind it. We are truly and spiritually joined to Christ. By virtue of our union with him, becoming one with a prostitute implicates Christ in sin—it joins his members to the prostitute!

The Holy Spirit

Paul uses the images of being baptized and drinking a liquid to communicate that possession of the Spirit is essential to union with Christ: Christ baptized us "in one Spirit . . . into one body . . . and all were made to drink of one Spirit"

[2] Peter T. O'Brien, *The Letter to the Ephesians*, The Pillar New Testament Commentary (Grand Rapids: Eerdmans, 1999), 413.
[3] Herman Ridderbos, *Paul: An Outline of His Theology*, trans. John Richard de Witt (Grand Rapids: Eerdmans, 1975), 362.

(1 Cor. 12:13).[4] Interpreting the two statements of verse 13 together, Ciampa and Rosner conclude, "The drinking or drenching with the Spirit is the experience of the Spirit that is also referred to as the baptism by or of the Spirit here or elsewhere."[5] The Holy Spirit is the bond of living union with Christ and thereby with other believers. The Spirit is the nexus that links believers to Christ and one another in one body.

Corporate and Vertical

Just as our bodily members are a part of us, so believers belong to Christ. This metaphor is ideal for teaching the relationship of believers, the members, to Christ, their Head (Rom. 12:4–8). It stresses the corporate aspect of union. But this is based always on vertical union with the Head.

When Paul speaks of his ministry of proclaiming the gospel (Col. 1:23, 25), he says that in his flesh he fills up "what is lacking in Christ's afflictions" (v. 24). Union with Christ involves sharing now in his sufferings and the power of his resurrection. As he toils and struggles in ministry, Paul shares in the power of the risen Christ, "with all his energy that he powerfully works within me" (v. 29). The sufferings in which Paul rejoices are those that he experiences in his body as he identifies with Christ's sufferings on the cross (v. 24). Of course, Paul's sufferings are not redemptive, as Christ's were.

Corporate and Horizontal

Just as our bodily members are a part of us, so believers belong to Christ. And to each other! This idea is also corporate. Even as a human body, although it has many members with various functions, is still one body, so it is with the church, the body of Christ (Rom. 12:5). Paul encourages various members of Christ's body with different gifts to serve the Lord appropriately (vv. 6–8).

The apostle treats various aspects of horizontal union with Christ in 1 Corinthians 12:14–27. He discusses the interdependence of the various members in verses 14–26. Those who consider themselves inferior to their fellows are mistaken (vv. 15–20). Each member is important to the functioning of the body (vv. 15–17), as God so ordered (v. 18). He planned to have many members playing their various parts in one body (vv. 19–20). Furthermore, those who consider themselves superior to others are mistaken also (vv. 21–26).

---

[4] For treatment of various interpretations of aspects of 1 Cor. 12:13, see Roy E. Ciampa and Brian S. Rosner, *The First Letter to the Corinthians*, The Pillar New Testament Commentary (Grand Rapids: Eerdmans, 2010), 589–96.
[5] Ibid., 592.

No part of the body can claim it does not need the other parts (v. 21). In fact, parts of our human bodies we cover in modesty are indispensable (vv. 22–24). "God has so composed the body, giving greater honor to the part that lacked it" (v. 24). His purpose was "that there may be no division in the body, but that the members may have the same care for one another" (v. 25). Paul says of the church, "If one member suffers, all suffer together; if one member is honored, all rejoice together" (v. 26).

Corporate and Individual

We see this over and over as we explore the headings under our summary of the Pauline pictures of union with Christ. God called us individually to himself in salvation and also called us into the people of God. Union with Christ is the link between individual salvation and belonging to the church. With one comes the other. There is no such thing as a solitary Christian. Rather, by virtue of union, every saved individual belongs to Christ the Head and his body. It is no wonder, then, that Christians are called to promote harmony and unity when we are "called in one body" (Col. 3:15).

Divine and Human Work

O'Brien offers a succinct summary, "While the empowering for growth comes from above, members of the body themselves are fully involved in the process."[6] Church leaders are to equip believers to do the work of the ministry to build up the body of Christ (Eph. 4:12). The body needs to grow not only in the sense of adding members but also in unity, maturity, and theological stability. Note that both Christ and his body are active in causing the body to grow. Christ provides the stimulus for growth. But it is also true that "when each part is working properly, [Christ] makes the body grow so that it builds itself up in love" (v. 16). Both the Head and parts of the body work together to produce growth.

Christ is the Head, "from whom the whole body, nourished and knit together through its joints and ligaments, grows with a growth that is from God" (Col. 2:19). Once again we see that growth of the body of Christ has divine and human elements. The body's growth is from its Head, that is, Christ (as in Eph. 4:16), and its growth is "from God." But it is also "nourished" by its "joints and ligaments" as its members fulfill their roles in the body.

---

[6] O'Brien, *Letter to the Ephesians*, 314.

Organic and Dynamic

Church leaders are to equip believers to do the work of the ministry to build up the body of Christ (Eph. 4:12). This is an organic and dynamic reference to the church as Christ's body. The Head and parts of the body work together to produce growth. And the whole body "grows with a growth that is from God" (v. 19). The body image is dynamic, not static; the body grows and matures.

Conclusion

I want to highlight two points. First, the supremacy of Christ. He is the "head of the church, his body, and is himself its Savior" (Eph. 5:23). Christ, preeminent in creation and redemption, is as the risen one the source of eternal life for his church (Col. 1:18). As its Head he also directs the church to do his will in the world. Moo highlights these truths against the background of the Colossian heresy:

> Just as Christ is preeminent in the universe, so he is preeminent within the new creation, the assembly of new covenant believers. But there is this difference: as the metaphor of body and head implies, Christ is in organic relationship to his people in a way that is not true of the creation in general.[7]

This leads right to the second point, which appears toward the end of Ridderbos's great summary statement:

> The most typical description of the church in Paul is that of the body of Christ. Although the idea that underlies this designation certainly occurs elsewhere in the New Testament—one need only think of the figure of the vine and the branches in John 15—nevertheless the qualification "body of Christ" is typically Pauline. In general it gives a further explication of significance of the church as the people of God. It describes the Christological mode of existence of the church as the people of God; it speaks of the special bond with Christ that the church has as the people of God, and the new Israel.[8]

Ridderbos underscores the importance of the corporate nature of the church and of salvation. The image of the church as the body of Christ is sufficient

---

[7] Douglas J. Moo, *The Letters to the Colossians and to Philemon*, The Pillar New Testament Commentary (Grand Rapids: Eerdmans, 2008), 128.

[8] Ridderbos, *Paul: An Outline of His Theology*, 362.

to chastise American believers for carrying their rugged individualism into church life. Burger is spot-on: "The body-metaphor always implies a certain corporateness, showing that the Christian existence is not an individual one."[9]

Temple

In four texts Paul employs the image of a building, which turns out to be a temple, to picture the church:

> Do you not know that you are God's temple and that God's Spirit dwells in you? If anyone destroys God's temple, God will destroy him. For God's temple is holy, and you are that temple. (1 Cor. 3:16–17)

> Do you not know that your body is a temple of the Holy Spirit within you, whom you have from God? You are not your own, for you were bought with a price. So glorify God in your body. (1 Cor. 6:19–20)

> What agreement has the temple of God with idols? For we are the temple of the living God; as God said,

>> "I will make my dwelling among them and walk among them,
>>   and I will be their God,
>>   and they shall be my people." (2 Cor. 6:16)

> You are no longer strangers and aliens, but you are fellow citizens with the saints and members of the household of God, built on the foundation of the apostles and prophets, Christ Jesus himself being the cornerstone, in whom the whole structure, being joined together, grows into a holy temple in the Lord. In him you also are being built together into a dwelling place for God by the Spirit. (Eph. 2:19–22)

Audacity

We too easily miss the sheer audacity of Paul's teaching. Ciampa and Rosner, focusing on the three Corinthian texts, highlight this notion against the backdrop of the magnificence and magnitude of Solomon's temple:

> We should not miss the audacity, if not patent ludicrousness, of Paul's claim. . . . The early Christians were a tiny Jewish sect. . . . To Paul's mind,

---

[9] Hans Burger, *Being in Christ: A Biblical and Systematic Investigation in a Reformed Perspective* (Eugene, OR: Wipf and Stock, 2009), 236.

its [Solomon's temple's] denouement was not the return from exile, nor the building of Herod's temple, but the existence of a small squabbling band in Corinth of mainly Gentile believers in Israel's murdered Messiah: *you yourselves are God's temple*.[10]

The Holy Spirit

It is important to underscore the role of the Holy Spirit; it is he who joins believers to Christ: "In him you also are being built together into a dwelling place for God *by the Spirit*" (Eph. 2:22). Our understanding of the Spirit's role is sharpened against the background of Greco-Roman temples, as Thiselton explains:

> The universal presence of images of the deities in Graeco-Roman temples would have made the principle more vivid to first-century readers. The image of the god or goddess usually dominated the temple either by size or by number (or both), and Paul declares that the very person of the Holy Spirit of God, by parity of reasoning, stands to the totality of the bodily, everyday life of the believer . . . in the same relation of influence and molding of identity as the images of deities in pagan temples.[11]

Corporateness

The temple/building metaphors effectively communicate that the church is a corporate entity. Murray Harris is succinct: "Corporately the Christian community is the new divine sanctuary, the place where the living God most fully expresses his presence."[12] In each of the four passages God's presence is evident. Indeed, "God's presence *constitutes* the temple status of his people, and without it they are no temple," Thiselton declares.[13] As we keep seeing, union with Christ, a corollary of God's presence with his people, is both an individual and a communal reality. As soon as individuals are joined to Christ, they are joined to every other believer in Christ.

Explicitness

In Ephesians 2:21–22 alone Paul explicitly teaches incorporation into Christ. He does so in three ways. He says it is he "in whom" the building grows into

---

[10] Ciampa and Rosner, *First Letter to the Corinthians*, 159.

[11] Anthony C. Thiselton, *The First Epistle to the Corinthians*, New International Greek Testament Commentary (Grand Rapids: Eerdmans, 2000), 475.

[12] Murray J. Harris, *The Second Epistle to the Corinthians*, New International Greek Testament Commentary (Grand Rapids: Eerdmans, 2005), 505.

[13] Thiselton, *First Epistle to the Corinthians*, 317, emphasis original.

a temple, "in him" it is being built into God's dwelling place, and this holy temple is "in the Lord" (vv. 21–22). The purpose of God's effecting this union is worship of the Holy Trinity, which takes place in this temple, for believing Jews and Gentiles "through him [Christ] . . . have access in one Spirit to the Father" (v. 18). And God makes this "holy temple in the Lord . . . a dwelling place for God by the Spirit" (vv. 21–22).

Dynamism

Paul mixes metaphors, describing the temple as dynamic and organic (vv. 21–22). He depicts a building as growing into a temple before our eyes. And this dynamic action is ongoing—believers "are being built" together progressively by the Spirit. O'Brien draws out an implication: "The building is still under construction . . . which is another way of saying that the new community of God is growing and progressing to its ultimate goal of holiness, an objective that is not simply personal or individual but in the present context must be corporate as well."[14]

Conclusion

Putting things together, we see Paul employing the building/temple imagery in a variety of ways. He uses it once directly (Eph. 2:19–22) and three times indirectly (1 Cor. 3:16–17; 6:19–20; 2 Cor. 6:16) to portray God's people audaciously replacing the divinely commissioned magnificent temple of King Solomon. Christians *are* God's temple!

The Holy Spirit builds this living temple and occupies the place of God in it. God's presence is what makes a temple a temple. Though he dwells in his people individually, the emphasis is on his dwelling in them corporately as God's temple. Paul portrays this temple—comprising God's holy people, where the Trinity is worshiped—as in the process of being built before our eyes (Eph. 2:22).

Marriage

Paul paints the image of Christ and his church as Groom and bride in three passages, which we will examine in turn: 1 Corinthians 6:15–20; 2 Corinthians 11:1–5; and Ephesians 5:22–32.

---

[14] O'Brien, *Letter to the Ephesians*, 219.

1 Corinthians 6:15–20

> Do you not know that your bodies are members of Christ? Shall I then take the members of Christ and make them members of a prostitute? Never! Or do you not know that he who is joined to a prostitute becomes one body with her? For, as it is written, "The two will become one flesh." But he who is joined to the Lord becomes one spirit with him. Flee from sexual immorality. Every other sin a person commits is outside the body, but the sexually immoral person sins against his own body. Or do you not know that your body is a temple of the Holy Spirit within you, whom you have from God? You are not your own, for you were bought with a price. So glorify God in your body.

Paul's most intimate picture of union with Christ—that of the marriage union between husband and wife—appears in three passages. And this is the most intimate of those passages, for it concerns the human body and sexual union. Paul rebukes some men in the Corinthian congregation who use theological arguments to defend their use of temple prostitutes. As people of the Spirit, they claim the use of their bodies as a point of Christian freedom. The offended apostle makes three appeals to the idea of union. First, Paul argues that from creation God ordained that "the two," Adam and Eve, would "become one flesh" (v. 16, citing Gen. 2:24). The first pair sets the pattern for human life. God wills for men and women to marry and within marriage to enjoy exclusive sexual intercourse.

Second, contrary to that exclusivity, Paul addresses a different union: "Do you not know that he who is joined to a prostitute becomes one body with her?" (1 Cor. 6:16). For Corinthian men to have sex with prostitutes violates the oneness and permanence God ordained for marriage. Paul offers a high view of the body and its behavior to a church needing his message. Sexual intercourse with prostitutes, then, is not inconsequential, as some Corinthian men claimed. The powerful emotional, psychological, and physical unity of sex is reserved for those who have covenanted lifetime fidelity to each another.

Third, not only does sex with a prostitute violate the Creator's marriage ordinance; Ciampa and Rosner insist that it also violates a believer's spiritual marriage to Christ:

> Genesis 2:24 draws attention to the spiritual marriage of the believer to Christ, a union that Paul assumes calls for faithfulness and purity. Paul presents two mutually exclusive alternatives in 6:16–17: cleaving to a pros-

titute and cleaving to the Lord. Thus the Genesis test is used not only to prove the seriousness of sexual union with a prostitute, but to introduce the notion of the believer's nuptial union with Christ.[15]

Paul's argument is weighty because he piles up these three appeals to union (vv. 16–17). Although this passage lacks the word *marriage*, *bride*, or *groom*, Paul describes the relationship between Christ and his people as a spiritual marriage. This is most clear when Paul says, "He who is joined to the Lord becomes one spirit with him," which parallels, "He who is joined to a prostitute becomes one body with her." Both speak of persons' being "joined" and becoming "one" with the one to whom they are joined. Here the similarities end, for in the one case one is joined to *a prostitute* and becomes one *body* with her. In the other case one is joined to *the Lord Jesus* and becomes one *spirit* with him. Fee concludes that Paul refers to the Holy Spirit and union with Christ, and this makes believers' union with prostitutes even worse, because believers' bodies belong to Jesus, who purchased them.[16]

2 Corinthians 11:1–5

> I wish you would bear with me in a little foolishness. Do bear with me! For I feel a divine jealousy for you, since I betrothed you to one husband, to present you as a pure virgin to Christ. But I am afraid that as the serpent deceived Eve by his cunning, your thoughts will be led astray from a sincere and pure devotion to Christ. For if someone comes and proclaims another Jesus than the one we proclaimed, or if you receive a different spirit from the one you received, or if you accept a different gospel from the one you accepted, you put up with it readily enough. Indeed, I consider that I am not in the least inferior to these super-apostles.

Paul, defending his apostolic ministry against enemies, ironically asks the Corinthians to put up with a "little foolishness" on his part (v. 1). His speech is ironic—they "put up with it readily enough" when "these super-apostles" preach a different gospel than his (vv. 4–5).

Paul speaks paternally as he who "betrothed" them to "one husband," even Christ (v. 2). According to ancient Eastern culture, it was a father's role to promise his daughter in marriage to a potential husband. Furthermore, the father assumed "responsibility for her virginal fidelity to her betrothed in the

---

[15] Ciampa and Rosner, *First Letter to the Corinthians*, 259–60.

[16] See Gordon D. Fee, *The First Epistle to the Corinthians*, The New International Commentary on the New Testament (Grand Rapids: Eerdmans, 1987), 260.

period between the betrothal and the marriage."[17] Likewise Paul, their spiritual father, desires to present the Corinthians in purity to Jesus on the day of his second coming. In lovely language Paul articulates union with Christ as the marriage of Christians, the bride, to Jesus, their Groom.

The apostle fears lest "as the serpent deceived Eve by his cunning," the Corinthians' "thoughts will be led astray from a sincere and pure devotion to Christ" (v. 3). Professed believers must be faithful to Jesus, their betrothed spouse. In Harris's words, there must be no "adulterous flirting with a false gospel."[18] We too must be on guard against seduction by imposters so we do not commit spiritual adultery. Instead, we are to love and live for our Divine Husband until he comes again to take us home.

Ephesians 5:22–32

> Wives, submit to your own husbands, as to the Lord. For the husband is the head of the wife even as Christ is the head of the church, his body, and is himself its Savior. Now as the church submits to Christ, so also wives should submit in everything to their husbands.
>
> Husbands, love your wives, as Christ loved the church and gave himself up for her, that he might sanctify her, having cleansed her by the washing of water with the word, so that he might present the church to himself in splendor, without spot or wrinkle or any such thing, that she might be holy and without blemish. In the same way husbands should love their wives as their own bodies. He who loves his wife loves himself. For no one ever hated his own flesh, but nourishes and cherishes it, just as Christ does the church, because we are members of his body. "Therefore a man shall leave his father and mother and hold fast to his wife, and the two shall become one flesh." This mystery is profound, and I am saying that it refers to Christ and the church.

If 1 Corinthians 6:16–17 is the most intimate of Paul's passages depicting union as the marriage of Christ and believers and 2 Corinthians 11:1–3 makes the most powerful application, then Ephesians 5:23–32 is the most direct, for, after citing Genesis 2:24, Paul writes, "This mystery [of two becoming one in human marriage] is profound, and I am saying that it refers to Christ and the church" (Eph. 5:32). Remarkably, here Paul employs the picture of mar-

---

[17] Paul Barnett, *The Second Epistle to the Corinthians*, The New International Commentary on the New Testament (Grand Rapids: Eerdmans, 1997), 499.
[18] Harris, *Second Epistle to the Corinthians*, 739.

riage between Christ and his people as a model for proper relations between husband and wife.

I cannot improve on the three conclusions for union with Christ that Constantine Campbell draws from this text. First, the marriage of Christ and his own does not obliterate distinctions between the two. Christ and his bride are intimately joined, but the marriage metaphor does not confuse the two. Second, as a human bride submits to her loving husband in marriage, so the church submits to Christ, her loving Head: "Christ is the head of the church. . . . The church submits to Christ" (vv. 23–24). The union neither undermines Christ's lordship nor gives the church license to disobey her Lord.

> Third, the marriage is prepared, instigated, and sustained by Christ, with the wife identified as the recipient of his care. Christ is the Saviour of the body (5:23), having loved her and given himself for her (5:25). He makes her holy in order to present her to himself without blemish (5:26–27). He sustains her through provision and care (5:29).[19]

Moreover, all of this puts the spotlight on God's marvelous grace shown to his bride. The church does not earn Christ's love; she is entirely the beneficiary of her suitor's advances in her direction.

Conclusion

In three texts Paul gifts the church with the intimate picture of union with Christ as marriage union.

Definition. Paul explicitly presents union with Christ in terms of the marriage of Christ and believers in Ephesians 5:22–32. In 1 Corinthians 6:15–17 he also speaks of the relationship between Christ and the church as spiritual marriage: "He who is joined to the Lord becomes one spirit with him" (v. 17). The marriage between Christ, the Groom, and the bride, his church, does not erase distinctions between them. The two are intimately joined, but the marriage metaphor does not confuse the two, unlike forms of mysticism in which adherents are supposedly absorbed in the deity.

Intimacy. This is Paul's most intimate picture of union with Christ, that of the closest human relationship—marriage and sexual union between husband and wife. In his most intimate passage he focuses on the human body and sexual relations (1 Cor. 6:16). Believers are spiritually joined to Christ in mar-

---

[19] Constantine R. Campbell, *Paul and Union with Christ: An Exegetical and Theological Study* (Grand Rapids: Zondervan, 2012), 308–9.

riage. Campbell draws good applications: the metaphor of marriage to Christ "underpins ethical constraints related to sexual immorality, prohibits spiritual unfaithfulness, and requires submission of the church to her husband."[20]

The Holy Spirit. Paul's treatment of the believer's marriage to Christ in 1 Corinthians 6 likely refers to the Holy Spirit: "He who is joined to *the Lord* becomes one *spirit* with him" (v. 17). Fee speaks of the impossibility of a sexual union between a Christian and a prostitute "because the believer's body already belongs to the Lord, through whose resurrection one's body has become a "member" of Christ by his Spirit.[21]

Grace. We must not miss the place of God's grace in the marriage metaphor of union with Christ. It is he who prepares the marriage, takes the initiative, and sustains the relationship. His bride, the church, is the object of his affection and the recipient of his care. Christ "himself is the Savior of the body" (Eph. 5:23, my translation), who loves his bride and gives himself unto death for her (v. 25). He lavishes upon her provision and care (v. 29). All of this highlights Christ's wonderful grace shown to his bride. The church does not earn Christ's love; she is entirely the beneficiary of her lover's advances in her direction.

Faithfulness and obedience to Christ, our Husband. Paul speaks as a father who "betrothed" the Corinthians to "one husband," even Christ (2 Cor. 11:2). Paul aims to present the Corinthians in purity to Jesus at his second coming. Paul does not want his readers to be "led astray from . . . pure devotion to Christ" (v. 3). We too must be on guard against imposters and their attempts to seduce us into spiritual adultery.

Moreover, as a bride submits to her loving husband in the bonds of matrimony, so the church submits to Christ, her loving Husband (Eph. 5:23–24). Campbell's words fittingly conclude our summary of Paul's nuptial ideas of union: "The metaphorical joining of husband and wife and their becoming one flesh indicate a profound union between Christ and the church. The metaphor is personal and implies a bond of intimacy that goes well beyond the other metaphors that Paul uses in portraying union with Christ."[22]

New Clothing

In two passages Paul directly speaks of union with Christ in terms of believers' putting on Christ as they would new clothes.

---

[20] Ibid., 310.
[21] Fee, *First Epistle to the Corinthians*, 260.
[22] Campbell, *Paul and Union with Christ*, 308.

Direct Passages

Put on the Lord Jesus Christ, and make no provision for the flesh, to gratify its desires. (Rom. 13:14)

As many of you as were baptized into Christ have put on Christ. (Gal. 3:27)

As we get dressed to cover our bodies, so Christians "clothe themselves" with Christ; they "put" him "on." As clothing comes into contact with our bodies, so we come into contact with Christ; we are joined to him spiritually. The apostle uses this imagery as a statement of a fact: in initial salvation you "have put on Christ" (Gal. 3:27). He uses it also in exhortation: in the Christian life believers are to "put on the Lord Jesus Christ" (Rom. 13:14).

Baptism/conversion involves putting on Christ figuratively as one puts on clothes. Baptism thus identifies believers with Christ and they share in his identity. In this way, baptism signifies union with Christ.[23]

In Galatians 3:27 Paul does not command believers, "Put on the Lord Jesus Christ," as in Romans 13:14, but says that they already "have put on Christ." The clothing metaphor, then, is used here not as an imperative but as an indicative. This is not to deny an ethical element in Paul's words here, however. As Richard Longenecker explains, "The figurative use of ἐνδύω (*enduo*, 'put on' or 'clothe') with a personal object means to take on the characteristics, virtues, and/or intentions of the one referred to, and so to become like that person."[24]

So, once and for all in conversion, believers put on Christ. But the apostle's clothing imagery does not end here, for in Romans 13:14 he commands: "Put on the Lord Jesus Christ." The apostle commands them to put on Christ himself, to live for him and as he lived. Here Paul speaks not of initial union with Christ but of our need "consciously to embrace Christ in such a way that his character is manifested in all that we do and say," as Moo states.[25]

Campbell offers a pithy summary: "Putting on Christ offers an alternative lifestyle. . . . There is a kind of shorthand at work," and Paul intends to "convey the idea of union with Christ through the phrase *put on the Lord Jesus Christ* and assume the ethical corollaries that flow from such union."[26]

---

[23] See Burger, *Being in Christ*, 243.
[24] Richard N. Longenecker, *Galatians*, Word Biblical Commentary (Nashville: Thomas Nelson, 1990), 156.
[25] Douglas J. Moo, *The Epistle to the Romans*, The New International Commentary on the New Testament (Grand Rapids: Eerdmans, 1996), 825–26.
[26] Campbell, *Paul and Union with Christ*, 312.

Related Passages

Paul uses the imagery of getting dressed in two other types of passages that do not speak of union with Christ. One type of passage speaks of believers' putting on clothing to indicate the new Christian lifestyle.[27] The apostle says that Christians were "taught in him, as the truth is in Jesus, to put off your old self, which belongs to your former manner of life . . . and to put on the new self, created after the likeness of God in true righteousness and holiness" (Eph. 4:21–22, 24).

In another place he commands, "Do not lie to one another, seeing that you have put off the old self with its practices and have put on the new self, which is being renewed in knowledge after the image of its creator" (Col. 3:9–10). And shortly thereafter he resumes, "Put on then, as God's chosen ones, holy and beloved, compassionate hearts, kindness, humility, meekness, and patience. . . . And above all these put on love, which binds everything together in perfect harmony" (vv. 12, 14).

In these two texts Paul urges believers to live for Christ. They are to "take off" the old ways and not return to their former pre-Christian lifestyle. They are to "put on" the new qualities of godliness, love, and patience. In fact, using the indicative–imperative pattern, he says they *have* had a change of clothes and should act like it (Colossians 3); they *are* to change their clothes as befits God's people (Ephesians 4). In these two passages, then, Paul exhorts Christians in ethical behavior.

A second type of passage uses language of a change of clothing to indicate the eschatological transformation that believers will undergo. Paul writes: "This perishable body must put on the imperishable, and this mortal body must put on immortality. When the perishable puts on the imperishable, and the mortal puts on immortality, then shall come to pass the saying that is written: 'Death is swallowed up in victory'" (1 Cor. 15:53–54). While the details of another text are debated, its main idea is clear enough:

> In this tent we groan, longing to put on our heavenly dwelling, if indeed by putting it on we may not be found naked. For while we are still in this tent, we groan, being burdened—not that we would be unclothed, but that we would be further clothed, so that what is mortal may be swallowed up by life. (2 Cor. 5:2–4)

---

[27] I am excluding two passages that might be included, two that speak of Christians' putting on spiritual armor: Eph. 6:11–17 and 1 Thess. 5:8.

The focus of these two texts is not on lives that please God but on what God will do for Christians when Christ returns. He will "clothe" them with immortality and eternal life. That is, God will transform them, fit them with resurrected bodies, and equip them for everlasting life on the new earth.

Though these two types of texts do not speak of union with Christ, they integrate well with union. The passages that enjoin believers to cultivate good ethical attributes speak of the results of union with Christ. Because we have put on Christ, we are to put on holiness, humility, patience, and compassion. The texts that predict believers' putting on new bodies in the resurrection speak also of the results of union with Christ, this time describing final salvation as putting on new clothes. I conclude that only two passages speak directly of union with Christ as donning new clothes—Romans 13:14 and Galatians 3:27. But several others use the imagery of a change of clothes to communicate the results of that union in moral transformation now and bodily transformation at the second coming.

Conclusion

Two passages directly use the metaphor of getting dressed to signify union with Christ. Paul uses the indicative: "As many of you as were baptized into Christ have put on Christ" (Gal. 3:27). Believers have clothed themselves with Christ; they have been united with him. Paul uses the imperative also: "Put on the Lord Jesus Christ, and make no provision for the flesh, to gratify its desires" (Rom. 13:14). Paul exhorts readers to live for Christ and to live as he lived. We put on Christ once and for all, but we live out that change of clothes the rest of our lives.

Two other kinds of texts relate indirectly to union with Christ. One kind of text speaks of believers' putting on clothing to indicate the new Christian lifestyle (Eph. 4:21–24; Col. 3:9–14). They are to "take off" the old ways and "put on" the new qualities of holiness, compassion, and patience.

Another kind of text related indirectly to union with Christ uses language of a change of clothing to point to the eschatological change believers will experience (1 Cor. 15:53–54; 2 Cor. 5:2–4). These texts focus on what God will do for Christians when Christ comes back. He will "clothe" them with immortality and eternal life. That is, God will transform them, equipping them with resurrected bodies for eternal life on the new earth.

Filled to All the Fullness

Four times Paul speaks of the church in exalted terms as the "fullness" of Christ or of God, or as "filled in" or "with" Christ or God. Twice explicitly and twice implicitly these passages pertain to union with Christ:

> He put all things under his feet and gave him as head over all things to the church, which is his body, the fullness of him who fills all in all. (Eph. 1:22–23)

> . . . to know the love of Christ that surpasses knowledge, that you may be filled with all the fullness of God. (3:19)

> . . . until we all attain to the unity of the faith and of the knowledge of the Son of God, to mature manhood, to the measure of the stature of the fullness of Christ. (4:13)

> In him the whole fullness of deity dwells bodily, and you have been filled in him, who is the head of all rule and authority. (Col. 2:9–10)

Ephesians 1:22–23

> He put all things under his feet and gave him as head over all things to the church, which is his body, the fullness of him who fills all in all.

Paul asks God the Father to give the Ephesians deeper insight into three areas: their hope of final salvation, how highly God esteems them as his inheritance, and his mighty strength toward them (vv. 16–19). The apostle portrays this great strength in two ways. First, it is the strength of God that raised Christ and exalted him to God's right hand (vv. 19–20). Second, it is the strength Christ exerts from that exalted position, the highest place of authority (vv. 21–23).

This strength of Christ is in turn viewed from three angles. Seen from above, he is over all things, the whole creation, including angels, good and bad. Seen from below, God "put all things under his feet" (v. 22; citing Ps. 8:6). Christ is the second Adam, who in exaltation regains the original dominion given to Adam and Eve that fallen human beings lost.

Seen from above once more, God "gave him as head over all things to the church" (Eph. 1:22). Paul's teaching here (and in Col. 1:18–19) represents a further development over that in Romans 12 and 1 Corinthians 12 concerning Christ's relation to the church, because now, to quote O'Brien, the apostle here deals with the "relationship which the church, as the body of Christ, bears to Christ as head."[28] The Father appointed the Son as Head of the church, his body. Christ has supreme authority over the church. And he wields this authority as he who is Head over "all things," not only the church. But he exerts that universal authority for the sake of his church.

Paul elevates the church in relation to Christ: God "gave him as head over all things to the church, which is his body, *the fullness of him who fills all in all*" (Eph. 1:22–23). This remarkable statement is best understood in the light of its Old Testament background: "Am I a God at hand, declares the LORD, and not a God far away? Can a man hide himself in secret places so that I cannot see him? declares the LORD. Do I not fill heaven and earth? declares the LORD" (Jer. 23:23–24). Even as God fills heaven and earth, so the ascended Christ "fills all in all" (Eph. 1:23). Ridderbos explains, "The whole universe falls within the reach of his mighty presence. He is the one . . . who in every respect fills the universe."[29] And, astoundingly, Paul says that Christ's church is the "fullness of him who fills all in all." That is, the church "can be called his *plērōma* [fullness] in a special sense, the domain filled and ever increasingly to be filled by him."[30]

It is necessary to distinguish the fullness of Christ from that of the church. His fullness belongs to both his person and work. As God incarnate, "In him the whole fullness of deity dwells bodily" (Col. 2:9). And as the crucified, risen Lord exalted to God's right hand, he "fills all in all" (Eph. 1:23). The church too has fullness, but its fullness is only Christ's fullness given to it. Notice the movement from Christ's fullness to the church's: "In him the whole fullness of deity dwells bodily, and you have been filled in him, who is the head of all rule and authority" (Col. 2:9–10).

Christ grants fullness to his church in two ways: as a status given and a task to be performed. As the triumphant Lord who fills all things with his mighty presence, he grants the church the status of fullness. The church is "filled in him" (Col. 2:10) and is already his "fullness" (Eph. 1:23). At the same time, Christ gives fullness to his church as a task to perform and a goal to be attained. Paul prays that the Ephesians "may be filled with all the fullness of God" (Eph. 3:19). Paul's goal is that the churches attain the "measure of the stature of the fullness of Christ" (Eph. 4:13).

O'Brien offers this summary:

---

[28] O'Brien, *Letter to the Ephesians*, 148.
[29] Ridderbos, *Paul: An Outline of His Theology*, 390.
[30] Ibid., 391.

God has given Christ as head over all things for the church. His supremacy over the cosmos is seen to be for the benefit of his people. . . . The church is said to be Christ's body. This is not stated of the cosmos. . . . The final clause in v. 23 makes the additional point that the church is Christ's *fulness*. In Colossians the term "fullness" was applied to Christ; here in Ephesians its referent is the church. As head over all things Christ exercises his sovereign rule by "filling" the universe. But only the church is his body, and he rules it, that is, fills it in a special way with his Spirit, grace, and gifts: it is his fulness.[31]

Ephesians 3:14–19

I bow my knees before the Father, from whom every family in heaven and on earth is named, that according to the riches of his glory he may grant you to be strengthened with power through his Spirit in your inner being, so that Christ may dwell in your hearts through faith—that you, being rooted and grounded in love, may have strength to comprehend with all the saints what is the breadth and length and height and depth, and to know the love of Christ that surpasses knowledge, that you may be filled with all the fullness of God.

Paul asks the Father to strengthen the Ephesians by the Holy Spirit's working within. The apostle's goal is "that Christ may dwell in your hearts through faith" (v. 17). The problem arises: all believers already have Christ in their hearts. Thielman aids our understanding:

Paul does not imply by this that Christ is absent from their hearts. . . . What they apparently lack is the inner strength and encouragement they should draw from these truths. . . . Union with Christ by faith brings personal, inner strength that allows the believer to live in a world dominated by rebellion against God.[32]

Paul's next words are simply grand: "that you, being rooted and grounded in love, may have strength to comprehend with all the saints what is the breadth and length and height and depth, and to know the love of Christ that surpasses knowledge, that you may be filled with all the fullness of God" (vv. 17–19). Believers are to appreciate better God's love from their increasing awareness that Christ makes his home in them.

---

[31] O'Brien, *Letter to the Ephesians*, 152.
[32] Frank Thielman, *Ephesians*, Baker Exegetical Commentary on the New Testament (Grand Rapids: Baker Academic, 2010), 230–31.

This works in three ways. First, Christ's love is the foundation of the Christian life; we are "rooted and grounded in love" (v. 17). Second, this foundation helps us to understand how measureless is God's love for us in Christ (v. 18).

Third, consequently we are to be "filled with all the fullness of God" (v. 19); that is, we are to grow to be the mature believers God intends. Paul here presents the church's fullness as a task to be done, a goal to be reached. Although according to 1:23 the church has already attained this fullness, here the church must aspire to it. This fits the common Pauline pattern of the "already" and the "not yet." Already in Christ we believers have the status of divine fullness; not yet have we attained the lifestyle in keeping with this exalted status. O'Brien is succinct: "They are to become what they already are."[33]

Ephesians 4:11–16

He gave the apostles, the prophets, the evangelists, the shepherds and teachers, to equip the saints for the work of ministry, for building up the body of Christ, until we all attain to the unity of the faith and of the knowledge of the Son of God, to mature manhood, to the measure of the stature of the fullness of Christ, so that we may no longer be children, tossed to and fro by the waves and carried about by every wind of doctrine, by human cunning, by craftiness in deceitful schemes. Rather, speaking the truth in love, we are to grow up in every way into him who is the head, into Christ, from whom the whole body, joined and held together by every joint with which it is equipped, when each part is working properly, makes the body grow so that it builds itself up in love.

Paul pleads for subjective unity for the church (vv. 1–3) and then lists the seven objective unities that should inspire it (vv. 4–6). The ascended Christ gave gifted men to his church to train the saints to perform the church's ministry so as to reach goals, including edification, unity, maturity, and doctrinal stability (vv. 12–14). Our present concern is with the goal of maturity. Paul prays that believers will "all attain . . . to mature manhood, to the measure of the stature of the fullness of Christ" (v. 13). Here as in 3:19 Christ's fullness is a task of the church. When the apostle holds up the "measure of the stature," he sets forth Christ as the church's impossible standard of maturity. This drives believers to seek grace to aspire to be what it has already received as a gift— the status of having been filled with Christ's fullness (1:23; Col. 2:10). Once

---

[33] O'Brien, *Letter to the Ephesians*, 265.

more the already/not yet tension assures the church of God's love in Christ and motivates the church to keep on its toes in pursuit of holiness and love.

Colossians 2:9–10

> In him the whole fullness of deity dwells bodily, and you have been filled in him, who is the head of all rule and authority.

This passage is vital to understanding the church's filling and fullness. Paul speaks first of Christ's union with God and then of our union with Christ. Paul tells of Christ's divine fullness and of our being filled in union with him. In this way Paul makes a key connection between Christ and believers. In Christ, their Lord and Savior, all the fullness of deity is embodied. As a result, when Christians are joined to him spiritually, they too come in close contact with the living God. They are "filled in him" (v. 10). This passage (along with Eph. 1:23) speaks of the "already" of the church's status in Christ. This status is possible only because of the "all-embracing character of the 'fullness of God' represented by Christ, controlled by him, and standing at his disposal," as Ridderbos puts it.[34]

In context of the Colossian heresy, Paul's message to the church is that they are complete in union with this glorious Christ. Being "filled in him" (v. 10), they lack nothing. F. F. Bruce is eloquent:

> Christians by their union with him participated in his life. If the fullness of deity resided in him, his fullness was imparted to them. There is an affinity here with the language of the Johannine prologue: "from his fullness have we all received, grace upon grace" (John 1:16). Without him his people must remain forever *disiecta membra*—incomplete, unable to attain the true end of their existence. But united with him, incorporated in him, they are joined with him in a living bond in which he and they complement each other (although they are not essential to his fullness as he is to theirs).[35]

Conclusion

This magnificent theme is illuminated by three distinctions.

First, we distinguish Christ's fullness from that of his church. All the full-

---

[34] Ridderbos, *Paul: An Outline of His Theology*, 390.
[35] F. F. Bruce, *The Epistles to the Colossians, to Philemon, and to the Ephesians*, The New International Commentary on the New Testament (Grand Rapids: Eerdmans, 1984), 101.

ness of deity is embodied in Christ. He is the fullness of God incarnate. As the crucified, risen Lord exalted to God's right hand, he "fills all in all" (Eph. 1:23). Out of his fullness the divine-human Christ gives fullness to the church: "In him the whole fullness of deity dwells bodily, and you have been filled in him" (Col. 2:9–10).

Second, we distinguish the church's fullness as status and task. Christ gives fullness to his church as both a status granted and a task to be accomplished. As Lord, who fills all things with his mighty presence, he grants the church the status of fullness. The church is "filled in him" (Col. 2:10) and is his "fullness" (Eph. 1:23). But at the same time, Christ gives fullness to his church as a task to do and a goal to be reached. Paul prays that the Ephesians "may be filled with all the fullness of God" (3:19). Paul's goal is that the churches attain to the "measure of the stature of the fullness of Christ" (4:13).

Third, we distinguish the "already" and "not yet." Already, in Christ we believers have the status of divine fullness (1:23; Col. 2:10) and are assured of God's love. Not yet have we attained a lifestyle corresponding to this exalted status. This motivates the church to keep on its toes in pursuit of holiness and love.

Indwelling

The Holy Spirit savingly unites God's people to Christ and takes up residence in and with them in a special relationship. I count at least sixteen places where Paul teaches indwelling.

> Hope does not put us to shame, because God's love has been poured into our hearts through *the Holy Spirit who has been given to us*. (Rom. 5:5)

> You, however, are not in the flesh but in the Spirit, if in fact *the Spirit of God dwells in you. Anyone who does not have the Spirit of Christ* does not belong to him. *But if Christ is in you*, although the body is dead because of sin, the Spirit is life because of righteousness. *If the Spirit of him who raised Jesus from the dead dwells in you*, he who raised Christ Jesus from the dead will also give life to your mortal bodies through *his Spirit who dwells in you*. (8:9–11)

> Do you not know that you are God's temple and that *God's Spirit dwells in you*? (1 Cor. 3:16)

Do you not know that *your body is a temple of the Holy Spirit within you, whom you have from God*? You are not your own, for you were bought with a price. So glorify God in your body. (6:19–20)

It is God who establishes us with you in Christ, and has anointed us, and who has also put his seal on us and *given us his Spirit in our hearts* as a guarantee. (2 Cor. 1:21–22)

We are the temple of the living God; as God said,

"*I will make my dwelling among them* and walk among them,
      and I will be their God,
      and they shall be my people." (6:16)

Examine yourselves, to see whether you are in the faith. Test yourselves. Or do you not realize this about yourselves, that *Jesus Christ is in you*?— unless indeed you fail to meet the test! (13:5)

I have been crucified with Christ. It is no longer I who live, but *Christ who lives in me*. (Gal. 2:20)

Christ redeemed us from the curse of the law by becoming a curse for us—for it is written, "Cursed is everyone who is hanged on a tree"—so that in Christ Jesus the blessing of Abraham might come to the Gentiles, *so that we might receive the promised Spirit* through faith. (3:13–14)

Because you are sons, *God has sent the Spirit of his Son into our hearts*, crying, "Abba! Father!" (4:6)

In him you also are being built together into *a dwelling place for God by the Spirit*. (Eph. 2:22)

For this reason I bow my knees before the Father . . . *so that Christ may dwell in your hearts through faith*—that you, being rooted and grounded in love . . . (3:14, 17)

To them God chose to make known how great among the Gentiles are the riches of the glory of this mystery, which is *Christ in you*, the hope of glory. (Col. 1:27)

Here there is not Greek and Jew, circumcised and uncircumcised, barbarian, Scythian, slave, free; but *Christ is all, and in all*. (3:11)

Whoever disregards this, disregards not man but *God, who gives his Holy Spirit to you.* (1 Thess. 4:8)

By *the Holy Spirit who dwells within us,* guard the good deposit entrusted to you. (2 Tim. 1:14)

The apostle employs many different expressions to portray the delightful reality that the Trinity makes its home in and with God's people as individuals and as the church. Usually Paul speaks of the Spirit. He says that the Spirit indwells us or was given to us, we have the Spirit, we received the Spirit, and the Father sent the Spirit into our hearts.

Six times he ascribes indwelling to the Son. He says that Christ is in us, lives in us, or dwells in our hearts (Rom. 8:10; 2 Cor. 13:5; Gal. 2:20; Eph. 3:17; Col. 1:27; 3:11).

Two times he associates indwelling with God the Father. He says that believers are a temple for God who dwells among us and are a dwelling place for God the Father (2 Cor. 6:16; Eph. 2:22).

It is correct to give pride of place to the Holy Spirit as the person of the Godhead who indwells the saints. Scripture does this because the Spirit is the prime mover in the application of salvation or, said differently, in uniting us to Christ. Most passages attribute indwelling to the Spirit, but it is incorrect to limit indwelling to the Spirit. Christians are indwelt by the Father, Son, and Holy Spirit. This should not surprise us, because it already is entailed in the orthodox doctrine of the Trinity, which I summarize this way:

- There is one God.
- He eternally exists in three persons, or modes, as Father, Son, and Holy Spirit.
- These persons are never separated in essence but must be distinguished.
- The three Trinitarian persons mutually indwell one another.
- The operation of the three divine persons is inseparable.

The unity of essence and inseparability of operation of the three persons should have led us to conclude via systematics, even if Scripture never said so, that believers are indwelt by the Trinity. But Scripture *does* say so. This incredible corollary to union with Christ would have come as no surprise to orthodox Lutheran and orthodox Reformed theologians. Listen as Richard Muller includes indwelling in his definition of union with Christ for the post-Reformation orthodox: "The orthodox therefore define the *unio mystica* [mystical union] as the spiritual conjunction (*coniunctio spiritualis*) of the Triune God with the believer in and following justification. It is a substantial and graciously effective indwelling."[36]

Being united to Christ by grace through faith in the gospel means being indwelt by the Holy Trinity! From the beginning God dwelt with his people in the garden of Eden, the tabernacle, the temple, the incarnation, and now the church. Indeed, as God's presence defines the tabernacle and temple, so the Spirit's indwelling defines the church universal and every particular church. In a word, it is the indwelling of God that makes a church a church. Marvelously, he dwells within every believer individually and dwells within believers corporately as they gather to worship him. We will explore implications of this warm truth in the chapter "Union with Christ in the Christian Life."

---

[36] Richard A. Muller, *Dictionary of Latin and Greek Theological Terms: Drawn Principally from Protestant Scholastic Theology* (Grand Rapids: Baker, 1985), 314.

Chapter 17

Union with Christ
in Hebrews

Hebrews 3:12–14

Take care, brothers, lest there be in any of you an evil, unbelieving heart, leading you to fall away from the living God. But exhort one another every day, as long as it is called "today," that none of you may be hardened by the deceitfulness of sin. For we have come to share in Christ, if indeed we hold our original confidence firm to the end.

Using Psalm 95, the author to the Hebrews issues a strong warning to his readers: They dare not imitate the Israelites in the wilderness, who became hardened, rebelled against the Lord, put him to the test, and went astray in their hearts (vv. 7–11). Now he applies the warning to his hearers: "Take care, brothers, lest there be in any of you an evil, unbelieving heart, leading you to fall away from the living God" (v. 12). He urges members of the house churches to whom he writes to examine themselves. His words "lest there be in *any of you*" convey a concern for each person. They must beware lest they, professed Jewish Christians, imitate their ancestors. They must guard their hearts from sin and unbelief so they do not fall away from the Lord.

What antidote does the writer prescribe to protect his readers from the poison of rebellion? Using a key word from Psalm 95, he prescribes the medicine of mutual exhortation: "But exhort one another every day, as long as it is called 'today,' that none of you may be hardened by the deceitfulness of sin" (v. 13). Standing alone, they are more likely to waver; holding each other accountable strengthens each of them. Mutual encouragement helps to keep professed believers from turning away from the living God. Philip E. Hughes's words are apt: "While this time lasts, each succeeding day is a fresh 'To-day' in which they may heed the psalmist's warning to hear the voice of God and render Him heart-obedience."[1] If they fail to heed the warning, they become susceptible to sin's "deceitfulness"; it is out to harden them to the things of God and to lead them astray.

Then the writer declares, "For we have come to share in Christ, if indeed we hold our original confidence firm to the end" (v. 14). As he does frequently, the author urges the readers to persevere in faith (cf. v. 6; 10:23, 36; 12:1–2). He wants them to maintain their original profession of faith "firm to the end." If they do, they "have come to share in Christ." Exegetes disagree as to whether this phrase, the only candidate for union with Christ in Hebrews, really teaches that concept. The words "for we have come to share in Christ"— μέτοχοι γὰρ τοῦ Χριστοῦ γεγόναμεν—are capable of two interpretations, each of which makes sense in Hebrews.

Hughes sets forth clearly the rival interpretations:

There is, indeed, a certain ambiguity associated with the Greek noun used here since it may mean either "partakers with" someone in a particular activity or relationship, in which case it denotes "companions" or "partners," as in 1:9 and Luke 5:7 (the only occurrence of the noun outside the Epistle to the Hebrews in the New Testament), or "partakers of," as in 3:1 ("partakers of a heavenly call"), 6:4 ("partakers of the Holy Spirit"), and 12:8 ("partakers of discipline").[2]

Although I acknowledge that competent scholars disagree with me and opt for the first interpretation,[3] I favor the second one for three reasons.[4] First, as Harold Attridge maintains, the first view yields "the rather jejune [dull] sense of 'fellows.'"[5] Indeed, it seems devoid of significance, and the suggestive

[1] Philip E. Hughes, *A Commentary on the Epistle to the Hebrews* (Grand Rapids: Eerdmans, 1977), 67.
[2] Ibid., 149.
[3] These include F. F. Bruce, *The Epistle to the Hebrews*, The New International Commentary on the New Testament (Grand Rapids: Eerdmans, 1964), 67–68; Hugh Montefiore, *A Commentary on the Epistle to the Hebrews*, Harper's New Testament Commentaries (New York: Harper and Row, 1964), 78; and James Moffatt, *A Critical and Exegetical Commentary on the Epistle to the Hebrews*, International Critical Commentary (Edinburgh: T&T Clark, 1924), 47.
[4] These reach the same conclusion as I do: Hughes, *Epistle to the Hebrews*, 150; Harold W. Attridge, *A Commentary on the Epistle to the Hebrews*, Hermeneia (Philadelphia: Fortress, 1989), 17–18; Paul Ellingworth, *The Epistle to the Hebrews*, New International Greek Testament Commentary (Grand Rapids: Eerdmans, 1993), 227; and Peter T. O'Brien, *The Letter to the Hebrews*, The Pillar New Testament Commentary (Grand Rapids: Eerdmans, 2010), 150.
[5] Attridge, *Epistle to the Hebrews*, 117n65.

language implies more than this. Second, 3:6 offers a key parallel: "Christ is faithful over God's house as a son. And we are his house if indeed we hold fast our confidence and our boasting in our hope." We do not merely *live in* God's house together; we *are* that house.[6] In a similar vein, we are not simply Christ's companions; we partake of him. Third, "participation not in one or other respect but in an inclusive and radical sense seems to be intended here," as Hughes argues.[7]

I conclude then, that this text in Hebrews contributes to our investigation of union with Christ. O'Brien is correct in saying: "Theologically, this would be akin to the Pauline references to being 'in Christ' . . . although this precise conception is not apparent elsewhere in Hebrews."[8] The writer to the Hebrews, then, after warning and encouraging his readers in the two previous verses, expounds: we have come to partake of the person of Christ and his saving benefits if we persevere to the end in faith. Authentic union with Christ entails more than a profession of faith; it entails steadfastness, even in the difficult circumstances of the original audience of Hebrews. And true saving faith, which according to Hebrews perseveres to the end, joins believers to Christ so that they "come to share in" him.

O'Brien helpfully correlates this understanding with other things Hebrews teaches that believers share with Christ as a result of their spiritual union with him:

[Being] sharers *in* Christ: as companions of the Son of God they share his joy (1:9); and since he is the heir of all things (1:2), they participate in his inheritance (1:14). Since they are his brothers and sisters (2:11–12), their hope is of sharing with him in the honour and glory attained through his death and exaltation (2:8–9), and so of participating in his heavenly, unshakable kingdom (12:28).[9]

Conclusion

Though the matter is debated, I view Hebrews 3:14 as pertaining to union with Christ. When the writer pens, "We have come to share in Christ, if indeed we hold our original confidence firm to the end," he is saying more than that we are Christ's companions or partners. He is saying that we share

[6] So Ellingworth, *Epistle to the Hebrews*, 227.
[7] Hughes, *Epistle to the Hebrews*, 150.
[8] O'Brien, *Letter to the Hebrews*, 150.
[9] Ibid., emphasis original.

in Christ—we partake of him. Other instances of the word the writer uses in Hebrews 3:14, "sharers" or "partakers" (μέτοχοι/*metochoi*), bear this out:

- "you who *share in* a heavenly calling" (3:1)
- "those who . . . have *shared in* the Holy Spirit" (6:4)
- "discipline, *in* which all have *participated*" (12:8)

The writer teaches, then, that we share in who Christ is and what he has accomplished for us. That means we partake of the Son of God and his saving benefits. By God's grace through faith we participate in his person and work.

This truth plays an important role in Hebrews and can do the same for our lives today. The original readers of Hebrews, whom the writer repeatedly exhorts to persevere amid trying circumstances, need encouragement to do so. The writer provides this encouragement at key places, even among his warnings (see 6:9 and 10:39). And 3:14 provides a great encouragement. To those tempted to quit the Christian marathon because of dire temptations and the hardening effects of sin, the writer proclaims, "We have come to share in Christ, if indeed we hold our original confidence firm to the end." Christ's church around the world needs to hear these same words today.

Chapter 18

Union with Christ
in 1–2 Peter

1 Peter

1 Peter 2:4–5

> As you come to him, a living stone rejected by men but in the sight of God chosen and precious, you yourselves like living stones are being built up as a spiritual house, to be a holy priesthood, to offer spiritual sacrifices acceptable to God through Jesus Christ.

After exhorting his readers to reject evil attitudes and behavior, Peter urges them, "Like newborn infants, long for the pure spiritual milk" to grow spiritually (vv. 1–2). He then turns attention to Christ. Even as Old Testament priests and believers "came" to God in worship and service,[1] so New Testament believers approach Christ as "a living stone" (v. 4). It is unusual to speak of Christ as a "living stone." In fact, the expression itself applied to a person is an anomaly, for a stone is something that is not alive.[2] The stone imagery is influenced by the words following in the text, taken from Isaiah 28:16; Psalm 118:22; and Isaiah 8:14:

> ". . . a stone,
> a cornerstone chosen and precious. . . ."

---

[1] Ex. 12:48; 16:9; Lev. 9:7–8; 10:4–5. Similar New Testament usage occurs in Heb. 4:16; 7:25; 10:22.
[2] Though the expression "living stone" could be used to describe massive unquarried rock, it was not used of human beings. Cf. Paul J. Achtemeier, *1 Peter*, Hermeneia (Minneapolis: Fortress, 1996), 154.

"The stone that the builders rejected
    has become the cornerstone,"

and

"A stone of stumbling,
    and a rock of offense." (1 Pet. 2:6–8)

But the idea of a "living stone" is Peter's own. In keeping with his thought, it speaks of Christ as alive from the dead and the source of spiritual life for his people (cf. 1:3, 23). As Peter Davids elucidates, it "designates Christ not as a monument or dead principle, but as the living, resurrected, and therefore life-giving one."[3] Humankind's faulty estimation of the "living stone" led to his rejection and crucifixion, but God esteems him as choice and "precious" (2:4).

Peter then expands his "stone" imagery to include the people of God: "As you come to him . . . you yourselves like living stones are being built up as a spiritual house" (vv. 4–5). Peter portrays believers in Christ, the "living stone," as "living stones" themselves. They are living because of their relationship to Christ; they have come in contact with the living stone and receive spiritual life from him. "Jesus' resurrection life becomes theirs, even while they live in the midst of a hostile world."[4] What is God doing with these stones? He is using them to build a building, "a spiritual house," where believers serve as believer-priests to "offer spiritual sacrifices acceptable to God through Jesus Christ" (v. 5).

Ernest Best gives the significance of the fact that the same adjective, "living," is applied to both Christ and his people: "*living stones*: the same designation was applied to Christ in v. 4. 'Living' again indicates that 'stones' is used metaphorically and also that the life of Christians ('born anew' 1:23) is derived from the life of Christ."[5] J. Ramsey Michaels draws the same conclusion from Peter's conception of believers' "coming to" Christ. "The notion of 'coming to' the Stone presupposes that it is not only living but life-giving."[6]

It is good to compare Peter's words—"You yourselves like living stones *are being built up* as a spiritual house" (2:5)—with what Paul wrote—"In him you *also are being built together* into a dwelling place for God by the Spirit" (Eph.

---

[3] Peter H. Davids, *The First Epistle of Peter*, The New International Commentary on the New Testament (Grand Rapids: Eerdmans, 1990), 85.

[4] Thomas R. Schreiner, *1, 2 Peter, Jude*, New American Commentary (Nashville: Broadman and Holman, 2003), 105.

[5] Ernest Best, *1 Peter*, The New Century Bible Commentary (1971; repr., Grand Rapids: Eerdmans, 1977), 101, emphasis original.

[6] J. Ramsey Michaels, *1 Peter*, Word Biblical Commentary (Waco, TX: Word, 1988), 98.

2:22). Both passages refer to the people of God as a temple, use the divine passive to imply that God is the builder, and employ a progressive verb to describe a building process.

First Peter 2:4–5 paints a beautiful picture of union with Christ. Christians derive their life from Christ. When they come to him, they receive spiritual life and are united to him who is "a cornerstone chosen and precious" (v. 6). Michaels's words are apt: "The readers of the epistle are identified . . . as 'living stones' themselves. Christ's life is theirs as well. . . . Only momentarily does he focus attention on Christian believers individually (i.e., as a plurality of 'stones'), for his real interest is in their corporate identity."[7] When joined to the living stone they become living stones and immediately are joined to all other living stones. Union with Christ is here a principle of both individual and communal salvation. We should not miss its purpose: "You yourselves like living stones are being built up as a spiritual house, to be a holy priest-hood, to offer spiritual sacrifices acceptable to God through Jesus Christ" (v. 5). Christians are both temple and priesthood, and therefore union serves the worship of God through his Mediator.

1 Peter 3:14–16

> Have no fear of them, nor be troubled, but in your hearts honor Christ the Lord as holy, always being prepared to make a defense to anyone who asks you for a reason for the hope that is in you; yet do it with gentleness and respect, having a good conscience, so that, when you are slandered, those who revile your good behavior in Christ may be put to shame.

Peter seeks to hearten his readers who are suffering for their faith. Though for the most part believers are not persecuted when they do good, Peter writes, "Even if you should suffer for righteousness' sake, you will be blessed" (v. 14). The apostle counsels them not to fear but instead "in your hearts honor Christ the Lord as holy, always being prepared to make a defense to anyone who asks you for a reason for the hope that is in you; yet do it with gentleness and respect" (v. 15). Believers are to honor Christ within as they ready themselves to explain to any inquirers why they believe in Jesus. And they are to do so gently and respectfully. They are also to be careful to walk in holiness so as to have clean consciences. In that way, when unbelievers speak against Christians' godly lives, the unbelievers "may be put to shame" (v. 16).

---

[7] Ibid., 99.

Peter describes their godly lives in this manner: "your good behavior in Christ." Paul Achtemeier captures the function of "in Christ" in this setting. "While much of the behavior exhibited by Christians would also be recognized as good in the general culture, the addition of the phrase ἐν Χριστῷ [*en Christō*, "in Christ"] makes clear that 'good' is here defined not by cultural norms but by the Christian faith."[8]

Although some do not see union with Christ in this verse,[9] I follow Davids, who does:

> The "good conduct" is "in Christ." This is a characteristically Pauline phrase, found 164 times in Paul's letters. Apparently Paul coined the expression, for it does not appear before him, although later writers use it (especially John). Peter's meaning is quite simply that good conduct flows out of and is determined by the Christian's relationship to Christ, that is, his or her union with Christ. Christ, then, defines what is good conduct, and Christ is the power and motivation for good conduct in even the most provoking situations.[10]

Peter thus envisions two scenarios, both of which require defenses. In the first, unbelievers ask believers to explain the reason for their lifestyle, and a verbal defense is appropriate. In the second, unbelievers falsely accuse believers of wrongdoing, and a nonverbal defense is required. In both cases believers are to keep trusting God and to conduct themselves in a manner of which he would approve. Peter's use of "in Christ" language implies where the power for this God-honoring living comes from, as Best recognizes: "When the Christian is united to Christ in fellowship on the basis of what God has done for him in the death and resurrection of Christ, then his 'behaviour' is 'good' and will be his defence against his accusers."[11]

1 Peter 5:10–11

> After you have suffered a little while, the God of all grace, who has called you to his eternal glory in Christ, will himself restore, confirm, strengthen, and establish you. To him be the dominion forever and ever. Amen.

[8] Achtemeier, *1 Peter*, 236.
[9] So ibid., who instead views "in Christ" here "as signifying what the adjective 'Christian' does in English: to think and act within the sphere of the influence of Christ." Schreiner, *1, 2 Peter, Jude*, agrees (177).
[10] Davids, *First Epistle of Peter*, 133.
[11] Best, *1 Peter*, 134.

Peter exhorts his readers to humble themselves before the Lord, to cast their cares on him, and to take seriously the spiritual battle in which they find themselves (vv. 6–8). The Devil desires to devour them, but they are to "resist him, firm in [their] faith," realizing that their sufferings are not unique but shared by believers around the globe (v. 9).

Peter has spoken previously about Christ's suffering and glory (1:11; 4:13; 5:1); here he applies these concepts to believers: "after you have suffered . . . God . . . who has called you to his eternal glory . . ." (v. 10). Because Jesus suffered and entered into his glory, Christians do the same. Peter's description of God fits their situation: they who are suffering need "the God of all grace." Indeed, he is that God and he will enable them to persevere to the end to receive "eternal glory" in the resurrection. In light of "eternal glory," all present suffering is for "a little while"—a noticeable echo of 1:6, as Thomas Schreiner observes.[12]

The apostle uses four future verbs—God "will himself restore, confirm, strengthen, and establish you" (5:10)—but, as Schreiner teaches, "There is no need to distinguish carefully between the meanings of the verbs, for together they emphatically make the same point. The God who has called believers to eternal glory will strengthen and fortify them, so that they will be able to endure until the end."[13]

God has called his people, including Peter's readers, "to his eternal glory *in Christ*" (v. 10). Here for the second time we encounter "in Christ" language in 1 Peter. Scholars debate whether "in Christ" goes with the whole phrase, with the verb "called," or with the noun "glory."[14] I favor the latter because of its proximity to "glory." Peter, then, probably uses "in Christ" to show means; God will bring us to his eternal glory *through Christ*, the Mediator. It is no wonder that Peter immediately bursts forth in doxology: "To him be the dominion forever and ever. Amen" (v. 11).

1 Peter 5:14

Peace to all of you who are in Christ.

Peter concludes his epistle with these words. As Paul did in fully one-half of his epistolary greetings, so here Peter includes an "in Christ" reference in a final greeting. He uses "in Christ" to describe his readers. He grants peace to

---

[12] Schreiner, *1, 2 Peter, Jude*, 245.
[13] Ibid.
[14] See Davids, *First Epistle of Peter*, 195, for discussion.

all of them "who are in Christ." This does not mean that Peter assumes "that some of them are not in Christ, but that it [peace] is for them because they are in Christ."[15]

The New Testament does not use the word *Christian* frequently, as we do, to describe believers. Best tells how this fact illumines Peter's words: "The present phrase ["in Christ"], which Paul made popular, implies the same as 'Christian' but is more profound since it includes the concept of personal fellowship with Christ."[16] "In Christ" here goes beyond "Christian" to speak of Peter's readers' new relationship with Christ. "The believer has moved into a new sphere of existence: he is united with Christ and shares His risen life," as J. N. D. Kelly explains.[17]

Given "the fiery trial" (4:12) his readers are enduring, it is very fitting for Peter, "a fellow elder" (5:1), to offer a pastoral prayer that God would bless them with his peace. "Their peace, then, is not the peace of this world, but the blessings of the coming age and its ruler, experienced in his 'family' in foretaste in this life."[18] Peter wants this peace to comfort them now and spawn the hope of a fully realized salvation in the resurrection of the dead on the last day.

Commenting on 5:14, Wayne Grudem offers a theological summary of larger scope: "To be *in Christ* is to be united with him for all the benefits of redemption: it is the status of all true believers as soon as they have become Christians, and they remain *in Christ* for all eternity."[19]

2 Peter

2 Peter 1:3–4

His divine power has granted to us all things that pertain to life and godliness, through the knowledge of him who called us to his own glory and excellence, by which he has granted to us his precious and very great promises, so that through them you may become partakers of the divine nature, having escaped from the corruption that is in the world because of sinful desire.

These verses immediately follow Peter's salutation. He says that Christ's divine power has given his people all they need to gain eternal life and to lead

---

[15] Ibid., 205.
[16] Best, *1 Peter*, 180. Schreiner holds that "'in Christ' simply means 'Christian' here"; *1, 2 Peter, Jude*, 252.
[17] J. N. D. Kelly, *A Commentary on the Epistles of Peter and of Jude*, Black's New Testament Commentary (Grand Rapids: Baker, 1969), 221.
[18] Davids, *First Epistle of Peter*, 206.
[19] Wayne Grudem, *1 Peter*, Tyndale New Testament Commentary (Grand Rapids: Eerdmans, 1988), 202.

lives pleasing to God. These are obtained through knowing Christ, who effectively summons us to himself. The end of our calling is Christ's own "glory and excellence," his beauty and moral perfection (v. 3). By his grace, when Jesus returns we will be like him (cf. 1 John 3:2). Because of Christ's moral excellence, he has given us wonderful promises. His twofold purpose? That we might partake of God's nature and escape the world's corruption (2 Pet. 1:4).[20]

Peter's words, that "you may become partakers of the divine nature"—γένησθε θείας κοινωνοὶ φύσεως/*genēsthe theias koinōnoi physeōs*—are bold and controversial. Richard Lucas and Christopher Green say that they make "a claim without equal in the New Testament."[21] This language has a history in Greek thought and in Hellenistic Judaism. Greeks commonly held to an ontological dualism between the divine and material worlds. The former was regarded as permanent and immortal; the latter, transient and mortal. Richard Bauckham explains, "A strong tradition of Greek thought held that the superior, spiritual part of man really belongs to the divine world and can recover its true, godlike nature and participate in the immortality of the gods."[22]

This strong tradition manifested itself in various ways in different Greek religions and philosophies. In the mystery religions immortality was sought through the performance of rituals and sometimes through asceticism. In the Platonic tradition the soul sought a return to its divine status through contemplation and detachment from the body. In the Hermetic literature persons sought divinization through obtaining knowledge. "In general the soul's attainment of godlike immortality, and its liberation from the material world in which it is involved through its confinement in the body, were necessarily closely connected."[23]

Although Peter was probably aware of some of these Greek ideas, he was more familiar with Hellenistic Judaism. "In 4 Maccabees and the Wisdom of Solomon, human destiny is presented as the soul's attainment of immortality and incorruptibility after death. . . . Pseudo-Phocylides . . . boldly combines the Jewish doctrine of physical resurrection with the Greek language of divinization."[24] But more than anyone else, Philo uses Platonic language. It is important to note that none of these Jewish writers portrays a pantheistic ab-

---

[20] In referring to Christ rather than God the Father in this paragraph, I follow Douglas J. Moo, *2 Peter, Jude*, NIV Application Commentary (Grand Rapids: Zondervan, 1996), 40–43.
[21] Richard Lucas and Christopher Green, *The Message of 2 Peter and Jude*, The Bible Speaks Today (Leicester, UK: Inter-Varsity, 1995), 51.
[22] Richard J. Bauckham, *Jude, 2 Peter*, Word Biblical Commentary (Waco, TX: Word, 1983), 180.
[23] Ibid.
[24] Ibid.

sorption of the soul into the being of God. They observe the Creator/creature distinction, but as Bauckham clarifies, "they do hold that the human soul, created in God's image, is capable of resembling God in his immortality and incorruptibility."[25] This is divinization only in a loose sense, and to these Jewish writers it is attainable by human beings only with the aid of divine grace.

Against this Greek and Jewish background, interpreters of 2 Peter have variously understood Peter's teaching that believers can, in some sense, "become partakers of the divine nature." Some regard the phrase as "metaphysical, patterned on that used in contemporary Hellenistic religion. The believer shares in a divine nature instead of a worldly."[26] Some have concluded that Peter's words refer to becoming immortal and incorruptible at death.[27] Others have reasoned that the apostle refers to sharing in God's or Christ's moral qualities, both in part now and fully in the future.[28] Still others hold that Peter means "they will enter into true union with God, participating in His glory, immortality, and blessedness."[29]

What are we to conclude concerning Peter's bold words? It is important to prevent misunderstandings. The apostle does not break down the distinction between God and his creatures. Never is the line between creatures and Creator trespassed. We do not become God or a part of God. When Peter writes, "become partakers of the divine nature," he speaks of Christians' sharing in God in some sense. There is a real union with God.

Schreiner is correct: "Believers will share in the divine nature in that they will be morally perfected; they will share in the moral excellence that belongs to God (1:3)."[30] He cites the conclusions of J. M. Starr's study of Peter's terminology: "He concludes from his comparative study that sharing in the divine nature does not mean 'deified.' Instead Peter maintained that believers will share in the moral qualities of Christ."[31] Of course, this moral perfection is not obtained in this life; it will be obtained only at Christ's return. "Nevertheless, it is doubtful that Peter referred *only* to the future. Even now believers are indwelt by the Holy Spirit and are like God to some extent."[32]

---

[25] Ibid.

[26] E. M. Sidebottom, *James, Jude, 2 Peter*, The New Century Bible Commentary (Grand Rapids: Eerdmans, 1967), 106–7.

[27] So Bauckham, *Jude, 2 Peter*, 181.

[28] So Peter H. Davids, *The Letters of 2 Peter and Jude*, The Pillar New Testament Commentary (Grand Rapids: Eerdmans, 2006), 176; Moo, *2 Peter, Jude*, 43; and Schreiner, *1, 2 Peter, Jude*, 294–95, who cites J. M. Starr, *Sharers in Divine Nature: 2 Peter 1:4 in Its Hellenistic Context*, Coniectanea Biblica New Testament (Stockholm: Almqvist & Wiksell, 2000).

[29] Kelly, *A Commentary on the Epistles of Peter and Jude*, 301–2.

[30] Schreiner, *1, 2 Peter, Jude*, 294.

[31] Ibid., 295. He cites Starr, *Sharers in Divine Nature*.

[32] Schreiner, *1, 2 Peter, Jude*, 295.

The view that Peter intends a real sharing in God's moral excellence is reinforced by the context of 2 Peter 1:4. Above I spoke of Peter's twofold purpose in that verse: partaking of God's nature and escaping the world's corruption. Here I add that our understanding of the former is corroborated by the latter, as Davids argues:

> Since this escape from the corruption in the world that parallels participating in the divine nature is ethical, . . . the character of the divine nature must also be ethical and not simply another way of indicating immortality. . . . The immortal permanence of the divine . . . is connected to holiness, purity, and goodness. . . . And so it is likely that what 2 Peter has in mind when he claims participation in the divine nature is the reception of an ethical nature like God's which then leads to immortality.[33]

Moreover, the five verses immediately following 1:4 further corroborate our understanding of believers' becoming partakers of God's nature as sharing in some of God's attributes (in a creaturely way, of course) and escaping the world's corruption due to sinful desire. The verses that follow are a call to virtue, including some of the very same divine qualities of which we partake: "virtue" (v. 5) and "godliness" (vv. 6–7).

Davids summarizes:

> The "escape" is likely an ongoing process, beginning indeed with Christian initiation (as Kelly and others argue), but not ending there (and not limited to attaining immortality at death, as Bauckham and Vögtle argue). Recognition that escape is a process brings a healthy humility to the follower of Jesus. It is this process of escape that leads directly to the call to grow in virtue in the next verse.[34]

Conclusion

Peter depicts believers in Christ, *the* "living stone," as "living stones" themselves when they come to him in service (1 Pet. 2:4). They are living because they have come in contact with the living stone and received eternal life from him who died for them and arose. By virtue of union with Christ, they receive resurrection life and are "born again" (1:23). God uses these "living stones" to build "a spiritual house" where believer-priests worship God through Christ

---

[33] Davids, *Letters of 2 Peter and Jude*, 176.
[34] Ibid.

(2:5). Peter's image of the church as a spiritual temple conveys the ideas of both individual and communal union with Christ.

Peter exhorts believers to persevere in faith and piety, even when falsely accused of wrongdoing for their faith in Christ. They must be ready to share their faith in a gentle and respectful manner with any who ask about it (3:15). And they are to live exemplary lives before unbelievers so that, Peter says, "those who revile your good behavior in Christ may be put to shame" (v. 16). Their "good behavior in Christ" speaks of godly conduct that derives from their union with Christ. Peter's use of "in Christ" language implies where the power for this God-honoring living comes from—from the living Christ, residing within.

Having previously told of Christ's suffering and glory (1:11; 4:13; 5:1), Peter now applies them to Christians: "After you have suffered . . . God . . . who has called you to his eternal glory in Christ, will himself restore, confirm, strengthen, and establish you" (5:10). Even as Christ suffered and entered into his glory, Christians follow him. "The God of all grace" will enable the suffering believers whom Peter addresses to endure to the end, where they will receive "eternal glory" in the resurrection. God has summoned his people to "his eternal glory *in Christ*" (v. 10). Taking "in Christ" to go with "glory," I understand Peter to mean that God will bring us to his eternal glory *through Christ*, the Mediator. Ernest Best sums up Peter's message: believers are members of Christ's church and are assured of final participation in his glory "only because of God's activity in and through Christ."[35]

Peter, "a fellow elder and a witness of the sufferings of Christ, as well as partaker in the glory that is going to be revealed" (5:1), prays that God would grant his readers peace in the midst of their "fiery trial" (4:12). He concludes his epistle thus: "Peace to all of you who are in Christ" (5:14). Like Paul, Peter includes an "in Christ" reference in this final greeting. He grants peace to all his readers "who are in Christ." "In Christ" here not only means "Christian" but also speaks of Peter's readers' new relationship with Christ, their spiritual bond with him.

Davids ties together Peter's three uses of "in Christ" language when he says of Peter's audience, "Their good life-style (3:16), their future hope (5:10), and their present peace are all due to their relationship with Christ, their identification with him."[36]

---

[35] Best, *1 Peter*, 176.
[36] Davids, *Letters of 2 Peter and Jude*, 205–6.

Peter famously said that through God's "precious and very great promises . . . you may become partakers of the divine nature" (2 Pet. 1:4). These words do not obliterate the distinction between God and his creatures. The apostle does not mean that we become God or a part of God. Rather, when he writes, "become partakers of the divine nature," he speaks of Christians' sharing in some of God's moral "excellence" (v. 3). The very next words confirm this interpretation, for Peter adds, "having escaped from the corruption that is in the world because of sinful desire" (v. 4). Participating in God's nature means escaping from the world's corruption. God wills for believers to share in the moral qualities of Christ. Although these moral qualities will be perfected in us only at the second coming, even now through the indwelling Spirit we are enabled to be like God to a degree.

Chapter 19

Union with Christ
in 1 John

Although union does not appear in 2–3 John, it is a prominent theme in 1 John. Believers are said to be "in" God, and he is said to be "in" them. The major motif pertaining to union is the concept of abiding. Like the Fourth Gospel, 1 John speaks of believers abiding in God/Christ and of God/Christ abiding in them.

1 John 2:4–6

> Whoever says "I know him" but does not keep his commandments is a liar, and the truth is not in him, but whoever keeps his word, in him truly the love of God is perfected. By this we may know that we are in him: whoever says he abides in him ought to walk in the same way in which he walked.

First John was written to give assurance to discouraged believers who had been rejected by false teachers (2:18–25; 5:13). But it has other purposes too, one of which is to distinguish true religion from counterfeits. Here John insists that the person who professes to know the Lord but disobeys him belies his profession and shows that God's Word does not dwell in his heart. On the other hand, God's love attains its goal in the one who obeys his Word.

In fact, John insists, obedience brings assurance to Christians. Those who claim to abide in Christ (2:6) and follow his example of faithfulness to and love for God gain confidence that they are "in him" (v. 5). These verses contain two pictures of union. The first motif is being in Christ. This resembles Paul's expression "in Christ (Jesus)." Robert Yarbrough explains:

> To be in Christ or God, as 1 John depicts the state, is to . . . know God the Father fully through relationship to him via the Son. It is to have the Father living in oneself, doing his work, if Jesus's own description of being "in the Father" and having "the Father . . . in me" is any indication: "Don't you believe that I am in the Father, and that the Father is in me? . . . It is the Father, living in me, who is doing his work" (John 14:10 NIV).[1]

The second picture of union is abiding in Christ. This is the first occurrence of a leading theme of 1 John. It speaks not only of initially believing in Jesus but also of persevering in faith, love, and godliness—three other important themes of the epistle. "Abiding" is not to be thought of as chiefly external; it speaks of a warm, ongoing attachment to the Son of God, as Stephen Smalley says: "The use of μένειν [*menein*, "to abide"] at this point suggests an intensely personal knowledge of God; it presupposes an intimate and committed relationship with him, through Jesus, which is both permanent and continuous."[2]

1 John 2:24–26

> Let what you heard from the beginning abide in you. If what you heard from the beginning abides in you, then you too will abide in the Son and in the Father. And this is the promise that he made to us—eternal life.
> I write these things to you about those who are trying to deceive you.

The readers rejected the "antichrists" (vv. 18, 22), false teachers and deceivers who espoused an errant christology and faulty ethic. The false teachers' leaving the Johannine Christians displayed that they were inauthentic (v. 19). John builds his readers up in their faith by assuring them that they have the Holy Spirit and know God's truth. They do not need to listen to the false teachers (vv. 20–21), antichrists who deny the Father and the Son. By contrast, the readers confess the Father (and the Son) (vv. 22–23). They are to continue believing and living out the truth they were told when they first believed the gospel. They are not to change the message or listen to those

---

[1] Robert W. Yarbrough, *1–3 John*, Baker Exegetical Commentary on the New Testament (Grand Rapids: Baker Academic, 2008), 87.
[2] Stephen S. Smalley, *1, 2, 3, John*, Word Biblical Commentary (Waco, TX: Word, 1984), 52.

who do. If they persist in the truth, they "too will abide in the Son and in the Father" (v. 24). Again Yarbrough appeals to the Gospel of John to provide understanding of "abiding" in 1 John.

> [Abiding] connotes a particular mode of living in which Christ himself is the root and branches upon which human lives are dependent like leaves on a grapevine. This is the imagery of John 15, a passage that crystallizes and defines the "abide" concept in John's cognitive world as known to us from his writings. There Jesus utters the word "abide" (or a form of it) eleven times in seven verses. To abide is to be assured fruitfulness (15:4 [3x], 5; cf. 15:16), preservation from destruction (15:6), and hearing of petitions (15:7a). With his words abiding in them (15:7b; cf. 5:38; 8:31), believers are to abide in Christ and in Christ's love (15:9).[3]

The closest John 15 comes to defining what it means to abide is when Jesus says, "As the Father has loved me, so have I loved you. Abide in my love" (John 15:9). To abide in Jesus is to abide in his love, to persist in a relationship with him begun with his love for us. To abide, then, is to love him in return, which involves worship, obedience, and much more. True disciples will continue in a personal relationship with the Son and Father, indicative of union with them. They will continue to enjoy eternal life, which is to know the Father and the Son (1 John 2:25; cf. John 17:3).

1 John 2:27–28

> The anointing that you received from him abides in you, and you have no need that anyone should teach you. But as his anointing teaches you about everything, and is true, and is no lie—just as it has taught you, abide in him.
>
> And now, little children, abide in him, so that when he appears we may have confidence and not shrink from him in shame at his coming.

The readers have God's "anointing," the Holy Spirit, poured out on the church by the ascended Christ. The Spirit continues to live within them and teach them the things of God in fulfillment of Jesus's promise, "The Spirit of truth . . . will guide you into all the truth" (John 16:13). Because they have the Spirit, they are able to reject the false teachers and their aberrant teachings. And they are to continue in the message about Christ that, combined with faith, brought them salvation.

---

[3] Yarbrough, *1–3 John*, 159–60.

Twice John commands, "Abide in him [Christ]" (1 John 2:27–28). Within the matrix of the thought of 1 John, this has doctrinal, behavioral, and relational aspects. It involves holding fast their confession of Christ amid opposition, living out in purity the reality of continuing in him, and loving him and other believers.[4] Viewed from the larger purview of 1 John, believers abide in him and are commanded to do so because he abides in them (3:24 [2x]; 4:12, 13, 15, 16). Thus, union with Christ, expressed as abiding, has both indicative and imperative features. Because God abides in us, we abide in him (indicative) and are commanded and exhorted to abide in him (imperative).

In addition, for the first time in the "abiding" passages, we find an eschatological element. Christians are to abide in Jesus, says John, "so that when he appears we may have confidence and not shrink from him in shame at his coming" (2:28). This means that abiding in Christ will enable believers to avoid condemnation and will increase their confidence at his return.

1 John 3:5–8

> You know that he appeared in order to take away sins, and in him there is no sin. No one who abides in him keeps on sinning; no one who keeps on sinning has either seen him or known him. Little children, let no one deceive you. Whoever practices righteousness is righteous, as he is righteous. Whoever makes a practice of sinning is of the devil, for the devil has been sinning from the beginning. The reason the Son of God appeared was to destroy the works of the devil.

Basic to 1 John is the message that "God is light, and in him is no darkness at all" (1:5). If people profess to know him and do not walk in holiness and truth, they lie (v. 6). If they believe the truth and live for God ("walk in the light"), it is not their performance but Christ's atonement that makes them acceptable to God (v. 7). If believers claim not to have sin or not to have sinned, they are fooling themselves and bringing shame on the Name they profess (vv. 8, 10). "If we confess our sins, he is faithful and just to forgive us our sins and to cleanse us from all unrighteousness" (v. 9).

The passage at hand must be understood against this backdrop. The sinless Christ came to "take away sins," to bring forgiveness and abolish sin in daily life (3:5). For professed Christians to live a life given over to sin, therefore, contradicts Christ's saving accomplishment. Of course, believers are not

---

[4] So ibid., 165.

perfect in this life; they still sin. But they do not "practice sin" as they did before salvation and as unsaved people in general do. John does not want his readers to be deceived: "Whoever practices righteousness is righteous, as he is righteous. Whoever makes a practice of sinning is of the devil" (vv. 7–8). Saved persons live basically godly lives; unsaved people do not and thereby reveal their paternity—they are the Devil's children. John's ethic is dualistic: "By this it is evident who are the children of God, and who are the children of the devil: whoever does not practice righteousness is not of God" (v. 10).

We are ready to understand verse 6: "No one who abides in him keeps on sinning; no one who keeps on sinning has either seen him or known him." Smalley accurately defines those who abide in Christ as those who enjoy an "intimate and ongoing relationship with Jesus."[5] John's point is that such people do not make a practice of sinning. People joined to Christ by grace through faith union bring honor to Jesus's cross by living for him. Jesus had promised his disciples, "If you abide in my word, you are truly my disciples, and you will know the truth, and the truth will set you free" (John 8:31–32). Yarbrough applies this to 1 John 3:6: "Part of this freedom is liberation from the tyranny of a life lived in darkness rather than in God's good light."[6]

However, those who live lives under the tyranny of sin reveal that they do not know the Lord. Yarbrough does not mince words: "In the immediate context, the upshot would be that the behavior presumed in 3:4, 6 would render profession of faith in Jesus null and void."[7]

1 John 3:21–24

> Beloved, if our heart does not condemn us, we have confidence before
> God; and whatever we ask we receive from him, because we keep his com-
> mandments and do what pleases him. And this is his commandment, that
> we believe in the name of his Son Jesus Christ and love one another, just
> as he has commanded us. Whoever keeps his commandments abides in
> God, and God in him. And by this we know that he abides in us, by the
> Spirit whom he has given us.

Though John has just spoken of believers' hearts condemning them for lack of love for fellow Christians, he has also spoken of such persons relying on God (who is great and all-knowing) for forgiveness and restoration (vv.

---

[5] Smalley, *1, 2, 3, John*, 158–59.
[6] Yarbrough, *1–3 John*, 186.
[7] Ibid.

19–21). The result is "confidence before God" (v. 21). And this confidence of acceptance by him overflows into confidence in prayer (v. 22). This confidence increases for those who love God's commandments and do what pleases him (as Jesus did, according to John 8:29).

As he so often does, John intertwines ethical, doctrinal, and relational themes. "And this is his commandment, that we believe in the name of his Son Jesus Christ and love one another, just as he has commanded us" (1 John 3:23). Obeying God's commandments includes trusting Christ and loving other believers. Then, for the first time, he speaks not only of believers' abiding in God (which he has done several times), but also of God's abiding in them: "Whoever keeps his commandments abides in God, and God in him" (v. 24). "Here, for the first time . . . we hear of a reciprocal 'abiding' between God in Christ and the Christian," says Smalley.[8] Obedient believers abide in God, and amazingly, he abides in them. I. Howard Marshall expresses something of the wonder of this: "The person who is obedient lives in God, and God lives in him. This formula, similar to Paul's language about the mutual indwelling of Christ and the believer, indicates the closest possible union between man and God."[9]

Here is union with Christ communicated in John's familiar idiom of abiding. But this time the abiding is reciprocal between God and believers and is correlated with reference to the indwelling Spirit: "And by this we know that he abides in us, by the Spirit whom he has given us" (v. 24). The Holy Spirit enables believers to know that God dwells in them. As Yarbrough summarizes, "Believers know, by the Spirit that God (or Christ) gives them, that they abide in Christ and Christ in them as they keep his commandments to trust and love."[10]

1 John 4:1–4

Beloved, do not believe every spirit, but test the spirits to see whether they are from God, for many false prophets have gone out into the world. By this you know the Spirit of God: every spirit that confesses that Jesus Christ has come in the flesh is from God, and every spirit that does not confess Jesus is not from God. This is the spirit of the antichrist, which you heard was coming and now is in the world already. Little children, you are

---

[8] Smalley, *1, 2, 3, John*, 210.
[9] I. Howard Marshall, *The Epistles of John*, The New International Commentary on the New Testament (Grand Rapids: Eerdmans, 1978), 202.
[10] Yarbrough, *1–3 John*, 216.

from God and have overcome them, for he who is in you is greater than he who is in the world.

First John issues stern warnings concerning doctrinal error. John calls readers to "test the spirits to see whether they are from God" (v. 1). They are not to trust every spirit, for there are many false prophets. Apparently, the spirits energize the prophets to speak, so to believe a false prophet's message is to believe the evil spirit within him. John gives a test to distinguish true and false prophets, to distinguish "the Spirit of truth and the spirit of error" (v. 6).

True prophets believe in the incarnation of the Son of God, while false prophets do not. Denying the incarnation is the work of the "spirit of the antichrist" (v. 3). Readers need not fear, for God is their Father (they are "from God") and gives them the victory through his Son. In fact, they have already "overcome" their foes.[11] Why? Because "he who is in you is greater than he who is in the world" (v. 4). The word rendered "in" (ἐν) should probably be translated "among."[12] Either way it speaks of their union with Christ, as Yarbrough underscores:

> John's confidence, while it extends to his readers, is not grounded in them. They will prevail only because "the one who is among you is greater than the one who is in the world." The one "in the world" is antichrist and the beings or forces he commands. The one whom believers share is Christ. He is, in traditional Johannine parlance, the one "who holds the seven stars in his right hand and walks among the seven golden lampstands" of the churches (Rev. 2:1 NIV). His powerful presence guarantees his followers' arrival at the destination to which he beckons them.[13]

Union with the powerful, risen Christ, then, bolsters John's readers in their spiritual battles against Antichrist and his allies, both spiritual and human. Because he is Christus Victor, they too are victors in him.

1 John 4:7–16

Beloved, let us love one another, for love is from God, and whoever loves has been born of God and knows God. Anyone who does not love does not know God, because God is love. In this the love of God was made

---

[11] John uses the perfect tense "you . . . have overcome" [νενικήκατε/*nenikēkate*] to indicate that the victory is a *fait accompli.*
[12] I gratefully acknowledge help on this point from my former student Jake Neufeld.
[13] Yarbrough, *1–3 John*, 227.

manifest among us, that God sent his only Son into the world, so that we might live through him. In this is love, not that we have loved God but that he loved us and sent his Son to be the propitiation for our sins. Beloved, if God so loved us, we also ought to love one another. No one has ever seen God; if we love one another, God abides in us and his love is perfected in us.

By this we know that we abide in him and he in us, because he has given us of his Spirit. And we have seen and testify that the Father has sent his Son to be the Savior of the world. Whoever confesses that Jesus is the Son of God, God abides in him, and he in God. So we have come to know and to believe the love that God has for us. God is love, and whoever abides in love abides in God, and God abides in him.

As Paul's supreme exposition of God's love is 1 Corinthians 13, so John's is 1 John 4:7–16. In his unique style John exhorts his readers to love one another, for love finds it source in God. God's love also has powerful results—love shown by Christians demonstrates regeneration and knowledge of God (v. 7). Therefore, regardless of profession of faith, a man or woman devoid of love reveals that he or she does not know God, "because God is love" (v. 8). Love is as inherent in God's nature as holiness ("God is light," 1:5). Because he is characterized by love, those who truly know him exhibit the same attribute, because his love is transformative, as Yarbrough reminds us: "No trait is more inherent in God as depicted by 1 John than the active will to love. Therefore, to know God results, quite simply, in loving like God loves."[14]

God displayed his love supremely in the incarnation. God sent his Son to be the Savior of the world, that those who were spiritually dead might be spiritually resurrected and have new life through him. In fact, it is misleading to begin a definition of love "from below," with human initiative. It is much wiser to begin "from above," with divine initiative: "In this is love, not that we have loved God but that he loved us" (v. 10). What is the supreme demonstration of this love? The fact that God "sent his Son to be the propitiation for our sins" (v. 10). Though salvation is free for everyone who believes, it was costly to the holy Son of God. It cost him his life given in propitiatory atonement to satisfy God's justice and turn away his wrath.[15]

Again, 1 John exhorts, "Beloved, if God so loved us, we also ought to love

---

[14] Ibid., 237.
[15] For a treatment of penal substitution, see Robert A. Peterson, *Salvation Accomplished by the Son: The Work of Christ* (Wheaton, IL: Crossway, 2012), 362–412. For responses to objections, see 396–407.

one another" (v. 11). God's active love for us energizes us to show active love to one another. His love, given in Christ's atoning death, transforms us into lovers of both God and human beings. Here this is expressed as an obligation true believers are glad to fulfill, for it is the overflow of God's boundless love for them.

In the next five verses "abide" occurs six times, all but one communicating believers' abiding in God and God's abiding in them:

- "God abides in us" (v. 12).
- "We abide in him and he in us" (v. 13).
- "Whoever confesses . . . Jesus . . . God abides in him, and he in God" (v. 15).
- "Whoever abides in love abides in God, and God abides in him" (v. 16).

This, the greatest concentration of "abiding" language in 1 John, deserves careful attention.

Though God is invisible, if his children demonstrate compassion for each other, God truly dwells in them and his love becomes visible and reaches its goal in their lives (v. 12). One way that God's people recognize that they abide in him and he in them is his Holy Spirit's dwelling in their hearts and lives (v. 13). John speaks with apostolic authority when he says, "We have seen and testify that the Father has sent his Son to be the Savior of the world" (v. 14). First John's exhortations to love are based not on pious pipe dreams but on apostolic eyewitness and testimony (cf. 1:1–4).

Although mutual abiding between God and human beings is mystical, it is based not on mysticism but on a confession of Jesus's divine sonship (v. 15). Let no one claim to dwell in God who has not professed Jesus as Lord and Savior. But for the person who truly professes Christ, "God abides in him, and he in God" (v. 15). Astonishingly, as revealed in the Fourth Gospel (John 6:56; 14:20; 15:4–5; 17:21), so here there is a mutual indwelling between God and his people. Christians have come to recognize and accept God's love in Christ (1 John 4:16). This is not a natural but a supernatural event. Only as God works in us do we know, taste, and believe that God loves us.

As was said near the beginning of this passage, here again "God is love" resounds (v. 16). And in light of all he has taught about God's love, John draws an inescapable conclusion: "Whoever abides in love abides in God, and God abides in him" (v. 16). Because the very nature of God is compassion, and because that compassion is transformative, people who continue in genuine love continue to be attached to God, and he to them.

It is no wonder, then, that such love gives true believers "confidence for the day of judgment" (v. 17). This is because God's perfect love drives out of our hearts all fear of his wrath (v. 18). First John is pithy in summary: "We love because he first loved us" (v. 19).

1 John 5:20

> We know that the Son of God has come and has given us understanding, so that we may know him who is true; and we are in him who is true, in his Son Jesus Christ. He is the true God and eternal life.

In contrast to the rebellious world (cf. 2:15–17), which "lies in the power of the evil one," believers "are from God" (5:19). Being "from God" here parallels being "born of God" in verse 18. Both expressions point to divine paternity. God is believers' Father; they are his children, born of him into his family. While the world languishes under the Evil One's sway, Christians belong to their heavenly Father. His unique Son protects them from the Evil One's great harm, and they do not live lives characterized by rebellion against their Father (v. 18).

God's people know that his Son has come in the incarnation and "has given" them "understanding" of spiritual reality, so they love God with their minds and "know him who is true" (v. 20). This is a reference to Christ, concerning whom the end of 1 John says exalted things: he is "true," "the true God and eternal life" (v. 20). These are three ways of affirming the deity of Christ. Yarbrough summarizes the first two: "It is fair to say that in John's usage this adjective ['true'] most frequently points to an object or person who is 'made of' the divine nature. . . . Wallace . . . rightly concludes that 'there is no grammatical reason for denying' that John here calls Jesus 'the true God.'"[16] And Raymond Brown correctly maintains that the third description, "eternal life," also refers to Jesus:

> The second predicate identifying *houtos* ["this"] is "eternal life," which, since it lacks the definite article, is closely joined to the first predicate—the true God who is (for us) eternal life. . . . This predicate fits Jesus better than it fits God. . . . If the reference here is to Jesus, then there is an inclusion

---

[16] Yarbrough, *1–3 John*, 319–20. He refers to Daniel B. Wallace, *Greek Grammar beyond the Basics: An Exegetical Syntax of the New Testament* (Grand Rapids: Zondervan, 1996), 327.

with the I John Prologue (1:2): "This eternal life which was in the Father's presence . . . was revealed to us."[17]

John says more; he says that "we are in him who is true, in his Son Jesus Christ. He is the true God and eternal life" (5:20). Here for the second time 1 John teaches that believers are "in Christ" (cf. 2:5). This is a plain reference to union with Christ. As Yarbrough notes (while including "abiding" language):

> Not only does John commend knowledge of the Son. . . . He also declares that believers are "in" the one for whom any adjective, even "true," is an inadequate approximation. The mutual indwelling of believers in the Son or the Father or vice versa has been a frequent theme of the epistle wherever there is talk of "abiding." . . . This positioning of believers begs comparison with Paul's notion of being "in Christ."[18]

Conclusion

First John has much to teach concerning union with Christ. Revisiting expressions of union from his Gospel, John employs two metaphors for union in his first epistle. First, he speaks of God or Christ being "in" us and of our being "in" Christ. Second, he says we "abide" in Christ or God and that Christ or God "abides" in us.

God or Christ in Us and We in Christ

One time 1 John says God or Christ is "in you": "Little children, you are from God and have overcome them, for he who is in you is greater than he who is in the world" (4:4). The context warns of spiritual warfare; it tells of the "spirit of antichrist" that energizes false prophets who deny the Son's incarnation (vv. 1–3). John's readers are not to cower in fear, for their mighty Victor has overcome the enemy for them. As a result, "You . . . have overcome them, for he who is in you is greater than he who is in the world" (v. 4).

Neither John nor his readers are to put their confidence in themselves. Rather, their victory is assured because of Christ's accomplishment in his death and resurrection and because of his presence in their lives. It is this powerful, overcoming presence that John points to when he says, "He who is

---

[17] Raymond E. Brown, *The Epistles of John*, Anchor Bible (Garden City, NY: Doubleday, 1982), 626.
[18] Yarbrough, *1–3 John*, 319–20.

in you is greater than he who is in the world." Christ is stronger than Satan and Antichrist and has overcome them. Moreover, this conquering Christ indwells his people, assuring them of eventual victory through his mighty presence.[19]

Twice, referring to Jesus, 1 John says "we are in him":

> Whoever says "I know him" but does not keep his commandments is a liar, and the truth is not in him, but whoever keeps his word, in him truly the love of God is perfected. By this we may know that *we are in him*: whoever says he abides in him ought to walk in the same way in which he walked. (2:4–6)

> We know that the Son of God has come and has given us understanding, so that we may know him who is true; and *we are in him* who is true, in his Son Jesus Christ. He is the true God and eternal life. (5:20)

The expression "we are in him [Jesus]" is equivalent to "we have eternal life" or "we know the Son." They are three of 1 John's ways of talking about possessing salvation. To be an authentic believer is to be in the Son, to exist in union with him. In the first passage, being "in him" is inseparable from obeying God. In the second passage, being "in him" is correlative with knowing Christ cognitively and personally.

Yarbrough's words bear repeating: "To be in Christ or God, as 1 John depicts the state, is to . . . know God the Father fully through relationship to him via the Son. It is to have the Father living in oneself, doing his work."[20] To be in the Son of God is a *sine qua non* of salvation, according to 1 John. It presupposes being indwelt by the Son, and it means dwelling in or being in him. And this takes us back to the Fourth Gospel's exalted teaching of mutual indwelling, which is an aspect of the second metaphor for union in 1 John.

Abiding in Christ or God, and Christ or God Abiding in Us

First John also speaks of union in terms of abiding. Frequently John speaks of believers abiding in Christ, which has moral ramifications. The one who claims to abide in Christ ought to follow Jesus's example (2:6). Similarly, John explains that "no one who abides in him keeps on sinning" (3:6). Twice in short compass John commands Christians to abide in Christ. The first time

---

[19] See ibid., 227.
[20] Ibid., 87.

this command is attached to the teaching of believers by the Holy Spirit ("[his] anointing") (2:27). The second time obeying this command prepares believers for the return of Christ (v. 28). Once John announces that if they persist in the truth they were taught when they first believed the gospel, they "will abide in the Son and in the Father" (v. 24). This is the only time Christians are said to continue "in" more than one divine person.

All of this should be viewed as extension and application of Jesus's teaching on abiding in the Gospel of John. Rudolf Schnackenburg distinguishes between the Son's relationship to the Father and that of Christians: "The Christian can never say like Christ: 'The Father and I are one' (John 10:30; cf. 17:11)."[21] Nevertheless, having made this crucial distinction, Schnackenburg captures the intimacy of relationship believers enjoy with God. "But through Christ the Christian is brought into a profound fellowship with God, as profound as is possible without the loss of one's personality."[22] As Yarbrough summarizes, abiding "has come to be almost ubiquitous shorthand in 1 John for believers' habitual personal attachment to Christ (e.g., 2:6, 28) or for the presence in believers of God's saving truth (e.g., 2:24, 27; 3:9)."[23]

Hand in hand with this profound personal relationship with God and Christ come the ethical obligations we observed above. John does not endorse easy-believism. To the contrary, 1 John is ethically rigorous, as Schnackenburg notes: "Johannine mysticism is distinctive because of its strong ethical orientation."[24]

John raises believers' personal relationship with God in Christ and the corresponding ethical responsibility to a higher level by teaching that abiding is reciprocal between God and his people. Twice 1 John says God "abides in us" (3:24; 4:12). Four times it speaks of this abiding with God as reciprocal:

Whoever keeps his commandments abides in God, and God in him. (3:24)

By this we know that we abide in him and he in us, because he has given us of his Spirit. (4:13)

Whoever confesses that Jesus is the Son of God, God abides in him, and he in God. (4:15)

---

[21] Rudolf Schnackenburg, *The Johannine Epistles: A Commentary*, trans. Reginald and Ilse Fuller (New York: Crossroad, 1992), 102.
[22] Ibid.
[23] Yarbrough, *1–3 John*, 202.
[24] Schnackenburg, *Johannine Epistles*, 103.

God is love, and whoever abides in love abides in God, and God abides in him. (4:16)

First John 3:24 assumes an important role, because here for the first time we encounter mutual abiding between God and Christians, as Smalley observes:

> It is the children of God who can lay claim to the personal and intimate relationship of "living" or "abiding" in him. . . . Elsewhere in this letter John speaks of disciples living in God and/or Jesus (2:5–6, 24, 27–28; 3:6; cf. 5:20), and/or God dwelling in the believer (4:12; cf. 2:14; 3:9). Here, for the first time, . . . we hear of a reciprocal "abiding" between God in Christ and the Christian (see also 4:13, 15, 16). The OT prophets had promised, as a part of the new covenant, that the dwelling-place of God would be with his people (Ezek. 37:27); and John now depicts the fulfillment of the hope (cf. Rev. 21:3). Obedience leads to a mutual indwelling: God in man, as well as man in God.[25]

We not only enjoy such a "personal and intimate relationship" with Christ, but he has such a relationship with us! This is the amazing truth of believers' sharing in a certain sense by grace through faith in the divine perichoresis we found in John's Gospel. And, of course, such a privilege carries ethical connotations. John combines mutual-abiding language with moral obligation. Reciprocal abiding is true of those characterized by obedience to God's commands (1 John 3:24), confession that Jesus is God's Son (4:15), and continuance in love (3:14).

For the sake of our study we separated John's speaking of God or Christ being "in" us and of our being "in" Christ from John's saying that we "abide" in Christ or God and that Christ or God "abides" in us. But now it is time to admit that the two are basically synonymous, as Brown indicates, "The expressions *einai en*, 'to be in,' and *menein en*, 'to abide in,' are almost interchangeable."[26]

It is worthwhile to address one more topic—the role of the Holy Spirit in believers' abiding. Twice John speaks of this:

> Whoever keeps his commandments abides in God, and God in him. And by this we know that he abides in us, by the Spirit whom he has given us. (3:24)

---

[25] Smalley, *1, 2, 3, John*, 210.
[26] Brown, *Epistles of John*, 259.

No one has ever seen God; if we love one another, God abides in us and his love is perfected in us. By this we know that we abide in him and he in us, because he has given us of his Spirit. (4:12–13)

While John does not attribute to the Holy Spirit as large a role as he plays in Paul's thought, the Spirit does play a minor role in 1 John. In the two texts above, the Spirit's ministry is to make Christians aware of their abiding in Christ. Yarbrough helpfully underscores this truth:

John and his readers know or recognize their abiding in God and his abiding in them, by virtue of the Spirit, whom God has given them (see 2:18–3:8). This is similar to the statement John already made in 3:24. . . . The Spirit is the link, even agent, who permits believers to see this reciprocity for what it is: a token of God's very presence among them, assuring them of the veracity of the message they have received and the importance of the ethic they are being called to embrace.[27]

---

[27] Yarbrough, *1–3 John*, 246.

Chapter 20

Union with Christ
in Revelation

Although Revelation is commonly neglected in treatments of union with Christ, by my count the book has three passages that have to do with union: 1:9–11; 14:13; and 19:7, 9.

Revelation 1:9–11

> I, John, your brother and partner in the tribulation and the kingdom and the patient endurance that are in Jesus, was on the island called Patmos on account of the word of God and the testimony of Jesus. I was in the Spirit on the Lord's day, and I heard behind me a loud voice like a trumpet saying, "Write what you see in a book and send it to the seven churches, to Ephesus and to Smyrna and to Pergamum and to Thyatira and to Sardis and to Philadelphia and to Laodicea."

After the prologue and greeting to seven churches in first-century Roman Asia, John begins to describe his amazing vision of the Son of Man. John says that he was exiled to the prison-island of Patmos for preaching the gospel. In rapture in the Spirit, he hears a loud voice commissioning him to record his visions in a book and to send the messages to the churches.

John describes himself as "your brother and partner in the tribulation and the kingdom and the patient endurance that are in Jesus" (v. 9). He is a spiritual brother to Christian readers, who like him belong to the family of God. He is their "partner" in tribulation, kingdom, and perseverance. At first blush this combination may seem strange. But for those familiar with Paul's teaching that believers participate in Jesus's story in his death and resurrection, there is no problem. We are joined to Christ in his death, and that sometimes involves trials that require endurance. We are joined to Christ in his resurrection, and so we are members of his kingdom now and await its fuller manifestation at his return.

Most important for our purposes is John's description of himself as a "partner [συγκοινωνός] in the tribulation and the kingdom and the patient endurance that are *in Jesus*" (v. 9). Does John's use of "in Jesus" approximate Paul's familiar "in Christ [Jesus]"? Beasley-Murray answers affirmatively: "The phrase *in Jesus* reminds us of Paul's favourite expression 'in Christ,' and has a not dissimilar meaning, viz., fellowship with the Lord who suffered and rose from death for humankind, and so fellowship with all who belong to him."[1] And Beasley-Murray is not alone.[2]

I too agree. Here at the beginning of Revelation John refers to himself as one who is actively involved (he is a "partner") with all other Christians in both struggles and victories by virtue of his union with Christ. I take "in Jesus" as a locative of sphere indicating Christ's realm, his domain. This realm involves cross and crown, which Christ himself taught and showed, as Beasley-Murray reminds us: "Tribulation and kingdom belong to the messianic pattern (Luke 24:26). To be *in Jesus*, therefore, is to experience the reality of both, and it enables that patient endurance of tribulation which ensures participation in the kingdom."[3]

Revelation 14:13

Blessed are the dead who die in the Lord from now on.

These comforting words follow one of Scripture's strongest passages on hell. Idolaters "will drink the wine of God's wrath, poured full strength into the cup of his anger" (v. 10). That is, they will personally experience God's wrath. As is common in the Bible, fire imagery depicts the suffering of the lost; they "will be tormented with fire and sulfur" (v. 10). How long will this suffering last? John's answer is chilling: "And the smoke of their torment goes

---

[1] George R. Beasley-Murray, *Revelation*, The New Century Bible Commentary (Grand Rapids: Eerdmans, 1974), 63.
[2] These writers agree: George E. Ladd, *A Commentary on the Revelation of John* (Grand Rapids: Eerdmans, 1972), 30; Henry Barclay Swete, *The Apocalypse of St. John*, 3rd ed. (London: Macmillan, 1911), 12.
[3] Beasley-Murray, *Revelation*, 64.

up forever and ever, and they have no rest, day or night" (v. 11). This is conscious punishment without end.

After issuing a summons for God's people to persevere in faith and obedience (v. 12), John draws a stark contrast to unbelievers' eternal lack of rest. God will bless believers who die, and they will "rest from their labors" (v. 13). Before John says this, however, he utters perplexing words: "Blessed are the dead who die" (v. 13). Truly happy are the dead? This is so counterintuitive. But what makes all the difference is the way John finishes his sentence: "Blessed are the dead who die *in the Lord* from now on."

Once more John uses words ("in the Lord") similar to Paul's "in Christ" language. The contrast between the realms of hell and heaven with their respective pain and bliss suggests that "in the Lord" is a locative used metaphorically to point to the sphere of Christ's rule. Christians do not belong to the kingdom of "the beast" but to the kingdom of Christ. Beasley-Murray explains, "Death has lost its terror for *the dead who die in the Lord*, for they are united to him who by his death and resurrection conquered death for them."[4]

Although Revelation tells of martyrs who give their lives in service to Christ, this passage speaks in broader terms, as George Ladd affirms: "To die *in the Lord* is the state of all believers, who both die and live in Christ (1 Cor. 15:18; 1 Thess. 4:16). It does not designate a special group of Christians."[5] It is no wonder that this text is so popular with preachers who preside at funerals of believers in Christ. For, in the words of Robert Mounce, "It pronounces blessed those who meet death in a state of spiritual union with Christ Jesus."[6]

Revelation 19:7, 9

"Let us rejoice and exult . . .
for the marriage of the Lamb has come,
    and his Bride has made herself ready; . . ."

"Blessed are those who are invited to the marriage supper of the Lamb."

Here again a text teaching union with Christ follows terrible words of woe for God's enemies. This time it is Babylon the harlot, the great city of this

---

[4] Ibid., 227, emphasis original.
[5] Ladd, *Commentary on the Revelation*, 198.
[6] Robert H. Mounce, *The Book of Revelation*, The New International Commentary on the New Testament (Eerdmans, 1977), 277.

world that opposes everything devoted to God. God's destruction of that evil city brings forth praise in heaven:

> After this I heard what seemed to be the loud voice of a great multitude in heaven, crying out,
>
> > "Hallelujah!
> > Salvation and glory and power belong to our God,
> > > for his judgments are true and just;
> >
> > for he has judged the great prostitute
> > > who corrupted the earth with her immorality,
> >
> > and has avenged on her the blood of his servants."
>
> Once more they cried out,
>
> > "Hallelujah!
> > The smoke from her goes up forever and ever." (19:1–3)

Over against "Babylon the great, mother of prostitutes and of earth's abominations" (17:5) is the bride of Christ, the church. Just after hearing the voice of the multitude praising God for Babylon's overthrow, John hears another voice singing a very different song:

> Hallelujah!
> For the Lord our God
> > the Almighty reigns,
>
> Let us rejoice and exult
> > and give him the glory,
>
> for the marriage of the Lamb has come,
> > and his Bride has made herself ready;
>
> it was granted her to clothe herself
> > with fine linen, bright and pure. (19:6–8)

In the next verse John obeys the angel's command to write, "Blessed are those who are invited to the marriage supper of the Lamb" (v. 9). Taking the colors of his palette from the Old Testament (Isa. 49:18 and especially 61:10), John creates his own painting of the preparation for the marriage of the Lamb and his bride. Jesus told a parable of a wedding feast for a king's son (Matt. 22:1–14). In John's Gospel, Jesus is referred to as the "bride-groom" (John 3:29). And, of course, Paul speaks of union with Christ using the metaphor of Christ and his bride (1 Cor. 6:15–17; 2 Cor. 11:2–3; Eph. 5:23–32).

John does not actually record the marriage supper or the marriage of the Lamb to his bride. But the place Revelation 19:6–8 occupies in the book shows it to be an image of union with Christ, fulfilled in the ultimate union between Christ and the church as depicted in 21:2–3:

> I saw the holy city, new Jerusalem, coming down out of heaven from God, *prepared as a bride adorned for her husband*. And I heard a loud voice from the throne saying, "Behold, the dwelling place of God is with man. He will dwell with them, and they will be his people, and God himself will be with them as their God."

Ladd accurately describes John's employment of the image of the marriage of the Lamb:

> The voice announces the marriage of the Lamb; it does not describe it. It proclaims that the marriage of the Lamb is about to take place. . . . [In Paul] believers are thus united to the Lord in the bonds of spiritual marriage. . . . It is this eschatological event—the perfect union of Christ and his church—which John announced under the metaphor of the marriage of the Lamb. . . . The actual event is nowhere described; it is a metaphorical way of alluding to the final redemptive fact when "the dwelling of God is with men. He will dwell with them, and they shall be his people, and God himself will be with them" (Rev. 21:3).[7]

Another reason for regarding the marriage of the Lamb as a picture of union with Christ is the Old Testament background of John's imagery in Isaiah:

> I will greatly rejoice in the LORD;
>   my soul shall exult in my God,
> for he has clothed me with the garments of salvation;
>   he has covered me with the robe of righteousness,
> as a bridegroom decks himself like a priest with a beautiful headdress,
>   and as a bride adorns herself with her jewels. (Isa. 61:10)

G. K. Beale drives home the point: "The marital metaphors at the end of Isa. 61:10 signify the intimate relationship initiated by God with his latter-day

---

[7] Ladd, *Commentary on the Revelation*, 246, 248.

people. . . . The metaphorical significance is . . . that God's people are finally entering into the intimate relationship with him that he has initiated."[8] That relationship is final union with Christ.

So, once again, though he uses different language than he did in 1:9 and 14:13, John presents union with Christ. Beasley-Murray helpfully draws big-picture theological conclusions from John's combining the images of wedding supper and marriage:

> The eschatological aspect of the figure [of marriage] is emphasized here through its conjunction with another image for the kingdom of God, namely, that of a feast prepared by the Lord for the world, in which his people will be guests. . . . By this means a whole wealth of associations relating to salvation are brought together: the prior love of God for man, revealed in the deeds of grace which win the love of the bride; the depth of fellowship between God and man, established in the love of God and the grace of Christ and mediated through the Holy Spirit . . . ; the joy of that relationship, when the trials of the former days are forgotten in laughter and happiness around the table of the Lord in his kingdom.[9]

Conclusion

Although Revelation does not contain many references to union with Christ, it contains three, and they deserve attention. In light of this small number it is striking to find references to union at the beginning and end of the book. At the beginning, John says he is his readers' "brother and partner [συγκοινωνός] in the tribulation and the kingdom and the patient endurance that are *in Jesus*" (1:9).

"Kingdom" appears to have strange companions in "tribulation" and "patient endurance." But if we note the reference to union with Christ, they are not strange at all. Ladd clarifies, "All of these hardships are experienced *in Jesus*. Here is John's parallel to Paul's frequent expression, 'in Christ,' signifying the believer's spiritual union with his Lord."[10] We are united to Christ in his crucifixion and as a result experience trials that demand perseverance. We are united to Christ in his resurrection, which entails membership in his kingdom now and forever.

[8] G. K. Beale, *The Book of Revelation*, New International Greek Testament Commentary (Grand Rapids: Eerdmans, 1999), 939–40.
[9] Beasley-Murray, *Revelation*, 272.
[10] Ladd, *Commentary on the Revelation*, 30.

Jesus taught that to belong to him and his kingdom involves cross and crown for him *and* his followers. Here at the beginning of Revelation John shows that he learned Jesus's lesson well. Consequently, he refers to himself as one who shares (as a "partner") with all other believers in struggles and victories, both of which are "in Jesus." Henry Barclay Swete concisely sums up the matter: "The whole life of a Christian, whether he suffers or reigns or waits, is in union with the life of the Incarnate Son."[11]

John refers to union again at the end of Revelation, this time without the words "in Jesus" (as in 1:9) or "in the Lord" (as in 14:13). Instead, he builds on the Old Testament picture of God's people adorning herself as his bride for her husband (Isa. 61:10). John uses this eschatological image of the intimacy of the relationship between God and his people to describe the culmination of God's covenantal promises of intimacy between himself and his saints, as Beale notes.[12] That intimate relationship is final union with Christ.

The church, the chaste bride of Christ, is set against Babylon, the "great prostitute who corrupted the earth with her immorality" (19:2). John reports praise directed to God in heaven for Babylon's demise (19:1–5). He also announces delight in heaven at the glorious prospect of the wedding of Christ and his church, preceded by the joyous marriage supper:

> "Let us rejoice and exult . . .
> for the marriage of the Lamb has come,
>   and his Bride has made herself ready; . . ."

> "Blessed are those who are invited to the marriage supper of the Lamb."
> (Rev. 19:7, 9)

John announces but does not record the supper or the wedding of the Lamb to his bride. But Revelation 21:2–3 interprets the wedding imagery of 19:6–8 in terms of the ultimate union between Christ and the church:

> I saw the holy city, new Jerusalem, coming down out of heaven from God, *prepared as a bride adorned for her husband*. And I heard a loud voice from the throne saying, "Behold, the dwelling place of God is with man. He will dwell with them, and they will be his people, and God himself will be with them as their God."

---

[11] Swete, *Apocalypse of St. John*, 12.
[12] Beale, *Book of Revelation*, 939–40.

Ian Boxall captures the main idea of verse 2: "It proclaims the most intimate of relationships between God in Christ, God's people and the community of which they are part."[13] Indeed, it proclaims the consummate union of Christ and his church under the picture of the marriage of the Lamb.

Following on the heels of strong words about hell and a call for believers to persevere (14:9–12), John delivers comforting words: "Blessed are the dead who die in the Lord from now on" (v. 13). John contrasts the blissful "rest" of believers "from their labors" (v. 13) with the never-ending lack of rest for lost persons (v. 11).

At first blush John's words are puzzling: "Blessed are *the dead*" (v. 13)! But by the time we reflect on the whole sentence, our bewilderment turns to joy: "Blessed are the dead who die *in the Lord* from now on" (v. 13).

The context juxtaposes two realms—hell and heaven—and their occupants. In light of the suffering of hell and the joy of heaven, John uses "in the Lord" in a manner resembling Paul's "in Christ" language. Beasley-Murray hits the nail on the head: "Death has lost its terror for *the dead who die in the Lord*, for they are united to him who by his death and resurrection conquered death for them."[14]

Revelation 14:13 does not mark out a special group of believers but describes them all. This text is often quoted at believers' funerals, for, as Mounce explains, it "pronounces blessed those who meet death in a state of spiritual union with Christ Jesus."[15]

---

[13] Ian Boxall, *The Revelation of Saint John*, Black's New Testament Commentary (Peabody, MA: Hendrickson, 2006), 294.
[14] Beasley-Murray, *Revelation*, 227, emphasis original.
[15] Mounce, *Book of Revelation*, 277.

PART TWO

UNION WITH CHRIST IN THEOLOGY

Chapter 21

Union with Christ and the Biblical Story

Union with Christ is understood properly only if viewed within the broad sweep of the biblical story. In this chapter we will explore only the theological highlights of that story. For this reason, we omit the important material covered in three chapters of the foundations of union with Christ in the Old Testament, Synoptic Gospels, and Acts, and will focus instead on six stages in the biblical narrative:[1]

- union and eternity past
- union and creation
- union and the fall
- union and the incarnation
- union and Christ's work
- union and the new creation

Union and Eternity Past

Two Pauline passages teach that God chose his people for salvation before creation:

> Blessed be the God and Father of our Lord Jesus Christ, who has blessed
> us in Christ with every spiritual blessing in the heavenly places, even as

---

[1] See chapters 1–3: "Foundations in the Old Testament," "Foundations in the Synoptic Gospels," and "Foundations in Acts."

> he chose us in him before the foundation of the world, that we should be holy and blameless before him. (Eph. 1:3–4)

> Do not be ashamed of the testimony about our Lord, nor of me his prisoner, but share in suffering for the gospel by the power of God, who saved us and called us to a holy calling, not because of our works but because of his own purpose and grace, which he gave us in Christ Jesus before the ages began. (2 Tim. 1:8–9)

In the former passage Paul teaches that before creation God chose to save sinners with the goal of final sanctification. In the latter the apostle encourages Timothy to spiritual boldness amid suffering by pointing him to God's power. God saves us and calls us to present sanctification. We are saved not by our performance but by God's purpose, plan, and grace—his favor bestowed against our merit. And—similar to what Paul said in Ephesians 1:4—this grace was granted us "before the ages began [lit. "before eternal ages"]" (2 Tim. 1:9).

It is arresting that in the two passages where Paul teaches that divine election was eternal, he also teaches that it was "in Christ":

> Even as he chose us *in him* before the foundation of the world . . . (Eph. 1:4)

> God, who saved us . . . not because of our works but because of his own purpose and grace, which he gave us *in Christ Jesus* before the ages began. (2 Tim. 1:8–9)

How are we to understand these two unusual usages of the common Pauline phrase "in Christ"?

Ephesians 1:3–4

There are at least three approaches to understanding the words "[God] chose us *in him* before the foundation of the world" (Eph. 1:4). The first approach, advanced by Arminians, is to understand "in Christ" as indicating a condition for salvation that people must meet. Jack Cottrell takes this approach:

> God foreknows whether an individual will meet the *conditions* for salvation which he has sovereignly imposed. . . . The basic and all-encompassing condition is whether a person is *in Christ*, namely whether one has entered into a saving union with Christ by means of which he shares in all the benefits of

Christ's redeeming work. . . . This is the import of Eph. 1:4, which says that "He chose us in Him"—in Christ.[2]

A second approach, also used by Arminians, is to understand Paul's words to mean that God primarily chose Christ and secondarily chose human beings for salvation, namely, those whom he foresaw would believe in Christ. Jerry Walls and Joseph Dongell adopt this approach:

> Jesus Christ himself is the chosen one, the predestined one. Whenever one is incorporated into him by grace through faith, one comes to share in Jesus' special status as chosen by God. . . . This view of election most fully accounts for the corporate nature of salvation, the decisive role of faith and the overarching reliability of God's bringing people to their destined end.[3]

Before introducing the third approach, I will critique the first two. The first view errs because when Paul writes, "He chose us in him before the foundation of the world," he does not mention a condition sinners must meet to be chosen by God. Paul's words do not tell of any human response; they tell of God's sovereign plan. Cottrell and other Arminian believers read foreseen faith into the apostle's words in an attempt to harmonize their view of conditional election with Paul's words.[4]

Moreover, the second approach also fails by reading ideas into Paul. God did choose Christ to be the divine-*human* Redeemer, but that is not Paul's point in Ephesians 1. Instead, Paul teaches that God "chose *us* in him" (v. 4). Verse 4 does not speak of the "decisive role of faith." Walls and Dongell read into the passage the idea that "whenever one is incorporated into him by grace through faith, one comes to share in Jesus' special status as chosen by God."[5] Instead, the passage emphasizes the decisive roles of God's sovereignty and grace (vv. 5–6, 11).

I take a third approach to Paul's words, "He [God] chose us in Christ before the foundation of the world." As we saw in the chapters on Paul's epistles, the apostle frequently employs "in Christ," "in him," and synonyms to refer to union with Christ. How does Paul's regular use of "in Christ," referring to

---

[2] Jack Cottrell, "Conditional Election," in *Grace Unlimited*, ed. Clark H. Pinnock (Minneapolis: Bethany House, 1975), 61, emphasis original.
[3] Jerry L. Walls and Joseph R. Dongell, *Why I Am Not a Calvinist* (Downers Grove, IL: InterVarsity, 2004), 76.
[4] For discussion, see Robert A. Peterson, *Election and Free Will*, Explorations in Biblical Theology (Phillipsburg, NJ: P&R, 2007), 103–8.
[5] Walls and Dongell, *Why I Am Not a Calvinist*, 76.

union in time, differ from his use of it in the context of pre-temporal election? The difference is temporal. Paul almost always speaks of people being joined to Christ in history. But in Ephesians 1:4 (and 2 Tim. 1:9), he speaks of election in Christ before creation. In these two places "in Christ" does not indicate actual union, because we did not exist before creation. Rather, Paul tells of God's sovereign plan to unite us to Christ. Thus, when Paul writes, "He chose us in him before the foundation of the world," he means that prior to creation God, out of his own will and love, both chose to save his people and also planned the means to save them. He planned to bring them into spiritual union with his Son and all his spiritual benefits.

2 Timothy 1:9

It is the same for 2 Timothy 1:9. We are delivered from our sins "not because of our works but because of his own purpose and grace." Note that neither does this text make God's election of his people contingent upon human beings' response to the gospel. It explicitly denies that our efforts can rescue us and focuses instead on God, who grants salvation "because of his own purpose and grace," that is, his sovereign will and compassion. When Paul says this grace was granted us "in Christ Jesus before the ages began," he means that God's gracious choice of us in eternity involved his plan to join us to his Son so that we would experience salvation. Saving grace would unfailingly come to God's chosen people due to God's sovereign and gracious plan.

These two passages teach that union was far from an afterthought on God's part. Amazingly, even his choice of sinners prior to creation included union with Christ. When God chose sinners for salvation, he chose also to unite them to Christ so they would experience salvation. That is, he planned to send his Son in the incarnation to live a sinless life, die, arise, and pour out the Spirit at Pentecost. The Spirit would apply the salvation that Jesus accomplished by spiritually joining us to Christ. Thus the Father "chose us *in Christ*" and "gave us grace *in Christ Jesus* before the ages began."

Anthony Hoekema is accurate in saying:

> "He chose us in him" further implies that our election (that is, our being chosen by God to be saved) should never be thought of apart from Christ. Union between Christ and his people was planned already in eternity, in the sovereign pretemporal decision whereby God the Father selected us as his own. . . . Those chosen to be saved, in other words, were never contemplated by the Father apart from Christ or apart from the work Christ was

to do for them—they were chosen *in Christ*. . . . Union with Christ is not something "tacked on" to our salvation; it is there from the outset, even in the plan of God. As Herman Bavinck used to say, Christ must never be thought of apart from his people, nor his people apart from Christ.[6]

Union and Creation

Union with Christ, planned from eternity, takes place in time. The Holy Spirit effectively brings believing sinners together with Christ in salvation; by grace through faith he joins them to the Son of God. But to move immediately from election in Christ to faith union with him is to skip three essential steps in the story. Moving backward, Pentecost, the incarnation, and mankind's being created in God's image are all necessary preconditions for union with Christ.

First, Christ's pouring out the Holy Spirit at Pentecost was necessary for the Spirit to unite sinners to Christ. Second, the incarnation of the eternal Son, his becoming one with us in our humanity, was essential for his accomplishing our salvation, including dying, rising, and bestowing the Spirit. It is also essential in establishing a fraternity between him and us so that we can be joined to him spiritually. And third, going back to the beginning, human beings' creation in the image and likeness of God, which established a compatibility between us and him, was necessary for us to be joined to Christ. This is our current occupation.

The Image of God

Union with Christ rests on the fact of humans' special creation by God. Though as creatures we are very different from God, in important ways as his image bearers we are like him. Robert Letham is succinct: "Union with Christ rests on the basis of the creation of man to be compatible with God."[7] This is a consequence of our being made like God. Genesis records:

> God said, "Let us make man in our image, after our likeness. And let them have dominion over the fish of the sea and over the birds of the heavens and over the livestock and over all the earth and over every creeping thing that creeps on the earth."

---

[6] Anthony A. Hoekema, *Saved by Grace* (Grand Rapids: Eerdmans, 1989), 56–57, emphasis original.
[7] Robert Letham, *Union with Christ: In Scripture, History, and Theology* (Phillipsburg, NJ: P&R, 2011), 9. I acknowledge a debt to Letham for help throughout this section.

So God created man in his own image,
    in the image of God he created him;
      male and female he created them. (Gen. 1:26–27)

The image of God in men and women as God's creatures is elusive; many elements seem to be involved, including our very structure, our roles, and our capacity for relationships.[8] It is this last element that concerns us now. "Because man was created in the image of God, he was made for communion with God, to rule God's creation on his behalf," writes Letham.[9] God made us for himself and in fellowship with himself. Adam and Eve were created neither as sinners nor as innocent beings (not good or evil) but as holy beings in fellowship with a holy God.

To appreciate that God made us compatible with himself and for fellowship with him, it is important to underline the immense differences between God and us.

It is he who sits above the circle of the earth,
    and its inhabitants are like grasshoppers. (Isa. 40:22)

The LORD is the everlasting God,
    the Creator of the ends of the earth. (v. 28)

[He is] the One who is high and lifted up,
    who inhabits eternity, whose name is Holy. (57:15)

He declares,

Heaven is my throne,
    and the earth is my footstool. (66:1)

Compared with him,

All the nations are as nothing before him,
    they are accounted by him as less than nothing and emptiness.
      (40:17)

He is unique who asserts, "I am the LORD, and there is no other" (45:5, 6, 18; cf. 22).

---

[8] For discussion, see Anthony A. Hoekema, *Created in God's Image* (Grand Rapids: Eerdmans, 1986), 11–101.
[9] Letham, *Union with Christ*, 15.

Astonishingly, though there is such a great divide between the great God and us, he made us in his image, and thus we are like him in important ways. Philip Hughes explains:

> The knowledge that the being of God is essentially and eternally personal is, indeed, of particular moment for our theme, because in creating man God was creating a *personal* being, who, in a manner impossible for other animate creatures, is capable of personal fellowship with and personal response to his personal Creator. . . . The fact that man is a person from Person explains his ability to interact as person to Person.[10]

Christ the True Image

Perhaps some were surprised to see that even God's eternal election involved Christ; we were chosen in him and were given grace in him. But it should come as no surprise that when contemplating humankind as created in God's image, we turn our attention to Christ, the true image of God. For Paul says that Christ "is the image of God" (2 Cor. 4:4), "the image of the invisible God" (Col. 1:15).

In fact, Christ as God's image forms a bridge between human beings as made in God's likeness and Christ's incarnation. Christ as image helps us to understand humankind as image bearers. Letham elucidates:

> Genesis states that the man and his wife were created *in* the image of God. The image of God is identified for us in the N.T. Paul points out that it is Christ who *is* the image of God (2 Cor. 4:4; Col. 1:15). . . . In Paul's thought, Christ as the second Adam *is* the image of God. Adam was created *in* Christ and then fell from that condition, but now, in grace, we are being renewed in the image of God, *in Christ the second Adam*, and thus in knowledge, righteousness, and holiness.[11]

The image of God in humankind both puts us under God (and over the other creatures) and at the same time makes us compatible with God himself. That Christ is the true image of God means we were made like Christ in the beginning, as Hughes explains:

> Man alone has affinities that reach both downward within the world over which he has been placed and upward to the Creator who is the Lord of all being. The truth that lies behind this double linkage is, first of all,

---

[10] Philip E. Hughes, *The True Image: The Origin and Destiny of Man in Christ* (Grand Rapids: Eerdmans, 1989), 5, emphasis original.
[11] Letham, *Union with Christ*, 14, emphasis original.

that man is God's *creature*; secondly, that man alone of God's creatures is formed *in the image of God*; and thirdly, that the eternal Son is *the Image* in accordance with which man was formed. The deeply intimate bond that binds man to the Second Person of the Godhead is thus constitutional to the very being of man.[12]

Our compatibility with God because we were made in the image of his Son helps us to begin to understand the incarnation of the eternal Son. We shall return to this theme after we consider union with Christ and the fall.

Union and the Fall

It is a mistake to emphasize the one prohibition God gave our first parents Adam and Eve so as to minimize the many blessings that were theirs:

> The LORD God took the man and put him in the garden of Eden to work it and keep it. And the LORD God commanded the man, saying, "You may surely eat of every tree of the garden, but of the tree of the knowledge of good and evil you shall not eat, for in the day that you eat of it you shall surely die." (Gen. 2:15–17)

They could eat of "every tree" but were refused only one.

The Death Sentence

Nevertheless, in spite of God's abundant goodness to the first pair, we know how the story unfolds. Eve and then Adam disobey God by eating the forbidden fruit. What form does the sentence of death take? How does it play out? Jack Collins answers these questions:

> We are now in a position to address the meaning of the death threat of Genesis 2:17. God takes his solemn command with the utmost seriousness and may be relied upon to do as he said. In the light of what happens (the actions and changed attitudes of the humans), we can see that the part of the semantic range of "death" that is present here is spiritual death, estrangement from God. Physical mortality, which 3:19 predicts, is a consequence of the humans' disrupted condition—which even those who have been morally recovered will have to undergo.[13]

[12] Hughes, *The True Image*, 213–14, emphasis original.
[13] C. John Collins, *Genesis 1–4: A Linguistic, Literary, and Theological Commentary* (Phillipsburg, NJ: P&R, 2006), 175.

This is a travesty: God made our first parents for himself. He created them in fellowship with him. He gave them each other, gave them dominion over the rest of creation, and showered them with blessings. Still, they listened to the Dark Power, who used the serpent as his agent, and rebelled against their Maker.

Scripture lists many results of the fall, including guilt and condemnation, corruption, suffering, shattered relationships, bondage, alienation from God, and disorder. Even the very creation is marred, for God cursed the ground because of Adam's transgression (Gen. 3:17–18).

Wonderfully, God in his grace overturns every one of those results of the fall through the work of Christ. The result of the fall that best illustrates humankind's need for union with Christ is given most clearly in Ephesians 2:

> Remember that at one time you Gentiles in the flesh, called "the uncircumcision" by what is called the circumcision, which is made in the flesh by hands—remember that you were at that time separated from Christ, alienated from the commonwealth of Israel and strangers to the covenants of promise, having no hope and without God in the world. (vv. 11–12)

Paul describes the horrible plight of his Gentile readers (and all unsaved people!) before they came to Christ. In doing so, he expresses most clearly why lost human beings need to be joined spiritually to Christ—because they are "separated from Christ" (v. 12). Thielman tells why Paul puts this first in his list of "five deficiencies of the Gentiles":

> This is the most important item in the list, as its position indicates: it is at the head of the list, outside the two couplets . . . used to express the other four problems. If every spiritual blessing of 1:4–13 is available only to those "in Christ" (1:3), and if rescue from the grim plight detailed in 2:1–3 comes only to those "in Christ" (2:5–6), then being "outside Christ" poses a problem of the first rank.[14]

Separation from Christ

Our need for union with Christ is that we are separated from Christ. At its root, union is a spatial concept used to communicate relational truth. It is as if Christ were "over there," having all the blessings of salvation, including

---

[14] Frank Thielman, *Ephesians*, Baker Exegetical Commentary on the New Testament (Grand Rapids: Baker Academic, 2010), 154.

forgiveness of sins and eternal life; and we are "over here," separated from his person and all his benefits. It is only as the Holy Spirit bridges the gap and unites us to the Savior that we experience salvation. Until that time, we are outside of Christ and therefore "having no hope and without God in the world" (v. 12).

Paul goes on to describe the remedy to our plight:

> Now in Christ Jesus you who once were far off have been brought near by the blood of Christ. . . . So then you are no longer strangers and aliens, but you are fellow citizens with the saints and members of the household of God, built on the foundation of the apostles and prophets, Christ Jesus himself being the cornerstone, *in whom* the whole structure, being joined together, grows into a holy temple *in the Lord. In him* you also are being built together into a dwelling place for God by the Spirit. (vv. 13, 19–22)

The remedy for separation from Christ is union with him, being "brought near by [his] blood," being incorporated into God's family, made part of his spiritual temple. (Notice "in Christ" language appears three times in vv. 21–22.)

Union and the Incarnation

Before time God chose to save us by uniting us to Christ. In time he created us in his image, like him and for fellowship with him. In fact, he made us in the image of his Son, the true image of God. But we rebelled in our first parents and as a result were separated from Christ. Although God could have given up on us, he did not. He came to us in the incarnation of his Son.

Hughes helpfully connects Christ as image of God to the incarnation:

> The doctrine of the Image of God is the key to the factuality of the incarnation no less than to the understanding of the true nature of man. The problem, arising from the limitation of our being and horizon, is: How can God become what he is not? How can God become one with his creatures for the purpose of restoring all things? The answer to that problem is . . . in the line that connects man to the Second Person of the Holy Trinity, that links image to Image, that is, the image of God at the center of man's being to the Image who is God the Son.[15]

---

[15] Hughes, *The True Image*, 214.

The Son's Deity and Humanity

Of course, in becoming one with us in the incarnation the eternal Son does not cease to be the eternal Son. He continues to be God after the incarnation. "The incarnation is God the Son actively taking to himself our human nature without in any sense ceasing to be God," Hughes says.[16] Consequently, after the incarnation Christ is both God and man in one person. He who alone was the true image of God and in whose image human beings were created took true humanity to himself in the incarnation. God used the virgin birth to accomplish this miracle. Hughes wastes no words: "The virgin birth of Jesus, then, is God in action uniting the human and the divine in the one theanthropic person of the incarnate Son."[17]

So we confess the deity of the incarnate Son; this is crucial, for only *God* can rescue us. Yet the incarnation is necessary, for only the God-*man* can rescue *us*. He had to become one of us to die for us, defeat our enemy, and deliver us, as Hebrews insists: "Since therefore the children share in flesh and blood, he himself likewise partook of the same things, that through death he might destroy the one who has the power of death, that is, the devil, and deliver all those who through fear of death were subject to lifelong slavery" (Heb. 2:14–15).

The Son's Incarnation and Union

Moreover, the incarnation is necessary also for union with Christ to occur, as Letham explains: "The basis of our union with Christ is Christ's union with us in the incarnation. We can become one with him because he first became one with us. By taking human nature into personal union, the Son of God has joined himself to humanity. He now has a human body and soul, which he will never jettison."[18] This is a vital point. Without the incarnation of the Son of God, sinners could never be joined to him. His humanity establishes a link between God and us, as I note in a previous book:

> Calvin expresses the fraternity Jesus' humanity established between Christ and the believer in many ways. Christ is "comrade and partner in the same nature with us," so that we share a "fellowship of nature" with him. "God's only Son put Himself on equal terms with us wishing to be our brother." We do not have to seek salvation "at long range," but in the Lord's human-

---

[16] Ibid.
[17] Ibid. For outstanding discussion of the theological significance of the virgin birth, see Donald Macleod, *The Person of Christ*, Contours of Christian Theology (Downers Grove, IL: InterVarsity, 1998), 21–43.
[18] Letham, *Union with Christ*, 21.

ity, "it was set at the hand of every man." This is because God in Christ "came near and opened Himself to us at close quarters."[19]

It is no accident, then, that the two New Testament authors who most emphasize union with Christ also place heavy emphasis on the incarnation. This volume has 46 pages presenting John's doctrine of union in his Gospel, first epistle, and Revelation. It has 161 pages presenting Paul's doctrine of union, which appears in every epistle except Titus. It is noteworthy, then, that John and Paul teach the incarnation as well as union with Christ.

John begins his Gospel with his famous prologue. He uses a chiasm to present Christ first as the Word (1:1–4) and then as the light (vv. 7–8). Regular parallelism would present the Word and the light, in that order, in action. John instead uses inverted parallelism (chiasm) and reverses the two:

> The true light, which gives light to everyone, was coming into the world. (v. 9)

> The Word became flesh and dwelt among us, and we have seen his glory, glory as of the only Son from the Father, full of grace and truth. (v. 14)

John's prologue thus moves in a particular direction. Its structure underlines the presupposition for the rest of the Gospel of John—the incarnation. The light comes into a very dark world (sinful and ignorant of spiritual matters) and illuminates, with the knowledge of God, all who hear Jesus's sermons or see his signs. And the eternal Word becomes a man of flesh and blood in Jesus of Nazareth and reveals the glory, grace, and truth of God.

One quotation from 1 John is sufficient to show John's very high regard for the incarnation of the eternal Son:

> Beloved, do not believe every spirit, but test the spirits to see whether they are from God, for many false prophets have gone out into the world. By this you know the Spirit of God: every spirit that confesses that Jesus Christ has come in the flesh is from God, and every spirit that does not confess Jesus is not from God. This is the spirit of the antichrist, which you heard was coming and now is in the world already. (4:1–3)

Confession or denial of the incarnation is the litmus test between orthodoxy and heresy!

---

[19] Robert A. Peterson, *Calvin and the Atonement* (Fearn, Ross-shire, UK: Mentor, 1999), 36.

It is the same for the apostle Paul, who speaks most of union with Christ. He puts great emphasis on the incarnation of the Son. Here are two key texts:

> When the fullness of time had come, God sent forth his Son, born of woman, born under the law, to redeem those who were under the law, so that we might receive adoption as sons. (Gal. 4:4–5)

> Have this mind among yourselves, which is yours in Christ Jesus, who, though he was in the form of God, did not count equality with God a thing to be grasped, but emptied himself, by taking the form of a servant, being born in the likeness of men. And being found in human form, he humbled himself by becoming obedient to the point of death, even death on a cross. (Phil. 2:5–8)

Like John, Paul holds the incarnation to be essential to Christ's mission, including pouring out the Spirit to effect union with Christ. In fact, it is difficult to overemphasize the importance of the incarnation when speaking of union with Christ. The incarnation does not in itself unite us to Christ. But it is an essential precondition for union. Letham is terse in saying, "Christ's union with us in the incarnation is the foundation for our union with him, both now and in the eternal future."[20]

The next step in understanding the biblical story of union with Christ involves his saving accomplishment, including what he did at Pentecost. The connection between the incarnation and Pentecost is drawn by Letham: "Christ has completely identified himself with us. He is one with us. He everlastingly took our nature into personal union. . . . The incarnation is the indispensable basis for union with Christ. Since Christ has united himself to us in the incarnation, we can be united to him by the Holy Spirit."[21]

Union and Christ's Work

Before discussing the relationship between union with Christ and his saving work, it is important to relate the incarnation to that work. The Son of God became a human being to be Mediator between God and human beings, to be the Savior of the world. In a book to which this is the sequel, I set forth nine saving events of Christ: incarnation, sinless life, death, resurrection, ascension, session, Pentecost, intercession, and return. The heart and soul of his

---

[20] Letham, *Union with Christ*, 41.
[21] Ibid., 40.

saving work are his death and resurrection. His incarnation and sinless life are essential preconditions for the crucifixion and empty tomb. And the five events from his ascension to his return are essential results of his death and resurrection.

Here is my conclusion to a chapter on the incarnation:

> So then, does Christ's incarnation save? The answer depends on what exactly is being asked. Does Christ's incarnation save in and of itself? The answer is no. Salvation does not come automatically to humankind when the eternal Son of God becomes a man. But does Christ's incarnation save as the essential precondition for the saving deeds that follow? The answer is yes. Only a divine-human Redeemer would do. If the Son had not become a human being, he could not have lived a sinless human life, died, and risen again to deliver his people. He could not have ascended, sat down at God's right hand, poured out the Holy Spirit, interceded for his own, and come again. To perform these saving works, he had to become one of us. In that important sense, Christ's incarnation saves.[22]

Pentecost

What does Christ's saving accomplishment have to do with union with him? The key here is Pentecost, for the coming of the Spirit at Pentecost enables faith union with Christ. Pentecost is as much Christ's saving deed as are his crucifixion and resurrection. We rightly think of the Holy Spirit when we think of Pentecost. But it is important to realize that Christ was the one who poured out the Spirit on the day of Pentecost.

This is in fulfillment of Joel's prophecy, as the Lord speaks through him:

> And it shall come to pass afterward,
> that I will pour out my Spirit on all flesh. (Joel 2:28; cf. Acts 2:17)

Pentecost is also in fulfillment of John the Baptist's prophecy in each of the four Gospels: "I baptize you with water for repentance, but he who is coming after me is mightier than I, whose sandals I am not worthy to carry. He will baptize you with the Holy Spirit and fire" (Matt. 3:11; see also Mark 1:7–8; Luke 3:16; John 1:32–34). And it is in fulfillment of Jesus's words in Acts 1: "While staying with them he ordered them not to depart from Jerusalem, but to wait for the promise of the Father, which, he said, 'you heard from me; for

---

[22] Robert A. Peterson, *Salvation Accomplished by the Son: The Work of Christ* (Wheaton, IL: Crossway, 2012), 39.

John baptized with water, but you will be baptized with the Holy Spirit not many days from now'" (vv. 4–5).

Pentecost is Jesus the Messiah's work as much as dying on the cross and rising from the dead are. It is as singular and unrepeatable as those works too. It is a unique event in which the risen, ascended Lord Jesus baptizes his church with the Holy Spirit once for all time, accomplishing by this action great things. Pentecost is a *public* event in which Christ proclaims the new covenant, inaugurates the new creation, and bestows the Spirit on the new community. It is the last of these that concerns us at present.[23]

It is the Holy Spirit who unites believers to Christ, as Paul teaches: "Just as the body is one and has many members, and all the members of the body, though many, are one body, so it is with Christ. For in one Spirit we were all baptized into one body—Jews or Greeks, slaves or free—and all were made to drink of one Spirit" (1 Cor. 12:12–13). Christ baptizes believers with the Spirit, thus incorporating them into Christ's spiritual body, the church. He causes all believers to drink the same spiritual drink—the Spirit.

The Spirit, whom Christ poured out on the church at Pentecost, is the one who joins us to Christ. Thus, Pentecost is the sending of the Spirit, who enables faith union with Christ, as Letham affirms:

> Christ, the eternal Son, having united human nature in himself, now unites us with himself by the Holy Spirit, as the Spirit draws us to him in faith. This is not a personal union, as we saw in the incarnation of the Son. In this case, the Holy Spirit enters, indwells, saturates, and pervades countless human persons and so brings them into union with Christ the Son.[24]

Letham is correct: the Holy Spirit, sent by Christ at Pentecost, brings human beings separated from Christ into saving faith union with him. We will explore this truth in more detail in a chapter titled, "The Most Important Work of the Holy Spirit." At present we round out the panorama of the biblical story by considering the goal of union with Christ.

Union and the New Creation

The goal of union with Christ is nothing less than the final salvation of the people of God and the deliverance of the heavens and earth!

---

[23] For exposition of these three themes see ibid., 215–26.
[24] Letham, *Union with Christ*, 54.

The Creation Itself Will Be United to Christ

The creation itself was subject to the curse of the fall. After Adam's sin God said to him,

> Because you have . . .
>   eaten of the tree
> of which I commanded you,
>   "You shall not eat of it,"
> cursed is the ground because of you;
>   in pain you shall eat of it all the days of your life;
> thorns and thistles it shall bring forth for you. (Gen. 3:17–18)

Scripture also predicts the deliverance of the cosmos, the coming of a new heaven and a new earth (Isa. 65:17–25; 66:22–23; Matt. 19:28; Rom. 8:20–22; 2 Pet. 3:10–13; Revelation 21–22).[25]

In God's plan the work of Christ is the remedy for creation's malady. Christ's death and resurrection have cosmic effects: "God was pleased . . . through him to reconcile to himself all things, whether on earth or in heaven, making peace by the blood of his cross" (Col. 1:19–20). Christ's saving accomplishment rescues not only human beings but the world:

> The creation was subjected to futility, not willingly, but because of him who subjected it, in hope that the creation itself will be set free from its bondage to corruption and obtain the freedom of the glory of the children of God. For we know that the whole creation has been groaning together in the pains of childbirth until now. (Rom. 8:20–22)

Remarkably, Paul teaches that God will ultimately unite all things in Christ:

> In him we have redemption through his blood, the forgiveness of our trespasses, according to the riches of his grace, which he lavished upon us, in all wisdom and insight making known to us the mystery of his will, according to his purpose, which he set forth in Christ as a plan for the fullness of time, to unite all things in him, things in heaven and things on earth. (Eph. 1:7–10)

Paul expands the bounds of time and space when, after speaking of Christ's violent redemptive death (his "blood"), he says that God revealed the

---

[25] For discussion of these passages and conclusions, see Dan C. Barber and Robert A. Peterson, *Life Everlasting: The Unfolding Story of Heaven*, Explorations in Biblical Theology (Phillipsburg, NJ: P&R, 2012), 17–31.

"mystery of his will . . . set forth *in Christ* as a plan for the fullness of time, to unite all things in him" (vv. 9–10). This is one of several times Paul uses "in Christ" to show union with Christ directly.

When Paul says that God's plan is to "unite all things *in him*," he uses union-with-Christ language to present Christ as the focal point. God's plan is to bring together "all things" in heaven and earth in Christ. O'Brien is correct: "Christ is the one *in whom* God chooses to sum up the cosmos, the one in whom he restores harmony to the universe. . . . The emphasis is now on a universe that is centered and reunited . . . in Christ as focal point."[26] A qualification is in order: This summation and harmony of the cosmos is not universalism, the ultimate salvation of all humankind. Lost persons will spend eternity in hell, separated from the bliss of God.[27]

Believers Will Be United to Christ

Union with Christ, the Spirit's application of Christ's death and resurrection, thus has cosmic effects in the end: "No longer will there be anything accursed" (Rev. 22:3). And, of course, union also has marvelous effects for the apple of God's eye, the people whom he made for himself, who rebelled against him, for whom the incarnate Son died and arose, and to whom the Spirit applies Jesus's saving work.

Indeed, Paul says that individual believers are already a part of the new creation: "If anyone is in Christ, he is a new creation. The old has passed away; behold, the new has come. All this is from God, who through Christ reconciled us to himself" (2 Cor. 5:17–18). Paul speaks of believers' change of status, "If anyone is in Christ, he is a new creation" (v. 17). "In Christ" characterizes Christ's new realm in which Christians find themselves. Being in his realm means being part of God's new creation. The apostle continues to describe this state of affairs: "The old has passed away; behold, the new has come" (v. 17). This "new" includes reconciliation (v. 18) and justification (v. 21), both of which are "in Christ." And being in Christ's new creation has ultimate consequences, as Paul often teaches.

One blessing of faith union with Christ is divine indwelling. In fact, indwelling *is* ongoing and living union with Christ. God gives us his Spirit when he unites us to his Son. Indwelling assures us of final salvation ex-

---

[26] Peter T. O'Brien, *The Letter to the Ephesians*, The Pillar New Testament Commentary (Grand Rapids: Eerdmans, 1999), 111–12, emphasis original.
[27] See Christopher W. Morgan and Robert A. Peterson, eds., *Hell under Fire: Modern Scholarship Reinvents Eternal Punishment* (Grand Rapids: Zondervan, 2004).

pressed in terms of resurrection: "If Christ is in you, although the body is dead because of sin, the Spirit is life because of righteousness. If the Spirit of him who raised Jesus from the dead dwells in you, he who raised Christ Jesus from the dead will also give life to your mortal bodies through his Spirit who dwells in you" (Rom. 8:10–11). Notice how the apostle regards Christ's indwelling and the Spirit's indwelling as interchangeable. The Father who raised the Son from the dead will do the same for us through his indwelling Spirit.

The apostle also says that indwelling, expressed as receiving the Spirit, assures us of adoption now and glorification and final adoption at the end of the age:

> You have received the Spirit of adoption as sons, by whom we cry, "Abba! Father!" The Spirit himself bears witness with our spirit that we are children of God, and if children, then heirs—heirs of God and fellow heirs with Christ, provided we suffer with him in order that we may also be glorified with him. (vv. 15–17)

As God's sons or daughters by grace through faith in Christ, we are also his heirs. Genuine children of God suffer with Christ now and await future glorification with him. Note that the suffering and glorification are in union with Christ—both are "with him." And the indwelling Spirit, whose presence is a mark of union, assures God's children of their adoption while they await its final manifestation: "And not only the creation, but we ourselves, who have the firstfruits of the Spirit, groan inwardly as we wait eagerly for adoption as sons, the redemption of our bodies" (v. 23).

In the strongest passage affirming God's preservation of his people, Paul asks, "What then shall we say to these things? If God is for us, who can be against us?" (v. 31). He answers with the greatest imaginable demonstration of the fact that God is "for us": "He who did not spare his own Son but gave him up for us all, how will he not also with him graciously give us all things?" (v. 32). The Father's giving the Son to die in our place proves unequivocally that he is our God and is on our side. Because Christ died and "was raised— who is at the right hand of God, who indeed is interceding for us," the apostle has great assurance that "neither death nor life, nor angels nor rulers, nor things present nor things to come, nor powers, nor height nor depth, nor anything else in all creation, will be able to separate us from the love of God in Christ Jesus our Lord" (vv. 34, 38–39).

Because of God's great love for us in Christ, he has graciously allowed us to participate in his Son's saving events. Paul teaches in Colossians:

- "With Christ you died" (2:20).
- "You have been raised with Christ" (3:1).
- "You have died, and your life is hidden with Christ in God" (v. 3).
- "When Christ who is your life appears, then you also will appear with him in glory" (v. 4).

We died with Christ, were raised with him, and ascended and sat down with him so that our "life is hidden with Christ in God" (v. 3). Shockingly, there is a sense in which we will even come again with him! When Paul says, "when Christ who is your life appears," he uses "appears" to refer to Christ's return. In the same sentence he says we also will "appear": "Then you also will appear with him in glory" (v. 4). Our faith union with Christ, once begun by grace, is so permanent that Paul says we will come again ("appear") with Christ.

Paul does not confuse believers and their Savior. His meaning is that union with Christ is so intimate that we share in his redemptive events, including his second coming. Our existence as his people is so closely connected to him that his return is our return, so to speak. Our identity is so bound up with the One to whom we are united that our full "revelation" will not occur until Jesus returns. That is why the apostle says also that "creation waits with eager longing for the revealing of the sons of God" (Rom. 8:19). Paul literally wrote "the *revelation*" of the sons of God, using the same word found in Revelation 1:1: "The *revelation* of Jesus Christ, which God gave him to show to his servants the things that must soon take place."

John also refers to union at the end of Revelation, when he builds on the Old Testament picture of God's people adorning herself as his bride for her husband (Isa. 61:10). John sets the church, the chaste bride of Christ, against Babylon, the "great prostitute who corrupted the earth with her immorality" (Rev. 19:2). He announces delight in heaven at the glorious prospect of the wedding of Christ and his church, preceded by a joyous marriage supper (vv. 6–9).

Revelation 21:2–3 interprets the wedding imagery of 19:6–9 in terms of the ultimate union between Christ and the church:

> I saw the holy city, new Jerusalem, coming down out of heaven from God, *prepared as a bride adorned for her husband.* And I heard a loud voice

from the throne saying, "Behold, the dwelling place of God is with man. He will dwell with them, and they will be his people, and God himself will be with them as their God."

Conclusion

This completes our survey of union with Christ in the biblical storyline. God the Father's eternal plan to save his people included planning to join them spiritually to his Son. He made human beings in his image for fellowship with himself. This means he made them in the likeness of the true image, his Son. In the fall, however, they rebelled against his goodness and were separated from God and Christ. The Son stooped to become a human being in the incarnation; he became one of us so we could be united to him by grace through faith in the gospel. The incarnation enabled Jesus to live a sinless life, die, and rise, accomplishing the work of salvation. After ascending, he poured out the Holy Spirit on the church, thereby joining believers to Christ. This bond of the Spirit known as faith union with Christ is individual and corporate, present and permanent, definitive and growing, already and not yet. When Jesus returns, union will be complete and whole as God's resurrected people will be joined to the Holy Trinity for all eternity on the new earth.

Chapter 22

The Holy Spirit Who Unites Us to Christ: His Personality and Deity

The chief role of the Holy Spirit in salvation is to apply salvation to believers; another way of saying this is that his chief role is to unite believers to Christ. Before we study this role, we must examine his person and other roles. This will enable us to understand that the Spirit who joins us to Jesus is a divine person who plays a part in the works of creation, providence, and inspiration of Scripture and who works extensively in the ministries of Jesus and his apostles. Only after doing so will we properly appreciate his work of uniting us to Christ.

Because the Son of God is the star of the biblical story, he is more prominent in Scripture than the Holy Spirit. It is therefore easier to demonstrate the personality and deity of Christ than the personality and deity of the Spirit. Nevertheless, Scripture testifies that the Spirit is a person—a divine person.

The Personality of the Holy Spirit in John's Gospel

Because most biblical teaching on union with Christ appears in John's Gospel and Paul's epistles, I will seek to prove the Spirit's personality and deity from those books.

The Holy Spirit is a person rather than an impersonal force. He has the attributes of personality. I say this for the following three reasons from the Fourth Gospel:

- The Spirit is like Jesus.
- The Spirit can be known.
- The Spirit does what only persons do.

The Spirit Is Like Jesus

Four times in John's Gospel Jesus says that he will send the Spirit as "another Helper" (John 14:16), "the Helper, the Holy Spirit," or "the Helper" (14:26; 15:26; 16:7). Although the word *paraklētos* (παράκλητος) is variously translated (the ESV renders it "Helper," and the NIV "Helper" or "Counselor"), there is no doubt that it refers to the Spirit as a person. This is especially true in light of Jesus's words, "I will ask the Father, and he will give you another Helper, to be with you forever, even the Spirit of truth" (14:16–17). Jesus means that the Father will send "another Helper" like Jesus, as D. A. Carson explains:

> "Another Paraclete" in the context of Jesus' departure implies that the disciples already have one, the one who is departing. Although Jesus is never in the Fourth Gospel explicitly referred to as a *parakletos*, the title is applied to him in 1 John 2:1. . . . That means that Jesus' *present* advocacy is discharged in the courts of heaven; John 14 implies that *during his ministry* his role as Paraclete, strengthening and helping his disciples, was discharged on earth. "Another Paraclete" is given to perform this latter task.[1]

"Another Helper" like Jesus is a person, not an impersonal force.

The Spirit Can Be Known

If we expand the words quoted above, Jesus says: "I will ask the Father, and he will give you another Helper, to be with you forever, even the Spirit of truth, whom the world cannot receive, because it neither sees him nor knows him. You know him, for he dwells with you and will be in you" (vv. 16–17). The world cannot receive the Spirit because the world is hopelessly empiricist; it

---

[1] D. A. Carson, *The Gospel according to John*, The Pillar New Testament Commentary (Grand Rapids: Eerdmans, 1991), 500, emphasis original.

does not believe what it cannot see. And, as its response to Jesus makes clear, it does not even always believe what it does see.

Though believers will not see the Spirit, in answer to Jesus's prayer to the Father, the Spirit will dwell with and in them, and they will *know* him (vv. 16–17). Impersonal forces cannot be known; only persons can be known. Since the Spirit can be known, he is a person.

The Spirit Does What Only Persons Do

The most prominent demonstration of the Spirit's personality in the Fourth Gospel is the fact that he repeatedly does things only persons can do. Here is a list of what Jesus says the Spirit will do when Jesus returns to the Father and he and the Father send the Spirit:

- He will teach and remind. (John 14:26)
- He will bear witness about Jesus. (15:26)
- He will convict the world. (16:8)
- He will guide into truth. (v. 13)
- He will speak. (v. 13—2x)
- He will hear. (v. 13)
- He will declare. (v. 13)
- He will glorify Jesus. (v. 14)
- He will take what is Jesus's and declare it. (vv. 14–15)

For these three reasons I conclude that the Gospel of John presents the Holy Spirit as a person.

The Personality of the Holy Spirit in Paul's Epistles

In addition, the apostle Paul frequently assumes the Spirit's personality. This is shown in the following seven ways in Paul's letters:

- The Spirit thinks.
- The Spirit communicates.
- The Spirit wills.
- The Spirit feels.
- The Spirit helps.
- The Spirit saves.
- The Spirit fellowships.

The Spirit Thinks

Forces cannot think, but persons can. And the Spirit thinks. Paul speaks of the "mind of the Spirit" (Rom. 8:27). And he offers a glimpse of the Spirit's mind: "The Spirit searches everything, even the depths of God. For who knows a person's thoughts except the spirit of that person, which is in him? So also no one comprehends the thoughts of God except the Spirit of God" (1 Cor. 2:10–11). The Spirit searches the deep things of God and knows God's thoughts, things only persons can do.

The Spirit Communicates

The apostle shows at least four ways the Spirit communicates. "The Spirit himself bears witness with our spirit that we are children of God" (Rom. 8:16). Even when we don't know what to pray, "The Spirit himself intercedes for us with groanings too deep for words. . . . The Spirit intercedes for the saints according to the will of God" (Rom. 8:26–27). The Spirit cries out, for "God has sent the Spirit of his Son into our hearts, crying, 'Abba! Father!'" (Gal. 4:6). The Spirit also sounds warnings: "The Spirit expressly says that in later times some will depart from the faith by devoting themselves to deceitful spirits and teachings of demons" (1 Tim. 4:1). Impersonal forces do not testify, pray, cry out, or warn. The Holy Spirit uses all these forms of communication. Therefore, he is a person.

The Spirit Wills

Paul summarizes his discussion of spiritual gifts: "All these are empowered by one and the same Spirit, who apportions to each one individually as he wills" (1 Cor. 12:11). The Spirit exercises volition in the distribution of gifts, something only persons do.

The Spirit Feels

Forces do not have desires and cannot be hurt. But Scripture ascribes desires to the Spirit: "For the desires of the flesh are against the Spirit, and the desires of the Spirit are against the flesh" (Gal. 5:17). And by commanding, "Do not grieve the Holy Spirit of God, by whom you were sealed for the day of redemption" (Eph. 4:30), Scripture implies that the Spirit can be hurt.

The Spirit Helps

Paul teaches concerning prayer, "The Spirit helps us in our weakness" (Rom. 8:26). And the imprisoned apostle looks to the Spirit for aid: "I know that through your prayers and the help of the Spirit of Jesus Christ this will turn out for my deliverance" (Phil. 1:19).

The Spirit Saves

Impersonal forces cannot rescue anyone. But in various ways Paul ascribes our salvation to the Spirit. The Spirit gives life: "The letter kills, but the Spirit gives life" (2 Cor. 3:6). He sanctifies: "God chose you as the firstfruits to be saved, through sanctification by the Spirit and belief in the truth" (2 Thess. 2:13). He also brings renewal. The apostle says that God "saved us, not because of works done by us in righteousness, but according to his own mercy, by the washing of regeneration and renewal of the Holy Spirit" (Titus 3:5). Only persons can give life, sanctify, and grant spiritual renewal. The Spirit is a person.

The Spirit Fellowships

The Spirit dwells in believers as God does in his temple. "Do you not know that you are God's temple and that God's Spirit dwells in you?" (1 Cor. 3:16). Again Paul writes, "Do you not know that your body is a temple of the Holy Spirit within you, whom you have from God?" (6:19). And in the apostle's most famous benediction, he prays, "The grace of the Lord Jesus Christ and the love of God and the fellowship of the Holy Spirit be with you all" (2 Cor. 13:14). Only persons can have fellowship. The Spirit, with whom believers fellowship, must then be a person.

Conclusion

The Gospel of John in at least three ways and Paul's epistles in at least seven ways present the Holy Spirit as a person and not a mere force. And that is not all. The two apostles also present the Spirit as a divine person. The Holy Spirit is a person, and he is a person in the Godhead.

The Deity of the Holy Spirit in John's Gospel

It is important to reiterate—the Son, not the Spirit, is the main actor in the Bible's story. The Spirit is a supporting actor to the Son, who is the star. And accordingly, while Scripture shouts the deity of the Son, it whispers the deity of the Spirit. Nevertheless, for those who have ears to hear, the whisper is unmistakable.

Because union with Christ, the subject of this book, is paramount in John's Gospel and Paul's letters, we will appeal primarily to those books to demonstrate the Spirit's deity.

First, the Gospel of John witnesses to the divinity of the Holy Spirit in at least three ways:

- The Spirit has divine attributes.
- The Spirit indwells believers.
- The Spirit does divine works.

The Spirit Has Divine Attributes

Two of the Spirit's divine qualities are bound up in his names and are therefore frequently overlooked. Three times Jesus says the Spirit is the "Spirit of truth" (John 14:17; 15:26; 16:13). He is called this because he performs the divine work of revealing Jesus to his disciples (15:26; 16:13–15). According to Jesus, the knowledge revealed by the Spirit of truth is divine knowledge, known only to the Trinitarian persons: the Spirit "will take what is mine and declare it to you. All that the Father has is mine; therefore I said that he will take what is mine and declare it to you" (16:14–15).

Christians are so familiar with the name Holy Spirit that it has lost its power; it packs no punch (14:26). That is unfortunate, because this name associates the Spirit with the holiness of God in a way only appropriate to God himself. Thus truth and holiness are bound up with the Spirit's names and show him to be a divine person.

The Spirit Indwells Believers

In the New Testament only God indwells believers. A half-dozen times God the Son is said to indwell them: Romans 8:10; 2 Corinthians 13:5; Galatians 2:20; Ephesians 3:17; and Colossians 1:27; 3:11. Usually, however, the Holy Spirit is said to indwell believers: for example, Romans 8:9, 11; 1 Corinthians 3:16; and 2 Corinthians 1:22. In the Fourth Gospel Jesus predicts that the Spirit will indwell believers: "I will ask the Father, and he will give you another Helper, to be with you forever, even the Spirit of truth .... You know him, for he dwells with you and will be in you" (John 14:16–17). Only God indwells his people. The Spirit does so; therefore, the Spirit is divine.

The Spirit Does Divine Works

In Scripture there are certain works that only God performs. One of those is giving life to those who are spiritually dead. That is what the Spirit does in John. While Jesus mystifies Nicodemus, the "teacher of Israel" (John 3:10), by speaking of the new birth, Jesus declares, "That which is born of the flesh is flesh, and that which is born of the Spirit is spirit" (v. 6). He means that human beings give rise to that which belongs to the human realm, while the Holy Spirit gives rise to that which belongs to the divine realm. After repeating his claim, "You must be born again" (v. 7), Jesus likens the Spirit to the wind: "The wind blows where it wishes, and you hear its sound, but you do not know where it comes from or where it goes. So it is with everyone who is born of the Spirit" (v. 8).[2] The Holy Wind of God, as unpredictable and sovereign as the wind, causes people to be born from above, to be born again. The Spirit does the divine work of giving life to those spiritually dead.

John communicates the same truth in different words in chapter 6. After presenting himself as the Bread of Life, the source of spiritual life, Jesus is met with a crowd grumbling at his difficult words (John 6:60–61). In response, Jesus does not back off but gives even more difficult words, speaking of his ascension (v. 62). Then he proclaims, "It is the Spirit who gives life; the flesh is no help at all. The words that I have spoken to you are spirit and life" (v. 63). Jesus's words bring spiritual life. And that is because the Spirit of God works in and through his words, for the "Spirit . . . gives life." Human striving ("the flesh") is "no help at all." Here again the Spirit is the source of eternal life, a role assumed only by God.

Plainly, Jesus in the Gospel of John, in these three ways—presenting the Spirit as possessor of God's qualities of truth and holiness, predicting that he will indwell believers, and portraying him as the giver of spiritual life—implies that the Holy Spirit is a divine person.

The Deity of the Holy Spirit in Paul's Epistles

Paul in his epistles also presents the deity of the Spirit. He does so in at least seven ways:

- The Spirit raises Jesus from the dead.
- The Spirit has divine attributes.

---

[2] Jesus here makes a play on words—the Greek word *pneuma* (πνεῦμα) means "breath, wind, or spirit (Spirit)."

- The Spirit indwells believers.
- The Spirit is equated with God.
- The Spirit is linked to the Father and Son.
- The Spirit applies salvation.
- The Spirit is indispensable to salvation.

The Spirit Raises Jesus from the Dead

Usually Scripture presents the Father as the one who raises Jesus from the dead. We see this in Acts 4:10; Romans 10:9; Ephesians 1:19–22; and 1 Peter 1:21, to cite four examples.[3] John's Gospel in two places teaches that Jesus raises himself from the dead (2:19–22 and 10:17–18). Scripture teaches that the Holy Spirit also plays a role in Jesus's resurrection. Paul begins Romans by speaking of the "gospel of God," which concerns God's "Son, who was descended from David according to the flesh," that is, who is a human being (Rom. 1:1, 3). But he was also "declared to be the Son of God in power according to the Spirit of holiness by his resurrection from the dead," that is, he is also divine (v. 4). Indeed, "Jesus Christ our Lord" is both God and man in one person.

Note that when the apostle speaks of Jesus's resurrection, he says that it was "according to the Spirit of holiness" (v. 4). God the Holy Spirit has a part to play in the powerful resurrection of Jesus that shows him to be the Son of God. Only God—Father, Son, and Spirit—is involved in raising Jesus from the dead. That the Spirit is so involved shows his deity.

The Spirit Has Divine Attributes

Only God possesses certain qualities. Scripture ascribes to the Holy Spirit the divine quality of power. Paul tells of his fulfilling the "ministry of the gospel of Christ" by preaching and miracles (Rom. 15:18–19). How does the apostle perform "signs and wonders"? "By the power of the Spirit of God" (v. 19). It is the powerful Holy Spirit who works through Paul to perform apostolic miracles.

The Spirit also evinces that he has the divine attribute of knowledge. Paul teaches that the apostles' preaching includes revelation about heaven that exceeds human knowing. But, amazingly, "these things God has revealed to us through the Spirit" (1 Cor. 2:10). How does the Spirit have access to the secret things of God, things that are inaccessible to human beings?

---

[3] Most frequently this is done by using the divine passive, as in 1 Cor. 15:4, 20.

"The Spirit searches everything, even the depths of God. For who knows a person's thoughts except the spirit of that person, which is in him? So also no one comprehends the thoughts of God except the Spirit of God" (vv. 10–11). Only a person knows his or her own inmost thoughts. Similarly, only the Holy Spirit knows the inmost thoughts, the "depths," of God. Surely this shows that the Spirit is privy to divine knowledge and therefore is God himself.

The Spirit Indwells Believers

Paul writes:

> We are the temple of the living God; as God said,
>
> > "I will make my dwelling among them and walk among them,
> >   and I will be their God,
> >   and they shall be my people." (2 Cor. 6:16)

As proof of believers' being God's temple, the apostle adapts Leviticus 26:11–12, which begins with God saying, "I will make my dwelling among you." In Scripture only God indwells his people. And in at least seven places (italicized here) the Holy Spirit is said to indwell believers:

> You, however, are not in the flesh but in the Spirit, if in fact *the Spirit of God dwells in you.* Anyone who does not have the Spirit of Christ does not belong to him.... *If the Spirit of him who raised Jesus from the dead dwells in you,* he who raised Christ Jesus from the dead will also give life to your mortal bodies through *his Spirit who dwells in you.* (Rom. 8:9, 11)

> Do you not know that you are God's temple and that *God's Spirit dwells in you*? (1 Cor. 3:16)

> Do you not know that your body is a temple of *the Holy Spirit within you,* whom you have from God? (1 Cor. 6:19)

> It is God who establishes us with you in Christ, and has anointed us, and who has also put his seal on us and *given us his Spirit in our hearts* as a guarantee. (2 Cor. 1:21–22)

> By *the Holy Spirit who dwells within us,* guard the good deposit entrusted to you. (2 Tim. 1:14)

Since only God indwells his people, and the Spirit does this, the conclusion is irresistible: the Spirit is God.

The Spirit Is Equated with God

In two of the passages just cited, the Spirit is equated with God. Paul tells the church corporately, "Do you not know that you are God's temple and that God's Spirit dwells in you?" (1 Cor. 3:16). He tells believers individually, "Do you not know that your body is a temple of the Holy Spirit within you, whom you have from God?" (6:19). Christians are "God's temple," a "temple of the Holy Spirit." The Spirit is thus interchangeable with God. His name is equated with God's.

The Spirit Is Linked to the Father and Son

Furthermore, the Spirit is linked with the Father and the Son in ways in which only God can be linked. Paul teaches concerning the gifts of the Holy Spirit: "There are varieties of gifts, but the same Spirit; and there are varieties of service, but the same Lord; and there are varieties of activities, but it is the same God who empowers them all in everyone" (1 Cor. 12:4–6). The apostle teaches that there are varieties of gifts, service, and activities, but the same Holy Spirit, the same Lord Jesus, and the same God the Father. That is, the unity of the persons of the Trinity undergirds the church's ministries. There are different spiritual gifts given by the Spirit, used in different varieties of service done for the Lord Jesus, and resulting in different activities performed by the Father. Note that the Holy Spirit is tied to the other two Trinitarian persons in various aspects of the church's life. Only God gives spiritual gifts, and he is here called the "same Spirit" (v. 4).

Paul's most famous benediction reads: "The grace of the Lord Jesus Christ and the love of God and the fellowship of the Holy Spirit be with you all" (2 Cor. 13:14). This demonstrates not only that the Holy Spirit is a person rather than a force—human beings cannot have "fellowship" with a force. It demonstrates also the Spirit's deity, for divine blessings are given by the Son, the Father, and the Spirit, respectively.

Paul spells out the historic seven unities of the Christian church: "There is one body and one Spirit—just as you were called to the one hope that belongs to your call—one Lord, one faith, one baptism, one God and Father of all, who is over all and through all and in all" (Eph. 4:4–6). God the Father is named, and there is no doubt as to the identity of "one Lord": it is Jesus. The "one

Spirit" refers to the Holy Spirit, who establishes the "one body," the church. Again the Spirit is associated with the Father and Son in a way that only God could be associated. Putting the name of an angel or apostle in the linguistic slot occupied by the Spirit does not work.

Thus in these three Pauline passages the Spirit is tied to the Father and Son as only God could be tied.

The Spirit Applies Salvation

Perhaps the greatest proof of the Spirit's deity is his role in applying salvation, a role in keeping with his servanthood. The Spirit applies adoption to believers; he enables them to call God "Father" in truth: "You did not receive the spirit of slavery to fall back into fear, but you have received the Spirit of adoption as sons, by whom we cry, "Abba! Father!" (Rom. 8:15). The Spirit applies regeneration to God's people: "Our sufficiency is from God, who has made us sufficient to be ministers of a new covenant, not of the letter but of the Spirit. For the letter kills, but the Spirit gives life" (2 Cor. 3:5–6; see also Gal. 5:25; Titus 3:5).

The Spirit applies sanctification to the people of God: "God chose you as the firstfruits to be saved, through sanctification by the Spirit and belief in the truth" (2 Thess. 2:13; see also Rom. 15:16). Although it is largely unknown, the Spirit also applies justification to believers: "You were washed, you were sanctified, you were justified in the name of the Lord Jesus Christ and by the Spirit of our God" (1 Cor. 6:11).

Christ baptizes us into his church "in the Spirit"; the Spirit thus unites us to Christ: "In one Spirit we were all baptized into one body—Jews or Greeks, slaves or free—and all were made to drink of one Spirit" (12:13). Along with the Father, the Spirit will also play a role in our final salvation, our resurrection from the dead: "If the Spirit of him who raised Jesus from the dead dwells in you, he who raised Christ Jesus from the dead will also give life to your mortal bodies through his Spirit who dwells in you" (Rom. 8:11).

Adoption, regeneration, sanctification, justification, union with Christ, and resurrection are six different ways of describing salvation. And the Spirit plays a role in all six; therefore, the Spirit is God.

The Spirit Is Indispensable to Salvation

The Spirit plays an important role in salvation—he applies it to the lives of God's people. In fact, Scripture goes so far as to teach that the Spirit is absolutely indispensable to salvation: "Anyone who does not have the Spirit of Christ does not belong to him" (Rom. 8:9).

In sum, in these seven ways Paul's epistles agree with John's Gospel—the Holy Spirit is divine.

Conclusion

Millard Erickson draws conclusions from the truths of the Spirit's personality and deity that seem irrefutable to me:

1. The Holy Spirit is a person, not a vague force. Thus, he is someone with whom we can have a personal relationship, someone to whom we can and should pray.
2. The Holy Spirit, being fully divine, is to be accorded the same honor and respect that we give to the Father and the Son. It is appropriate to worship him as we do them. He should not be thought of as in any sense inferior in essence to them, although his role may sometimes be subordinated to theirs.
3. The Holy Spirit is one with the Father and the Son. His work is the expression and execution of what the three of them have planned together. There is no tension among their persons and activities.
4. God is not far off. In the Holy Spirit, the Triune God comes close, so close as to actually enter into each believer. He is even more intimate with us now than in the incarnation.[4]

---

[4] Millard J. Erickson, *Christian Theology*, 2nd ed. (Grand Rapids: Baker, 1998), 879.

Chapter 23

The Works of the Holy Spirit

The previous chapter argued from John's Gospel and Paul's letters for the personality and deity of the Holy Spirit. This chapter deals with the works of the Spirit. My goal is to talk about the Spirit's work of joining people to Christ. But before doing so, it is good to focus on other works of the Spirit. I want us to view union with Christ in the context of the Spirit's "greater" works.

I will treat the Spirit's work in five spheres:

- the work of the Spirit in creation
- the work of the Spirit in Scripture
- the work of the Spirit in the world
- the work of the Spirit in the apostles
- the work of the Spirit in Jesus

The Work of the Spirit in Creation

The Holy Spirit is seldom mentioned in Scripture in relation to creation. Even the few texts that I believe support that notion are debated. The Bible begins: "In the beginning, God created the heavens and the earth. The earth was without form and void, and darkness was over the face of the deep. And the Spirit of God was hovering over the face of the waters" (Gen. 1:1–2). The word translated "Spirit" (*ruakh*) means "breath, wind, spirit, or Spirit." And some, therefore, have understood verse 2 to refer to wind. But this is probably not correct for three reasons, which I credit to my colleague Jack Collins: (1) *Ruakh* is used not by itself here but in a composite expression whose consistent Old Testament usage is "Spirit of God." (2) The verb *hovering* or *brooding* fits better with *Spirit* as its subject than with wind. (3) The Spirit is associated with a bird in other Scriptures, such as Matthew 3:16.[1]

I thus take "the Spirit of God was hovering over the face of the waters" (v. 2) as a reference to the Holy Spirit's playing a part in the divine activity of creation. Bruce Waltke explains: "Spirit better fits the context. Hovering eaglelike over the primordial abyss, the almighty Spirit prepares the earth for human habitation."[2]

Another passage that presupposes the Spirit's part in creation is Job 33:4, where Elihu says,

> The Spirit of God has made me,
>   and the breath of the Almighty gives me life.

Scripture regularly ascribes the work of creation to the Father. The New Testament in a number of places ascribes it also to the Son as the Father's agent (John 1:3, 10; 1 Cor. 8:6; Col. 1:16; Heb. 1:2, 10). We should not be surprised that Scripture says less about the Spirit's role in creation, because he is the agent of the Father and the Son. Certainly, because Christian theology teaches an indivisible Holy Trinity, we must say that creation is the work of Father, Son, and Holy Spirit.

The Work of the Spirit in Scripture

The Holy Spirit is also involved in the production of Holy Scripture. Peter, discussing the prophetical writings of the Old Testament, affirms, "No prophecy of Scripture comes from someone's own interpretation. For no prophecy was ever produced by the will of man, but men spoke from God as they were carried along by the Holy Spirit" (2 Pet. 1:20–21). Peter asserts that prophecies were not the product of mere human impulse; the prophets were impelled by the Holy Spirit so that they spoke from God himself. Richard Bauckham agrees: "The only point which the author of 2 Peter is concerned to deny is that the prophets themselves were the originating source of their message.

---

[1] C. John Collins, *Genesis 1–4: A Linguistic, Literary, and Theological Commentary* (Phillipsburg, NJ: P&R, 2006), 45.
[2] Bruce K. Waltke, *Genesis: A Commentary* (Grand Rapids: Zondervan, 2001), 60.

To counter this view he affirms that the Holy Spirit was the source of their prophecy, enabling them to speak as God's own spokesmen."[3]

Scripture sometimes refers to the Holy Spirit as the "Spirit of Christ." Peter does this in his first epistle when he points to the true source of Old Testament prophets' predictions of Christ's passion and exaltation: "Concerning this salvation, the prophets who prophesied about the grace that was to be yours searched and inquired carefully, inquiring what person or time the Spirit of Christ in them was indicating when he predicted the sufferings of Christ and the subsequent glories" (1 Pet. 1:10–11). The prophets did not fully understand their own predictions of the Christ. But the Spirit of Christ within them did. Again Peter ascribes the production of Scripture to the Holy Spirit.

The Work of the Spirit in the World

The Holy Spirit also plays important roles vis-à-vis the world. Jesus tells the disciples that it is good for him to go away because he will then send the Helper. What will the Helper do? "When he comes, he will convict the world concerning sin and righteousness and judgment: concerning sin, because they do not believe in me; concerning righteousness, because I go to the Father, and you will see me no longer; concerning judgment, because the ruler of this world is judged" (John 16:8–11). How merciful Jesus is! He will send the Spirit to convict sinners of their sin "because they do not believe in" him (v. 9). On their own, sinners would never believe, but a ministry of the Spirit is to convict the world of its need for Christ. He will convict the world also of its self-righteousness and faulty spiritual judgment.[4]

Furthermore, the Spirit is included in the chorus of witnesses to Jesus in the Fourth Gospel. Jesus declares, "When the Helper comes, whom I will send to you from the Father, the Spirit of truth, who proceeds from the Father, he will bear witness about me" (15:26). The Spirit thus joins John the Baptist, Jesus's miracles, the Old Testament, the Father, the disciples, and Jesus himself in witnessing to Jesus.

In addition, the Holy Spirit invites people to come to Christ. In very nearly the Bible's last words we read: "The Spirit and the Bride say, 'Come.' And let the one who hears say, 'Come.' And let the one who is thirsty come; let the one who desires take the water of life without price" (Rev. 22:17). God graciously

---

[3] Richard J. Bauckham, *Jude, 2 Peter*, Word Biblical Commentary (Waco, TX: Word, 1983), 234.
[4] Here I follow the interpretation of D. A. Carson in *The Gospel according to John*, The Pillar New Testament Commentary (Grand Rapids: Eerdmans, 1991), 537–39.

ends his story with both the Spirit and the church warmly inviting readers to come to Jesus to quench their spiritual thirst.

And in fact, when anyone does believe in Jesus, it is because the Spirit has been at work to enable faith, as Paul testifies: "No one can say 'Jesus is Lord' except in the Holy Spirit" (1 Cor. 12:3). The primitive Christian confession is "Jesus is Lord" (Rom. 10:9–10; 1 Cor. 12:3; Phil. 2:11). It is the Spirit who enables people to make this confession, to say "Jesus is Lord" in truth. That is, it is the Spirit who gives the gift of saving faith to sinners.

The Work of the Spirit in the Apostles

In addition, Scripture presents the Spirit of God as active in the apostles and their ministries. He equips them for service to God. He speaks through them (Matt. 10:20), teaches them what to say (Luke 12:12), gives them "a mouth and wisdom" (21:15), and clothes them with power from on high at Pentecost so they might witness to Jesus's death and resurrection (24:49). Dwelling within them, the Spirit will be their Helper forever (John 14:16–17).

The Spirit leads the apostles into the work he has prepared for them (Acts 13:2, 4). He leads them to make wise corporate judgments for the life of the church (15:28). He sometimes shuts and sometimes opens doors of ministry for the apostles, guiding them to preach the Word where God calls them (16:6–10).

Through the apostles' ministry the Spirit builds the church as a holy temple to the Lord. Amazingly, God takes Gentiles, those foreign to God and his covenants, and incorporates them into the people of God:

> You are no longer strangers and aliens, but you are fellow citizens with the saints and members of the household of God, built on the foundation of the apostles and prophets, Christ Jesus himself being the cornerstone, in whom the whole structure, being joined together, grows into a holy temple in the Lord. In him you also are being built together into a dwelling place for God by the Spirit. (Eph. 2:19–22)

The cornerstone of the church's foundation is Christ. And his apostles and New Testament prophets are a part of the foundation. The church is built on the foundation of Christ and the apostles. It is the Holy Spirit who builds this structure, the church, by adding believing Jews and Gentiles to God's people. The Spirit joins them to Christ as individuals constituting a "holy temple in the Lord. . . . a dwelling place for God" (vv. 21–22).

The Spirit also intercedes for all believers, including the apostles. Whether we realize it or not, in ourselves we are weak; we need the Lord's strength. Sometimes we do not even know what to pray for. "But the Spirit himself intercedes for us with groanings too deep for words. And he who searches hearts knows what is the mind of the Spirit, because the Spirit intercedes for the saints according to the will of God" (Rom. 8:26–27). The Spirit prays to the Father in our behalf; he intercedes for us.

The Work of the Spirit in Jesus

None of these is the most important work of the Spirit for our purposes. Rather, pride of place belongs to the Spirit's work in Jesus. Remarkably, the same Spirit who was at work in the earthly ministry of Jesus works in us, primarily to join us to the person of Christ and his many spiritual benefits. The Spirit was at work in Old Testament predictions and in Jesus's conception, earthly ministry, death, resurrection, and baptizing the church with the Spirit.

Old Testament Predictions

The Old Testament foretells that the Spirit will be at work in the Promised One:

> There shall come forth a shoot from the stump of Jesse,
>   and a branch from his roots shall bear fruit.
> And the Spirit of the LORD shall rest upon him,
>   the Spirit of wisdom and understanding,
>   the Spirit of counsel and might,
>   the Spirit of knowledge and the fear of the LORD.
> And his delight shall be in the fear of the LORD. (Isa. 11:1–3)

He will be a descendant of King David (whose father was Jesse). God's Spirit will rest on him and grant him great wisdom and strength. Consequently, his life will be characterized by the "fear of the LORD" (vv. 2–3).

> Behold my servant, whom I uphold,
>   my chosen, in whom my soul delights;
> I have put my Spirit upon him;
>   he will bring forth justice to the nations.
> He will not cry aloud or lift up his voice,
>   or make it heard in the street;
> a bruised reed he will not break,

and a faintly burning wick he will not quench;
   he will faithfully bring forth justice.
He will not grow faint or be discouraged
   till he has established justice in the earth;
   and the coastlands wait for his law. (42:1–4)

The Lord will choose him to be his servant and will delight in him. He will give him his Spirit to enable him to act justly, to be gentle, and to persevere in his pursuit of justice in all the earth.

The Spirit of the Lord God is upon me,
   because the Lord has anointed me
to bring good news to the poor;
   he has sent me to bind up the brokenhearted,
to proclaim liberty to the captives,
   and the opening of the prison to those who are bound;
to proclaim the year of the Lord's favor,
   and the day of vengeance of our God;
   to comfort all who mourn. (61:1–2)

The Lord will anoint the Promised One with his Spirit. This will enable him to preach good news to the poor, the brokenhearted, the captives, and the imprisoned. His message will bring comfort to some and vengeance to others.

Jesus's Conception

We see the Spirit at work in the life of Jesus from the very beginning. His conception in Mary's womb is the work of the Spirit. Even as the Holy Spirit came upon people in the Old Testament, so Mary is told by the angel, "The Holy Spirit will come upon you" (Luke 1:35). The angel continues, "The power of the Most High will overshadow you; therefore the child to be born will be called holy—the Son of God" (v. 35). The same Spirit hovered over the waters in creation, overshadowed the people of Israel in the pillars of cloud and fire in the wilderness, and dwelled in the tabernacle and first temple. The shekinah cloud of the Spirit's presence was absent from the second temple. And Ezekiel prophesied that, even as he had seen the glory depart from the temple, so it would reappear in the new temple (Ezek. 43:1–5).[5]

Jesus is that promised glory. And from his conception the Spirit of glory

---

[5] I received much help from Sinclair B. Ferguson, *The Holy Spirit*, Contours of Christian Theology (Downers Grove, IL: InterVarsity, 1996), 39. In fact, Ferguson helped me in this whole section treating the Spirit's work in Jesus.

"overshadowed" his mother with the result that her baby boy was born the "holy . . . Son of God" (Luke 1:35). Even before Jesus's birth, then, the Spirit was active in preparing for him a human body and soul so he could save his people from their sins.

Jesus's Earthly Ministry

The Spirit is also extremely active in every aspect of Jesus's earthly ministry, as the summary in Acts indicates: "God anointed Jesus of Nazareth with the Holy Spirit and with power. He went about doing good and healing all who were oppressed by the devil, for God was with him" (Acts 10:38). It is the Spirit who officially descends "on him like a dove" at his baptism so he can fulfill his threefold messianic office of prophet, priest, and king (Mark 1:10). The same "Spirit immediately" drives him "out into the wilderness," where he is tempted by Satan for forty days (v. 12–13).

In his very first sermon Jesus quotes Isaiah 61:1–2:

> The Spirit of the Lord is upon me,
>> because he has anointed me
>> to proclaim good news to the poor.
> He has sent me to proclaim liberty to the captives
>> and recovering of sight to the blind,
>> to set at liberty those who are oppressed,
> to proclaim the year of the Lord's favor. (Luke 4:18–19)

Indeed, the Spirit is upon Jesus and anoints him as prophet, priest, and king. As a result his earthly ministry is empowered by the Spirit. "Jesus returned in the power of the Spirit to Galilee, and a report about him went out through all the surrounding country. And he taught in their synagogues, being glorified by all" (vv. 14–15). Contrary to the Pharisees' blasphemous claims that Jesus casts out demons by the Devil, he casts them out by the Spirit of God (Matt. 12:28). In fact, the Father gives the Son "the Spirit without measure" (John 3:34). Jesus not only performs mighty deeds by the Spirit. The Spirit, his constant companion, also moves him in more mundane matters. For example, "he rejoiced in the Holy Spirit" and prays to the Father (Luke 10:21).

Jesus's Death

Jesus is not only conceived by the Holy Spirit and empowered by the same Spirit for ministry. The Spirit also has a role to play in his atoning death. The writer to the Hebrews declares that if Old Testament sacrifices "sanctify for the purification of the flesh, how much more will the blood of Christ, who through the eternal Spirit offered himself without blemish to God, purify our conscience from dead works to serve the living God" (Heb. 9:13–14). The Trinitarian persons must be distinguished. Only the Son becomes incarnate and dies for sinners. But the persons must never be separated. Thus we learn that the Father takes part in Christ's atonement, for "in Christ God was reconciling the world to himself" (2 Cor. 5:19). And the Spirit was not inactive when Jesus hung on the cross, for "through the eternal Spirit" Christ "offered himself . . . to God" (Heb. 9:14).

Peter O'Brien brings the priestly context to bear on this text: "The Holy Spirit anointed Jesus as high priest for every aspect of his ministry, including his sacrificial death."[6] William Lane is more specific: the writer "indicates what makes Christ's sacrifice absolute and final. . . . The fact that his offering was made . . . 'through the eternal Spirit' implies that he has been divinely empowered and sustained in his office."[7] Moreover, the Spirit is active in Jesus's ministry from womb to tomb, as the next section clarifies.

Jesus's Resurrection

The Spirit is active also in Jesus's resurrection, as both Peter and Paul testify. Peter writes: "Christ also suffered once for sins, the righteous for the unrighteous, to bring you to God. He was put to death in the body but made alive in the Spirit" (1 Pet. 3:18 NIV). Although the matter is debated, I favor this translation.[8] J. Ramsey Michaels agrees: "He was put to death in the flesh, but made alive in the Spirit."[9] Thomas Schreiner clarifies, "Christ was put to death with reference to or in the sphere of his body, but on the other hand he was made alive by the Spirit."[10]

The best explanation I have found is Paul J. Achtemeier's:

Yet a most natural construal of ζῳοποιηθεὶς δὲ πνεύματι [*zōopoiētheis de pneumati*] would be to take it as a dative of instrument: Christ was

---

[6] Peter T. O'Brien, *The Letter to the Hebrews*, The Pillar New Testament Commentary (Grand Rapids: Eerdmans, 2010), 324–25.

[7] William L. Lane, *Hebrews 9–13*, Word Biblical Commentary (Dallas: Word, 1991), 240.

[8] The translation of *pneumati* as either "spirit" or "Spirit" is debated. The ESV reads, "Christ also suffered once for sins, the righteous for the unrighteous, that he might bring us to God, being put to death in the flesh but made alive in the spirit." This contrasts two spheres, that of the flesh with that of the spirit. I regard Paul J. Achtemeier's reasoning for adopting "Spirit" as cogent. Achtemeier, *1 Peter*, Hermeneia (Minneapolis: Fortress, 1996), 250–51.

[9] J. Ramsey Michaels, *1 Peter*, Word Biblical Commentary (Waco, TX: Word, 1988), 203.

[10] That is, the two prepositional phrases ("in the body" and "in the Spirit") are not parallel in use. Thomas R. Schreiner, *1, 2 Peter, Jude*, New American Commentary (Nashville: Broadman and Holman, 2003), 184.

raised "by the (divine) Spirit," that is, by God, a central affirmation of the NT. . . . Christ was put to death by unbelieving humanity, but raised by (God's) Spirit. Such a construal has the advantage of allowing us to understand Christ's resurrection in the second member of the parallel phrase in its normal form, as a bodily resurrection, since the resurrection is being described in terms of the one who brought it about (Spirit), not in terms of the sphere within which it occurred (spirit). Such a construal would therefore allow the interpretation of the phrase to remain within the normal boundaries of NT tradition.[11]

In at least two places Paul confesses the same truth:

Paul, a servant of Christ Jesus, called to be an apostle, set apart for the gospel of God, which he promised beforehand through his prophets in the holy Scriptures, concerning his Son, who was descended from David according to the flesh and was declared to be the Son of God in power according to the Spirit of holiness by his resurrection from the dead, Jesus Christ our Lord. (Rom. 1:1–4)

When the apostle unfolds the gospel of God, he concentrates on his Son. Specifically he contrasts the Son of God's humanity (he was "descended from David according to the flesh," v. 3) and deity (he was "declared to be the Son of God in power . . . by his resurrection from the dead," v. 4). The latter is declared "according to the Spirit of holiness," that is, the Holy Spirit. The Father, then, proclaims the divinity of his Son by powerfully raising him from the dead through the agency of the Spirit.

Schreiner emphasizes the newness of the Spirit's work in Jesus's life:

The reference to the resurrection demonstrates that Jesus's experience with the Spirit on earth is excluded here. The resurrection of Jesus inaugurates the new age. When Jesus lived on earth as the Son of David, he lived his life in the old age of the flesh that was characterized by weakness, sin, and death. At his resurrection, however, Jesus left the old age behind and inaugurated the new age of the Spirit.[12]

Paul teaches the activity of the Spirit in Jesus's resurrection also in his confession of the "mystery of godliness" in a christological hymn or poem:

---

[11] Achtemeier, *1 Peter*, 250.
[12] Thomas R. Schreiner, *Romans*, Baker Exegetical Commentary on the New Testament (Grand Rapids: Baker Academic, 1998), 44.

He was manifested in the flesh,
>   vindicated by the Spirit,
>   seen by angels,
> proclaimed among the nations,
>   believed on in the world,
>   taken up in glory. (1 Tim. 3:16)

Paul includes in this confession everything from Christ's incarnation to his resurrection, to his proclamation, to his being the object of faith, to his ascension. Specifically, Jesus's "vindication" from the dead is "by the Spirit." Remember that Jesus died the death of a criminal, a condemned man. In that regard his resurrection from the dead is his justification (vindication). The Father justifies his Son by raising him from the dead. And he does so "by the Spirit," as George Knight explains: "Paul is here speaking of the vindication of Jesus by the Holy Spirit through his resurrection."[13]

Thus in three different contexts and in three different ways—Jesus "was put to death in the body but made alive in the Spirit" (1 Pet. 3:18 NIV), "declared to be the Son of God in power according to the Spirit of holiness by his resurrection from the dead" (Rom 1:1–4), and "vindicated by the Spirit" (1 Tim. 3:16)—Peter and Paul teach the same truth: the Holy Spirit is active in Jesus's resurrection from the dead.

Jesus's Baptizing the Church with the Spirit

The Holy Spirit thus works in Jesus from his conception through his resurrection. Why include Pentecost, devoting three pages to it? Because Pentecost is the bridge connecting the Spirit's working in Jesus's life to the Spirit's working in our lives, of which union with Christ is his major work.

Why did Christ receive the Spirit at his baptism? Remember that later the Father through Peter proclaims Jesus the "Christ [or "Anointed One"], the Son of the living God" (Matt. 16:16). Why was he the Anointed One? There are a number of reasons, including to equip him for his earthly ministry. But the main reason Jesus is anointed with the Spirit is to give the Spirit. Our survey of the Spirit's work in Jesus would be incomplete, therefore, without a look at his pouring out the Spirit on the church at Pentecost.

The prophets Joel (Joel 2:28) and John the Baptist (Matt. 3:11; Mark. 1:7–8; Luke 3:16; John 1:32–34) and Jesus himself (Luke 24:49) foretell this great

---

[13] George W. Knight III, *The Pastoral Epistles*, New International Greek Testament Commentary (Grand Rapids: Eerdmans, 1992), 185.

event. Jesus recalls John the Baptist's prophecy at the beginning of Acts (Acts 1:4–5). The Baptist predicted that the Messiah would baptize the church with the Holy Spirit, and in Acts 2 he does that very thing.

The Jewish feast of Pentecost after Jesus's death and resurrection is like none other. God uses wind and fire to symbolize the coming of the Holy Spirit (Acts 2:2–3). Peter identifies the events of Pentecost with "what was uttered through the prophet Joel" (v. 16). It is crucial to understand that *Jesus* pours out the Spirit on the church on the day of Pentecost. This is as much Jesus's saving work as dying for our sins and rising again. Pentecost is a saving action of Christ whereby he applies the benefits of his death and resurrection to the church. It is his unique and unrepeatable redemptive-historical deed.

Acts does not elaborate on Pentecost. Instead it tells the results of that stunning event—the apostles are equipped by the Spirit to spread the gospel across the first-century world. If we view Jesus's ministry at Pentecost in light of the Bible's whole story, we learn several ways in which his giving the Spirit applies and extends his saving work.

At Pentecost Jesus publicly proclaims the new covenant. The Old Testament promises of a new covenant (e.g., in Jer. 31:31) find their fulfillment in him, the "one mediator between God and men" (1 Tim. 2:5). He is the Mediator of the new covenant (Heb. 9:15; 12:24; 13:20), which he ratifies by his death and resurrection (Luke 22:20). But this grand news is broadcast only when Jesus publicly heralds it at Pentecost. He does this through the Holy Spirit whom he pours out on his apostles.

Though the new creation will be fully disclosed only at the end, Christ begins the new creation when he dies and rises. But it is only publicly manifested at Pentecost. After his resurrection Jesus says to his disciples, "As the Father has sent me, even so I am sending you" (John 20:21). He thereby connects their ongoing ministry to his own. He then performs a prophetic action to equip them for their mission. John writes: "When he had said this, he breathed on them and said to them, 'Receive the Holy Spirit. If you forgive the sins of any, they are forgiven them; if you withhold forgiveness from any, it is withheld'" (John 20:22–23). Jesus's breathing on the disciples recalls God's breathing into Adam the breath of life (Gen. 2:7). Even as God the Creator granted his human creature life by a divine act of in-breathing, so the risen Christ, the re-Creator, by his prophetic act promises to give spiritual life to his disciples. Christ's breathing on his disciples while saying "Receive the Holy Spirit" foretells that Pentecost will be the beginning of God's new creation.

Furthermore, the sounds of Pentecost point to another Old Testament connection. "Suddenly there came from heaven a sound like a mighty rushing wind, and it filled the entire house where they were sitting" (Acts 2:2). This recalls the picture of the Spirit of God's powerful work in creation (Gen. 1:2). One Hebrew word means "breath, wind, spirit, or Spirit," and the same is true for one Greek word. So when Luke refers to the "mighty rushing wind" that fills the house, he symbolically speaks of the mighty Spirit of God that Jesus the Christ pours on his apostles. Dennis Johnson explains the significance of the wind in Acts 2:2, which recalls the Spirit of God of Genesis 1:2: "The sound of wind signaled the arrival of the Spirit, who makes the dead alive. The 'wind' was the breath of God, breathed into the new humanity. Pentecost was a new creation. . . . The coming of the Spirit at Pentecost marked a major step in God's restoration of his creation in the last days."[14]

Jesus on the day of Pentecost gives the Holy Spirit to the people of God in a new and powerful manner. Pentecost does not represent the beginning of the Holy Spirit's work in the world. Instead, it represents the work of salvation in a grander and fuller way than previously. The Spirit comes with newness and power and brings the fullness of salvation. And that salvation manifests itself in many ways, including heretofore unprecedented witness. Christ forms a new community, the New Testament church, when he gives the Spirit at Pentecost.

Conclusion

We have considered the work of God the Holy Spirit in five spheres: in creation, in Scripture, in the world, in the apostles, and supremely in Jesus. We have seen that Spirit at work in Jesus's conception, earthly ministry, death, and resurrection. We learned that Jesus poured out the Spirit on the church at Pentecost and thereby publicly proclaimed the new covenant, inaugurated the new creation, and bestowed the Spirit on the new community.

All this prompts important questions: What is the most important saving ministry of the Spirit? With what one act does he bestow on God's people all of the blessings of salvation? What is the most comprehensive way of describing the application of salvation? What does the Spirit do to connect believers to both the person and work of the Mediator? These four questions have the same answer: union with Christ. And this glorious ministry of the Spirit is the focus of the next chapter.

---

[14] Dennis E. Johnson, *The Message of Acts in the History of Redemption* (Phillipsburg, NJ: P&R, 1997), 58.

Chapter 24

The Most Important
Work of the Holy Spirit

The last two chapters have shown that the Holy Spirit is a divine person who does the divine works of creation, giving Scripture, and working in the world, the apostles, and Jesus. The most important work of the Holy Spirit in the realm of salvation is union with Christ. Each person of the Trinity plays a role in this union. The Father planned to join us to his Son before creation. Interestingly, two texts speak of a pre-creation election, and both contain a reference to union with Christ. The Father "chose us in him before the foundation of the world" (Eph. 1:4). God "saved us . . . because of his own purpose and grace, which he gave us in Christ Jesus before the ages began" (2 Tim. 1:9).

Of course, the Son is crucial in union because it is union with *Christ*. The Holy Spirit joins us to the Son's person and saving accomplishments. By grace through Spirit-generated faith we become participants in Jesus's story, chiefly his death and resurrection. Scripture says we died, were buried, rose, ascended, sat down at God's right hand, and even in a sense will come again, all with him! And participation in Christ's saving deeds brings us salvation in its many expressions.

But the chief worker in faith union with Christ is the Holy Spirit. The focus of this chapter is on the most important work of the Spirit pertaining to salvation—joining us to the Son. Paul is the biblical writer who teaches this. He does so in at least three ways. First, Paul directly ascribes our union with Christ to the Spirit. The Spirit is the bond of union. Second, the apostle teaches that people who do not have the Holy Spirit do not belong to Christ, implying that union (belonging to Christ) is essential for salvation. Third, Paul ascribes to the Spirit's work aspects of salvation that occur in union with Christ. These include regeneration, justification, adoption, sanctification, preservation, and glorification.

- The Spirit is the bond of union with Christ.
- People who lack the Spirit do not belong to Christ.
- The Spirit brings about aspects of salvation that occur in union.

The Spirit Is the Bond of Union with Christ

The most straightforward passage teaching that the Holy Spirit is essential to spiritual union between believers and Christ is 1 Corinthians 12:12–13: "Just as the body is one and has many members, and all the members of the body, though many, are one body, so it is with Christ. For in one Spirit we were all baptized into one body—Jews or Greeks, slaves or free—and all were made to drink of one Spirit." Paul compares the human body, which is one in spite of its many parts, to the church, the body of Christ (v. 12). Though the church has many members, it is one body. Why? Because all members of the church participate in one Holy Spirit when they are incorporated into Christ's body. These are two different ways—sharing in the Spirit and being made a member of Christ's body—of describing the same reality: union with Christ. Paul then employs the images of baptism and drinking of liquid to underscore that it is the Spirit who is the necessary nexus between believers and Christ (v. 13).

I regard it a sound assumption to consider the two lines of verse 13 as referring to the Corinthian believers' common reception of the Holy Spirit at conversion:[1]

In one Spirit we were all baptized into one body . . .
and [we] all were made to drink of one Spirit.

Although it is possible to translate the first phrase "by the Spirit" and regard him as the baptizer, Gordon Fee argues that "nowhere else does this dative with 'baptize' imply agency (i.e., that the Spirit does the baptizing), but it always refers to the element 'in which' one is baptized."[2] Sinclair Ferguson elaborates:

---

[1] I acknowledge help from Gordon D. Fee, *The First Epistle to the Corinthians*, The New International Commentary on the New Testament (Grand Rapids: Eerdmans, 1987), 603.
[2] Ibid., 606.

While [the preposition] *en* may be translated as "by," "with," or "in," the conclusion that Paul sees the Spirit as the medium ("with/in the Spirit") and not the agent ("by the Spirit") is irresistible. For one thing, the language of Spirit-baptism remains essentially unchanged wherever we encounter it, and thus the New Testament consistently sees Christ, not the Spirit, as the Baptizer: "he will baptize."

In 1 Corinthians 12:13, Paul's point is that the body is one because all of its members share in the one Spirit whom they have received simultaneously with their incorporation into Christ's body.[3]

Paul uses two pictures to communicate the key truth that the Holy Spirit is indispensable for union with Christ to occur.[4] In the second of these pictures we "all were made to drink of one Spirit" (v. 13). William Baker correctly summarizes the two possibilities for the verb used here (ποτίζω/*potizō*): "This word can refer to the irrigation of crops or to someone drinking a cup of water."[5] It speaks of either watering plants or taking a drink. So Paul portrays either believers' being drenched by the Spirit (in baptism?[6]) or believers' drinking the Spirit. Most commentators prefer the second option. Support for this interpretation is found in 1 Corinthians 10:1–4 (shown here along with 12:13 for comparison):

> Our fathers were all . . . baptized into Moses . . . and all drank the same spiritual drink. (10:1, 2, 4)

> We were all baptized into one body . . . and all were made to drink of one Spirit. (12:13)

That is, Paul's words in 12:13 seem to "echo his interpretive description of Israel's exodus and wilderness experience in 10:2–4," as Ciampa and Rosner note.[7] Some see being "made to drink of one Spirit" as a reference to drinking the cup of the Lord's Supper (cf. 10:4; 11:25),[8] but that probably is too specific. Surely it is a mistake to conclude from the figure of watering or drinking that "its effect is to give a somewhat impersonal view of the Spirit" akin to

---

[3] Sinclair B. Ferguson, *The Holy Spirit*, Contours of Christian Theology (Downers Grove, IL: InterVarsity, 1996), 194.
[4] For refutation of Pentecostal attempts to make Pentecost normative, see ibid., 80–87.
[5] William Baker, *1 Corinthians*, Cornerstone Biblical Commentary (Carol Stream, IL: Tyndale House, 2009), 182.
[6] So ibid., 183.
[7] Roy E. Ciampa and Brian S. Rosner, *The First Letter to the Corinthians*, The Pillar New Testament Commentary (Grand Rapids: Eerdmans, 2010), 591–92.
[8] So Raymond F. Collins, *First Corinthians*, Sacra Pagina (Collegeville, MN: Liturgical Press, 1999), 463.

Hellenistic philosophical views.[9] That is to misunderstand the function of the imagery.

What is the apostle's point, then? Ben Witherington answers, "There are no Christians without the Spirit. At conversion the Christian is united to the body by the Spirit and is given the Spirit to drink."[10] And again, "The image is both external and internal: The Spirit works on believers to unite them to the body and works in them as an ongoing source of life and spiritual sustenance."[11]

Paul's words are reminiscent of themes reflected in the Fourth Gospel:

> Jesus said to her, "Everyone who drinks of this water will be thirsty again, but whoever drinks of the water that I will give him will never be thirsty again. The water that I will give him will become in him a spring of water welling up to eternal life." (John 4:13–14)

> Jesus stood up and cried out, "If anyone thirsts, let him come to me and drink. Whoever believes in me, as the Scripture has said, 'Out of his heart will flow rivers of living water.'" Now this he said about the Spirit, whom those who believed in him were to receive, for as yet the Spirit had not been given, because Jesus was not yet glorified. (7:37–39)

In sum: Paul uses two images to communicate the same reality—the indispensability of the Spirit of God for union with Christ. Sinclair Ferguson helps us: the first image says, "All Christians are . . . baptized into one body by Christ; the Spirit is the medium of that baptism."[12] The second image tells of "the initial reception of the Spirit, the river of living water of whom believers may drink and never thirst again."[13] In short, the Holy Spirit is the bond of union with Christ.

People Who Lack the Spirit Do Not Belong to Christ

Indeed, the Holy Spirit is so indispensable for union with Christ that, according to Paul in Romans 8:9, to lack the Spirit means not to belong to Christ. In the preceding context he contrasts two antithetical realms: that of the flesh and that of the Spirit (vv. 5–11). To be "in the flesh" is to be unsaved, to hate

---

[9] C. K. Barrett, *A Commentary on the First Epistle to the Corinthians* (Peabody, MA: Hendrickson, 1968), 289.
[10] Ben Witherington III, *Conflict and Community in Corinth: A Socio-Rhetorical Commentary on 1 and 2 Corinthians* (Grand Rapids: Eerdmans, 1995), 258.
[11] Ibid., 258n18.
[12] Ferguson, *The Holy Spirit*, 194.
[13] Ibid.

God, to be unable to please God, and to be headed for eschatological condemnation. To be "in the Spirit" is to be saved, to love God, to be able to please God, and to be headed for eschatological salvation.

After describing the miserable condition of those "in the flesh," Paul assures his readers that they do not belong to that group: "You, however, are not in the flesh but in the Spirit, if in fact the Spirit of God dwells in you" (v. 9). We misunderstand the apostle if we take "if" here to suggest that the Roman believers might be "in the flesh." Rather, as Schreiner asserts, "He assures them that they are in the Spirit. . . . Paul summons the readers to consider whether the Spirit indwells them, wanting them to draw the conclusion that he does."[14] That conclusion is that they are not in the flesh but in the Spirit because, in fact, the Spirit does indwell them.

Moreover, "Anyone who does not have the Spirit of Christ does not belong to him" (v. 9). Though it is cast in negative terms, in context the purpose of this statement is mainly positive, as C. E. B. Cranfield notes: "It is clear that its purpose here is the positive one of asserting that every Christian is indwelt by the Spirit."[15] Nevertheless, its secondary purpose is to deny that anyone lacking the Spirit is a Christian, regardless of any profession of faith. That is, possession of the Holy Spirit is necessary to salvation.

James Dunn gives us wisdom:

> Paul can make this assumption because belonging to Christ and having the Spirit are for him one and the same thing. Possession of the Spirit is what constitutes a Christian, so naturally he assumes that the members of the Roman congregations have received the Spirit. It is possession of the Spirit which makes the difference; Christ's lordship is realized, documented, and made effective by the presence of the Spirit in a life. In what amounts to the nearest thing to a definition of "Christian" in his writings, Paul defines a Christian, albeit in negative formulation, as one who has the Spirit of Christ.[16]

Because the Holy Spirit is the bond of union with Christ, both negative and positive results obtain. Negatively, those who lack the Spirit do not belong to Christ. Positively, the Spirit brings about aspects of salvation that occur in union with Christ.

---

[14] Thomas R. Schreiner, *Romans*, Baker Exegetical Commentary on the New Testament (Grand Rapids: Baker Academic, 1998), 413.

[15] C. E. B. Cranfield, *The Epistle to the Romans*, International Critical Commentary (Edinburgh: T&T Clark, 1975), 388.

[16] James D. G. Dunn, *Romans 1–8*, Word Biblical Commentary (Dallas: Word, 1988), 444.

The Spirit Brings about Aspects of Salvation That Occur in Union

The Holy Spirit is responsible chiefly for bringing those separated from Christ into saving union with him. He is the person of the Godhead who joins believers to Christ. Therefore, it should not surprise us to find the Spirit active in the aspects of the application of salvation that make up union. John Murray is correct in saying, "Union with Christ is in itself a very broad and embracive subject. It is not simply a step in the application of redemption; when viewed, according to the teaching of Scripture, in its broader aspects it underlies every step of the application of redemption."[17]

Union is the large set of which these elements are subsets: regeneration, justification, adoption, sanctification, preservation, and glorification. They all occur in union with Christ and are all brought about by the Spirit. My strategy for each aspect of the application of salvation will involve two steps. First, I will demonstrate that the aspect in question accompanies union with Christ. Second, I will show that the Holy Spirit is the one who brings about that aspect.

Regeneration

First, regeneration takes place in union with Christ. Paul teaches this in Ephesians 2. Before prescribing the remedy, he gives the terrible diagnosis of unsaved persons: they are spiritually dead and unable to rescue themselves (v. 1); they follow Satan (usually without realizing it), who is at work in them (v. 2); and from birth their sins merit God's wrath (v. 3). But thanks be to God for providing the remedy to the disease of sin! Because of his mercy, love, and grace, he saves believers through Christ's death and resurrection.

Specifically, because he highlights people's spiritual death apart from Christ, Paul accents regeneration, God's making sinners alive to him: "God, being rich in mercy, because of the great love with which he loved us, even when we were dead in our trespasses, made us alive together with Christ" (vv. 4–5). The parenthetical clause that immediately follows is vital—"by grace you have been saved" (v. 5). For Paul the epitome of God's grace is his making persons alive who were dead in their sins.

The most important thing for our present purposes is to see that regeneration takes place in union with Christ: "God . . . made us alive together with Christ" (vv. 4–5). Andrew Lincoln explains:

---

[17] John Murray, *Redemption Accomplished and Applied* (Grand Rapids: Eerdmans, 1955), 161.

Salvation for those whose plight is spiritual death must involve a raising to life. This is in fact what God has accomplished for believers. He made them alive with Christ. At this point also, Ephesians is reminiscent of Colossians [2:13]. . . . The thought in both instances is that new life comes to believers because they share in what has happened to Christ. . . . A relationship with Christ is in view which affects believers' future destinies because it involves sharing in Christ's destiny.[18]

Regeneration takes place not apart from Christ but in union with him.

Second, regeneration is the work of the Holy Spirit. The Trinity is at work in regeneration. The Father takes the initiative: "According to his great mercy, he has caused us to be born again to a living hope" (1 Pet. 1:3). The Father does this "through the resurrection of Jesus Christ from the dead" (v. 3). The Father is the initiator of regeneration, and the Son supplies the power for the new life through his resurrection. The Spirit applies regeneration to those spiritually dead so that they come alive to God, as the Gospel of John teaches.

Jesus gives Nicodemus, a Pharisee, member of the Sanhedrin, and important teacher in Israel, what he needs—strong correction. He surprises Nicodemus by telling him, "Truly, truly, I say to you, unless one is born again he cannot see the kingdom of God" (John 3:3). Nicodemus does not understand what Jesus is talking about (v. 4), so Jesus issues a restatement: "Truly, truly, I say to you, unless one is born of water and the Spirit, he cannot enter the kingdom of God" (v. 5). I follow Linda Belleville, and her teacher D. A. Carson, in asserting that John distinguishes here between *spirit* used with and without the definite article. The key is verse 6: "That which is born of the flesh is flesh, and that which is born of the Spirit is spirit." The first occurrences of "flesh" and "spirit" have the article and should be understood as humankind and the Holy Spirit, respectively. The second uses of both words lack the article and refer to two realms, that of humanity and that of God, respectively. Also important is Jesus's criticizing Nicodemus for not knowing about the new birth. Evidently Jesus had in mind Ezekiel's joining of water and spirit to speak of cleansing ("clean water," Ezek. 36:25) and heart transformation ("a new spirit," v. 26) in the last days.

Carson summarizes,

In short, *born of water and spirit* (the article and the capital "S" in the NIV should be dropped: the focus is on the impartation of God's nature as

---

[18] Andrew T. Lincoln, *Ephesians*, Word Biblical Commentary (Dallas: Word, 1990), 101.

"spirit" [cf. 4:24], not on the Holy Spirit as such) signals a new begetting, a new birth that cleanses and renews, the eschatological cleansing and renewal promised by the Old Testament prophets.[19]

This prepares us to understand John 3:7–8: "Do not marvel that I said to you, 'You must be born again.' The wind blows where it wishes, and you hear its sound, but you do not know where it comes from or where it goes. So it is with everyone who is born of the Spirit." Jesus makes a word play, because *pneuma* means "breath, wind, or spirit." He likens the effects of the Holy Spirit to those of the wind. The wind is free and beyond human control; it blows where it wants, and we cannot figure out its course ahead of time. We can only know where it has been by its effects. So are those "born of the Spirit" (v. 8). Carson is correct: "The person who is 'born of the Spirit' can be neither controlled nor understood by persons of but one birth. . . . Both the mysteriousness and the undeniable power of the Spirit of God are displayed in the Scriptures to which Nicodemus had devoted so many years of study."[20]

We have surveyed regeneration in Ephesians 2 and John 3. Hoekema sums up the gist of the first passage: "The point Paul is making is that this 'making alive' takes place in union with Christ. . . . In other words, regeneration occurs when we are for the first time savingly united with Christ."[21] And Leon Morris captures the point of the second passage, "Jesus makes it clear that no man can ever fit himself for the kingdom. Rather he must be completely renewed, born anew, by the power of the Spirit."[22] We thus conclude: the Holy Spirit acts in regeneration to unite us to Christ and bring us new life.[23]

Justification

First, justification takes place in union with Christ. Paul teaches this in 2 Corinthians. Before speaking of justification the apostle treats reconciliation. Reconciliation is peacemaking. God makes peace between himself and alienated rebels and between them and him. He does this through Jesus, the peace-

---

[19] D. A. Carson, *The Gospel according to John*, The Pillar New Testament Commentary (Grand Rapids: Eerdmans, 1991), 195, emphasis original. Carson acknowledges Linda Belleville, "'Born of Water and Spirit': John 3:5," *Trinity Journal* 1 (1980): 125–41.

[20] Carson, *Gospel according to John*, 198, emphasis original.

[21] Anthony A. Hoekema, *Saved by Grace* (Grand Rapids: Eerdmans, 1989), 59.

[22] Leon Morris, *The Gospel according to John*, The New International Commentary on the New Testament (Grand Rapids: Eerdmans, 1971), 219.

[23] See also Titus 3:4–5: "God . . . saved us, not because of works done by us in righteousness, but according to his own mercy, by the washing of regeneration and renewal of the Holy Spirit."

maker, specifically through his death and resurrection. Paul accents two aspects of reconciliation in this chapter: (1) God reconciled us to himself (5:18–19) and (2) gave us the ministry of reconciliation (vv. 18–20).

If we ask how God reconciles sinners to himself, Paul has a ready answer, for after imploring sinners to be reconciled to God, he says, "For our sake he made him to be sin who knew no sin, so that . . . we might become the righteousness of God" (v. 21). This is the language of justification. God made the righteous Christ to be sin in his sight so that we sinners might become God's righteousness. There is imputation, or reckoning, of our sin to Christ and his righteousness to us, as Murray Harris underlines:

> V. 21a stands in stark contrast to v. 19b. Because of God's transference of sinners' sin on to the sinless one, because sin was reckoned to Christ's account, it is now not reckoned to the believer's account. This total identification of the sinless one with sinners at the cross, in assuming the full penalty and guilt of their sin, leaves no doubt that substitution as well as representation was involved.[24]

I deliberately omitted two words when I quoted 2 Corinthians 5:21. Paul writes: "For our sake he made him to be sin who knew no sin, so that *in him* we might become the righteousness of God." Although rarely do the words "in him" indicate union with Christ in Paul without further nuance, here they do that very thing. Even as Christ shared in the plight of sinners to the point of dying (vicariously) as a sinner, so believers are declared righteous by God when they believe in Christ and share in his perfect righteousness.[25]

Paul teaches the same thing in Philippians 3. He discounts his pedigree and performance, the very things he once regarded as making him acceptable to God (vv. 4–8). Why? In order to "gain Christ and be found in him" (vv. 8–9). Here again the words "in him" denote union with Christ. Paul declares his desire to "gain Christ and be found in him, not having a righteousness of my own that comes from the law, but that which comes through faith in Christ, the righteousness from God that depends on faith" (vv. 8–9). As in 2 Corinthians 5:21, so here union is elaborated in forensic terms. Paul eschews a merited righteousness of law keeping for a faith-righteousness that comes from God. Hoekema explains:

---

[24] Murray J. Harris, *The Second Epistle to the Corinthians*, New International Greek Testament Commentary (Grand Rapids: Eerdmans, 2005), 453.
[25] So Constantine R. Campbell, *Paul and Union with Christ: An Exegetical and Theological Study* (Grand Rapids: Zondervan, 2012), 186–87.

> The words "be found in him" . . . tie in justification with union with Christ. . . . Most incontrovertibly, therefore, this passage sets forth the truth that we are justified not on the basis of any works which we do ourselves, but solely on the basis of what Christ has done for us. The righteousness of God thus obtained through faith is a treasure of such incomparable worth that in comparison with it we too should count every other gain but loss.[26]

Justification takes place not apart from Christ but in union with him, as both 2 Corinthians 5:21 and Philippians 3:8–9 show.

Second, justification is the work of the Holy Spirit. Hoekema is emphatic: "Our justification . . . is inseparable from the work of the Holy Spirit."[27] We see this in 1 Corinthians 6:11. In a context in which Paul condemns Christians' taking other Christians to court before unbelievers, he speaks against the greed and fraud that provoked this discussion (v. 8). Such behavior is unworthy of the name of Christ. Paul immediately launches into a condemnation of sinful lifestyles with these words: "Do you not know that the unrighteous will not inherit the kingdom of God?" (v. 9).

After listing evil lifestyles characteristic of lost persons rather than saints, Paul gives a word of encouragement: "Such were some of you" (v. 11). Some of the Corinthian Christians had pursued these lifestyles before they believed. Paul continues, "But you were washed, you were sanctified, you were justified" (v. 11). He uses three verbs to describe their salvation. They were "washed" from the pollution of their sins, probably a reference to baptism. They were "sanctified" with initial or definitive sanctification, that powerful work of the Holy Spirit in setting sinners apart to God and constituting them his saints. They were "justified" or declared righteous by the Father on the basis of Christ's saving accomplishment.

The key for our present study is the pair of prepositional phrases that follow: "in the name of the Lord Jesus Christ" and "by the Spirit of our God" (v. 11). Probably the two phrases go with all three verbs, but they certainly go with the last one—"you were justified." When we ask what the connection is between justification and the "name of the Lord Jesus Christ," the answer is that we are justified by believing in Christ's name, that is, his person. The first phrase thus denotes the object of faith. But how were they "justified . . . by the Spirit of our God"? The answer is that the Spirit enables us to believe in the name of Christ. The Spirit grants the gift of saving faith.

---

[26] Hoekema, *Saved by Grace*, 160.
[27] Ibid., 30.

Fee comments helpfully on this phrase, "The reference to the Spirit reflects Paul's understanding of the Spirit as the means whereby God in the new age effects the work of Christ in the believer's life."[28] Indeed he does, and here he effects Christ's work in believers' lives by enabling them to believe in Jesus's name for justification, which (according to 2 Cor. 5:21; Phil. 3:8–9) is inseparable from union with Christ. In conclusion: the Holy Spirit acts in justification to unite us to Christ and bring us forgiveness and a righteous standing before God.

Third, the past twenty years have witnessed vigorous debates concerning justification. Though most of these are beyond the scope of this book, some attention to them is warranted here; thus the addition of this third point.[29] After summarizing my own understanding of justification, I will focus on justification and union with Christ. I hold to a traditional evangelical and Reformed doctrine of justification, emphasizing the Trinity and the "already" and "not yet," and benefiting from the work of Richard Gaffin and Michael Bird.

God the Father is the Judge who legally declares believing sinners righteous. This declaration is based on the saving accomplishment of the Son in his death ("a propitiation" [Rom. 3:25–26] and "one act of righteousness" [Rom. 5:18]) and resurrection (Rom. 4:24–25). The Holy Spirit's part in justification is sometimes neglected. In keeping with his other ministries in applying salvation to the people of God, he gives the gift of faith, enabling guilty sinners to believe and be justified (1 Cor. 6:11; see exposition above).

As with every other aspect of the application of salvation, justification is most properly and finally eschatological. On the last day God the Judge will declare believers in Christ righteous before humankind and angels (Matt. 12:36–37; Rom. 5:19; Gal. 5:5). The judgment will be based on thoughts (1 Cor. 4:5), words (Matt. 12:36), and deeds (2 Cor. 5:10; Rev. 20:12–13) that demonstrate the reality of faith in Christ. This is the "not yet" aspect of justification. The miracle of the gospel is that there is also an "already" aspect.

---

[28] Fee, *First Epistle to the Corinthians*, 246.

[29] Proponents of the New Perspective on Paul (NPP) include James D. G. Dunn, *The Theology of Paul the Apostle* (Grand Rapids: Eerdmans, 1998); and N. T. Wright, *Justification: God's Plan and Paul's Vision* (Downers Grove, IL: IVP Academic, 2009). Opponents of the NPP include Michael S. Horton, *Covenant and Salvation: Union with Christ* (Louisville: Westminster John Knox, 2007); and Stephen Westerholm, *Perspectives Old and New on Paul: The "Lutheran" Paul and His Critics* (Grand Rapids: Eerdmans 2004). Valuable collections of essays on justification include James K. Beilby and Paul Rhodes Eddy, eds., *Justification: Five Views* (Downers Grove, IL: IVP Academic, 2011); and Mark Husbands and Daniel J. Trier, *Justification: What's at Stake in the Current Debates?* (Downers Grove, IL: InterVarsity, 2004). An important but neglected resource is Richard B. Gaffin Jr., *Resurrection and Redemption: A Study in Paul's Soteriology*, 2nd ed. (Phillipsburg, NJ: P&R, 1987). Recent insightful treatments include R. Michael Allen, *Justification and the Gospel: Understanding the Contexts and Controversies* (Grand Rapids: Baker Academic, 2013); and Michael F. Bird, *The Saving Righteousness of God: Studies on Paul, Justification and the New Perspective* (Milton Keynes, UK: Paternoster, 2006).

"Since we have been justified by faith . . ." (Rom. 5:1). "There is therefore *now* no condemnation for those who are in Christ Jesus" (Rom. 8:1). The word "now" in this verse alludes to the new era in redemptive history inaugurated by Jesus's death and resurrection and the resultant positive relation with God enjoyed in the present by those who know the Judge's future verdict. With different vocabulary John's teaching overlaps Paul's: "Whoever believes in him [the Son] is not condemned. . . . And this is the judgment" (John 3:18–19).

Richard Gaffin convinces me that justification (as well as adoption, sanctification, and glorification) is first of all a christological category and secondarily a soteriological one.[30] Vicariously the sinless Christ in his resurrection was justified (1 Tim. 3:16), adopted (Acts 13:33; Rom. 1:4), sanctified (Rom. 6:9–10), and glorified (1 Cor. 15:20, 42–44). Then, by virtue of union with the risen Christ, believers are justified, adopted, sanctified, and glorified in him.

Furthermore, Michael Bird, building on N. T. Wright's work, has taught me that "justification is *covenantal* since it confirms the promises of the Abrahamic covenant and legitimates the identity of Jews, Greeks, and barbarians as full and equal members of God's people."[31]

Two major issues are disputed concerning justification and union with Christ: the relationship between justification and union, and whether imputation is involved. I will address these in turn. First, three views compete concerning how union with Christ and justification are related. Some so emphasize justification that there is little place for union. A recent example is Robert Reymond's treatment of the two doctrines in his systematic theology. Although he grants that union with Christ is "all-embracive" and the "fountainhead from which flows the Christian's every spiritual blessing," he allots less than four pages to it. On the other hand, he allots eighteen pages to justification.[32] Union seems to play a small role in his overall soteriology.

Some reverse this and allow union to swallow justification so that it occupies little place. Albert Schweitzer is a seminal example of this approach. Wright summarizes: "Schweitzer, for his part, famously regarded 'justification' and the other 'forensic' language of Paul as a second-order way of thinking, a 'secondary crater' within the 'primary crater' which, for him, was 'being in Christ.'"[33]

---

[30] Gaffin, *Resurrection and Redemption*, 114–34.

[31] Michael F. Bird, *Evangelical Theology: A Biblical and Systematic Introduction* (Grand Rapids: Zondervan, 2013), 567, emphasis original.

[32] Robert L. Reymond, *A New Systematic Theology of the Christian Faith* (Nashville: Thomas Nelson, 1998), 736, 739. He devotes pp. 736–39 to union with Christ and pp. 739–56 to justification.

[33] Wright, *Justification*, 84, citing Albert Schweitzer, *The Mysticism of Paul the Apostle* (London: A & C Black, 1931), 225.

I favor a mediating position that acknowledges union as the larger category of which justification is a subcategory. This is what I demonstrated above when arguing, "Justification takes place in union with Christ." Campbell aptly summarizes this position: "Justification occurs through and in Christ. . . . Union is an originating theme through which others derive. On that score, justification is likewise derived through union with Christ and coheres with Christ's other works by virtue of their common source in Christ."[34] But at the same time, I am eager to give proper weight to justification as a key way of expressing the gospel and not to allow union to overwhelm justification.

A second issue concerns union with Christ and imputation. Carson begins an essay in defense of imputation thus:

> For many Protestants today, the doctrine of imputation has become the crucial touchstone for orthodoxy with respect to justification. For others, imputation is to be abandoned as an outdated relic of a system that focuses far too much attention on substitutionary penal atonement and far too little attention on alternative "models" of what the cross achieved.[35]

Carson correctly cites John Piper, and Joel Green and Mark Baker, as proponents of these two views, respectively.[36]

More specifically, some have argued against imputation in Paul. Rather, they say, believers receive Christ's righteousness in union with him, and there is no need for imputation. Daniel Powers, who maintains that salvation for Paul is corporate participation in Christ, rejects outright the idea of imputation.[37] Many others affirm imputation in Paul and connect it to union with Christ, including Brian Vickers and Lane Tipton.[38]

I side with this second position. I believe in the imputation of Christ's righteousness as the ground of justification.[39] But I do not regard it as the touchstone of orthodoxy. Many true believers in Christ have never heard of it, and some even deny it. I do not endorse the latter course, but acknowledge

[34] Campbell, *Paul and Union with Christ*, 396.
[35] D. A. Carson, "The Vindication of Imputation: On Fields of Discourse and Semantic Fields," in Beilby and Eddy, *Justification: Five Views*, 46.
[36] John Piper, *Counted Righteous in Christ: Should We Abandon the Imputation of Christ's Righteousness?* (Wheaton, IL: Crossway, 2002); Joel B. Green and Mark D. Baker, *Recovering the Scandal of the Cross: Atonement in the New Testament and Contemporary Contexts* (Downers Grove, IL: InterVarsity, 2000).
[37] Daniel G. Powers, *Salvation through Participation: An Examination of the Notion of the Believers' Corporate Unity with Christ in Early Christian Soteriology* (Leuven, Belgium: Peeters, 2001).
[38] Brian Vickers, *Jesus' Blood and Righteousness: Paul's Theology of Imputation* (Wheaton, IL: Crossway, 2006); Lane G. Tipton, "Union with Christ and Justification," in *Justified in Christ: God's Plan for Us in Justification*, ed. K. Scott Oliphint (Fearn, Ross-shire, UK: Mentor, 2007), 23–49.
[39] See the cogent defense of this Reformed view in Vickers, *Jesus' Blood* and *Righteousness*.

that among those who trust Jesus as Lord and Savior in his death and resurrection are some who deny imputation. Nevertheless, I affirm that imputation belongs to Paul's doctrine of justification and urge acceptance of it.

As I argued above, justification is entailed in union with Christ. It is a key outworking of union. And, it seems to me, the imputation of Christ's righteousness is an important aspect of justification. I agree with Carson:

> In short, although the "union with Christ" theme has often been abused, rightly handled it is a comprehensive and complex way of portraying the various ways in which we are identified with Christ and he with us. In its connection with justification, "union with Christ" terminology, especially when it is tied to the great redemptive event, suggests that although justification cannot be reduced to imputation, justification in Paul's thought cannot long be faithfully maintained without it.[40]

Adoption[41]

First, adoption takes place in union with Christ. Paul teaches this in Galatians 3. He reviews redemptive history in 3:15–4:7, speaking of the Abrahamic, Mosaic, and new covenants in turn. Here he deals with the last, which has arrived "now that faith has come" (3:25).

Anticipating his treatment of adoption in 4:1–7, Paul writes, "In Christ Jesus you are all sons of God, through faith" (3:26). In translating, there is ambiguity concerning where to put the words "in Christ Jesus." The NIV puts them with "faith": "You are all sons of God through faith *in Christ Jesus.*" The ESV translates it, "*In Christ Jesus* you are all sons of God, through faith." As noted earlier, where the Greek is potentially ambiguous I assume that a Greek writer would use word order to clear up the ambiguity. In this instance, the NIV follows the Greek word order. Thus, although the ESV rendering would provide another reference to union with Christ, I assume Paul uses "in Christ Jesus" to present Christ as the object of faith (NIV).

A brief summary of adoption is in order. "Adoption is an act of God's free grace, whereby we are received into the number, and have a right to all the privileges of the sons of God."[42] The background for adoption is bondage to Satan and sin (4:3, 7). Christ, the eternal Son of God, became flesh to redeem

---

[40] Carson, "The Vindication of Imputation," 77.
[41] For a book-length treatment of adoption, see Robert A. Peterson, *Adopted by God: From Wayward Sinners to Cherished Children* (Phillipsburg, NJ: P&R, 2001).
[42] Westminster Shorter Catechism, q. 34.

spiritual slaves and make them God's sons (vv. 4–5). Like justification, adoption is by grace through faith, as the NIV rendering of 3:26 shows.

Adoption also takes place in union with Christ (according to 3:26–27). Verse 27 explains why the people mentioned in verse 26 are "sons of God": "As many of you as were baptized into Christ have put on Christ." Being "baptized into Christ" denotes union with Christ, as the image of putting on clothes suggests. Baptism/conversion involves figuratively putting on Christ as one puts on clothes. As clothing covers the body, so Christ "covers" believers.

In sum: To be "baptized into Christ" is to be joined to him.[43] And since verse 27 explains what it means to be "sons of God" (in v. 26), union is a bigger category of which adoption is a part. The word *for* is important: "You are all sons of God, through faith in Christ Jesus. *For* as many of you as were baptized into Christ have put on Christ" (vv. 26–27, my translation). Their baptism explains their status as God's adopted sons. (Paul does not teach that the act of baptism automatically saves the Galatians.)[44] Adoption takes place not apart from Christ but in union with him.

Second, adoption is the work of the Holy Spirit. Paul teaches this in Romans 8. After exhorting his readers to live not for sin but for God (vv. 12–13), Paul turns to adoption. In fact, verse 14 prevents a possible misunderstanding of verse 13, which sets forth two alternatives in strong terms: "If you live according to the flesh you will die, but if by the Spirit you put to death the deeds of the body, you will live." "You will die" and "you will live" denote the final states of damnation and salvation, respectively.

Some have concluded that verse 13 teaches that believers may fall from saving grace and be lost. This is a wrong conclusion for two reasons. First, it clashes with strong preservation passages that surround it in 8:1–4 and 28–39. Second, verse 14 clarifies verse 13 by giving assurance that God's children obey the Spirit: "All who are led by the Spirit of God are sons of God." That means they "put to death the deeds of the body" (v. 13). Paul thus gives God's condition for gaining eternal life in one verse and gives confidence to God's children that they will satisfy that condition and gain life in the next verse. In other words, God's children are identifiable; they acknowledge the Holy Spirit's leadership and live for their heavenly Father.

Paul next contrasts the "spirit of slavery" and the "Spirit of adoption": "You did not receive the spirit of slavery to fall back into fear, but you have

---

[43] See F. F. Bruce, *The Epistle to the Galatians*, New International Greek Testament Commentary (Grand Rapids: Eerdmans, 1982), 185.
[44] See ibid.

received the Spirit of adoption as sons" (v. 15). Here again we see that the background for adoption is slavery to sin and the fear that goes with it. God gives us the "Spirit of adoption as sons." He assures us of his fatherly love by giving us the Spirit.

The names of the first two persons of the Trinity are ideal to communicate God's grace of adoption. God is the Father who adopts us into his family. God is the Son who through death and resurrection enables us to become his brothers and sisters by faith. But the name Holy Spirit is not ideal to communicate God's love in adoption. So what does God do? He alters the name of the third person of the Trinity to communicate his adoptive love for us. He calls him "the Spirit of his [the Father's] Son" (Gal. 4:6) and "the Spirit of adoption as sons" (Rom. 8:15).

Paul's next words present the Holy Spirit as the agent of adoption: "You have received the Spirit of adoption as sons, by whom we cry, 'Abba! Father!'" (v. 15). It is the Spirit who enables sinners to cry out for salvation to God as Father. Douglas Moo is pithy: "Since the Spirit is presented as the Father's agent in conferring 'life' (see v. 11), it may be better to think of the Spirit as the agent through whom the believer's sonship is both bestowed and confirmed."[45]

Adoption, then, is the Spirit's work. He enables those who were enslaved to sin to believe in the unique Son and so become sons themselves. He enables them to call God "Father," "Abba," the very word Jesus uses to address his Father (Mark 14:36). By God's grace and the Spirit's agency believers thus have a relationship with God akin to Jesus's relationship to his Father (though his is eternal and by nature, while ours had a beginning and is by grace).

Cranfield waxes eloquent concerning these truths:

> The Spirit they have received has not led them back into bondage, and so into that anxiety which is its inseparable characteristic. . . . He has not betrayed their hopes by subjecting them to the same sort of anxious fear as they had experienced before. . . . Instead, He has proved Himself to be the Spirit of adoption, that is, the Spirit who brings about adoption, uniting men with Christ and so making them sharers in His sonship.[46]

Subsequent verses give even more blessings that follow adoption—the Spirit's internal witness, believers' inheritance, and future glory—but now it

---

[45] Douglas J. Moo, *The Epistle to the Romans*, The New International Commentary on the New Testament (Grand Rapids: Eerdmans, 1996), 502.
[46] Cranfield, *Epistle to the Romans*, 396–97.

is time to sum up: the Holy Spirit acts in adoption to unite us to Christ and bring us all the rights, privileges, and responsibilities that accompany it.

Sanctification

First, sanctification takes place in union with Christ. Paul teaches this in Romans 6, where he returns to the false charge of antinomianism previously lodged against him (cf. 3:8). He has just written, "Where sin increased, grace abounded all the more" (5:20), from which his enemies wrongly deduce that he is teaching antinomianism. They throw this question in his teeth: "Are we to continue in sin that grace may abound?" (6:1). Paul finds this repugnant and asks incredulously: "How can we who died to sin still live in it?" (v. 2).

Paul explains that we die to sin when we are baptized: "Do you not know that all of us who have been baptized into Christ Jesus were baptized into his death?" (v. 3). The apostle teaches that baptism denotes union with Christ in his death. We are baptized into Christ; we take part in his narrative. Just as he died, then, in union with him we also die to sin. Christ's atonement breaks the domination of sin over our lives; we no longer have to obey that harsh master. Instead, we belong to another Master, who bought us with his death and resurrection. We now love and serve him.

It saddens Paul that believers would keep living in sin after baptism (v. 2). To do so is to misunderstand baptism, in which God identifies us with Christ in his cross and empty tomb. "We were buried therefore with him by baptism into death, in order that, just as Christ was raised from the dead by the glory of the Father, we too might walk in newness of life" (v. 4). We must live, then, as those who with Christ died to sin and who live to God.

According to Paul, Christians share in Jesus's story. We are crucified with him (v. 6), participate in his death (vv. 5, 8) and resurrection (v. 5), and "will also live with him" (v. 8). Our union with Christ in his death and resurrection is the source of successful Christian living (vv. 4, 6–7, 11–14). That is why Paul commands, "Do not present your members to sin as instruments for unrighteousness, but present yourselves to God as those who have been brought from death to life, and your members to God as instruments for righteousness" (v. 13). Sanctification takes place not apart from Christ but in union with him.

Second, sanctification is the work of the Holy Spirit. Paul teaches this in 2 Thessalonians 2. He says that he, Silvanus, and Timothy (see 1:1) "ought always to give thanks to God for you, brothers beloved by the Lord, because

God chose you as the firstfruits to be saved" (2:13). Paul's ministry team should thank God always for loving and electing the Thessalonians for salvation.[47] Paul specifies that God chose them to be "saved through sanctification by the Spirit and belief in the truth." Here are the means God uses to bring his eternal plan into effect. He uses the Spirit's sanctifying work and the Thessalonians' resultant faith in the gospel to rescue them from their sins.

Gene L. Green's discussion is apt:

> [Paul] assured the Thessalonians that sanctification was a work of God (1 Thess. 5.23) that he effects through the agency of the Holy Spirit (1 Thess. 4.8). The process of sanctification began at their conversion (1 Pet. 1.2) and is being worked out throughout their lives so that the believers might be blameless before the Lord at his coming (1 Thess. 5.23 . . .). Far from its being auxiliary to their salvation, the apostle understands the *sanctifying work* as the action *of the Spirit* of God that brings about their salvation.[48]

Though we commonly restrict sanctification to its progressive aspect, Scripture presents it as initial or definitive, progressive or lifelong, and final or complete. We see the first in 1 Corinthians 7:11 and 1 Peter 1:2; the second in 1 Thessalonians 4:3, 7; and the third in Ephesians 5:25–27 and 1 Thessalonians 5:23.

Other passages bear witness to the Holy Spirit's sanctifying work in the people of God:

> On some points I have written to you very boldly by way of reminder, because of the grace given me by God to be a minister of Christ Jesus to the Gentiles in the priestly service of the gospel of God, so that the offering of the Gentiles may be acceptable, sanctified by the Holy Spirit. (Rom. 15:15–16)

> You were washed, you were sanctified, you were justified in the name of the Lord Jesus Christ and by the Spirit of our God. (1 Cor. 6:11)

> Peter, an apostle of Jesus Christ,

---

[47] There is a textual variant in v. 13 that yields either the translation "God chose you *from the beginning* to be saved" (NIV) or "God chose you *as the firstfruits* to be saved" (ESV). Both are true theologically, and neither has a bearing on our current investigation. For discussion, see Gordon D. Fee, *The First and Second Letters to the Thessalonians*, The New International Commentary on the New Testament (Grand Rapids: Eerdmans, 2009), 301–2. Fee concludes in favor of the second option.

[48] Gene L. Green, *The Letters to the Thessalonians*, The Pillar New Testament Commentary (Grand Rapids: Eerdmans, 2002), 326–27, emphasis original.

> To those who are elect exiles of the Dispersion in Pontus, Galatia, Cappadocia, Asia, and Bithynia, according to the foreknowledge of God the Father, in the sanctification of the Spirit, for obedience to Jesus Christ and for sprinkling with his blood. (1 Pet. 1:1–2)

Hoekema is correct: "That our sanctification is ascribed to the Spirit does not come as a surprise. In fact, the very name 'Holy Spirit' already suggests that the Spirit is associated with holiness or sanctification."[49] It is true: the Holy Spirit acts in sanctification to unite us to Christ, constitute us as God's saints, and begin the lifelong process of making us holy.

Preservation

First, preservation takes place in union with Christ. Paul teaches this twice in Romans 8, once at the beginning and once at the end of the chapter. He writes, "There is therefore now no condemnation for those who are in Christ Jesus" (Rom. 8:1). We saw earlier that the word "now" points to the "new era of salvation history inaugurated by Christ's death and resurrection," as Moo points out.[50] Paul employs legal language to affirm that Christ delivers his people from the penalty lawbreakers deserve—condemnation. Christ has saved believers from God's never-ending wrath. Cranfield is succinct when he says, "For those who are in Christ Jesus (cf. 6:2–11; 7:4) there is no divine condemnation, since the condemnation which they deserve has already been fully borne for them by Him."[51] Indeed, Scripture declares that Christ died in the place of his people:

> He was pierced for our transgressions;
> > he was crushed for our iniquities;
> upon him was the chastisement that brought us peace,
> > and with his wounds we are healed. (Isa. 53:5)

> Christ redeemed us from the curse of the law by becoming a curse for us—for it is written, "Cursed is everyone who is hanged on a tree." (Gal. 3:13)

> Christ also suffered once for sins, the righteous for the unrighteous, that he might bring us to God. (1 Pet. 3:18)

---

[49] Hoekema, *Saved by Grace*, 30.
[50] Moo, *Epistle to the Romans*, 472.
[51] Cranfield, *Epistle to the Romans*, 373.

"Those who are in Christ Jesus" (Rom. 8:1) refers to those in Christ's realm. Paul contrasts that realm with the one "of sin and death" (v. 2). People who are in Christ's realm are justified already and will not receive a verdict of condemnation at the last judgment. Rather, they will be declared righteous. Schreiner sums up the matter:

> Thus there is no condemnation for those in Christ because the future deliverance from death has invaded the present world. . . . Via union with Christ . . . they have already died with Christ and been raised with him (6:1–11). . . . The word κατάκριμα [*katakrima*, "condemnation"] is a forensic term . . . denoting the removal of the curse (cf. Gal. 3:13) from those who are descendants of Adam.[52]

The apostle also affirms that God preserves those who are "in Christ" at the end of Romans 8: "I am sure that neither death nor life, nor angels nor rulers, nor things present nor things to come, nor powers, nor height nor depth, nor anything else in all creation, will be able to separate us from the love of God in Christ Jesus our Lord" (vv. 38–39). These verses occur at the end of the strongest preservation passage in Scripture, Romans 8:28–39. There Paul, in turn, bases God's keeping his people safe on his sovereignty (vv. 28–30), power (vv. 31–32), justice (vv. 33–34), and love (vv. 35–39).[53]

Paul describes God's love as "in Christ Jesus our Lord," thereby telling where the love of God is most clearly seen. Because of God's love in Christ, nothing at all will ever separate believers from their Lord. Paul uses comprehensive language. What is not included in "neither death nor life"? For those whose past sins are forgiven, what could possibly be omitted from "nor things present nor things to come"? And just to make sure all his bases are covered Paul adds, "nor anything else in all creation." Cranfield sums up the matter well:

> The movement of thought surely requires that the list in these two verses should be *all*-embracing, and the presence of the next phrase shows that it is intended to be so. . . . ["Nor anything else in all creation"] stands . . . by itself, and concludes the list. It is apparently added in order to make the list completely comprehensive.[54]

---

[52] Schreiner, *Romans*, 398–99.
[53] For a theological exposition, see Robert A. Peterson, *Our Secure Salvation: Preservation and Apostasy*, Explorations in Biblical Theology (Phillipsburg, NJ: P&R, 2009), 60–67.
[54] Cranfield, *Epistle to the Romans*, 444, emphasis original.

Paul thus teaches emphatically that God's keeping believers is bound up with his love "in Christ Jesus our Lord." As Dunn, speaking of Paul, eloquently states:

> The sweep of his faith is truly majestic. No longer simply situations of stress and suffering within life, but the boundary situations of life and beyond life, the powers that determine eternal destiny, all fall under his gaze, with no different result: *nothing* can loose the embrace of God's love in Christ.... Whatever names his readers give to the nameless forces which threaten the Creator's work and purpose, they are in the end impotent before him who is God over all.... Nothing, but nothing, can separate from "God's love in Christ Jesus our Lord."[55]

In short, preservation takes place not apart from Christ but in union with him.

Second, preservation is the work of the Holy Spirit. Paul teaches this in two places in Ephesians, both concerning the Holy Spirit as seal. It is important to see the Spirit's role in broader theological context. Preservation is the work of the Trinity. "The God and Father of our Lord Jesus Christ . . . has caused us to be born again to a living hope . . . an inheritance that is . . . kept in heaven for you, who by God's power are being guarded through faith for . . . salvation" (1 Pet. 1:3–5). Jesus, referring to his sheep, says, "My Father, who has given them to me, is greater than all, and no one is able to snatch them out of the Father's hand" (John 10:29).

The Son also plays an important part in the preservation of the saints. He says, "Whoever comes to me I will never cast out" (6:37). Concerning the elect he says, "This is the will of him who sent me, that I should lose nothing of all that he has given me, but raise it up on the last day" (v. 39). And he also keeps the sheep safe in his arms: "My sheep hear my voice, and I know them, and they follow me. I give them eternal life, and they will never perish, and no one will snatch them out of my hand" (10:27–28).

The Holy Spirit plays a part in preservation; this is clearly seen when Paul presents him as the seal of our final redemption. In Ephesians 1:3–14 Paul offers praise to the triune God for salvation. This includes the Father's election (vv. 4–5, 11), the Son's redemption (v. 7), and the Holy Spirit as seal (vv. 13–14). We will focus on the last: "In him you also, when you heard the word of truth, the gospel of your salvation, and believed in him, were sealed with the promised Holy Spirit" (v. 13). Paul says that when the Ephesians heard

---

[55] Dunn, *Romans 1–8*, 512–13, emphasis original.

the gospel and believed in Christ, they were "sealed with the promised Holy Spirit."

In three places Paul presents the Spirit as the seal of salvation. In 2 Corinthians 1:21–22 he teaches that the Father is the sealer, distinguishing "God . . . who has also put his seal on us" from "Christ" and "his Spirit." In two other places he uses the divine passive to imply that the Father is the sealer (Eph. 1:13; 4:30). So in Ephesians 1:13 the apostle means that when the Ephesians believed, they "were sealed [by the Father] with the promised Holy Spirit." "Promised"[56] indicates that the Spirit has come in fulfillment of Old Testament prediction.

The key is the Spirit himself as seal. "In him you . . . were sealed with the promised Holy Spirit" (v. 13). The Father seals believers with the Spirit. Furthermore, the two words that begin the verse are crucial: "in him" is used as a locative (figuratively) to show realm. The Father seals believers with the Holy Spirit in Christ's domain. Here is the main point: God makes us part of Christ's realm permanently. And he gives us the Spirit as seal of that fact.

Verse 14 confirms our interpretation of verse 13: "the guarantee of our inheritance until we acquire possession of it, to the praise of his glory." "Guarantee" is the Aramaic loanword *arrabōn*, which means "first installment, deposit, down payment, pledge."[57] "It was a common commercial word denoting a pledge—some object handed over by a buyer to a seller until the purchase price was paid in full," as F. F. Bruce explains.[58] Paul thus teaches that the Father seals believers in Christ with the Holy Spirit as the pledge or "guarantee of our inheritance until we acquire possession of it" (v. 14). The Spirit is God's pledge to us that we will not fail to gain our final inheritance as God's children. The Spirit thus plays an important role in keeping God's people saved until the end.

Bruce beautifully applies Paul's message:

> The Spirit consciously received is "the guarantee of our inheritance," the pledge given to believers by God to assure them that the glory of the life to come, promised in the gospel, is a well-founded hope, a reality and not an illusion. . . . They can enter into the enjoyment of this everlasting portion here and now by the ministry of the Spirit. . . . Redemption is already

---

[56] Literally, "the Holy Spirit of promise," with the genitive "of promise" (τῆς ἐπαγγελίας/*tēs epangelias*) used as a qualitative genitive and correctly rendered "promised."

[57] BDAG, 2nd ed. (1979), 109.

[58] F. F. Bruce, *The Epistles to the Colossians, to Philemon, and to the Ephesians*, The New International Commentary on the New Testament (Grand Rapids: Eerdmans, 1984), 266.

theirs through the sacrifice and death of Christ (v. 7), but one aspect of that redemption remains to be realized. On the day of resurrection God will "redeem" his own possession, and the evidence of his commitment to do so is given in his "sealing" that possession with the Spirit.[59]

In Ephesians 4:30 Paul is even more emphatic. He commands, "Do not grieve the Holy Spirit of God, by whom you were sealed for the day of redemption." The apostle regards the Spirit as a (divine) person who can be hurt. In this context, Christians grieve the Spirit with sinful anger or speech. Once more Paul uses the divine passive to imply that the Father is sealer. He seals us with the "Holy Spirit of God . . . for the day of redemption." Here Paul plainly gives the Spirit a major part in keeping us for final salvation.

O'Brien's words are accurate and edifying:

> The "day of redemption," which is unique to Ephesians, refers to the final day of salvation and judgment, that is, the goal of history. . . . On the final day God will "redeem" his own possession, and the guarantee he has given of this is his sealing of them with the Spirit. . . . There is a fulfilment yet to come, and believers eagerly await it. For the moment, however, the apostle's gaze is on the presence of the Spirit in their midst. They are to live out the future in the here and now until that "day" of redemption arrives, and this reminder that the Holy Spirit is God's own seal should be an incentive to holy living and speaking.[60]

Hoekema's summary anticipates my own: "The Holy Spirit, in other words, in a mysterious but wonderful way, enables us to persevere in the Christian walk until the day when we shall enter into our final inheritance on the glorified new earth."[61] In other words, the Holy Spirit plays a part in our preservation, which takes place in union with Christ, because the Spirit is God's seal, protecting us until we enter final salvation.

Glorification

First, glorification takes place in union with Christ. Paul teaches this in Romans 8 and Colossians 3. In the former passage, after urging believers to live wholeheartedly for God and speaking of the glories of our adoption by the

---

[59] Ibid.
[60] Peter T. O'Brien, *The Letter to the Ephesians*, The Pillar New Testament Commentary (Grand Rapids: Eerdmans, 1999), 349.
[61] Hoekema, *Saved by Grace*, 31.

Father, he turns his attention to the Spirit. The Spirit enables people to cry out to the Father in saving faith. "You have received the Spirit of adoption as sons, by whom we cry, 'Abba! Father!'" (Rom. 8:15). The Spirit also testifies within believers' hearts that God is their Father: "The Spirit himself bears witness with our spirit that we are children of God" (v. 16).

Paul extends the adoption metaphor to include inheritance: "If children, then heirs—heirs of God and fellow heirs with Christ" (v. 17). As God's children by adoption we are also his heirs! Paul says the same thing in Galatians 4:7: "You are no longer a slave, but a son, and if a son, then an heir through God." If we take into account the Bible's big story, the inheritance of believers is startling: we inherit the Trinity and the new earth (1 Cor. 3:21–23; Rev. 21:1–7)!

There follows an important proviso: we are God's children and heirs "provided we suffer with him in order that we may also be glorified with him" (Rom. 8:17). When God adopts children, he not only places them in his family but also gives them his Spirit and changes them. They are identifiable: "All who are led by the Spirit of God are sons of God" (v. 14). This is because union with Christ involves union with his death and resurrection. Because we are joined to Christ in his death, we "suffer with him." And because we are joined to Christ in his resurrection, we will "also be glorified with him."

As we saw previously, it is impossible to be a Christian without the Holy Spirit. Those who lack the Spirit are not believers: "Anyone who does not have the Spirit of Christ does not belong to him" (v. 9). Conversely, those who have the Spirit *are* Christians. The Spirit's main job is to unite us to Christ in his death and resurrection, and that is why Paul can issue his proviso, as Moo explains concerning the inheritance promised in verse 17:

> Paul adds that this glorious inheritance is attained only through suffering. . . . Because we are one with Christ, we are his fellow heirs, assured of being "glorified with him." But, at the same time, this oneness means that we must follow Christ's own road to glory, "suffering with him." . . . Paul makes clear that this suffering is the condition for the inheritance; we will be "glorified with" Christ (only) *if* we "suffer with him." Participation in Christ's glory can come only through participation in his suffering. . . . For the glory of the kingdom of God is attained only through participation in Christ, and belonging to Christ cannot but bring our participation in the sufferings of Christ. Just as, then, Christ has suffered and entered into his

glory (1 Pet. 1:11), so Christians, "fellow heirs with Christ," suffer during this present time in order to join Christ in glory.[62]

In Colossians 3 also Paul teaches that glorification takes place in union with Christ. He opposes the false teachers and their asceticism, which has "no value in stopping the indulgence of the flesh" (2:8–23, quoting 23): "Set your minds . . . not on things that are on earth" (3:2). His chief concern, however, is positive: "Christ . . . seated at the right hand of God" (v. 1). For this reason he commands, "Seek the things that are above. . . . Set your minds on things that are above" (vv. 1–2). The antidote to destructive teaching and futile asceticism is Christ (2:8–15). This is why the apostle points the Colossians "above," where Christ is.

Paul underlines union with Christ in his narrative as motivation to "seek" him. When he tells his readers, "You have died" (3:3), he means with Christ (cf. 2:20). He specifically mentions union with Christ in his resurrection (3:1). Due to his readers' union with Christ in his death and resurrection, Paul concludes, "Your life is hidden with Christ in God" (v. 3).

Contrary to asceticism, Paul's readers are to pursue Christ above. This does not entail despising their earthly lives, for he teaches them how to relate to one another in church and home (3:18–4:1). This is "earthy" teaching. It does not involve denial of bodily appetites as a means of spirituality; instead, it means drawing strength from union with Christ in heaven for daily life on earth.

Astoundingly, Paul carries participation in Christ's story even further. We not only died with him, were buried with him, arose with him, ascended with him, and sat down in heaven with him. But in a sense we also come again with him! This is the meaning of Paul's words, "When Christ who is your life appears, then you also will appear with him in glory" (3:4). "When Christ . . . appears" refers to his return. And "you also will appear with him in glory" refers to *our* return, so to speak. Believers have a "second coming" in union with Christ, as O'Brien explains:

> For the moment their heavenly life remains hidden, secure with Christ in God. Their new life as Christians in Christ is not visible to others, and, in some measure, is hidden from themselves. It will only be fully manifest when Christ, who embodies that life, appears in his Parousia. Indeed, the day of the revelation of the *Son* of God will be the day of the revelation

[62] Moo, *Epistle to the Romans*, 505–6, emphasis original.

of the *sons* of God. That manifestation will take place "in glory" for it will involve the sharing of Christ's likeness and the receiving of the glorious resurrection body.[63]

Our union with Christ is so all-encompassing that we will (in a sense) come again with him. Only at his second coming will our true identities "in Christ" be disclosed. In the meantime we do not even come close to being the holy and glorious persons we will be in the resurrection.[64] Glorification takes place not apart from Christ but in union with him.

Second, glorification is the work of the Holy Spirit. I was surprised to find that Scripture does not teach this truth as directly as the previous five, concerning the Spirit's role in regeneration, justification, adoption, sanctification, and preservation. Nevertheless, Scripture implies it. Consider that the following texts serve as background for this truth by combining the Spirit and glory:

> If the ministry of death, carved in letters on stone, came with such glory that the Israelites could not gaze at Moses' face because of its glory, which was being brought to an end, will not the ministry of the Spirit have even more glory? (2 Cor. 3:7–8)

> We all, with unveiled face, beholding the glory of the Lord, are being transformed into the same image from one degree of glory to another. For this comes from the Lord who is the Spirit. (v. 18)

The text that best implies the Spirit's role in glorification is 1 Peter 4:13–14. In his first epistle Peter encourages persecuted believers to persevere in their faith by entrusting themselves to God and doing his will. So he writes in chapter 4, "Do not be surprised at the fiery trial when it comes upon you to test you, as though something strange were happening to you" (v. 12). Christians are to expect persecution, as he says elsewhere, a truth echoed by Paul: "All who desire to live a godly life in Christ Jesus will be persecuted" (2 Tim. 3:12).

Moreover, believers can even rejoice in persecution. "Rejoice insofar as you share Christ's sufferings, that you may also rejoice and be glad when his glory is revealed" (1 Pet. 4:13). Peter instructs his readers to be glad when they suffer for and in Christ now, because such suffering is an indication that they will share in his glory at his return. Underlying this verse is the doctrine of union

---

[63] Peter T. O'Brien, *Colossians, Philemon*, Word Biblical Commentary (Waco, TX: Word, 1982), 171, emphasis original.
[64] Although it is little known, Paul teaches the same truth in Rom. 8:19: "The creation waits with eager longing for *the revelation* of the sons of God" (my translation).

with Christ in his death and resurrection; or, as Peter is wont to say, in his past suffering and future glory. Davids captures Peter's thought remarkably:

> As the Christians suffer because of their identification with Christ, they enter into the experience of Christ's own sufferings. This experience creates a re-imaging of their own suffering, which will allow them to see the real evil as an advantage as their perspective shifts. This process is precisely what each of the passages in 1 Peter that use this language does: each encourages a re-imaging of suffering as an identification with Christ . . . that will lead to an eventual participation in glory.
>
> It is because of this re-imaging of suffering that the Christians can be instructed to "rejoice," . . . for they obtain an eschatological perspective on their problems. This perspective becomes explicit in the promise that they will "also rejoice, being glad when his glory is revealed." On the one hand, there will be a corresponding participation in the glory of Christ for those who now share in Christ's sufferings. . . . On the other hand, while this revelation of Christ's glory is future . . . they can rejoice now in the evidence that they belong to him (their suffering) because they anticipate the coming joy.[65]

This is where the Holy Spirit enters the picture: "If you are insulted for the name of Christ, you are blessed, because the Spirit of glory and of God rests upon you" (v. 14). Peter's wording agrees much with that of Isaiah 11:2 in the Septuagint: "The Spirit of God . . . will rest on him." He adapts for Christians words that refer to the Messiah, "probably on the basis of the application of 'the name of Christ' to Christians in the preceding clause."[66] The Greek syntax is awkward in the last clause of 1 Peter 4:14, and another interpretation is possible based on another translation option, as Schreiner, who favors this option, shows.[67]

I respectfully follow the translation of the ESV (the NIV is very similar): "The Spirit of glory and of God rests upon you." When believers suffer because they are Christians, Peter insists, they can rejoice because they have been joined to Christ and thereby participate in the Holy Spirit. The way Peter refers to the Spirit within this context implies that glorification is the work of the Spirit. Davids concludes:

---

[65] Peter H. Davids, *The First Epistle of Peter*, The New International Commentary on the New Testament (Grand Rapids: Eerdmans, 1990), 166–67.

[66] J. Ramsey Michaels, *1 Peter*, Word Biblical Commentary (Waco, TX: Word, 1988), 264.

[67] Thomas R. Schreiner, *1, 2 Peter, Jude*, New American Commentary (Nashville: Broadman and Holman, 2003), 222–23, offers this paraphrase: "The eschatological glory promised in v. 13 and the Spirit of God rest upon you."

Thus those suffering for Christ experience through the Spirit now the glory they are promised in the future (1:7; 5:4; cf. 2 Cor. 4:17; Col. 3:4). Indeed their very suffering is a sign that the reputation (glory) of God is seen in them, that the Spirit rests on them. They can indeed count themselves blessed.[68]

In 1 Peter 4:13, then, Peter promises suffering believers a share "when his [Christ's] glory is revealed," and then speaks of the "Spirit of glory and of God" resting on them in verse 14. The implication is that the "Spirit of glory" will enable each one of them to be a "partaker in the glory that is going to be revealed" (5:1). Schreiner is right in affirming, "Believers who suffer are blessed because they are now enjoying God's favor, tasting even now the wonders of the glory to come and experiencing the promised Holy Spirit."[69]

I conclude: the "Spirit of glory and of God" (4:14) will act in glorification to unite believers to Christ "when his glory is revealed" (v. 13).

Conclusion

"The key to our sharing in the Father-Son relationship is the work of the Holy Spirit, who enters us personally in order to bring us to trust in Christ and thereby to unite us through Christ to his Father."[70] Donald Fairbairn's summary of the church fathers' understanding holds true for this study: the most important work of the Holy Spirit in salvation is to join human beings to Christ.

We have seen three pieces of evidence for this statement. First, in 1 Corinthians 12:12–13 Paul uses two pictures to credit union with Christ to the Spirit. Christ baptizes all believers into his body with the one Spirit. And all believers have drunk of the one Spirit. It is reasonable to conclude, therefore, that the Spirit is indispensable to union with Christ, as the next piece of evidence says in no uncertain terms.

Second, the apostle says point-blank, "Anyone who does not have the Spirit of Christ does not belong to him" (Rom. 8:9). That is, the Spirit is the bond of union with Christ. This fact yields both negative and positive results. In negative terms, it is as simple as this: no Spirit, no union. In positive terms, the third piece of evidence is true.

---

[68] Davids, *First Epistle of Peter*, 168.
[69] Schreiner, *1, 2 Peter, Jude*, 223.
[70] Donald Fairbairn, *Life in the Trinity: An Introduction to Theology with the Help of the Church Fathers* (Downers Grove, IL: IVP Academic, 2008), 195.

Third, Paul ascribes aspects of salvation that occur in union with Christ to the Spirit's working. Different ways of talking about salvation applied to sinners include regeneration, justification, adoption, sanctification, preservation, and glorification. Each of these aspects of the application of salvation takes place in union with Christ, and each is the work of the Holy Spirit.

Marcus Johnson's words form a fitting conclusion to this chapter:

> We are united to Christ by the Holy Spirit. . . . To say that our union with Christ occurs by the power of the Spirit means that the Holy Spirit is himself the bond that united us to the living Christ. . . . The heart of the Spirit's ministry is to join us to the incarnate, crucified, resurrected, ascended, and living Lord Jesus Christ. J. I. Packer writes that "the distinctive, constant, basic ministry of the Holy Spirit in the New Covenant is . . . to mediate Christ's presence to believers." Therefore, describing union with Christ as a "spiritual" union can mean only that it is a union with *Christ* that takes place through the power of the Holy Spirit—it is a *Spiritual* union.[71]

---

[71] Marcus Peter Johnson, *One with Christ: An Evangelical Theology of Salvation* (Wheaton, IL: Crossway, 2013), 45, emphasis original. He cites J. I. Packer, *Keep in Step with the Spirit* (Grand Rapids: Fleming H. Revell, 1984), 49.

Chapter 25

The Christ to Whom We Are United

Mystical union . . . is that personal engrafting of believers into Christ which constitutes the foundation of the Christian life. As branches are joined with the vine, their source (John 15), or members of a body with their head (Eph. 4), so the elect are united with Christ.[1]

It may seem to go without saying, but P. Mark Achtemeier is correct to make it explicit: union with Christ is the foundation of the Christian life because such union is union with *Christ*. It is too common to focus on the benefits of union with Christ and lose sight of the Christ to whom we are united. Union with Christ is the application of *salvation*. Why is this so? Because the Christ to whom we are united by grace through faith is the Mediator between God and men and the Savior of the world. Who he is and what he has accomplished give union its saving significance and power. It is only fitting, then, that we devote a chapter to the Christ of union with Christ:

- the person of Christ
- the work of Christ
- Christ the object of saving faith

The Person of Christ

The last chapter rightly underscored the Holy Spirit's essential role in uniting believing sinners to Christ. But it is important to recognize that without

---

[1] P. Mark Achtemeier, "Union with Christ (Mystical Union)," in *Encyclopedia of the Reformed Faith*, ed. Donald K. McKim and David F. Wright (Louisville: Westminster John Knox, 1992), 379.

Christ's person and work there would be no one and nothing for the Spirit to join believers to for salvation. It is only because of Christ's identity and saving accomplishment that the Spirit's work is effective. Here we will summarize orthodox christology from Scripture.

The Preexistence of Christ

Christology begins "above," where God is. It is thus a rescue mission coming "down" from God to lost human beings. The Son's preexistence is taught in many passages. Simon Gathercole presents ten sayings in which angels say of Jesus, "Have you come [with an expressed purpose]?" or in which he says of himself, "I have come" with a stated purpose. I will cite two spoken by fallen angels and three from Jesus's lips:

> What have you to do with us, Jesus of Nazareth? Have you come to destroy us? I know who you are—the Holy One of God. (Mark 1:24)

> They cried out, "What have you to do with us, O Son of God? Have you come here to torment us before the time?" (Matt. 8:29)

> Those who are well have no need of a physician, but those who are sick. I came not to call the righteous, but sinners. (Mark 2:17)

> The Son of Man came not to be served but to serve, and to give his life as a ransom for many. (Mark 10:45)

> The Son of Man came to seek and to save the lost. (Luke 19:10)

Gathercole's conclusion to his exegesis of these passages bears repeating:

> There is good reason to see evidence of preexistence in the ten statements examined. Specifically, we have found that they confirm the hypothesis established earlier that the grammatical form and the angelic parallels point toward preexistence. The grammatical form points toward a deliberate action in coming with a purpose, and the angelic parallels confirm that it is heavenly beings who make such statements in their references to coming into the world.[2]

---

[2] Simon J. Gathercole, *The Preexistent Son: Recovering the Christologies of Matthew, Mark, and Luke* (Grand Rapids: Eerdmans, 2006), 170. See also Douglas McCready, *He Came Down from Heaven: The Preexistence of Christ and the Christian Faith* (Downers Grove, IL: InterVarsity, 2005).

Bethlehem does not mark the beginning of the Son of God's existence. He existed for all eternity with the Father and Holy Spirit in heaven. The Christ to whom we are united preexisted as the eternal Son of God. He, the preexistent Son, became a human being in his incarnation.

The Incarnation

Christology begins "above" in the preexistence of the divine Son. It moves "below" when the Son becomes a human being in Jesus of Nazareth. This is the incarnation, the eternal, almighty God becoming a man. We will examine texts in John, Paul, and Hebrews that teach the incarnation.

John, after speaking of the Word of God being in the beginning with God, being divine, and serving as God's agent in creation (John 1:1–3), writes, "The Word became flesh and dwelt among us, and we have seen his glory, glory as of the only Son from the Father, full of grace and truth" (John 1:14). The eternal Word became "flesh," σάρξ (*sarx*), an earthy, almost shocking word. Greeks held to gradations of reality, with spirit being the highest and matter less real. They had ethical gradations corresponding to the ontological ones, so that pure spirit (God) was good and matter was evil. Thus, according to Greek thought, immediate contact between God and matter—such as in the incarnation—was impossible. But not to John: "The Word became flesh," that is, God became man, a human being of flesh and blood. D. A. Carson says, "The Word, God's very Self-expression, who was both with God and who was God, became flesh: he donned our humanity, save only our sin. God chose to make himself known, finally and ultimately, in a real, historical man."[3]

Paul teaches the same truth in Philippians 2. There, after saying that Jesus "was in the form of God," Paul writes that the Son "emptied himself" by "taking the form of a servant" (vv. 6–7). The apostle thus juxtaposes two seemingly contradictory ideas: the "form of God" and the "form of a servant"![4] The Son existed in the outward form of God, something that could be said only of God himself. He then humbled himself to take the outward form of a bondslave, something that could be said only of a bona fide human being. The following words underline this truth: "being born in the likeness of men" (v. 7). All of this was so that he could become "obedient to the point of death, even death on a cross," to save his people from their sins (v. 8). And Paul follows these

---

[3] D. A. Carson, *The Gospel according to John*, The Pillar New Testament Commentary (Grand Rapids: Eerdmans, 1991), 127.
[4] I take "form" in both cases to be a near synonym to other words in the passage: "likeness" (v. 7) and "human form" (v. 8).

words with magnificent words telling of Christ's subsequent exaltation. But do not miss the key fact: without the incarnation, there would have been no cross, atonement, empty tomb, or exaltation—and consequently no salvation!

The writer to the Hebrews affirms the incarnation three times in one passage. In chapter 2 he presents Jesus as the second Adam, the Victor, and the Great High Priest. The author prefaces each picture with an affirmation of the truth that God became a man in Jesus:

> We see him who for a little while was made lower than the angels, namely Jesus, crowned with glory and honor because of the suffering of death, so that by the grace of God he might taste death for everyone. (v. 9, second Adam)

> Since therefore the children share in flesh and blood, he himself likewise partook of the same things, that through death he might destroy the one who has the power of death, that is, the devil, and deliver all those who through fear of death were subject to lifelong slavery. (vv. 14–15, Victor)

> He had to be made like his brothers in every respect, so that he might become a merciful and faithful high priest in the service of God, to make propitiation for the sins of the people. (v. 17, High Priest)

The Christ to whom we are united became a human being like us, apart from sin. As a result of the incarnation, Jesus of Nazareth is God and man in one person. He is both divine and human. I have argued for the deity of Christ elsewhere and will summarize five of those arguments here.[5]

The Deity of Christ

First, piggybacking on the fresh arguments of Richard Bauckham, I affirm that Scripture identifies Jesus with God.[6] His name is divine, for religious events occur in his name (Matt. 18:20; 28:19). Old Testament Yahweh passages are applied to him. Joel prophesies that "everyone who calls on the name of the LORD shall be saved" (Joel 2:32), and Peter, after citing that text, identifies the "Lord" whom his hearers must call upon to be saved—"this Jesus" (Acts 2:36).

The name Jesus is used interchangeably with God (1 Thess. 2:2 with 3:2;

[5] Robert A. Peterson, "Toward a Systematic Theology of the Deity of Christ," in *The Deity of Christ*, ed. Christopher W. Morgan and Robert A. Peterson, Theology in Community (Wheaton, IL: Crossway, 2011), 193–227.
[6] See Richard J. Bauckham, *Jesus and the God of Israel* (Grand Rapids: Eerdmans, 2008).

1 Thess. 2:13 with 1:8; Gal. 1:15 with 1:6; Eph. 1:11 with 5:17). Jesus is also called God. Murray Harris painstakingly concludes that there are six New Testament texts where this occurs: John 1:1; 20:28; Romans 9:5; Titus 2:13; Hebrews 1:8; and 2 Peter 1:1. Jesus is identified with God himself.[7]

Second, Jesus receives the devotion due God alone. Worship is directed toward him (John 5:22–23). He instructs his followers to perform Christian baptism in his name and the names of the Father and Holy Spirit (Matt. 28:19). Gordon Fee shows that the Lord's Supper is the "Christian version of a meal in honor of a deity," with Jesus as the Deity (1 Cor. 11:20).[8] New Testament writers exalt Jesus to God's status when they offer doxologies in his name (Heb. 13:20–21; 2 Pet. 3:18; Rev. 5:11–12). Hymns are sung to Jesus (Eph. 5:18–21; Col. 3:16). Prayers also are directed to him in John 14:13–14; Acts 7:59; and Revelation 22:20. Plainly, in numerous ways Jesus is the object of devotion and worship.

Third, Jesus brings the age to come. The New Testament contrasts the "present age" and the "age to come." The "present age," located between Christ's advents, fulfills many Old Testament predictions and anticipates the "age to come," the *eschaton*. The "present age" is marked by evil (Gal. 1:4) and spiritual blindness (2 Cor. 4:4). The "age to come" is marked by the resurrection (Luke 20:34–36) and eternal life (18:30).

Oscar Cullmann popularized another distinction—that between the "already" and the "not yet."[9] Viewed from the Old Testament, the New Testament presents the "already," the fulfillment of prophetic predictions and the hopes of God's people. Alongside the "already" in the New Testament stands the "not yet," the fact that many prophecies await fulfillment.

The transitions from the Old Testament to the "present age" and from the "present age" to the "age to come" are accomplished by God himself. Only he establishes the "already" and the "not yet." In the New Testament Jesus Christ inaugurates both the "already" and the "not yet." He brings both ages. In the Gospels the "already" and the "not yet" appear primarily as the coming of the kingdom of God, present and future. Jesus inaugurates the kingdom in his preaching (Matt. 13:11) and exorcisms (12:28). The same Jesus, the Son of Man, will yet bring the consummated kingdom. He will come back in great glory, sit on his glorious throne, judge the nations, and assign eternal destinies (25:41, 46).

---

[7] Murray J. Harris, *Jesus as God: The New Testament Use of* Theos *in Reference to Jesus* (Grand Rapids: Baker, 1992).
[8] Gordon D. Fee, *Pauline Christology: An Exegetical-Theological Study* (Peabody, MA: Hendrickson, 2007), 491.
[9] Oscar Cullmann, *Salvation in History*, trans. S. G. Sowers (New York: Harper and Row, 1967). See also Geerhardus Vos, *The Pauline Eschatology* (Grand Rapids: Eerdmans, 1953).

In the Epistles too Jesus brings the "already" and the "not yet." Believers' sins have been forgiven by Christ because we have been included in his kingdom (Col. 1:13–14). But the day has not yet appeared when we will be raised from the dead and God will outwardly rule over all. That will occur when Jesus Christ, the risen one, comes again and transfers the kingdom to the Father (1 Cor. 15:22–25). Finally, Revelation teaches the same things. Christ is already the one "who loves us and has freed us from our sins by his blood and made us a kingdom, priests to his God and Father" (Rev. 1:5–6). But that day is still future when his kingdom will be eternally established in the new heaven and new earth. Till then, we long for the time when the "kingdom of the world has become the kingdom of our Lord and of his Christ, and he shall reign forever and ever" (Rev. 11:15).

This validation of Christ's deity is as extensive as the New Testament. David Wells explains, "Jesus was the one in whom this 'age to come' was realized, through whom it is redemptively present in the church, and by whom it will be made cosmically effective at its consummation. He is the agent, the instrument, and the personifier of God's sovereign, eternal, saving rule."[10] Surely such roles can be undertaken only by God himself—in this case God the Son.

Fourth, Jesus does many works that only God can do. These include creation, providence, judgment, and salvation. Both Testaments say that God alone does the work of creation (Gen. 1:1; Isa. 40:25–26; Eph. 3:8–9; Rev. 4:11). The New Testament ascribes the work of creation to the Son of God (John 1:3; 1 Cor. 8:6; Col. 1:16; Heb. 1:2, 10).

Both Testaments teach that God alone does the work of providence. He alone sustains and directs his creation to his appointed ends (Ps. 104:24–30; Acts 17:24–28). The New Testament ascribes the work of providence to the Son of God (Col. 1:16; Heb. 1:3).

Both Testaments affirm that God alone does the work of judgment (Gen. 18:25; Ps. 50:6; Rom. 14:10; 1 Pet. 1:17). The New Testament ascribes the work of judgment to the Son of God (Matt. 16:27; John 5:22–23; Acts 10:42; 2 Thess. 1:7–8).

Both Testaments teach that God alone does the work of salvation. He alone is the Savior (Ex. 15:2; Ps. 62:1–2, 7; Luke 1:46–47; 1 Tim. 1:1). The New Testament ascribes the work of salvation to the Son of God in many ways. It calls Jesus the "Savior of the world" (John 4:42), ascribes the divine preroga-

---

[10] David F. Wells, *The Person of Christ* (Westchester, IL: Crossway, 1984), 172.

tive of forgiving sins to him (Luke 7:48–49; cf. Acts 5:31; Col. 1:13–14; Rev. 1:5–6), and says that in his death he makes purification for sins (Heb. 1:3). Because Jesus performs all these works that only God performs, he is equal with God.

Fifth, Jesus consummates salvation. The Old Testament ascribes to God alone the prerogatives of putting people to death and making them alive (Deut. 32:39; 1 Sam. 2:6). The New Testament applies this Old Testament principle to eternal destinies. Jesus warns: "Do not fear those who kill the body but cannot kill the soul. Rather fear him who can destroy both soul and body in hell" (Matt. 10:28). And the New Testament ascribes these same divine prerogatives to the returning Christ. Jesus will raise the dead, as the Gospel of John teaches (John 6:40, 44, 54). He also performs the divine role of assigning saints and sinners their final destinies (Matt. 25:34, 41).

In his first coming, Jesus, our Great High Priest, offered himself as an atoning sacrifice. In his second coming, he will bring final salvation: "Just as it is appointed for man to die once, and after that comes judgment, so Christ, having been offered once to bear the sins of many, will appear a second time, not to deal with sin but to save those who are eagerly waiting for him" (Heb. 9:27–28). Although we live on earth, "our citizenship is in heaven." From there "we await a Savior, the Lord Jesus Christ, who will transform our lowly body to be like his glorious body, by the power that enables him even to subject all things to himself" (Phil. 3:20–21). Our mortal bodies are lowly because they are subject to illness and death. At his return Christ will exert his almighty power and cause our lowly bodies to share his resurrection glory.

Jesus will bring cosmic restoration. Through Jesus "God was pleased . . . to reconcile to himself all things, whether on earth or in heaven, making peace by the blood of his cross" (Col. 1:19–20). Jesus's death and resurrection not only save all the people of God of all ages but are the reason why there will be a new heaven and a new earth (Rev. 21:1). His saving work has cosmic consequences. In all of these ways Jesus will consummate salvation, and here again Scripture identifies him with God.

The Christ to whom we are united is God. And he became a human being.

The Humanity of Christ

Of the many demonstrations of the humanity of Christ, I will mention six.

First, the incarnation proves Christ's humanity because in it the Son of God became like us in every way (though without sin), even capable of bodily death. In Hebrews 2 the incarnation serves the purpose of atonement: "Since therefore the children share in flesh and blood, he himself likewise partook of the same things, that through death he might destroy the one who has the power of death, that is, the devil, and deliver all those who through fear of death were subject to lifelong slavery" (Heb. 2:14–15). The Son became incarnate so he could die to defeat the Devil and deliver human beings. The incarnation is a strong affirmation of the humanity of the incarnate Son.

Second, Jesus had human weaknesses and needs that demonstrated his true humanity. The Fourth Gospel shows Jesus's divine power; it also shows his human weakness. We read concerning the Samaritan city of Sychar, "Jacob's well was there; so Jesus, wearied as he was from his journey, was sitting beside the well" (John 4:6). The same Jesus who shows supernatural knowledge (1:48–49), who raises himself from the dead (2:19–21; 10:17–18), and who bestows eternal life as a gift (10:28) was tired! The incarnate Son was God and man in one person, as John's Gospel bears ample witness.

While he was on the cross after caring for his mother, Mary, "Jesus, knowing that all was now finished, said (to fulfill the Scripture), 'I thirst.' A jar full of sour wine stood there, so they put a sponge full of the sour wine on a hyssop branch and held it to his mouth" (19:28–29). Once again we see Jesus exhibiting real human need—he was thirsty and asked for something to drink.

"God cannot be tempted with evil" (James 1:13), but God incarnate can! The Synoptic Gospels record Jesus's temptation in the wilderness by the Devil (Matt. 4:1–11; Mark 1:12–13; Luke 4:1–13). And the writer to the Hebrews tells the importance of Jesus's successfully undergoing temptation: "We do not have a high priest who is unable to sympathize with our weaknesses, but one who in every respect has been tempted as we are, yet without sin" (Heb. 4:15). Jesus knew the pain of temptation but, unlike us, never succumbed. Consequently, he empathizes with our struggles with sin, and because he is sinless and divine he (along with the Father) can give us mercy and grace in "time of need" (v. 16).

We see Jesus's human limitation and wisdom at the same time when he avoids danger: "After this Jesus went about in Galilee. He would not go about in Judea, because the Jews were seeking to kill him" (John 7:1). The Son of God on earth exhibited genuine human weaknesses and needs.

Third, our Lord incarnate had genuine human emotions. He was grieved at the hardness of heart of people in the synagogue in Nazareth who opposed his healing a man with a withered hand (Mark 3:5). He was "very sorrowful, even to death" in Gethsemane as he contemplated drinking the cup of God's wrath on the cross (Matt. 26:38). He showed both sorrow and love for his deceased friend Lazarus. John says Jesus was "deeply moved" as he stood outside Lazarus's tomb (John 11:33, 38). "See how he loved him!" the mourners cried at the sight of Jesus's tears for his friend (v. 36).

Fourth, Jesus had human experiences. He was born (Matt. 1:18, 24–25; Luke 2:6–7), lived approximately thirty-three years, was crucified (John 19:18), and died (vv. 30, 33). He experienced normal human growth. After the episode of Jesus as a boy with the teachers in the temple, "He went down with them [Joseph and Mary] and came to Nazareth and was submissive to them" (Luke 2:51). Luke then gives a wonderful summary statement of Jesus's growth: "Jesus increased in wisdom and in stature and in favor with God and man" (v. 52). He grew "in wisdom," that is, intellectually. He grew "in stature," that is, physically. He grew "in favor with God," that is, spiritually. And he grew in favor "with man," that is, socially. Jesus's experience of normal human growth is a potent statement of his true humanity.

Fifth, Jesus had a human relationship with God the Father. He was subordinate to the Father. In the upper room he told his disciples, "You heard me say to you, 'I am going away, and I will come to you.' If you loved me, you would have rejoiced, because I am going to the Father, for the Father is greater than I" (John 14:28; cf. 5:26; 17:2, 4).

Jesus honored the Father. After the Jewish leaders accused him of being a Samaritan and having a demon (8:48), Jesus replied, "I do not have a demon, but I honor my Father, and you dishonor me" (v. 49; cf. 7:18). Furthermore, Jesus obeyed God's commands. As he headed to the cross, he remarked to his disciples, "I do as the Father has commanded me, so that the world may know that I love the Father" (14:31; cf. 10:18; 12:49; 15:10).

Sixth, three times Hebrews says something found nowhere else in Scripture, something that sounds shocking—that Jesus was "made perfect." Three passages mention it, but only one expounds the theme: "Although he was a son, he learned obedience through what he suffered. And being made perfect, he became the source of eternal salvation to all who obey him, being designated by God a high priest after the order of Melchizedek" (5:8–10; cf. 2:10; 7:28).

The preceding verse speaks of Gethsemane, where Jesus with great sorrow poured out his heart to the Father (5:7). The Father answered the Son's prayer not by removing the cross but by raising him from the dead. Jesus's being made perfect pertains to his human struggles and climaxes in the cross. In what sense did the incarnate Son need to be made perfect? Hebrews 2:10 provides a hint when it says that God made Christ "perfect through suffering." This idea is expanded when Hebrews 5:8 says that Jesus "learned obedience through what he suffered." The Son was made perfect when, over the course of his earthly life, he learned to obey the Father, especially by enduring suffering.

To be Redeemer, Jesus must not only be God and man in one person. He must also be tried and found true. Jesus did not come as a thirty-three year-old to die and be raised. He came as an infant to experience human life triumphantly, with all of its trials and temptations. Only then could he save his people from their sins: "Being made perfect, he became the source of eternal salvation to all who obey him, being designated by God a high priest after the order of Melchizedek" (Heb. 5:9–10). This theme too, then, underscores Jesus's humanness.

It is crucial to add that Jesus's genuine humanity was sinless. This teaching so pervades the New Testament that I will cite only a few representative passages and give references to the rest. All parts of the New Testament testify that to accomplish his saving work, the Son of God was without sin: the Gospels, Acts, Pauline Epistles, General Epistles, and Revelation.

The Gospels affirm Jesus's sinless humanity. Mary was told, "The child to be born will be called holy—the Son of God" (Luke 1:35; cf. Mark 1:24; John 6:69). Acts testifies to Jesus's moral purity often. Peter preached to the Jews, "You denied the Holy and Righteous One" (Acts 3:14; cf. 4:27, 29–30; 7:51–52; 22:14).

Paul is also numbered among the witnesses to Jesus's sinlessness: "For our sake he made him to be sin who knew no sin, so that in him we might become the righteousness of God" (2 Cor. 5:21). The General Epistles contain numerous references to Jesus's moral excellence: "Christ also suffered once for sins, the righteous for the unrighteous, that he might bring us to God" (1 Pet. 3:18; cf. 2:22–23; Heb. 4:15). First John speaks frequently of Jesus's blamelessness: "If anyone does sin, we have an advocate with the Father, Jesus Christ the righteous" (1 John 2:1; cf. 2:20; 3:3, 5–7).

In one of the letters to the seven churches, Revelation joins the chorus praising Jesus's moral character: "To the angel of the church in Philadelphia write: 'The words of the holy one, the true one, who has the key of David, who opens and no one will shut, who shuts and no one opens'" (Rev. 3:7).

There is no question, then, that the writers of the New Testament thought that Jesus's sinlessness was very significant. From the Gospels through Revelation they agree that he who accomplished redemption by his death and resurrection was holy and without sin.

The Christ to whom we are united partook of genuine and sinless humanity when he became one of us. And though tested and tried, he never sinned and never will.

The Unipersonality of Christ

We have seen that Scripture teaches the preexistence, incarnation, deity, and humanity of the Son of God, Jesus Christ. We complete our survey of his identity by affirming the unity of his person. Scripture presents him as one person with divine and human natures. The early church affirmed the unity of his person over against two attacks against it. Nestorianism divided him into two, while Eutychianism (or monophysitism) denied the distinction between his two natures, in effect making him neither God nor man, but a *tertium quid*. The confession of faith (AD 451) from the famous Council of Chalcedon states that Jesus Christ was "truly God and truly man . . . made known in two natures without confusion, without change [against Eutychianism], without division, without separation [against Nestorianism]."[11] As J. N. D. Kelly says concerning this historic council, "Its distinctive theology is to be seen in the equal recognition it accords both to the unity and to the duality in the God-man."[12]

This magnificent Christ, who preexisted, became incarnate, and therefore is both God and man in one person, is the one to whom we are joined in saving union. When by grace through faith we are joined to his person, we also receive all the benefits of his saving work. We now turn our attention to that work.

The Work of Christ

This book is the sequel to *Salvation Accomplished by the Son: The Work of Christ*.[13] Here I summarize three themes from the conclusion to that work:

- Christ's saving deeds
- biblical pictures that interpret Christ's saving deeds
- the directions to which Christ's saving work points

---

[11] J. N. D. Kelly, *Early Christian Doctrines*, rev. ed. (San Francisco: Harper and Row, 1978), 339–40.
[12] Ibid., 341.
[13] Robert A. Peterson, *Salvation Accomplished by the Son: The Work of Christ* (Wheaton, IL: Crossway, 2012).

Christ's Saving Deeds

Although salvation is not based on our works, it is based on Christ's work. The heart of Jesus's saving accomplishment is his death and resurrection. Listen to Paul's summary of the gospel he proclaims: "That Christ died for our sins in accordance with the Scriptures, that he was buried, that he was raised on the third day in accordance with the Scriptures" (1 Cor. 15:3–4).

Christ's cross and empty tomb are the center of his saving work. They are preceded by two essential preconditions (the incarnation and Christ's sinless life) and are followed by five essential results (his ascension, session, pouring out the Spirit at Pentecost, intercession, and return). Each of these is a part of his saving work. A brief exposition of each event is in order.

As we noted previously, in the incarnation of the Son, almighty God became a human being. God the Son left the glory of heaven and the fellowship of the Father and Holy Spirit to become the "last Adam," the "second man" (1 Cor. 15:45, 47). God permanently took to himself genuine humanity! Why? "God sent forth his Son, born of woman, born under the law, to redeem those who were under the law, so that we might receive adoption as sons" (Gal. 4:4–5).

Christ's spotless life is another essential prerequisite for his saving death and resurrection. Despite the fact that Christ was "in every respect . . . tempted as we are," he was "without sin" (Heb. 4:15). He was, as God said through Isaiah, the "righteous one, my servant" (53:11). This qualified him "who knew no sin" to give himself for others "so that in him" they "might become the righteousness of God" (2 Cor. 5:21).

The central saving deeds of God's Son are his death and resurrection. The death of the sinless incarnate one saves in all of these ways. It reconciles sinners to God, redeems them from bondage to sin, pays the penalty for their sins, triumphs over their foes, undoes the disobedience of Adam, and purifies defiled human beings. These are six ways of saying the same thing: the cross saves believers from their sins! We will expand these six biblical pictures in the next section.

Jesus's death should not be separated from his resurrection, because together they constitute the very core of his saving accomplishment. If he had not died, he could not have risen, and if he had not risen, his death would not save. "But thanks be to God, who gives us the victory through our Lord Jesus Christ" by raising him from the dead (1 Cor. 15:57). Jesus's resurrection signals his mighty conquest of Satan, his demons, and all God's other enemies.

This is followed by Christ's going from earth to heaven in his ascension. He not only accomplished salvation on earth in his death and resurrection as the God-*man*, but continues to minister in heaven in his intercession as the God-*man*. The ascension moves Christ from the limited earthly plane to the transcendent heavenly one (Heb. 6:20). As a result, "We have . . . a sure and steadfast anchor of the soul, a hope that enters into the inner place behind the curtain" (v. 19). From heaven, the exalted Lord and Prince bestows gifts of "repentance . . . and forgiveness of sins" (Acts 5:31).

The ascension enabled the session, Christ's sitting at the "right hand of the Majesty on high" (Heb. 1:3). He sits as prophet, priest, and especially king. As heavenly prophet, he equips his servants with his Spirit to spread his word and advance his kingdom. As exalted priest, he sat down to demonstrate the completion, perfection, and efficacy of his sacrifice (10:12). As enthroned king, he reigns on high with his Father and awaits the time when "his enemies should be made a footstool for his feet" (10:13; cf. 1:13; Ps. 110:1).

Pentecost is as much Christ's saving deed as are his death and resurrection. He was the "Christ," or Anointed One, because he received the Spirit at his baptism so that after ascending, he would dispense the Spirit to the church. In fulfillment of Old Testament prediction, the exalted Lord baptizes his church by pouring out the Holy Spirit on it (Joel 2:28–32; Acts 2:17–18, 33). He thereby publicly proclaimed the new covenant and began the new creation.

Christ's ongoing work, his intercession, has two aspects. First, as crucified, risen, and ascended Lord, he prays for his people with understanding and compassion and grants them "mercy and . . . grace to help in time of need" (Heb. 4:15–16, quoting 16; cf. Rom. 8:34). Second, because of the "power of an indestructible life" (7:16), he is priest forever and thus "able to save to the uttermost those who draw near to God through him, since he always lives to make intercession for them" (7:24–25, quoting 25).

Christ's saving work culminates in his second coming. He will bring heaven down to earth, as Revelation reveals: John saw the "holy city Jerusalem coming down out of heaven from God" to earth (Rev. 21:10). Christ's second coming brings final salvation. "Christ, having been offered once to bear the sins of many, will appear a second time, not to deal with sin but to save those who are eagerly waiting for him" (Heb. 9:28). The returning Christ will initiate the resurrection of the dead, the last judgment, and the eternal state.

Four points deserve mention. First, all nine events—incarnation, sinless life, death, resurrection, ascension, session, Pentecost, intercession, and return—constitute one saving work of Christ. Each event is important and should be appreciated. Yet Christ's saving work consists of all nine. We should, then, have a holistic view of his salvation, which includes everything from his incarnation to his return. The nine events constitute his unified saving work.

Second, although all nine events are necessary to salvation, it bears repeating that two are central and inseparable. Christ's death and resurrection are the heart and soul of his saving accomplishment. Sometimes Scripture mentions both together (John 10:17–18; Acts 2:22–24; Rom. 4:25; 10:9–10; 1 Cor. 15:3–4; 2 Cor. 5:15; Phil. 3:10; Heb. 1:3; 1 Pet. 1:11), but usually it uses shorthand and mentions merely one, implying the other.[14]

Third, there are two essential preconditions to Christ's death and resurrection: his incarnation and sinless life. Fourth, there are five essential results that follow Christ's death and resurrection: his ascension, session, Pentecost, intercession, and second coming.

However, events—even Christ's saving events—are not self-interpreting. People who walked by Jesus's cross, some who stood at its foot, and even one of the robbers crucified with him did not understand its meaning (Matt. 27:39–44)! Thankfully, God graciously gives pictures in Scripture to help us understand Jesus's saving work.

Biblical Pictures That Interpret Christ's Saving Deeds

I count six major biblical pictures that interpret Jesus's saving accomplishment. First, the picture of reconciliation comes from the sphere of interpersonal relations. We need to be reconciled to God because of disrupted relations or alienation. Christ is portrayed as the peacemaker who by his death and resurrection reconciles God to human beings and human beings to God. The result is peace between God and us and between us and God (Rom. 5:10; 2 Cor. 5:18–20; Eph. 2:12–17; Col. 1:20–23).

Second, the theme of redemption comes from the sphere of the master-slave relationship. We need to be redeemed because we are in bondage to sin and Satan. Christ is portrayed as the Redeemer who by his death and resurrection delivers us from spiritual slavery. As a result we experience the freedom of the sons or daughters of God (1 Cor. 6:20; Heb. 9:15; 1 Pet. 1:19).

---

[14] John Calvin makes this point, *Institutes of the Christian Religion*, ed. John T. McNeill, trans. Ford Lewis Battles, 2 vols. (Philadelphia: Westminster, 1960), 1:521 (2.16.13).

Third, the picture of legal substitution comes from the sphere of law. We need to be justified because of the guilt of Adam's original sin and of our own actual sins. Christ is portrayed as our legal substitute who by his death and resurrection propitiates God and pays the penalty for our sins. The result is that a holy and just God declares righteous all who trust Christ (Rom. 3:25–26; Gal. 3:13; Col. 2:14).

Fourth, the theme of Christus Victor comes from the sphere of warfare. We need to be delivered because we have spiritual enemies far more powerful than we. Christ is portrayed as our champion who by his death and resurrection defeats our foes. As a result there is real victory in the Christian life (Col. 2:15; Heb. 2:14–15; Rev. 5:5).

Fifth, the picture of re-creation comes from the sphere of creation. We need to be restored because Adam's fall brought sin, death, and disorder into the world of humankind. Christ is portrayed as the second Adam who by his obedience unto death and resurrection reverses the effects of Adam's sin. The result is the restoration of our lost glory and dominion (Rom. 5:18–19; 1 Cor. 15:22; Col. 1:18).

Sixth, the theme of sacrifice comes from the sphere of worship. We need to be cleansed because we are defiled by our sin. Christ is portrayed as the Great High Priest who offers himself as a sacrifice and lives forever. As a result believers are purified (Eph. 5:2, 25–26; Heb. 9:12, 14; 10:14).

I conclude with three emphases. First, the six pictures do not portray six different realities. Rather, they are six different ways of looking at the same reality—the salvation that Christ accomplished. Why, then, does Scripture paint six major pictures? The answer seems to lie, as Leon Morris suggested years ago, in the Bible's depiction of sin. The multiplicity of images of salvation corresponds to the multiplicity of the images of sin.[15] The many ways of speaking about our plight correspond to the many ways God in his grace comes to our aid. Sin is so odious and salvation so glorious that God depicts them both in a variety of corresponding ways.

Each need, each way of describing sin, corresponds to God's way of overturning sin in Christ's work. So God overturns alienation with Christ's reconciliation. He overcomes bondage with Christ's redemption. He overturns guilt with Christ's propitiation. He overcomes our mighty enemies with a mightier champion's victory. He overturns Adam's disobedience with the second Adam's obedience. He overcomes our spiritual defilement with Christ's

---

[15] Leon Morris, *The Cross in the New Testament* (Grand Rapids: Eerdmans, 1965), 395.

cleansing blood. But the key point is that these are various ways of communicating the same truth—Jesus saves sinners through his death and resurrection!

Second, each one of the six major pictures is noteworthy. Scripture presents Christ's saving work using more than six themes, but I identify six main pictures. Each picture is important to gain a good understanding of the cross and empty tomb. Thus it is a mistake to champion one picture and downplay the others. For a full-orbed appreciation of the work of Christ, one must explore all six pictures. The picture of Adam/new creation has been the most neglected of the six, in my experience.

Third, though every picture is valuable and none is to be ignored, I conclude that penal substitution is foundational to the others.[16]

The Directions to Which Christ's Saving Work Points

A fruitful way of thinking about Christ's saving accomplishment is to consider it in terms of the directions to which it points. It points in three directions: toward God himself (an upward direction), toward our enemies (a downward direction), and toward human beings and the whole creation (a horizontal direction). All three directions are important. Christ's saving accomplishment, which centers in his death and resurrection, affects God himself, our spiritual enemies, and human beings and the creation.

The horizontal direction. The direction involving human beings is more prevalent in Scripture than the others. The six pictures tally scores of passages that tell of God's rescuing sinners through the Mediator's work. And some of those pictures teach that because of Christ's saving work there will be a new heaven and a new earth (Rom. 8:19–22; Eph. 1:19–20).

The upward direction. This direction is the most fundamental and profound. Christ's work influenced the life of God himself. The initiative for the work of Christ belongs to God the Trinity. That means God acts through the cross and empty tomb to influence himself. He satisfies his justice, reconciles himself, is pleased with the second Adam's obedience, and purifies heaven. God in Christ affects God.

This is profound for several reasons. First, it speaks to the greatness of God's grace in the initiative and the accomplishment of salvation. This story was not conceived on earth by human beings. It was conceived in heaven by God. What kind of a world religion posits that God became a man to die to

---

[16] For a defense of this point, see Peterson, *Salvation Accomplished by the Son*, 557–60.

satisfy the demands of his own character and thereby save his creatures? A divinely revealed, unique, and gracious one!

A second reason is the mystery of the incarnation itself. If we cannot fully understand the incarnation, how will we fully understand the cross and empty tomb? Third, the concept of God's entering into covenant with Abraham and eventually with us in the new covenant provides a framework for understanding how covenant keepers or breakers influence God. But at the end of the day, we confess we are out of our depth trying to understand God's influencing himself through Christ's cross and empty tomb because, although Christ is a covenant-keeping man, he also is God. These things are beyond understanding. They are too much for us.

This upward element is foundational to the horizontal and downward ones. Without the Godward direction of the work of Christ, the other two directions would not exist. They are very important but derivative of the influence of Christ's work on God himself. Because God propitiates himself, he defeats our foes and rescues us and the creation. I agree with Sinclair Ferguson: "A comprehensively biblical exposition of the work of Christ recognizes that the atonement, which terminates on God (in propitiation) and on man (in forgiveness), also terminates on Satan (in the destruction of his sway over believers). And it does this last precisely because it does the first two."[17] I would simply add that the atonement terminates on man and Satan because it terminates on God. In my terminology: both the horizontal and the downward aspects depend on the upward one.

The downward direction. This direction shows the effects of Jesus's death and resurrection on our enemies—it destroys them! Christus Victor is derivative of the upward direction. Ferguson says it well, referring to Gustav Aulén's *Christus Victor*, the book whose title became a label for a view of the atonement:

> In this respect, Gustav Aulén's view was seriously inadequate. He displaced the motif of penal satisfaction with that of victory. But, as we have seen, in Scripture the satisfaction of divine justice, the forgiveness of our sins, and Christ's defeat of Satan are not mutually exclusive but complementary. Each is an essential dimension of Christ's work. Each is vital for our salvation, and each provides an aspect of the atonement from which the other aspects may be seen with greater clarity and richness.

---

[17] Sinclair Ferguson, "Christus Victor et Propitiator: The Death of Christ, Substitute and Conqueror," in *For the Fame of God's Name: Essays in Honor of John Piper*, ed. Sam Storms and Justin Taylor (Wheaton, IL: Crossway, 2010), 185.

Moreover, these aspects are interrelated at the profoundest level. For the New Testament the dramatic aspect of the atonement involves a triumph that is secured through propitiation. Aulén therefore failed to recognize that in setting the dramatic view over against the penal view of the atonement he inevitably enervated the dramatic view of its true dynamic.[18]

This magnificent Christ, whose person we have summarized, was the one who accomplished a saving work like none else. Scripture interprets his nine saving events with six major pictures. His profound work negatively affects God's enemies and ours and positively affects God, believers, and the whole creation. And here is the whole point of this chapter's content up until now: it is to this Christ and his work that believers are joined when they are united to Christ by grace through faith!

Christ the Object of Saving Faith

Considered in its broadest terms, union with Christ is an overarching soteriological concept that includes election, Christ's atonement, the application of salvation, and its consummation. Indeed, "union with Christ is the central truth of the whole doctrine of salvation," as John Murray insists.[19]

While it is important to conceive of union with Christ in such a wide scope so as not to truncate it, it is also important to focus on actual union with Christ. Calvin's words in this regard are justly famous: "We must understand that as long as Christ remains outside of us, and we are separated from him, all that he has suffered and done for the salvation of the human race remains useless and of no value for us."[20]

Having set forth Christ's person and work, we are ready to talk about our becoming "actual partakers in the application of redemption" (Murray) and about Christ's no longer remaining outside us so that we continue to be separated from him (Calvin). It is time to consider actual union with Christ. This is the chief work of the Holy Spirit in salvation, as we have seen.[21] Here, while keeping the Spirit in view, I will underscore that actual union with Christ occurs when by God's sovereign grace sinners trust Christ as Lord and Savior.

---

[18] Ibid.
[19] John Murray, *Redemption Accomplished and Applied* (Grand Rapids: Eerdmans, 1955), 170.
[20] Calvin, *Institutes*, 1:537 (3.1.1).
[21] See chapter 24, "The Most Important Work of the Holy Spirit."

God's Grace Is Unconquerable

We will dwell on God's effective grace that brings us into actual union with Christ. *Irresistible grace* is the term used to describe God's grace that successfully brings sinners to salvation. The word *irresistible* gives the impression that God brings people into his kingdom kicking and screaming, but most often he is more like a lover who gently woos and draws us to himself.[22] Noting that many sinners do resist God's grace all their lives (but none of the elect "successfully" so resist), Hoekema wisely suggests the synonyms *invincible* or *unconquerable* grace for irresistible grace.[23] I previously offered five lines of biblical evidence for God's invincible grace and summarize them here.[24]

John 6:37 and Acts 13:48. God's choosing for salvation results in saving faith. Jesus teaches this: "All that the Father gives me will come to me, and whoever comes to me I will never cast out" (John 6:37). To understand these words we need to explore two ideas. When Jesus speaks of the Father's "giving" people to him, he tells of the Father's choosing people for salvation (cf. 17:2, 6, 9–10, 24). This is seen most clearly in Jesus's words to the Father in 17:2: "You have given him [Jesus] authority over all flesh, to give eternal life to all whom you have given him." Jesus says the Father gave him authority over all humankind so that Jesus can give eternal life "to all whom" the Father has "given him." Jesus is Lord over all people but grants salvation only to those whom the Father chose and gave to him.

We also need to understand people's "coming" to Jesus. He shows what this means when saying, "I am the bread of life; whoever comes to me shall not hunger, and whoever believes in me shall never thirst" (6:35). "Coming" to Jesus is parallel to believing in him. To "come" to him means to trust him as Savior.

These understandings for "giving" and "coming" help us better comprehend verse 37: "All that the Father gives me [chooses and entrusts to me] will come to me [believe in me], and whoever comes to me I will never cast out." Jesus teaches that those whom the Father chose for salvation *will* believe in Jesus. He also promises never to cast them out; that is, he will keep them saved until the end. When Jesus says that all those chosen will believe in him, he teaches the idea of unconquerable grace. God's grace successfully saves the people whom he chose.

[22] My students have taught me that God *did* bring some of them to himself as kicking and screaming recalcitrant souls!
[23] Anthony A. Hoekema, *Saved by Grace* (Grand Rapids: Eerdmans, 1989), 105.
[24] Robert A. Peterson and Michael D. Williams, *Why I Am Not an Arminian* (Downers Grove, IL: InterVarsity, 2004), 185–89.

We see God's choosing as resulting in saving faith also in Acts 13:48. On their first missionary journey, Paul and Barnabas minister in Antioch in Pisidia. At first their preaching to the Jews leads to a positive response, but a week later jealous Jewish leaders stir up the people against them (vv. 42–45). As a result they turn from the Jews to preach to the Gentiles (as the messianic prophecy in Isa. 49:6 implied). A dramatic response ensues: "When the Gentiles heard this, they began rejoicing and glorifying the word of the Lord" (Acts 13:48), and many put their faith in Christ. Luke's explanation is intriguing: "As many as were appointed to eternal life believed" (v. 48). People "appointed to eternal life" are those whom God chose for salvation. Luke says that as many as were chosen by God "believed." God's election results in saving faith; his grace is invincible.

John 6:44. The Father's drawing is effective. Jesus shocks his hearers: "No one can come to me unless the Father who sent me draws him." We saw that "coming" to Jesus means believing in him (according to v. 35). "Drawing" means God's bringing people to Jesus. It is John's language for Paul's idea of calling in Romans 8:28–30 and 9:22–24, both of which speak not of a general gospel call to all people but of a special and effective call to those whom God chose. Jesus teaches that no one can believe in him unless God the Father effectively brings (draws) them to Jesus. God's grace irresistibly summons people to faith in Jesus for salvation.

Acts 16:14. God opens hearts. On Paul's second missionary journey, he, Silas, and Timothy preached the gospel in Philippi to a group of women who had gathered to pray. Luke tells the story: "One who heard us was a woman named Lydia, from the city of Thyatira, a seller of purple goods, who was a worshiper of God. The Lord opened her heart to pay attention to what was said by Paul" (v. 14). God works in Lydia's heart to make her receptive to the gospel message. She believes in Christ, is baptized, and prevails upon the missionary team to spend the night in her home (v. 15). Luke thus simply and powerfully shows God's effective grace at work.

2 Corinthians 4:6. God illuminates people blinded by Satan. Paul describes the horrible plight of unsaved persons. They cannot believe the gospel because the "god of this world has blinded the minds of the unbelievers, to keep them from seeing the light of the gospel of the glory of Christ, who is the image of God" (v. 4). Satan, who is far stronger than human beings, is active in unsaved persons' minds to prevent them from trusting Christ as offered in the gospel. How then can they be saved? It is impossible for fallen humans, but nothing is impossible for God! The same almighty God who called light out of darkness in creation "has shone in our hearts to give the light of the knowledge of the glory of God in the face of Jesus Christ" (v. 6). The Creator is the same as the Redeemer. God, who is stronger than Satan and whose word effectively created the heavens and the earth, effectively uses the gospel message to illuminate those lost in Satan's darkness. God's grace cannot be defeated by Satan or unbelievers. It is unconquerable.

1 John 5:1. Regeneration unfailingly leads to faith. John writes to strengthen his readers' assurance of salvation (1 John 5:13). Five times he speaks of the results of the new life that regeneration brings in the lives of his readers. God's grace bears fruit in those born again.

> Everyone who practices righteousness has been born of him. (2:29)

> No one born of God makes a practice of sinning, for God's seed abides in him, and he cannot keep on sinning because he has been born of God. (3:9)

> Beloved, let us love one another, for love is from God, and whoever loves has been born of God and knows God. (4:7)

> Everyone who believes that Jesus is the Christ has been born of God. (5:1)

> We know that everyone who has been born of God does not keep on sinning. (5:18)

Three times John says that regeneration results in holiness (2:29; 3:9; 5:18). Once he says that the new life shows up in love (4:7). And once he says that regeneration produces faith: "Everyone who believes that Jesus is the Christ has been born of God" (5:1). Some misunderstand this verse to teach that faith is the cause of the new birth. But this is backward. In each of the five passages regeneration is the cause of the effect with which it is associated—whether godliness, love, or, in 5:1, faith. No one would say that holiness or love is the cause of regeneration. Rather, because of God's grace in regeneration, all those born again live for God, love him and other believers, and believe that Jesus is the Christ. That is, they trust him as God's promised Deliverer. Once again Scripture teaches that God's grace is irresistible; it always attains its goal in the lives of God's people.

Summary. What is the goal of God's invincible grace in people's lives? As the five examples just cited show, God's grace chooses them so they come to (believe in) Jesus (John 6:37), appoints them to eternal life so they believe (Acts 13:48), draws them so they come to (believe in) Jesus (John 6:44), opens hearts so hearers pay attention to and believe the gospel (Acts 16:14), overcomes Satanic blinding so they believe the gospel (2 Cor. 4:6), and leads them to believe in Jesus (1 John 5:1). In sum, God's unconquerable grace produces faith in Christ. Without fail, it moves sinners to trust Jesus as Lord and Savior. Moreover, Spirit-generated faith in him is the means of entering into union with Christ and his benefits. This means that faith union in Christ is the only way of salvation.

Faith in Christ Saves

The person and work of Jesus Christ are God's provision for salvation. We partake of Christ and his salvation when we are united to him by God's irresistible grace through faith in the gospel. This means that faith in Christ saves because it joins us to Christ.

In the Old Testament God alone is the proper object of his people's faith. This is apparent in the life of Abraham, the father of the Jews: "He believed the LORD, and he counted it to him as righteousness" (Gen. 15:6). It is also evident in God's dealings with Israel and Egypt in the exodus. At the stretching out of Moses's same hand that parted the waters so the Israelites could cross the sea, the waters crashed on the pursuing Egyptian army, killing them all. We then read: "Thus the LORD saved Israel that day from the hand of the Egyptians, and Israel saw the Egyptians dead on the seashore. Israel saw the great power that the LORD used against the Egyptians, so the people feared the LORD, and they believed in the LORD and in his servant Moses" (Ex. 14:30–31).

In the New Testament, God remains the primary object of faith. Jesus himself told his disciples, "Have faith in God" (Mark 11:22). Furthermore, "faith toward God" is one of the foundational principles of the Christian faith (Heb. 6:1).

The New Testament, however, declares an additional message. Over and over it portrays Jesus as the proper object of saving faith:

> Jesus came into Galilee, proclaiming the gospel of God, and saying, "The time is fulfilled, and the kingdom of God is at hand; repent and believe in the gospel." (Mark 1:14–15)

> For God so loved the world, that he gave his only Son, that whoever believes in him should not perish but have eternal life. (John 3:16)

Whoever believes in the Son has eternal life; whoever does not obey the Son shall not see life, but the wrath of God remains on him. (John 3:36)

I said, "Who are you, Lord?" And the Lord said, "I am Jesus whom you are persecuting. . . . I am sending you to open their eyes, so that they may turn from darkness to light and from the power of Satan to God, that they may receive forgiveness of sins and a place among those who are sanctified by faith in me." (Acts 26:15, 17–18)

Now the righteousness of God has been manifested apart from the law, although the Law and the Prophets bear witness to it—the righteousness of God through faith in Jesus Christ for all who believe. (Rom. 3:21–22)

We know that a person is not justified by works of the law but through faith in Jesus Christ, so we also have believed in Christ Jesus, in order to be justified by faith in Christ and not by works of the law. (Gal. 2:16)

Though you have not seen him [Jesus Christ], you love him. Though you do not now see him, you believe in him and rejoice with joy that is inexpressible and filled with glory (1 Pet. 1:8)

This is his commandment, that we believe in the name of his Son Jesus Christ and love one another, just as he has commanded us. (1 John 3:23)

Scripture is unmistakable: Jesus is the only proper object of faith that saves. He himself says "Believe in God; believe also in me. . . . I am the way, and the truth, and the life. No one comes to the Father except through me" (John 14:1, 6), and Peter proclaims, "There is no other name under heaven given among men by which we must be saved" (Acts 4:12). John Frame speaks precious truth: "Scripture presents Jesus, not primarily as a model or example of faith, but as the object of faith. We believe in Jesus for salvation (John 3:15–16; 6:29; 8:24; 16:9; 17:20; Acts 3:16; 10:43; 16:31; 1 John 3:23; 5:13)."[25]

Evangelical Christians agree that Jesus is the only Savior of the world. They unanimously reject pluralism, the view that all religions lead to God. But not all evangelicals agree that people must *believe* in Jesus for salvation. Inclusivists, while holding that Jesus is the only Savior and that no one will be saved apart from his death and resurrection, open the door for people to be saved by Jesus apart from the gospel. Some posit that God will count Jesus's

---

[25] John M. Frame, *The Doctrine of God*, A Theology of Lordship (Phillipsburg, NJ: P&R, 2002), 679–80.

saving work to those who respond positively to general revelation, to God's law written on the hearts, and the like.[26]

Exclusivists, on the other hand, though they agree with inclusivists that only Jesus saves, disagree with them by maintaining that faith in Christ in this life is necessary for salvation.[27] I concur with Andreas Köstenberger, who, at the end of his essay "The Gospel for All Nations," draws five conclusions, which I summarize:

1. The gospel is God's saving message to a world living in darkness and a humanity lost in its sin.
2. Acceptance of the gospel is not optional for salvation but rather required, owing to pervasive human sinfulness.
3. The gospel is not vaguely theological, as if it were amenable to various ways of salvation depending on a person's belief in a particular kind of god, or depending on the degree to which people were able to hear the gospel presented in a clear way; it is decidedly and concretely christo-logical, that is, centered on the salvation provided through the vicarious cross-death of the Lord Jesus Christ.
4. The messianic motif pervading all of Scripture and centering in the Lord Jesus Christ coupled with the risen Jesus's "Great Commission" for his fol-lowers to go and disciple the nations inextricably link an understanding of the gospel as the exclusive message of salvation in Jesus Christ with the church's mandate to engage in missionary outreach.
5. In light of the clear biblical passages examined above, and in light of the strong and pervasive trajectory of references to the gospel throughout Scripture, there seems to be no proper biblical way of salvation other than through explicit faith in Jesus Christ.[28]

Conclusion

This chapter has concentrated on the Christ to whom we are united in salva-tion. We explored an orthodox Christology, including the Son of God's preex-istence, incarnation, deity, humanity, and unipersonality. Then we pondered the work of this unique person of Christ. While stressing that the center of his saving accomplishment is his death and resurrection, we acknowledged

---

[26] The best evangelical arguments for inclusivism are those of Terrance L. Tiessen, *Who Can Be Saved? Reassessing Salvation in Christ and World Religions* (Downers Grove, IL: InterVarsity, 2004).

[27] See Christopher W. Morgan and Robert A. Peterson, eds., *Faith Comes by Hearing: A Response to Inclusivism* (Downers Grove, IL: IVP Academic, 2008).

[28] Ibid., 217–18.

that he performs a total of nine saving deeds, embracing two essential pre-
requisites to the cross and empty tomb (incarnation and sinless life) and five
essential results of his death and resurrection (ascension, session, giving the
Spirit at Pentecost, intercession, and second coming). These nine events constitute one saving work of the divine-human Christ.

Events are not self-interpreting, not even God's events, so he graciously
explains the meaning of Christ's saving work. He does so by painting six large
pictures in Scripture. Christ is the reconciler who through his work makes
peace between God and us and between us and God. He is the Redeemer who
buys us out of slavery to sin by his blood. He is our substitute, crucified to take
the penalty that we sinners deserve and raised for our justification. He is the
mighty champion who defeats our foes—the Devil, sin, and death. He is the
second Adam who by his obedience unto death and resurrection overcomes
the effects of Adam's sin. He is our Great High Priest who offers himself in
sacrifice to cleanse all believers' from the stain of their sin and who lives to
"save to the uttermost those who draw near to God through him" (Heb. 7:25).

This is the marvelous biblical Christ and a summary of what he did to save
his people from their sins. His saving work was directed toward God himself,
our enemies, us, and even the heavens and earth. And here is precisely where
actual union with Christ comes in. Though he is the unique God-man who
performs the astounding saving deeds we just rehearsed, all he is and has accomplished do not benefit us until we are joined to him in salvation. Trevor
Hart summarizes Calvin's attempt to combine Christ's saving accomplishment
and union: he "seeks to sketch a theology in which both substitution and
participation are central, and in which both rest upon the saving union which
God has established between this man and others."[29]

Actual union with Christ is the work of the Holy Spirit in effectively applying the grace of God to everyone who believes on the Lord Jesus Christ. This
grace is unconquerable and never fails to unite the elect to their Savior. By
God's invincible grace through faith we no longer are separated from Christ;
he no longer remains only outside us. Now we are spiritually connected to his
person and work. In faith union we partake of him and all his saving benefits.
The next three chapters will explore some of those superb benefits for God's
people.

---

[29] Trevor Hart, "Humankind in Christ and Christ in Humankind: Salvation as Participation in Our Substitute in the
Theology of John Calvin," *Scottish Journal of Theology* 42 (1989): 81.

Chapter 26

Union with Christ
in the Church

Our study of union with Christ would be incomplete without giving attention to the church and Christian living. For this reason, the next three chapters will tackle the church, its ordinances of baptism and the Lord's Supper, and the Christian life, all viewed in terms of union with Christ.

The Church

Because Paul is Scripture's main theologian of union with Christ, we expect him to say the most about union and the church, and he does not disappoint. Nevertheless, other biblical writers have important things to say about the topic, namely, Peter in his two epistles and John in his Gospel, first epistle, and Revelation.

- The church is a living temple.
- The church abides in the Father and the Son.
- The church is "in Christ."
- The church participates in Jesus's story.
- The church is the body of Christ.
- The church is the bride of Christ.

The Church Is a Living Temple

The apostles Peter and Paul paint the picture of a building-temple to render the people of God as a living sanctuary in which the Trinity is worshiped.

According to Peter

Peter mixes metaphors to present the church as a building that is alive, a living temple. Recalling Jesus's reference to himself as the "cornerstone" of Psalm 118:22 (in Matt. 21:42), Peter presents Christ as the "cornerstone" who saves those who believe and judges those who reject him (1 Pet. 2:6–8). Indeed, Peter creatively presents the risen Christ as the "living stone" (v. 4). The apostle thereby speaks of Christ as alive from death and the source of spiritual life for his people (cf. 1:3, 23).

Peter extends his "stone" imagery to encompass God's people: "As you come to him . . . you yourselves like living stones are being built up as a spiritual house" (2:4–5). Peter depicts believers in Christ, the "living stone," as "living stones" themselves. The same adjective applied to both Christ and his people indicates that the life of Christians is derived from Christ's life. They are living because of their relationship to Christ; they receive spiritual life from him.

Peter's focus is not so much on believers individually as on their corporate identity. When joined to the living stone they become living stones joined to all other living stones. Union with Christ is a principle of both individual and communal salvation. God uses these stones to build a building, a "spiritual house," where believers serve as believer-priests to "offer spiritual sacrifices acceptable to God through Jesus Christ" (v. 5). Christians are both temple and priesthood, and therefore union serves the worship of God through his new covenant Mediator.

Peter thus portrays the church as an organism. It is alive with the resurrection life of Jesus, the source of believers' eternal life. Through union with him, they are "born again to a living hope" (1:3) and form the church, a living temple where God is worshiped.

According to Paul

Paul also presents the church as a building, a temple. Against the background of Solomon's magnificent temple, he audaciously tells the Corinthian Christians twice in short compass, "You are God's temple" (1 Cor. 3:16; cf. v. 17). Paul includes a point not found in Peter—this temple is the place where the Spirit dwells.[1] Occupying the place of the god or goddess in a Greco-Roman temple, the Holy Spirit is the Deity in the temple. As such he connects

---

[1] Peter, of course, mentions the Holy Spirit in his letters. My point is that he does not make an explicit connection between the Spirit and the church.

believers to Christ: "In him you also are being built together into a dwelling place for God by the Spirit" (Eph. 2:22).

In fact, in the four passages treating the church as a temple (1 Cor. 3:16–17; 6:19–20; 2 Cor. 6:16; Eph. 2:19–22), Paul affirms it is God's presence that makes a church a church. "Corporately the Christian community is the new divine sanctuary, the place where the living God most fully expresses his presence," as Harris explains.[2]

Three times in Ephesians 2:21–22 Paul teaches incorporation into Christ: he is the one "in whom" the building grows into a temple; "in him" it is being built into God's dwelling place; and this holy temple is "in the Lord" (vv. 21–22). As in Peter, so in Paul: God brings about this union to promote Trinitarian worship in this temple, for believing Jews and Gentiles "through him [Christ] . . . have access in one Spirit to the Father" (v. 18).

Although Peter is more creative and overt, Paul too presents this spiritual temple of God's people as dynamic and organic (vv. 21–22). He portrays a building growing into a temple before our eyes. Furthermore, this dynamic action continues—believers "are being built" together increasingly by the Spirit.

Like Peter, Paul affirms that God dwells in his people individually, but his emphasis falls on his dwelling in them communally as God's temple. Union with Christ results in this marvelous reality—Christians *are* the temple of the living God! The Holy Spirit builds this living temple and occupies the place of God in it. God's presence is what makes a temple a temple. Paul depicts this temple, made up of God's holy people, where the Trinity is present and worshiped, as being built before our eyes (Eph. 2:22).

Though the two apostles have different emphases, Peter and Paul have important things in common when they present the church as a building-temple:

You yourselves like living stones *are being built up* as a spiritual house. (1 Pet. 2:5)

In him you *also are being built together* into a dwelling place for God by the Spirit. (Eph. 2:22)

Peter and Paul portray God's people as a temple, use the divine passive to imply that God is the builder, and use a progressive verb to communicate a building process. According to both apostles, the church is a living temple.

---

[2] Murray J. Harris, *The Second Epistle to the Corinthians*, New International Greek Testament Commentary (Grand Rapids: Eerdmans, 2005), 505.

The Church Abides in the Father and the Son

According to the Gospel of John

Using very different idiom and imagery, John presents a picture of the church that somewhat overlaps Peter and Paul's image of the church as a living temple. The church mutually indwells or abides in the Father and the Son. In order to understand this theme we must treat another one—the mutual indwelling or abiding of the Father and the Son in one another. In his Farewell Discourse and final prayer Jesus teaches that the Father is in him and indwells him:

> Do you not believe that I am in the Father and *the Father is in me*? The words that I say to you I do not speak on my own authority, but *the Father who dwells in me* does his works. (14:10)

> The glory that you have given me I have given to them, that they may be one even as we are one, I in them and *you in me*, that they may become perfectly one, so that the world may know that you sent me and loved them even as you loved me. (17:22–23)

In the same places and in the Good Shepherd Discourse Jesus teaches that he is in the Father, and he and the Father are in one another:

> If I am not doing the works of my Father, then do not believe me; but if I do them, even though you do not believe me, believe the works, that you may know and understand that *the Father is in me and I am in the Father*. (10:37–38)

> Do you not believe that *I am in the Father and the Father is in me*? The words that I say to you I do not speak on my own authority, but the Father who dwells in me does his works. Believe me that *I am in the Father and the Father is in me*, or else believe on account of the works themselves. (14:10–11)

> In that day you will know that *I am in my Father*, and you in me, and I in you. (14:20)

> I do not ask for these only, but also for those who will believe in me through their word, that they may all be one, just as *you, Father, are in me, and I in you*, that they also may be in us, so that the world may believe that you have sent me. (17:20–21)

The Father and Son indwell one another. Another way of saying this is that they are "in" one another. They mutually exist in one another. They share the divine life. Each person of the Trinity—Father, Son, and Holy Spirit—is wholly God.[3] That is why Jesus says that seeing him means seeing the invisible Father (14:9). The fact that God has eternally existed in three persons is a mystery superseding human intelligence. The mutual indwelling of the divine persons is a mystery within the mystery of the Holy Trinity, a mystery of mysteries, if you will. Theologians call it *perichoresis* (Greek), *circumincession*, or *co-inherence*.[4]

I began by saying that the Father is in the Son, and then I said the Father and Son indwell one another. Now we see that the Father and the Son are in believers as a precursor to saying that believers are, in a sense, in the Father and the Son. The Son is in believers:

> In that day you will know that I am in my Father, and you in me, and *I in you*. (14:20)

> The glory that you have given me I have given to them, that they may be one even as we are one, *I in them* and you in me, that they may become perfectly one, so that the world may know that you sent me and loved them even as you loved me. (17:22–23)

> I made known to them your name, and I will continue to make it known, that the love with which you have loved me may be in them, and *I in them*. (17:26)

In fact, the Father and the Son are in believers. We learn this from Jesus's message that he and the Father will make their home with believers. In 14:1–3 Jesus spoke of returning to heaven to prepare rooms for the disciples in the Father's house. Now he employs the image of a home to speak of his and the Father's coming to the disciples to make their home with them on earth: "If anyone loves me, he will keep my word, and my Father will love him, and we will come to him and make our home with him" (v. 23). Raymond Brown is right: "Here it ["dwelling place"] is used for the indwelling of the Father and the Son with the believer."[5]

---

[3] Working systematically, we include the Holy Spirit, although John does not explicitly say this. He ordinarily relegates the Spirit to a post-Pentecostal ministry (7:39; 14:17).

[4] "Circumincessio: *circumincession* or *coinherence*; used as a synonym of the Greek *perichoresis* . . . or *emperichoresis*. . . . *Circumincessio* refers primarily to the coinherence of the persons of the Trinity in the divine essence and in each other, but it can also indicate the coinherence of Christ's divine and human natures in their communion or personal union." Richard A. Muller, *Dictionary of Latin and Greek Theological Terms* (Grand Rapids: Baker, 1985), 67.

[5] Raymond E. Brown, *The Gospel according to John: XIII–XXI*, Anchor Bible (Garden City, NY: Doubleday, 1970), 648.

Jesus defines the church as the people who indwell the Father and the Son. Jesus and believers are in one another—they mutually abide in one another:

> In that day you will know that I am in my Father, and *you in me, and I in you.* (14:20)

> Whoever feeds on my flesh and drinks my blood *abides in me, and I in him.* (6:56)

> *Abide in me, and I in you.* As the branch cannot bear fruit by itself, unless it abides in the vine, neither can you, unless *you abide in me.* (15:4).

Most remarkably, one text says believers are in the Father and the Son: "I do not ask for these only, but also for those who will believe in me through their word, that they may all be one, just as you, Father, are in me, and I in you, *that they also may be in us,* so that the world may believe that you have sent me" (17:20–21).

It is amazing that Jesus sometimes uses the language of mutual indwelling with reference to himself (or himself and the Father) *and believers*! There are great differences between the way the persons of the Trinity mutually indwell one another and the way they and believers do this. The differences include that fact that the persons of the Trinity are divine and able ontologically to indwell one another—so that there is one God eternally existing in three persons. And this mutual indwelling is eternal. We maintain the Creator/creature distinction and insist that the persons of the Trinity do not share their deity with us. Moreover, our fellowship with them had a beginning (though it will last forever).

But there are similarities too between the Trinity's mutual indwelling and ours with the divine persons. These include the fact that the divine persons have fellowship with us (1 John 1:3), and we with them, due to the Trinity's grace! The initiative and glory belong to them alone, but the fellowship that results is also ours. It is mysterious and marvelous indeed to try to understand how Christians are "in" the Trinity. In a way fitting for creatures and only by grace, through and in Christ we participate in the divine love and life the Trinitarian persons have always shared.

Furthermore, it is noteworthy that John's purpose involves the disciples' witness in the world. Twice in John 17, after mentioning our mutual indwelling with the Father and/or the Son, John says:

. . . that they also may be in us, so that the world may believe that you have sent me. (v. 21)

. . . I in them and you in me . . . so that the world may know that you sent me and loved them even as you loved me. (v. 23)

According to 1 John

Frequently 1 John speaks of believers' abiding in Christ. This is to be viewed as extension and application of Jesus's teaching in John's Gospel. Yarbrough's summary is fitting: abiding "has come to be almost ubiquitous shorthand in 1 John for believers' habitual personal attachment to Christ (e.g., 2:6, 28) or for the presence in believers of God's saving truth (e.g., 2:24, 27; 3:9)."[6] Hand in hand with this warm personal relationship with God and Christ come moral obligations (cf. 2:6; 3:6). First John does not endorse easy-believism but is ethically rigorous.

John elevates believers' personal relationship with God in Christ and their corresponding ethical responsibility by teaching that abiding is reciprocal between God and his people. Twice 1 John says that God "abides in us" (3:24; 4:12). Four times it speaks of this abiding with God as reciprocal:

Whoever keeps his commandments abides in God, and God in him. (3:24)

By this we know that we abide in him and he in us, because he has given us of his Spirit. (4:13)

Whoever confesses that Jesus is the Son of God, God abides in him, and he in God. (4:15)

God is love, and whoever abides in love abides in God, and God abides in him. (4:16)

These passages have an important role because they tell of the mutual abiding between God and Christ and Christians. This is the amazing truth of believers' sharing in a certain sense by grace through faith in the divine perichoresis we found in John's Gospel. And, as noted earlier, such a privilege carries ethical connotations. John combines mutual-abiding language with moral obligation. Reciprocal abiding is true of those characterized by obedi-

---

[6] Robert W. Yarbrough, *1–3 John*, Baker Exegetical Commentary on the New Testament (Grand Rapids: Baker Academic, 2008), 202.

ence to God's commands (1 John 3:24), confession that Jesus is God's Son (4:15), and continuing in love (3:14; 4:16).

John says that God or Christ is "in" us and we are "in" Christ, and also says that we "abide" in Christ or God and that Christ or God "abides" in us. The two are basically synonymous. Twice, referring to Jesus, 1 John says, "We are in him":

> By this we may know that *we are in him*: whoever says he abides in him ought to walk in the same way in which he walked. (2:5–6)

> We know that the Son of God has come and has given us understanding, so that we may know him who is true; and *we are in him* who is true, in his Son Jesus Christ. (5:20)

The expression "we are in him [Jesus]" is one of 1 John's ways of talking about possessing salvation. To be an authentic believer is to be in the Son, to exist in union with him. In the first passage, being "in him" is inseparable from obeying God. In the second passage, being "in him" is correlative with knowing Christ cognitively and personally. To be in the Son of God is a *sine qua non* of salvation according to 1 John. It presupposes being indwelt by the Son, and it means dwelling in or being in him. And this takes us back to the Fourth Gospel's exalted teaching of mutual indwelling, which is an aspect of the second metaphor for union in 1 John.

According to 1 and 2 Thessalonians

Although it is commonly neglected, Paul too speaks to believers' being in the Father and the Son. He does so only in the first verses of 1 and 2 Thessalonians. Here he depicts Christians as "in God the Father and the Lord Jesus Christ," where the preposition "in" goes with both Father and Son. Though some discount the possibility that Paul writes of union with the Father and the Son, the apostle appears in fact to do so. F. F. Bruce notes that even as "in Christ" and it parallels are frequently used by Paul to denote union with Christ, so "here, then 'in God the Father' must be understood in the same way."[7]

I do not claim that Paul develops this idea as John does in his Gospel and first epistle. But it is noteworthy that there is more agreement between John and Paul on this matter than has usually been acknowledged. When Paul

---

[7] F. F. Bruce, *1 & 2 Thessalonians*, Word Biblical Commentary (Waco, TX: Word, 1982), 7.

speaks of the Thessalonian believers' being in the Father and the Son, he affirms the rudiments of a theology of mutual indwelling between believers and the Trinitarian persons.

Conclusion

When John depicts the church as abiding in the Father and the Son, he gives us an exalted and mysterious teaching. John's notion of mutual indwelling is perhaps the most mysterious aspect of the mysterious doctrine of union with the living Christ. On our own we would never have conceived of our mutually indwelling the Trinity. But that is what the Fourth Gospel reveals. By grace through faith we participate in the life of the Trinitarian persons and share in their love for one another and us! This is staggering.

Abiding in Christ the Bread of Life or abiding in Christ the Vine to be fruitful are themes related to eternal life. Like Peter's and Paul's depiction of the church as a living temple, the church as abiding in God is organic and dynamic. Through the work of Christ and in union with him, the church shares the life of the Trinity. It abides in Christ, continuing in a relationship of love with him.

The Gospel of John applies mutual indwelling or abiding to the church's mission. Christians are to share the love of the Trinity with those who don't know Christ. First John applies abiding relationally and ethically. Those who abide in the Father and the Son love, know, and obey them.

The Church Is "in Christ"

In our summary of union with Christ in Paul, we explored his use of "in Christ" language, acknowledging considerable help from Constantine Campbell's *Paul and Union with Christ*.[8] Here we consider insights of that summary that pertain to the church. It is a fallacy to regard every use of "in Christ" and equivalents ("in him," "in whom," "in the Lord") as referring to union with Christ in a narrow and direct sense. Most uses contain other nuances or shades of meaning.

These many and varied nuances are worth exploring, but most importantly for our present purposes is the one constant that holds true: regardless of nuance, each usage of "in Christ" language makes a connection to Christ.

---

[8] See pp. 185–95. Constantine R. Campbell, *Paul and Union with Christ: An Exegetical and Theological Study* (Grand Rapids: Zondervan, 2012).

This was true even for those uses of "in Christ" that did not narrowly and directly speak of union. We can safely say that Paul commonly speaks of the people of God, the church, in terms of "in Christ" language, and when he does, he has in mind a link between Christ's person and work and the church.[9]

Various Nuances

We found these diverse shades of meaning significant because they highlight the person and work of Christ applied to individuals and churches. Their diversity underscores different expressions of the application of salvation. Salvation always occurs "in Christ," always relating to who he is and what he has accomplished. And this relation is expressed in many ways, out of which I chose to examine agency, association, cause, instrument, manner, object of faith, periphrasis for "Christian," and realm.

I selected eight major nuances out of twenty or more. Both agency and instrumentality present Christ as the only Mediator between God and human beings. He alone is God's instrument in bringing salvation to his people. So Paul addresses the church in Corinth as "those sanctified in Christ Jesus" (1 Cor. 1:2). They are the assembly of Christians meeting in Corinth who have been set apart as holy through the mediation of Christ's person and work.

Paul also employs "in Christ" vocabulary to communicate an association between Christ and Christians. So when he begins to lay bare the basis of justification, he says believers are "justified by his grace as a gift, through the redemption that is in Christ Jesus" (Rom. 3:24). The church's redemption, its deliverance from spiritual bondage, is "in Christ Jesus," that is, not apart from but in close association with him.

Often Paul via "in Christ" language presents Christ as the cause of sundry things, including ministries. So he exhorts the believers in Thessalonica to respect and highly esteem their church leaders for their work. He refers to the leaders as those "over you in the Lord" (1 Thess. 5:12). Church leaders deserve respect and regard because of Jesus's person and accomplishment.

Sometimes "in Christ" language is used to show that the manner in which believers do things is affected by their relationship to Christ. So Paul wants the Romans to give Phoebe a warm welcome and meet any needs she has. He writes, "Welcome her in the Lord in a way worthy of the saints" (Rom. 16:2).

[9]Counts of "in Christ" language vary. Numbers range from a low of "151 references" (Mark A. Seifrid, "In Christ," in *Dictionary of Paul and His Letters*, ed. Gerald F. Hawthorne, Ralph P. Martin, and Daniel G. Reid [Downers Grove, IL: InterVarsity, 1993], 436) to a high of "some two hundred times" (R. David Rightmire, "Union with Christ," in *Evangelical Dictionary of Biblical Theology*, ed. Walter A. Elwell [Grand Rapids: Baker, 1996], 789).

Here "in the Lord" indicates the manner in which the Corinthians are to receive Phoebe, as the next words suggest—"in a way worthy of the saints." Church life is to be lived "in Christ," that is, in a way of which he would approve.

Many times Paul employs "in Christ" nomenclature to set forth Christ as the object of saving faith. Three times in one verse Paul brings into opposition two very different approaches to salvation: "We know that a person is not justified by works of the law but through faith in Jesus Christ, so we also have believed in Christ Jesus, in order to be justified by faith in Christ and not by works of the law, because by works of the law no one will be justified" (Gal. 2:16). Salvation is not by keeping the law but by believing in Christ, the only true object of saving faith. For good reason the Reformers taught that justification is the article by which the church stands or falls. If one tries to approach salvation in any other way than faith in Christ, the church will be filled with unbelievers.

Paul uses "in Christ" so commonly that it becomes a way for him to indicate the adjective or noun *Christian*. When Paul contrasts his role as sole spiritual father to the Corinthians with "countless guides in Christ" whom they had, he means "Christian guides." And when the apostle says he knows a "man in Christ" who was caught up to the third heaven, he means a "Christian man" (2 Cor. 12:2). "In Christ" vocabulary fills Paul's mouth when referring to members of Christ's church.

Again and again Paul uses "in Christ" and equivalents to depict the realm, domain, or sphere over which Christ rules. He commonly sets this realm over against that of Satan, sin, and death. Jesus is our mighty champion who by his death and resurrection routs our enemies and gives us the victory. God saves us by putting us "in Christ," transferring us into his sphere. This is very clearly seen in Colossians 1:13–14: "He has delivered us from the domain of darkness and transferred us to the kingdom of his beloved Son, *in whom* we have redemption, the forgiveness of sins." In another place Paul contrasts two representatives and leaders of the human race: "As in Adam all die, so also in Christ shall all be made alive" (1 Cor. 15:22). By grace through faith union, believers are transferred out of Adam's realm into Christ's. This, Paul's most frequent use of "in Christ," sets the church squarely in Christ's domain, with all the responsibilities and blessings that come with that status.

Union with Christ as a Nuance

Paul usually says that the church is "in Christ" in terms of the nuances or shades of meaning we just examined. But remember: every use still carries the idea of a link to Christ, though most bear one of the eight nuances above. R. David Rightmire's summary is accurate: "in Christ" language "is the apostle's favorite term to describe the personal and dynamic relation of the believer to Christ, and appears in a variety of contexts."[10]

However, nine occurrences speak of union with Christ in a narrow and direct sense. The nuance of these nine occurrences is union with Christ proper. Believers are joined to Christ individually and corporately. These nine occurrences, then, instruct us concerning union and the church.

Christians have a protected status before God and a new way of living shared with other Christians in the church. God the Father has caused the saints in Corinth, and all saints, to be "in Christ Jesus, who became to [them] wisdom from God, righteousness and sanctification and redemption" (1 Cor. 1:30). Justification, along with every other aspect of the application of salvation, comes to us in union with Christ. Believers, therefore, are declared righteous "in him" (2 Cor. 5:21). Paul deems union with Christ so foundational for salvation that he can describe saved persons as those having "Jesus Christ in" them (2 Cor. 13:5). Only those with Christ in them are truly a part of Christ's church. And this is just the beginning of their journey; as they serve God, they continue to participate in Christ's death and resurrection (v. 4).

Western Christians too easily focus on ourselves as individuals and the time in which we live. While not completely wrong, this is myopic in two ways. First, Scripture takes a bigger view: God joins individuals to his Son to constitute the church. Union with Christ necessarily means union with others joined to Christ. In addition, Paul shocks us by taking a bigger view yet: God plans to "unite *all things* in" Christ, "things in heaven and things on earth" (Eph. 1:10). Paul thus construes union with Christ and salvation in individual, corporate, and cosmic terms.

Second, although we are not to neglect the present, a biblical worldview insists that we expand our temporal vision in light of God's past eternal plan and future eternal goal. Both plan and goal involve the church. In eternity past (v. 4) God planned to merge all things in his Son. This will take place in the "fullness of time" (v. 10), namely, when Christ comes again. Christ will be the center because God planned to unite "all things" in Christ as goal. "All things" include the church triumphant and renewed world.

Paul directs church members to "put on the whole armor of God," for they struggle against "cosmic powers over this present darkness" (Eph. 6:11–12).

---

[10] Rightmire, "Union with Christ," 789.

Paul has in mind Isaiah's descriptions of Yahweh and Messiah engaged in war. When we view Ephesians 6 from this perspective, we see that the apostle paints an ecclesial picture of union with Christ. When Paul, therefore, writes, "Be strong *in the Lord* and in the strength of his might" (v. 10), he insists that readers find strength in their union with the triumphant Christ.

Christ is so important to Paul that he will give up everything, including heritage and standing, for the "surpassing worth of knowing Christ Jesus [his] Lord" (Phil. 3:8). Paul is willing to trade all for Christ, for in doing this he gains Christ and his righteousness. Being "found in him" (v. 9), Paul and we gain all the blessings of salvation, including justification.

Essential to understanding union with Christ is the news that "in him the whole fullness of deity dwells bodily, and you have been filled in him, who is the head of all rule and authority" (Col. 2:9–10). The apostle follows two steps. First, he tells of Christ's union with God. Second, he tells of the union of the church with Christ. The two ideas are inseparable. Only because Christ is God incarnate and therefore one with God do we in Christ become one with God. We carefully distinguish Christ's union from ours. His union is by nature and ours by grace. He is God incarnate; we are sinners joined to God in Christ. For that reason, Paul joins Christ, in whom all the fullness of deity exists bodily, and Christians, who are granted fullness in him. The Colossians and the whole church are made complete in a living union with Christ.

Only in Paul's 1 and 2 Thessalonians salutations does he depict a church as being "in God the Father and the Lord Jesus Christ" (1 Thess. 1:1; cf. 2 Thess. 1:1). Paul thus teaches that by God's grace Christians are in union with the Father and the Son. This wondrous teaching has affinities with Jesus's request of God the Father "that they also may be in us" (John 17:21).

The Church Participates in Jesus's Story

When Paul teaches that believers take part in Jesus's narrative, his focus is on the church. Almost all his uses of this theme appear in letters written to churches. The only exception is 2 Timothy 2:11–12, which, although written to an individual, contains a hymn sung corporately by the church. Participation in Jesus's story, then, is an ecclesial theme in Paul's epistles.

When individuals trust Christ for salvation, the Spirit joins them to him and all others who know him. By grace through faith they participate in his story. The church is joined to him in everything from his death to his return.

As we saw previously, believers share in many events in Jesus's narrative, including his

- suffering (Rom. 8:17; Phil. 3:10),
- death (Rom. 6:3, 6, 8; 7:4; 2 Cor. 4:10; Gal. 2:20; Phil. 3:10; Col. 2:20; 3:3; 2 Tim. 2:11),
- burial (Rom. 6:4; Col. 2:12),
- being made alive (Eph. 2:5; Col. 2:13) ,
- new life (1 Thess. 5:10; 2 Tim. 2:11),
- resurrection (Rom. 6:4–5, 8; 7:4; 2 Cor. 4:10–11, 14; Eph. 2:6; Col. 2:12; 3:1),
- being seated in heaven (Eph. 2:6),
- being hidden in God (Col. 3:3),
- return (Col. 3:4; cf. Rom. 8:19),
- glory (Rom. 8:17),
- reign (2 Tim. 2:12).

Again, the apostle says that believers communally take part in everything from Jesus's suffering and death to his return and reign. This is because they take part in *him*. When they are spiritually joined to him, his story becomes their story. The church does not participate in his incarnation, sinless life,[11] pouring out the Holy Spirit at Pentecost, or intercession for the church. These events are Christ's alone; the church does not share in them.

"Suffering," in the list above, refers to being united to Christ in his crucifixion and, as a result, suffering in the Christian life (Paul's theme in Col. 1:24–25). The church's union with Christ's saving events begins with his sufferings on the cross and concludes with his second coming. Colossians 3:4 and Romans 8:18–19 ascribe to believers a second coming in a sense. Our connection to Christ is so intimate, definitive, and permanent that we will return with him, in a manner of speaking. This is because our lives and identity are bound up with him in our union with him.

What is the takeaway of the church's participation in Christ's story? This theme effectively communicates that Christ's redemptive events applied are the only solution to the problem of sin. In total, Christ performs nine redemptive events: two essential preconditions (incarnation and holy life), the center of his saving accomplishment (death and resurrection), and five indispensable consequences of his death and resurrection (ascension, session, pouring out

---

[11] Although its effects are imputed to us in justification (2 Cor. 5:21).

the Spirit, intercession, and second coming). This point bears repeating: the core of his saving work is his death and resurrection.

Jesus's death and resurrection are the only solution to the problem of sin. This holds true for sin's past, present, and future dimensions. Christ's cross and empty tomb *saved* us from sin's *penalty* in justification (a subset of union with Christ). "There is therefore now no condemnation for those who are in Christ Jesus" (Rom. 8:1). Condemnation is the legal opposite of justification. Condemnation is God the Judge's declaration of damnation based on lost persons' thoughts, words, and actions. Justification is God the Judge's declaration of righteousness based on Christ's righteousness (in his life and death). Justification and condemnation are the decisions of the Judge at the last judgment. Amazingly, from the perspectives of the "already" and "not yet," those verdicts are announced *now* based upon humans' relationship to Christ. Of course, the words of Romans 8:1 apply only to those who have trusted Christ's saving work for their acceptance by God.

The Savior's atonement and resurrection life *save* us from sin's *power* in progressive sanctification (a subset of union with Christ). "We were buried therefore with him by baptism into death, in order that, just as Christ was raised from the dead by the glory of the Father, we too might walk in newness of life" (Rom. 6:4). Christ's death breaks the stranglehold of sin over the church. His resurrection unleashes the power believers need to live victoriously for him.

Christ's death and resurrection *will save* us from sin's *presence* in glorification (and final sanctification, subsets of union with Christ). "Since, therefore, we have now been justified by his blood, much more *shall we be saved* by him from the wrath of God. For if while we were enemies we were reconciled to God by the death of his Son, much more, now that we are reconciled, *shall we be saved* by his life" (Rom. 5:9–10).

We must not lose sight of the big picture. Justification, progressive sanctification, and glorification are all subsets of union with Christ. When we say there is no other solution to the problem of sin—past, present, or future—than Christ's saving work, we mean in union with Christ.

The Church Is the Body of Christ

The body of Christ, one of Paul's favorite images of the church, exalts Christ and blesses his people as organically united to their Head and to one another.

Perhaps more than any other, this Pauline picture of the church extols

Christ. In a context acclaiming Christ as paramount in creation and redemption, Paul pens, "[Christ] is the head of the body, the church" (Col. 1:18). Indeed, in Colossians and Ephesians Paul's emphasis is on Christ as Head and his people as body. As Head, Christ is the church's life-giver and Lord.

As Head he is the fount of the church's spiritual life, as the very next words express: "He is the beginning, the firstborn from the dead" (v. 18). As risen from the dead he inaugurates the new creation and gives eternal life to his people. Of course, the new heavens and new earth await their fullness. But the new creation was initiated by Christ's death and resurrection, so that his people have eternal life now in mortal bodies as they await eternal life in immortal bodies (Rom. 8:10–11).

As Head he also charges the church to obey him in the world. Paul alerts his readers to reject the religious errorists who have mistaught them. Rather, Christ's people must cling to the "Head," namely, Christ himself (Col. 2:19). He alone is the Head, the ultimate authority over his body, the church. Moreover, our Head and Savior "nourishes and cherishes" us (Eph. 5:23, 29–30).

Christ is the Head of his body, and we are the members of it. Paul explains, "You are the body of Christ and individually members of it" (1 Cor. 12:27). The very concept of the body of Christ speaks of incorporation into him. The designation "body of Christ" was so customary for Paul that he only had to say, "There is one body," and he and readers understood he was referring to the body of Christ, the church (Eph. 4:4).

The metaphor of believers as the body of Christ is more than a metaphor. We know this from Paul's revulsion at believers' taking Christ's members and making them "members of a prostitute" (1 Cor. 6:15). The reference is metaphorical, but at the same time there is a spiritual reality behind it. By God's grace through faith we are really, spiritually united to Christ. Because of our true union with him, becoming one flesh with a prostitute joins his members to the prostitute!

The chief role of the Holy Spirit in salvation is to join believers to Christ and one another in one body. Christ baptized us "in one Spirit . . . into one body . . . and all were made to drink of one Spirit" (1 Cor. 12:13). The Holy Spirit is God's bond of vital union with Christ and other believers. When Christ incorporates us into his body through the Spirit, he joins us to every other member of his body as well.

Union with Christ is vertical and horizontal, corporate and individual. Because it is corporate and vertical, even as many members of our body are part of us, so believers are a part of Christ; they belong to him. The image of the body works well to convey the relationship of believers, the members, to Christ, their Head (Rom. 12:6–8). It highlights the corporate side of union, but it is always based on vertical union with the Head.

Because union is also corporate and horizontal, just as our bodily members belong to us, so believers belong to Christ. And by virtue of union with him they belong to each other! This idea is also corporate. Paul urges the members of Christ's body with various gifts to serve the Lord in an appropriate manner (Rom. 12:6–8). He deals with different aspects of horizontal union with Christ in 1 Corinthians 12:14–27. The various church members are interdependent (vv. 14–26). Those who think they are inferior are misguided, for God plans all the members to play their various parts in one body (vv. 15–20). Moreover, those who think they are superior are also misguided (vv. 21–26). They should learn a lesson from their own bodies. The parts we cover in modesty are essential (vv. 22–24). And it is the same in Christ's body, the church: "God has so composed the body, giving greater honor to the part that lacked it" (v. 24). His purpose? That "there may be no division in the body, but that the members may have the same care for one another" (v. 25).

I have emphasized the corporate side of the church for two reasons. First, it is paramount in Scripture. Second, as Westerners we think in almost exclusively individualistic terms. Having emphasized the corporate side, for completeness we should affirm that union in Christ's body is also individual. God calls us individually to himself in salvation and also calls us into the people of God. By virtue of union with Christ, every saved individual belongs to Christ the Head *and* his body.

The work of Christ's church is entrusted to him and his people. One job of church leaders is to train members to engage in ministry to edify Christ's body (Eph. 4:12). The body needs to grow numerically and also in unity, maturity, and doctrinal stability. Christ provides the stimulus for growth, but both the Head of the body and its members are active in bodily growth (vv. 15–16). The body image is dynamic, for the body grows and matures (v. 19). This divine-human dynamic interplay is evident also in Colossians 2. Christ is the Head, "from whom the whole body, nourished and knit together through its joints and ligaments, grows with a growth that is from God" (v. 19). The body's growth is "from its Head," namely, Christ, and its growth is "from God." At the same the body is "nourished" by its "joints and ligaments," that is, when the members perform their roles in the body.

It is here under the metaphor of the body of Christ that Paul's amazing theme of the church as the "fullness" of Christ or of God, or as "filled in" or "with" Christ or God belongs. I will make three distinctions to explain this grand idea.

First, we should not confuse Christ's fullness with that of his church. All the fullness of deity lives in Christ in bodily form. He is the fullness of deity incarnate. And as the risen Lord exalted to God's right hand, he "fills all in all" (Eph. 1:23). Out of his fullness the God-man, Jesus Christ, grants fullness to the church: "In him the whole fullness of deity dwells bodily, and you have been filled in him" (Col. 2:9–10).

Second, Christ grants his church fullness as a status and also as a task. As the Lord who fills all things with his divine presence, he gives the church the status of fullness. The church is "filled in him" (Col. 2:10) and is his "fullness" (Eph. 1:23). But simultaneously Christ gives his church fullness as a task to perform and goal to be attained. Paul prays that the Ephesians "may be filled with all the fullness of God" (Eph. 3:19). The apostle's goal is that the churches attain the "measure of the stature of the fullness of Christ" (Eph. 4:13).

Third, we need to distinguish the "already" and "not yet." "Already" in Christ Christians have the status of divine fullness (Eph. 1:23; Col. 2:10) and know God's love. "Not yet" have they attained a lifestyle befitting this exalted status. This stimulates the church to press on in its quest for godliness and love.

Ridderbos captures something of the grandeur of this Pauline picture of the church: "It describes the Christological mode of existence of the church as the people of God; it speaks of the special bond with Christ that the church has as the people of God, and the new Israel."[12]

The Church Is the Bride of Christ

The final picture of the church we will examine is the church as Christ's bride. This warm and joyous picture appears in three Pauline texts as well as at the end of the book of Revelation.

Paul portrays union with Christ as the marriage of Christ and the church in Ephesians 5:22–32, and in 1 Corinthians 6:15–17 he presents the relationship between Christ and the church as spiritual marriage. It is important to keep in mind that although marriage joins Christ, the Groom, and his bride,

---

[12] Herman Ridderbos, *Paul: An Outline of His Theology*, trans. John Richard de Witt (Grand Rapids: Eerdmans, 1975), 362.

the church, it does not remove distinctions between them. He alone is the divine-human Lord and Savior, whose unique identity makes union with him the church's greatest blessing.

This, Paul's most intimate picture of union with Christ, corresponds to marriage and the physical union between husband and wife. When discussing this picture, Paul even focuses on the human body and sexual relations (1 Cor. 6:16). Believers are spiritually wed to Christ.

By now we are accustomed to finding Paul, when speaking of the church, alluding to the Holy Spirit (in 1 Cor. 6:17). I believe Fee is correct: "Paul's point is that the physical union of a believer with a prostitute is not possible because the believer's body already belongs to the Lord, through whose resurrection one's body has become a 'member' of Christ by his Spirit."[13]

This image of the church is replete with God's grace. It is God who initiates the marriage and sustains the relationship. His bride, the church, is the object of his love and care. Christ "himself is the Savior of the body" (Eph. 5:23, my translation), who, out of love for his bride, offers himself up in death for her (v. 25). He lavishes provision and care upon her (v. 29). All of this highlights Christ's abundant grace showered on his bride. The church does nothing to merit Christ's love; it is entirely the recipient of his loving advances.

While this metaphor underlines God's love and sovereignty, it also embraces our responsibility. Paul speaks paternally as he who "betrothed" the Corinthians to "one husband," even Christ (2 Cor. 11:2). Paul's goal is to present the Corinthians in purity to Jesus at his return. With godly jealousy Paul fears lest his readers "be led astray from . . . pure devotion to Christ" into spiritual adultery (v. 3).

Furthermore, as a bride submits to her loving husband in marriage, so the church submits to Christ, its loving Husband (Eph. 5:23–24). Campbell extols Paul's use of the one-flesh union of marriage to depict the union of Christ, the loving Husband, and his church: "The metaphor is personal and implies a bond of intimacy that goes well beyond the other metaphors that Paul uses in portraying union with Christ."[14]

Paul is not the only one to paint the picture of the church and Christ as bride and Groom. John also has some important things to say about it. In Revelation 19 he builds on the Old Testament picture of God's people adorning itself as a bride for her husband (Isa. 61:10) to depict the culmination of

---

[13] Gordon D. Fee, *The First Epistle to the Corinthians*, The New International Commentary on the New Testament (Grand Rapids: Eerdmans, 1987), 260.

[14] Campbell, *Paul and Union with Christ*, 308.

God's covenantal promises of intimacy between himself and his saints.[15] That relationship is final union with Christ. John celebrates heavenly praise of God for the ruin of God's enemy Babylon, the "great prostitute who corrupted the earth with her immorality" (Rev. 19:1–5, quoting 2) and counterfeit of the true bride of Christ.

John has even greater reason for praise: "It is this eschatological event—the perfect union of Christ and his church—which John announced under the metaphor of the marriage of the lamb," as Ladd brings to our attention.[16] John proclaims delight in heaven at the glorious prospect of the wedding of Christ and his church, preceded by the blissful marriage supper:

> "Let us rejoice and exult . . .
> for the marriage of the Lamb has come,
>   and his Bride has made herself ready; . . ."

> "Blessed are those who are invited to the marriage supper of the Lamb."
> (Rev. 19:7, 9)

John only announces but does not record the supper or the wedding of the Lamb and his bride. Nevertheless John interprets the wedding imagery of 19:6–8 in terms of the ultimate union between Christ and the church:

> I saw the holy city, new Jerusalem, coming down out of heaven from God, *prepared as a bride adorned for her husband.* And I heard a loud voice from the throne saying, "Behold, the dwelling place of God is with men. He will dwell with them, and they will be his people, and God himself will be with them as their God." (Rev. 21:2–3)

Philip Hughes captures the joyful anticipation of God's people at the prospect of being invited to the marriage supper and wedding of the Lamb and his bride, the church:

> There is good reason to *be joyful and exultant* [19:7, author's translation], to give expression to a superabundance of joy, because the inauguration of the everlasting kingdom coincides with *the marriage of the Lamb.* The imagery emphasizes in a striking way the intense love of the Lord for his own. In the Old Testament God speaks of himself as the husband of his

[15] G. K. Beale, *The Book of Revelation*, New International Greek Testament Commentary (Grand Rapids: Eerdmans, 1999), 939–40.
[16] George E. Ladd, *A Commentary on the Revelation of John* (Grand Rapids: Eerdmans, 1972), 248.

people (Is. 54:5; Ho. 2:19f., *etc.*); and in the New Testament the church is depicted as the bride of Christ whose advent as the Bridegroom to take her to himself she eagerly awaits (Eph. 5:25; Mt. 25:1ff.; Mk. 2:19; Jn. 3:29; 2 Cor. 11:2). Now the long desired moment has arrived when love blends with love in a union of everlasting perfection.[17]

---

[17] Philip E. Hughes, *The Book of the Revelation*, The Pillar New Testament Commentary (Grand Rapids: Eerdmans, 1990), 199, emphasis original.

Chapter 27

Union with Christ in the Sacraments

Baptism and the Lord's Supper have not received the attention they deserve in some treatments of union with Christ. And this study of union would be lacking without taking them into account.

The two ordinances of the church are dissimilar in a number of ways. Baptism is the initial rite of the Christian faith, and the Lord's Supper is its ongoing rite. Their material elements differ, for baptism involves water while the Supper involves bread and the fruit of the vine. Baptism, as Paul teaches, is to be performed only once: "There is one . . . baptism" (Eph. 4:4–5). By contrast, as Paul teaches, the Lord's Supper is to be observed repeatedly, "as often as" necessary "until he comes" (1 Cor. 11:26). In addition, both sacraments have multiple meanings.

Despite these differences, the ordinances have similarities as well. Both were instituted by Christ's command. Both have important roles to play in the Christian life. Neither bears new content, but both tell the "old, old story of Jesus and his love." That is, both portray the gospel in a ceremony. Jesus was very gracious to his church. He not only commanded preachers to "preach the word" (2 Tim. 4:2), he also built the Word into the church's two fundamental ceremonies. This is prominent in Augustine's and Calvin's idea that baptism and the Lord's Supper are "visible words." Indeed, as Paul teaches concerning the Supper, "as often as you eat this bread and drink the cup, you *proclaim* the Lord's death until he comes" (1 Cor. 11:26). The Supper and its words of institution are a proclamation of the gospel. It is the same for baptism, which carries the "promise" of the forgiveness of sins (Acts 2:38–39).

Although baptism and the Lord's Supper have several meanings, they hold their most basic and profound meaning in common—union with Christ. This chapter will trace their origin to Jesus's commands and study their description in Paul's epistles. It will highlight that baptism signifies union with Christ once and for all, while the Lord's Supper signifies ongoing union and communion with Christ.

Christ Institutes Baptism and the Lord's Supper

Baptism

The apostles did not come up with the ideas of baptizing converts or eating a meal to remember Jesus's death. Rather, the Mediator of the new covenant gave both ordinances to his church. The apostles' Lord and Savior gave them baptism as part of his Great Commission before his ascension: "Go therefore and make disciples of all nations, baptizing them in the name of the Father and of the Son and of the Holy Spirit" (Matt. 28:19).

The preposition "in" could be rendered "into," as the ESV note indicates. Either way the meaning is the same: baptism is in or into the three names of the Trinitarian persons. "Name" is used in the Old Testament sense of signifying the *person* who bears the name (cf. Ex. 34:5–7). To be baptized into (or in) one's name is to be brought into relation with the one or ones denominated by that name, in this case the Holy Trinity. Baptism is thus into union with the Father, the Son, and the Holy Spirit. I understand baptisms in Jesus's name in Acts to be shorthand (because Jesus is the only Mediator between God and men) for this longhand expression. Christian baptism, then, signifies union with Christ, even with the Trinity.

The Lord's Supper

The apostles did not originate the idea of the Lord's Supper, either. Instead, during his Last Supper before his crucifixion Jesus shared with his disciples a Jewish Passover meal, instituting the Lord's Supper.

Instituted in the Synoptic Gospels. Ever since they were old enough to remember, the disciples had observed the Passover, with their fathers serving as president of the meal. Most of the aspects of the meal Jesus shared with them they had experienced once a year for many years.

In fact, almost all of the meal was the same, except for two things. Their fathers always took bread and prayed over it, but they never said, "Take, eat; this is my body" (Matt. 26:26)! And their fathers always gave thanks for the third cup of the meal, the cup of redemption, before giving it to them. But their fathers never said, "Drink of it, all of you, for this is my blood of the covenant, which is poured out for many for the forgiveness of sins" (vv. 27–28)! With these radical words, Jesus instituted the Supper that would appropriately come to be known as the "Lord's supper" (1 Cor. 11:20).

What meaning did Jesus's symbolism convey? The question is not what meaning the disciples grasped from Jesus's words and actions. They were too upset to understand what he was saying and doing. (He had told them he was leaving and that one of them would betray him.) But later, perhaps when he taught them in the fifty days between his resurrection and Pentecost, they came to understand. What was Jesus's intended meaning? It is not hard to find. When he identifies the bread with his body and passes the loaf around for them each to break off and eat a piece, he is telling them to "ingest" him, so to speak. And when he identifies the fruit of the vine with his blood and tells them all to drink from the common cup, he is telling them to "drink" him, as it were. Via this simple symbolism he is communicating that they are to take him "into" themselves, as they would food and drink. Jesus's message, conveyed in such an unadorned manner, was union with himself and what he was about to accomplish.

Preached in the Gospel of John. Although the Fourth Gospel does not record the institution of baptism or the Lord's Supper, when many Christians read the Bread of Life Discourse, they think of the Supper:

> Truly, truly, I say to you, whoever believes has eternal life. I am the bread of life. Your fathers ate the manna in the wilderness, and they died. This is the bread that comes down from heaven, so that one may eat of it and not die. I am the living bread that came down from heaven. If anyone eats of this bread, he will live forever. And the bread that I will give for the life of the world is my flesh. (John 6:47–51)

Jesus again declares, "I am the bread of life" (v. 48; cf. v. 35). He is the reality the manna pointed to. The fathers were nourished in the wilderness by bread from heaven, but they nevertheless died. It was sufficient to sustain physical but not spiritual life. But Jesus is the true Bread of Life, true in John's sense of the fulfillment of Old Testament foreshadowing. The manna in the wilderness was a type of the "bread that comes down from heaven," that is, the Son of God's incarnation. Anyone who "eats" this bread will not die but live forever.

The terms "eat" and "feed on" Jesus appear eight times in this passage. They mean to appropriate Jesus in faith.[1] Jesus's reference to his flesh (σάρξ/ *sarx*, the same word as in 1:14) fits this conclusion: "The bread that I will give for the life of the world is my flesh" (v. 51). Jesus gives his flesh in his sacrifice on the cross. To eat the living bread, therefore, is to trust in his atoning death.

It is understandable that Jesus's hearers again trip over his words, which seem to imply cannibalism: "How can this man give us his flesh to eat?" (v. 52). Jesus, however, refuses to tone down his message but makes it more offensive to Jewish ears, because the law forbade eating blood:

> Truly, truly, I say to you, unless you eat the flesh of the Son of Man and drink his blood, you have no life in you. Whoever feeds on my flesh and drinks my blood has eternal life, and I will raise him up on the last day. For my flesh is true food, and my blood is true drink. Whoever feeds on my flesh and drinks my blood abides in me, and I in him. As the living Father sent me, and I live because of the Father, so whoever feeds on me, he also will live because of me. This is the bread that came down from heaven, not like the bread the fathers ate, and died. Whoever feeds on this bread will live forever. (vv. 53–58)

Jesus's words shock: refusing to eat his flesh and drink his blood bars people from eternal life; eating and drinking them brings eternal life now and resurrection life at the end of the age. His flesh and blood are true spiritual food and drink. Manna prolonged physical life; the living bread conveys eternal life. While the primary referent of these verses is Jesus's sacrificial death, Christians see in them overtones of the Lord's Supper. The blood speaks of violent death, whether of Old Testament sacrificial animals or of Jesus, "the Lamb of God, who takes away the sin of the world" (1:29).

What are we to make of Jesus's insistence that hearers must eat his flesh and drink his blood to have eternal life? Jesus's incarnation (vv. 50–51, 58) makes possible his death (and resurrection) (v. 51). Hearers must believe in him to gain eternal life (v. 47). Within this framework, Jesus's words allude to the Supper and convey the notion of union with Christ. Ingesting his flesh

---

[1] So D. A. Carson, *The Gospel according to John*, The Pillar New Testament Commentary (Grand Rapids: Eerdmans, 1991), 295.

and drinking his blood mean making him part of us, as our food and drink become part of us. This is embryonic language for union with him and his saving benefits. So, though Jesus in John's Gospel does not establish the two church ordinances, his Bread of Life message speaks eloquently of the most important theme of the Supper—union with Christ.

In sum: in the Synoptic Gospels Jesus, with few words, institutes the two ordinances of the Christian church. In his Bread of Life sermon in the Gospel of John he speaks to the most important meaning of the Lord's Supper—union with him. Acts, we may add, records baptisms and twice the celebration of the Lord's Supper, the "breaking of bread" (Acts 2:42; cf. 20:7). But it does not further our understanding of the meaning of the ordinances apart from communicating that baptism signifies the forgiveness of sins (Acts 2:38; 22:16). It would remain for the apostle Paul to describe baptism and the Supper more fully.

Paul Describes Baptism and the Lord's Supper

Paul is Scripture's main teacher concerning the meaning of the sacraments of baptism and the Lord's Supper. He assigns several meanings to each of them but teaches that the most fundamental and profound meaning of each is union with Christ.

In five passages Paul connects union with Christ and the sacraments or ordinances of the church. In Romans 6:1–14; Galatians 3:25–29; and Colossians 2:11–12 he connects union with Christian baptism. In 1 Corinthians 10:16–17 and 11:23–26 he joins union and the Lord's Supper. I do not hold that the sacraments work *ex opere operato*, as does the Roman Catholic Church. Both the Holy Spirit and faith are necessary to benefit from the grace offered in the ordinances. Nevertheless, Paul implies in these texts that God offers grace in the sacraments; they are means of grace parallel to the Word of God (cf. 1 Cor. 11:26). And the grace they communicate to believing participants brings the benefits of union with Christ. In fact, though baptism and the Supper have many meanings, the most important, comprehensive, and profound meaning of both is union—initial union in baptism, the rite of initiation, and ongoing union in the Lord's Supper, the rite of fellowship.

In light of their significance, I quote Paul's five passages at length:

What shall we say then? Are we to continue in sin that grace may abound? By no means! How can we who died to sin still live in it? Do you not know that all of us who have been baptized into Christ Jesus were baptized into his death? We were buried therefore with him by baptism into death, in order that, just as Christ was raised from the dead by the glory of the Father, we too might walk in newness of life.

For if we have been united with him in a death like his, we shall certainly be united with him in a resurrection like his. We know that our old self was crucified with him in order that the body of sin might be brought to nothing, so that we would no longer be enslaved to sin. For one who has died has been set free from sin. Now if we have died with Christ, we believe that we will also live with him. We know that Christ, being raised from the dead, will never die again; death no longer has dominion over him. For the death he died he died to sin, once for all, but the life he lives he lives to God. So you also must consider yourselves dead to sin and alive to God in Christ Jesus.

Let not sin therefore reign in your mortal body, to make you obey its passions. Do not present your members to sin as instruments for unrighteousness, but present yourselves to God as those who have been brought from death to life, and your members to God as instruments for righteousness. For sin will have no dominion over you, since you are not under law but under grace. (Rom. 6:1–14)

The cup of blessing that we bless, is it not a participation in the blood of Christ? The bread that we break, is it not a participation in the body of Christ? Because there is one bread, we who are many are one body, for we all partake of the one bread. Consider the people of Israel: are not those who eat the sacrifices participants in the altar? What do I imply then? That food offered to idols is anything, or that an idol is anything? No, I imply that what pagans sacrifice they offer to demons and not to God. I do not want you to be participants with demons. You cannot drink the cup of the Lord and the cup of demons. You cannot partake of the table of the Lord and the table of demons. Shall we provoke the Lord to jealousy? Are we stronger than he? (1 Cor. 10:16–22)

I received from the Lord what I also delivered to you, that the Lord Jesus on the night when he was betrayed took bread, and when he had given thanks, he broke it, and said, "This is my body which is for you. Do this in remembrance of me." In the same way also he took the cup, after supper, saying, "This cup is the new covenant in my blood. Do this, as often as you drink it, in remembrance of me." For as often as you eat this bread and drink the cup, you proclaim the Lord's death until he comes. (1 Cor. 11:23–26)

Now that faith has come, we are no longer under a guardian, for in Christ Jesus you are all sons of God, through faith. For as many of you as were baptized into Christ have put on Christ. There is neither Jew nor Greek, there is neither slave nor free, there is no male and female, for you are all one in Christ Jesus. And if you are Christ's, then you are Abraham's offspring, heirs according to promise. (Gal. 3:25–29)

In him also you were circumcised with a circumcision made without hands, by putting off the body of the flesh, by the circumcision of Christ, having been buried with him in baptism, in which you were also raised with him through faith in the powerful working of God, who raised him from the dead. (Col. 2:11–12)

Baptism

Baptism bears different meanings in the New Testament. It portrays salvation in general terms (1 Pet. 3:21), reception of the Spirit (Acts 2:38), forgiveness (2:38; 22:16), cleansing (1 Cor. 6:11; Col. 2:11–12), regeneration (Titus 3:5), and adoption (Gal. 3:27). In Paul's letters, three passages call for our attention.

Romans 6:1–11. Believers die with Christ to sin when they are baptized. They are united to Christ in his crucifixion, and sin's dominance over their lives is broken. As a result, Christians should not live as if ruled by sin. This is because sin's control over them is broken when they are joined to Christ in his death, as signified by baptism. Christians are also joined to Christ in his resurrection, with the result that "just as Christ was raised from the dead by the glory of the Father, we too might walk in newness of life" (v. 4). Believers have no place living as those who do not know the Lord. To live in that way is to disgrace Christ who loved us and gave himself for us. For Christians to live in sin is to forget that their baptism joins them to Christ in his death and resurrection (vv. 3–4). Rather they are to "consider" themselves "dead to sin and alive to God in Christ Jesus" (v. 11). That means they are to live out their union with Christ in his death and resurrection.

Galatians 3:26–29. Under the new covenant in Christ, the Mediator of that covenant, believers have been adopted into God's family by grace through faith in the Redeemer (v. 26). Adoption fits under the larger category of union with Christ, according to Paul: "As many of you as were baptized into Christ have put on Christ" (v. 27). The apostle links baptism and the figure of putting on Christ as clothing. Baptism/conversion involves putting on Christ as one puts on clothes. As clothes cover our bodies, so Christ "covers" us in baptism. The rite, then, "shows the total involvement of a believer in Christ. The believer is identified with Christ, sharing in his position, in his identity," as Hans Burger argues.[2]

Bruce accurately sums up the matter: "To be 'baptized into Christ' is to be incorporated into him by baptism, and hence to be 'in Christ.'"[3] Bruce also correctly asserts, "It is difficult to suppose that the readers would not have understood it as a statement about their initiatory baptism in water"; and he correctly denies that Paul ascribes *ex opere operato* efficacy to the baptismal rite.[4] In this passage, as in Romans 6:3–11, water baptism signifies but does not automatically effect union with Christ.

Faith in Christ and baptism are levelers and unifiers. "There is neither Jew nor Greek, there is neither slave nor free, there is no male and female, for you are all one in Christ Jesus" (v. 28). "In Christ Jesus" is used here, as often elsewhere, to show domain or sphere. The Galatian Christians are unified in Christ Jesus's domain, which transcends spheres of ethnicity, socioeconomics, and gender.

Colossians 2:11–12. It is much the same in this passage, where Paul says that "in him" the Colossian Gentile believers were spiritually circumcised when they were baptized. Christ circumcised them figuratively, so that the "body of the flesh" (their spiritual foreskin) was removed. That means their sins were forgiven when they were "buried with him in baptism" (v. 12). And they were resurrected to newness of life when they "were also raised with him through faith in the powerful working of God, who raised him from the dead" (v. 12). Christ conveys forgiveness by his spiritual circumcision in baptism.

Baptism signifies union with Christ in his death and resurrection. Union with Christ involves participation in Christ's redemptive events. As in Romans 6, so in Colossians 2 we participate in Christ's death, burial, and resurrection, so that in a sense they become *our* death, burial, and resurrection. Because we died with him, as is evidenced in our "having been buried with him," we are forgiven. His death counts for us. Because we were "raised with

---

[2] Hans Burger, *Being in Christ: A Biblical and Systematic Investigation in a Reformed Perspective* (Eugene, OR: Wipf and Stock, 2009), 243.
[3] F. F. Bruce, *The Epistle to the Galatians*, New International Greek Testament Commentary (Grand Rapids: Eerdmans, 1982), 185.
[4] Ibid.

him," we have new life through the "powerful working of God, who raised him from the dead" (Col. 2:12).

Speaking of the error threatening the Colossians, Bruce captures the thrust of Paul's message on baptism:

> If only they called to mind their baptism, and all that was involved and implied in it, they would be delivered from such inconsistent syncretism. . . . No longer is there any place for a circumcision performed by hands. . . . The death of Christ has effected the inward cleansing which the prophets associated with the new covenant, and of this Christian baptism is the visible sign. . . . Baptism not only proclaims that the old order is past and done with; it proclaims that a new order has been inaugurated. . . . Baptism, therefore, implies a sharing in Christ's resurrection as well as in his death and burial. . . . From now on that power energizes them and maintains the new life within them—the new life which is nothing less that Christ's resurrection life flowing through all the members of his body. In him they already enjoy eternal life, the life of the age to come.[5]

The Lord's Supper

It is good to start with the names Scripture gives to the Lord's Supper. It is called the "table of the Lord" and "Lord's supper" (1 Cor. 10:21; 11:20), which remind us it is a fellowship meal. Paul calls it a κοινωνία (*koinōnia*), which means "fellowship, sharing, or communion" (twice in 10:16) and reveals that the Supper communicates union with Christ (and one another, v. 17). Although the noun *eucharist* is not used, the related verb "to give thanks" appears in the Gospels (Matt. 26:27) and Epistles (1 Cor. 11:24). Acts calls the Lord's Supper the "breaking of bread" (2:42; cf. 20:7), which reminds us of the physical action that takes place in the meal and of Jesus's humanity to which it points. Two passages from Paul invite discussion.

1 Corinthians 10:16–22. Paul's most extensive treatment of the Supper appears in 1 Corinthians 11, where he corrects abuses in the Corinthian congregation. But his words on the topic in the preceding chapter, often overlooked, are crucial:

> Therefore, my beloved, flee from idolatry. I speak as to sensible people; judge for yourselves what I say. The cup of blessing that we bless, is it not

---

[5] F. F. Bruce, *The Epistles to the Colossians, to Philemon, and to the Ephesians*, The New International Commentary on the New Testament (Grand Rapids: Eerdmans, 1984), 103–5.

a participation in the blood of Christ? The bread that we break, is it not a participation in the body of Christ? Because there is one bread, we who are many are one body, for we all partake of the one bread. Consider the people of Israel: are not those who eat the sacrifices participants in the altar? What do I imply then? That food offered to idols is anything, or that an idol is anything? No, I imply that what pagans sacrifice they offer to demons and not to God. I do not want you to be participants with demons. You cannot drink the cup of the Lord and the cup of demons. You cannot partake of the table of the Lord and the table of demons. Shall we provoke the Lord to jealousy? Are we stronger than he? (1 Cor. 10:14–22)

Paul teaches via rhetorical questions: "The cup of blessing that we bless, is it not a participation in the blood of Christ? The bread that we break, is it not a participation in the body of Christ?" (v. 16). The negative particle he uses with both questions implies a positive answer. The cup and bread of the Supper signify "participation," a "sharing" with the blood and body of Christ.[6] This means that partaking of the elements in faith brings sharing in the benefits of Christ's atonement. God uses the Supper to give grace to believing partakers.

Paul employs an unusual order in verses 16–17—first the cup, then the bread. He chooses this order to set up a movement from vertical union between believers and Christ in verse 16 to horizontal union among believers themselves in verse 17: "Because there is one bread, we who are many are one body, for we all partake of the one bread." We share union with Christ with other believers, and this in nowhere better expressed than in the Lord's Supper.

With his use of the words "participation" and "participants," Paul draws powerful parallels to communicate what happens when believers partake of the Supper. He draws attention to Old Testament believers' participation in Jewish sacrifices and pagans' participation in pagan sacrifices (vv. 18–20). The former are "participants" with God in the sacrifices; believing worshipers receive the benefits of the sacrifice in the meal accompanying the fellowship (or peace) offering (v. 18; cf. Lev. 7:11–18). And, unknowingly, pagans participate with demons in pagan sacrifices and are thereby "participants with demons" (1 Cor. 10:20). Paul's point is clear: even as Old Testament believers received the benefits of peace offerings in the fellowship meal, and even as pagans participate with demons in their pagan sacrifices, so believing recipients participate with Christ in the Lord's Supper.

---

[6] BDAG, 2nd ed. (1979), 439.

Keith Mathison summarizes Paul's argument:

In verse 18, Paul points to the sacrificial meals of the Israelites to illustrate the idea of communion in the body and blood of Christ. . . . The participants of the meal appropriate the reality and benefits that the sacrifice represents and accomplishes. . . . In verses 19–20, Paul denies that idols possess any kind of ontological existence or reality, but he insists that those who worship them do unwillingly participate in a reality beyond man-made idols. They enter in the realm of demon worship. . . . To partake of the table of demons is to commit idolatry, break the covenant, fellowship with demons.[7]

By virtue of Paul's appeal to Old Testament and pagan worship, when he speaks of Christians' partaking of the Lord's Supper, he means that in doing so they participate in the body and blood of Christ. They partake of the benefits of Christ's once-for-all sacrifice on the cross.

This raises a problem. If baptism signifies initial union with Christ, what does the Lord Supper signify? Ongoing union with Christ. Our once-for-all-time union with Christ signified in baptism is strengthened and invigorated by partaking of the Lord's Supper in faith.

The Lord's Supper, like baptism, has many meanings. These are helpfully viewed in terms of past, present, and future. With regard to the past, the Supper fulfills what the Passover meal pointed to—remembrance of Christ's great redemptive act (1 Cor. 5:7; 11:24–25). In the present, it is a visible proclamation of Christ's atoning death (v. 26). With respect to the future, it points toward final redemption (Matt. 26:29; 1 Cor. 11:26; Rev. 19:9).

But its most significant, encompassing, and profound meaning is union with Christ, which pertains to all three temporal aspects. Believing participants in the Lord's Supper enjoy true fellowship with him and partake of the benefits of his atoning sacrifice. First Corinthians 10:16 tells of vertical fellowship with Christ in the Supper, and verse 17 tells of horizontal fellowship with other believers in the Supper based on that vertical fellowship.

The apostle intends for readers to keep in mind what he said in 10:16–17 when they read his more famous words of 11:23–26.

1 Corinthians 11:23–26. Paul's famous words concerning the Lord's Supper merit our attention:

---

[7] Keith A. Mathison, *Given for You: Reclaiming Calvin's Doctrine of the Lord's Supper* (Phillipsburg, NJ: P&R, 2002), 228–29.

I received from the Lord what I also delivered to you, that the Lord Jesus on the night when he was betrayed took bread, and when he had given thanks, he broke it, and said, "This is my body which is for you. Do this in remembrance of me." In the same way also he took the cup, after supper, saying, "This cup is the new covenant in my blood. Do this, as often as you drink it, in remembrance of me." For as often as you eat this bread and drink the cup, you proclaim the Lord's death until he comes.

Other apostles passed on to Paul authoritative tradition about the Lord's Supper. This tradition has Jesus's taking the role of a household head or patron who blesses the food and passes it out. The apostle repeats Jesus's words, "This is my body which is for you," and "This cup is the new covenant in my blood" (vv. 24–25), and his commands to partake. Jesus said these things at his final dinner with his disciples before his crucifixion, a first-century Passover meal. Though his disciples did not understand the meaning of Jesus's words and actions then, the symbolism effectively conveys union with Christ. Jesus identifies the bread with his body and the fruit of the vine with his blood and instructs his disciples to eat and drink. They are to "ingest" and "drink" him metaphorically so that he becomes a part of them. The symbolism communicates union between the partakers and that which is partaken, even the body and blood of the Son of God.

Ciampa and Rosner point out corroboration when they assert that Paul's words from 10:16–17 are "expected to inform our understanding of the present text."[8] Drinking and eating this meal in faith is a "participation in the blood of Christ" and a "participation in the body of Christ." As a result, "it is not merely a question of a group of individuals sharing in the redemption found through the breaking of Christ's body, but a group whose identity is formed in light of that in which they all share together—namely the redemption won through Christ's death on our behalf."[9] Consequently, in a nutshell, "The Lord's Supper . . . is designed to help Christians to nurture, deepen and strengthen their relationship or union with Christ, and with one another in him," as J. P. Baker remarks.[10]

Conclusion

Situating union with Christ within the contours of a sacramental theology shaped largely by a study of Paul, I hold to a sacramental theology in which

---

[8] Roy E. Ciampa and Brian S. Rosner, *The First Letter to the Corinthians*, The Pillar New Testament Commentary (Grand Rapids: Eerdmans, 2010), 552.
[9] Ibid.
[10] J. P. Baker, "Union with Christ," in *New Dictionary of Theology*, ed. Sinclair B. Ferguson, David F. Wright, and J. I. Packer, vol. 2 (Downers Grove, IL: InterVarsity, 1988), 698.

God acts, not merely humanity. The parallel between Word and sacraments helps. Baptism and the Lord's Supper are "visible words" that portray the gospel in ceremony. Jesus graciously ministers the gospel to his church via the preached Word and the visible words of baptism and communion.

I understand the Word/sacrament parallel as follows. Because they are two forms of the Word of God, Scripture ascribes saving efficacy to both written Word (2 Tim. 3:15) and sacrament (Acts 2:38; 22:16; 1 Cor. 10:16; 1 Pet. 3:21). But the sacraments do not save in and of themselves any more than the Word does. People are saved not by merely hearing the Word but by putting their faith in the Christ who comes to them in preaching (Rom. 10:17). Similarly, neither being baptized nor receiving the Lord's Supper automatically saves. But when someone believes the gospel, whether communicated through preaching or through the ordinances, he is saved. For example, people have believed in Christ for salvation as they have observed the Supper with the words of institution, for there "the Lord's death" is proclaimed (1 Cor. 11:26).

God works through both Word and ordinances. However, the Word is necessary for salvation, while the ordinances are not (1:14–17). Even as our response to the preached Word is important, so is our response to the gospel in the ordinances. Baptized persons who walk away from the faith are not saved; they bring condemnation on themselves. Persons who take Communion and reject its message reap judgment (11:27–32).

Who is the main worker in preaching and administering the ordinances? Any evangelical preacher would affirm that he is merely a spokesman for God, who is the main Preacher working through him (2 Cor. 5:20). Anyone who does not believe that should stop preaching. God also is the main Minister of the sacraments. It is not the human being who baptizes or serves the Lord's Supper who gives grace. It is God who works through the visible word in baptism and the Supper to make promises to his people, to which they must respond.

God makes a promise in the visible words of the Lord's Supper and fulfills his promise when it is met with faith. The mere performance of the sacramental act does not save. I thus reject both Roman Catholic and Lutheran understandings of the Eucharist. It is a mistake to focus on the bread and wine. Instead, the focus belongs on Christ, who loved us and gave himself for us. He grants grace from heaven through the Holy Spirit. The Spirit is the nexus between the ascended, seated Christ and faithful partakers. The Spirit truly and spiritually, but not physically, conveys the benefits of Christ's atonement to believing participants. The Supper is thus a Christ-ordained means by which he gives grace to believing partakers.

Ferguson elaborates:

> The role of the Spirit is so vital in the Supper. Only by understanding his work can we avoid falling into the mistakes which have dogged both Catholic (*ex opere operato*) and evangelical (memorialist) misunderstandings of the Supper. It is not by the church's administration, or merely by the activity of our memories, but through the Spirit that we enjoy communion with Christ, crucified, risen, and now exalted. For Christ is not localized in the bread and wine (the Catholic view), nor is he absent from the Supper as though our highest activity were remembering him (the memorialist view). Rather, he is known through the elements, *by the Spirit*. There is a genuine *communion* with Christ in the Supper. Just as in the preaching of the Word he is present not in the Bible (locally), or by believing, but by the ministry of the Spirit, so he is also present, in the Supper, not *in* the bread and wine but by the power of the Spirit. The body and blood of Christ are not enclosed in the elements, since he is at the right hand of the Father (Acts 3:21); but by the power of the Spirit we are brought into his presence and he stands among us.[11]

I conclude this chapter as I began it, by affirming that baptism and the Lord's Supper hold their most basic, comprehensive, and profound meaning in common—union with Christ. This raises a problem. If both baptism and the Supper signify union with Christ, what is the difference between them? Is Communion merely a repetition of baptism? The answer to these questions lies in distinguishing initial union with Christ, signified in baptism, from ongoing union with Christ, signified in Communion.

This prompts more questions. Is our initial union with Christ insufficient and in need of augmenting? What does the Supper do that baptism does not? The answers here lie in understanding that our once-for-all-time union with Christ signified in baptism is strengthened and invigorated by partaking of the Lord's Supper in faith. We understand this better if we compare it to forgiveness. We receive forgiveness from Christ once-and-for-all at conversion, yet receive daily forgiveness from him as we confess our sins.

An illustration from marriage helps. We are married permanently (no divorce is permitted in this illustration!). We do not get married again as we

---

[11] Sinclair B. Ferguson, *The Holy Spirit*, Contours of Christian Theology (Downers Grove, IL: InterVarsity, 1996), 201, emphasis original.

love our spouses and fellowship with them over the years. Our wedding day is not the end but the beginning of a lifelong relationship that grows as we communicate and walk together. It is the same in our spiritual lives. God joins us to his Son once and for all when we trust Christ as he is offered in the gospel. But our relationship with him grows as we love him, walk with him, and do his will. Mathison, summarizing Calvin's view, is succinct:

> The sacrament of baptism is connected with the believer's initial union with Christ. The sacrament of the Lord's Supper is connected with the believer's ongoing union with Christ. In the Lord's Supper, the believer is nourished and sustained, and his communion and union with Christ is strengthened and increased.[12]

---

[12] Mathison, *Given for You*, 275–76.

Chapter 28

Union with Christ in
the Christian Life

Union with Christ is a central New Testament description of Christian
identity, the life of salvation in Christ. It entails the giving of a new identity such that in Christ, forgiveness and new life are received through the
Spirit. Union with Christ involves abiding in Christ the Vine. It means
that through the Spirit, sinners are adopted in the household of God as co-
heirs with Christ. It means that God's Spirit is poured out to make the life
and teaching of Jesus real to us. It implicates our worship, our vocation in
the world, and our witness as the church. Union with Christ is theological
shorthand for the gospel itself—a key image that pulls together numerous
motifs in the biblical witness.[1]

J. Todd Billings is correct in the statement above: union with Christ is all this
and more. Having studied the biblical witness from the Old Testament to
Revelation, and having summarized the theology of union, we now focus on
the practical outworking of Scripture and theology. How should union with
Christ affect our Christian lives? This is a huge question, to which I will offer
many answers. But even before I attempt this, it is important to define union
briefly.

Why have I waited until the final chapter of the book to define its very
subject? The answer is that I wanted to treat union in Scripture and theol-

---

[1] J. Todd Billings, *Union with Christ: Reframing Theology and Ministry for the Church* (Grand Rapids: Baker Academic, 2011), 1.

ogy before trying to capture its meaning. On the basis of scriptural teaching and theological reflection, I now attempt to define union with Christ. I say "attempt" because it turns out the concept is elusive. This admission of our limitations should not discourage us, because union is mysterious.

Defining Union with Christ

It is for good reason that the most common name for union with Christ over the history of its investigation is "mystical union." "Mystical" is open to misunderstanding. It does not mean that union concerns mystical experience indifferent to reason. Rather, as Gaffin summarizes:

> Union with Christ is a mystery in the New Testament sense of what has been hidden with God in his eternal purposes but now, finally, has been revealed in Christ, particularly in his death and resurrection, and is appropriated by faith (Rom. 16:25–26; Col. 1:26–27; 2:2). Certainly, in its full dimensions this mystery is beyond the believer's comprehension (Eph. 3:18–19; cf. 1 Cor. 2:9).[2]

We are unable to plumb the depths of the mystery that is union with Christ because they are beyond our ability to understand. Nevertheless, we know much about union because Scripture says much about it. Having been chastened, we seek to summarize union before devoting our energies to applying it.

Various categories have been employed to define union with Christ. Once more I express gratitude for Campbell's *Paul and Union with Christ*, this time for the rubric he uses to summarize union in Paul. He rightly states that any one definition for union is inadequate because union is so expansive. He proposes instead four concepts to summarize Paul's teaching on union:

> *Union* gathers up faith union in Christ, mutual indwelling, Trinitarian, and nuptial notions. *Participation* conveys partaking in the events of Christ's narrative. *Identification* refers to believers' location in the realm of Christ and their allegiance to his lordship. *Incorporation* encapsulates the corporate dimensions of membership in Christ's body.[3]

---

[2] Richard B. Gaffin Jr., "Union with Christ: Some Biblical and Theological Reflections," in *Always Reforming: Explorations in Systematic Theology*, ed. A. T. B. McGowan (Downers Grove, IL: IVP Academic, 2006), 273.
[3] Constantine R. Campbell, *Paul and Union with Christ: An Exegetical and Theological Study* (Grand Rapids: Zondervan, 2012), 413–14, emphasis original.

Viewed from another angle, union is even broader. Systematic categories, based on the text of Scripture, are also helpful.[4] Ephesians 1 uses "in Christ" language to depict election, Christ's cross, the application of salvation (faith union), and final salvation for the church and cosmos!

- Election: "... even as he chose us *in him* before the foundation of the world" (v. 4).
- Christ's cross: "*In him* we have redemption through his blood, the forgiveness of our trespasses" (v. 7).
- The application of salvation: "Blessed be the God and Father of our Lord Jesus Christ, who has blessed us *in Christ* with every spiritual blessing in the heavenly places" (v. 3). "... to the praise of his glorious grace, with which he has blessed us *in the Beloved*" (v. 6).
- Final salvation for the church: "*In him* you also, when you heard the word of truth, the gospel of your salvation, and believed in him, were sealed with the promised Holy Spirit, who is the guarantee of our inheritance until we acquire possession of it" (vv. 13–14).
- Final salvation for the cosmos: "... making known to us the mystery of his will, according to his purpose, which he set forth *in Christ* as a plan for the fullness of time, to unite all things *in him*, things in heaven and things on earth" (vv. 9–10).

We might label these election in Christ, the cross in Christ, the application of salvation in Christ, and final salvation (of church and cosmos) in Christ. In this broad sense, then, union with Christ encompasses everything from election in eternity past to resurrection in the new heavens and new earth in eternity future. Gaffin's words are apt: "For those who are 'in Christ,' this union or solidarity is all-encompassing, extending in fact from eternity to eternity, from what is true of them 'before the creation of the world' (Eph. 1:4, 9) to their still future glorification (Rom. 8:17; 1 Cor. 15:22)."[5] I thus agree with Murray:

Union with Christ is the central truth of the whole doctrine of salvation. All to which the people of God have been predestined in the eternal election of God, all that has been secured and procured for them in the once-for-all accomplishment of redemption, all of which they become actual

---

[4] I acknowledge a debt to John Murray, *Redemption Accomplished and Applied* (Grand Rapids: Eerdmans, 1955), 162–64, and Richard B. Gaffin Jr., *By Faith, Not by Sight: Paul and the Order of Salvation*, 2nd ed. (Phillipsburg, NJ: P&R, 2013), 41–42.

[5] Gaffin, *By Faith, Not by Sight*, 41–42.

partakers in the application of salvation, and all that by God's grace they will become in the state of consummated bliss is embraced within the compass of union and communion with Christ.[6]

Nonetheless, in a special sense union with Christ refers particularly to the application of salvation. We can call this aspect faith union, the union with Christ that follows faith in him for salvation. Hoekema calls it "actual" union: "Actual union with Christ can only take place with actual people."[7] Previously I demonstrated that the various aspects of the application of salvation take place "in Christ"; here I will repeat only the conclusion: "Different ways of talking about salvation applied to sinners include regeneration, justification, adoption, sanctification, preservation, and glorification. Each of these aspects of the application of salvation takes place in union with Christ, and each is the work of the Holy Spirit."[8]

How are we to construe the relationship between faith union with Christ and the aspects of the application of salvation? Some, including Gaffin, regard faith union as the larger set of which the elements of the application of salvation are subsets: "This [union with Christ] . . . is the central truth of salvation for Paul, the key soteriological reality comprising all others."[9] On the other hand, Campbell opts for the metaphor of a web to describe the place of faith union in Paul's thought: "The metaphor of a web helpfully accounts for the structure of Paul's thought, and union is the webbing that holds it all together. It is not the centre of his thought, though possibly should be regarded as a key to rediscover the richness and vitality of Paul's theology."[10]

I think Gaffin and Campbell both are correct. Because the other elements of the application of salvation take place "in Christ," in union with him, union is properly regarded as the most comprehensive way to sum up the application of salvation. But Campbell makes a good point. Union also acts as webbing, or we might say glue, that connects many other features of Paul's thought. Union, then, is both embracive and connective; it is both all-encompassing and linking.

[6] Murray, *Redemption Accomplished and Applied*, 170.
[7] Anthony A. Hoekema, *Saved by Grace* (Grand Rapids: Eerdmans, 1989), 55n4.
[8] See "The Most Important Work of the Holy Spirit," p. 347.
[9] Gaffin, *By Faith, Not by Sight*, 41.
[10] Campbell, *Paul and Union with Christ*, 442.

Union with Christ and the Christian Life

When Paul thinks of salvation, he thinks of faith union with Christ. Another way of demonstrating this is to examine the twelve passages where Paul says that salvation is "in Christ" or that "in him we have" salvation. Only once does he actually use the word "salvation." In the other passages he uses synonyms for the idea of salvation.

> . . . are justified by his grace as a gift, through *the redemption that is in Christ Jesus*. (Rom. 3:24)

> The wages of sin is death, but the free gift of God is *eternal life in Christ Jesus our Lord*. (6:23)

> To the church of God that is in Corinth, to those *sanctified in Christ Jesus* . . . (1 Cor. 1:2)

> *In Christ God was reconciling the world to himself*, not counting their trespasses against them, and entrusting to us the message of reconciliation. (2 Cor. 5:19)

> Because of false brothers secretly brought in—who slipped in to spy out *our freedom that we have in Christ Jesus*, so that they might bring us into slavery . . . (Gal. 2:4)

> . . . that *in Christ Jesus the blessing of Abraham* might come to the Gentiles, so that we might receive the promised Spirit through faith. (3:14)

> Blessed be the God and Father of our Lord Jesus Christ, who *has blessed us in Christ with every spiritual blessing in the heavenly places*. (Eph. 1:3)

> *In him we have redemption* through his blood, the forgiveness of our trespasses, according to the riches of his grace. (1:7)

> *In him we have obtained an inheritance*, having been predestined according to the purpose of him who works all things according to the counsel of his will. (1:11)

> Be kind to one another, tenderhearted, forgiving one another, *as God in Christ forgave you*. (4:32)

> Paul, an apostle of Christ Jesus by the will of God according to the promise of *the life that is in Christ Jesus*. (2 Tim. 1:1)

> I endure everything for the sake of the elect, that they also may obtain *the salvation that is in Christ Jesus* with eternal glory. (2:10)

In these texts Paul refers to our deliverance from sin as blessing (twice), eternal life (twice), freedom, forgiveness, inheritance, reconciliation, redemption (twice), salvation, and sanctification. In a variety of contexts and with varied vocabulary he talks about salvation. And etched into his mind is a deep connection between salvation and faith union with Christ. We could categorize the nuance of the "in Christ" language used here as instrumental—it is through Christ's person and work that his people are saved. He is the new covenant Mediator of all the benefits of salvation. The central question of this chapter presents itself: What effect does union with Christ have on the Christian life? This is a big question deserving of answers, and three stand out:

- Union with Christ constitutes Christian identity.
- Union with Christ means belonging to Christ.
- Union with Christ means suffering and glory.

Union with Christ Constitutes Christian Identity

Ridderbos hits the nail squarely on the head: in Scripture, union with Christ

> does not have the sense of a communion that becomes reality only in certain sublime moments, but rather of an abiding reality determinative for the whole of the Christian life, to which appeal can be made at all times, in all sorts of connections, and with respect to the whole church without distinction.[11]

One of the most important consequences of faith union with Christ is that it defines believers. It gives them an identity in relation to Christ.

Believers Are "in Christ"

Simply put, believers are "in Christ." We studied this expression in all of Paul's letters and summarized its significance.[12] Here we reap some fruit. Although "in Christ" language has various shades of meaning, it always communicates a relationship between believers and Christ. And at least eight texts speak of union with Christ in an explicit sense. Therefore, when Paul says people are "in

---

[11] Herman Ridderbos, *Paul: An Outline of His Theology*, trans. John Richard de Witt (Grand Rapids: Eerdmans, 1975), 59.

[12] See pp. 185–95.

Christ," he defines them as those who stand in a saving relationship to Christ. He is their Lord and Savior, and they know him. In fact, union with Christ is so determinative of salvation that Paul describes Christians thus: "Jesus Christ is in you" (2 Cor. 13:5). That is, Christians are people who are "in Christ" and "in whom" he dwells.

Moreover, Scripture describes the saving union between Christ and believers in many important ways. It is brought about *by the Holy Spirit*. This is the Holy Spirit's most important work pertaining to salvation.[13] When we call union with Christ "spiritual," perhaps we should capitalize the word "Spiritual," for this union is initiated, kept, and brought to eschatological fulfillment by the Spirit.

It is *comprehensive*. As we saw above, union involves election before time, sharing in Christ's redemptive events at conversion, and resurrection on the last day. We distinguish these various aspects of union but must not forget they are one. Gaffin wisely cautions us, "These distinctions, it should be not be missed, point not to different unions, but to different aspects or dimensions of a single union."[14]

It is *vital*. Because the Spirit of life brings life, union is vital. The Spirit regenerates the people of God. When we were spiritually dead, devoid of the life of God, he "made us alive together with Christ" (Eph. 2:5). This life is not only initial but ongoing. As we abide in Christ, the living Vine, we experience spiritual life from him.

It is *permanent*. God joins us to Christ once and for all. So, Paul tells the Gentile believers in Ephesus, "In him you also, when you heard the word of truth, the gospel of your salvation, and believed in him, were sealed with the promised Holy Spirit" (Eph. 1:13). "In him" they "were sealed" with the Spirit, and that not just for a time but "for the day of redemption" (4:30). The Spirit is not only seal but "guarantee of our inheritance until we acquire possession of it" (1:14). Believers are thus safe in the grace of God given in union with Christ. We are saved and safe to love God, live for him, and tell others of his matchless grace.

Believers Are Corporately and Individually United to Christ

In addition, faith union with Christ means union with other believers. When people trust Christ for salvation, the Holy Spirit links them spiritually to

---

[13] See chapter 24, "The Most Important Work of the Holy Spirit."
[14] Gaffin, *By Faith, Not by Sight*, 42.

Christ and at the same time links them to all others who are "in him." Union with Christ is thus individual and corporate. Some biblical pictures of union underscore this. When believers as "living stones" are united to Christ the "living stone," they are corporately "built up as a spiritual house" to worship the Trinity (1 Pet. 2:4–5). Paul paints a similar picture, "In him [Christ] you also are being built together into a dwelling place for God by the Spirit" (Eph. 2:22). Joined to Christ the Head of his body, the church, we are joined to all other members of his body as well.

I have separated chapters on the church, its sacraments, and the Christian life because of space considerations. But thematically they belong together. Union with Christ puts us into the church of which Christ is the Head. We belong to the other members of his body and they to us. And we grow as we avail ourselves of God's ordained means of grace: the preaching of the Word, the sacraments, and prayer, all of which pertain to the church as the communal body of Christ. Union with Christ launches us not into a solitary life but into one of community with God's people who also have been joined to Christ by grace through faith union.

Paul takes an even larger view of salvation and teaches that God plans to "unite *all things* in" Christ (Eph. 1:10). Paul, then, views union with Christ in individual, corporate, and cosmic terms, and so should we.

Believers and the Trinity Mutually Indwell One Another

That we are indwelt by and indwell the Trinity is the most overwhelming thing I learned while writing this book. Not only do the Trinitarian persons mutually indwell one another. And not only do the Trinitarian persons indwell believers. But the Trinitarian persons and believers mutually indwell one another! This is taught by John (John 6:56; 14:20; 15:4–5; 17:21) and Paul (1 Thess. 1:1; 2 Thess. 1:1). Of course, we must exercise caution in talking about this. We guard the Holy Trinity by observing the Creator/creature distinction. We do not become gods or part of God. We acknowledge that there is not a beginning to the Trinitarian mutual indwelling; it is eternal. By contrast believers and the Trinity begin to mutually indwell one another at conversion. The Trinity's mutual indwelling is by nature; ours with the persons of the Trinity is entirely by grace through faith in Christ, the supreme covenant Mediator.

Having made those qualifications, I stand in awe that Jesus could speak of present and future believers in him as being "in" the Father and Son (John

17:21). I understand why many Pauline scholars shrink at Paul's declaring that the Thessalonian church is "in God the Father and the Lord Jesus Christ" (1 Thess. 1:1; cf. 2 Thess. 1:1). But I do not shrink from this but, putting it alongside John's testimony, rejoice in such a union between the Holy Trinity and forgiven sinners! Surely this should issue in much praise to God, lives devoted to him who loved us this much, and a desire to fulfill Jesus's missional purpose for saying these things by our involvement in God's world mission (John 17:20–26).

Believers Are Participants in Jesus's Story

Paul teaches that when the Holy Spirit unites believers to Christ, they participate in his story. Because they share in *him*, they are united to him in everything, from his death to his second coming and beyond. His story becomes their story. Certain events of Christ are his alone and not shared: incarnation, sinless life, Pentecost, and intercession. Nevertheless, by grace through faith we share in his death, burial, resurrection, ascension, and session—even his return.

Our identity is so bound up with our union with Christ that it will be fully revealed only when he comes again. This is what Paul means when in two texts he ascribes a kind of "second coming" to believers. In Colossians 3:4 the apostle says that when Christ "appears," we also "will appear with him in glory." And in Romans 8:19 he speaks of believers' "revelation" (my translation). Of course, Jesus's second coming, his "revelation," is the cause of ours! He alone is the Redeemer; we are the redeemed. Nevertheless, our faith union with him so identifies us that there is a sense in which we will return and reign with him. Only then will it be disclosed what beautiful daughters or handsome sons we are, spiritually speaking.

Paul's teaching that we participate in Christ's narrative conveys the message that Jesus's death and resurrection are the only provision for us to overcome sin. This is true of sin's three temporal dimensions: past, present, and future. Our union with Christ's cross and empty tomb *saved* us from sin's *penalty* in justification (Rom. 8:1). As a result, it is useless to try to save ourselves. Only faith in Jesus saves. Our union with Christ's death and resurrection *save* us from sin's *power* in progressive sanctification (6:4). Consequently, self-help programs will not produce real spiritual growth. We not only are saved once and for all by grace through faith; we also live the Christian life the same way. Our union with Christ's death and resurrection *will save* us from sin's *presence* in glorification and final sanctification (5:9–10). This gives great confidence to God's people, for their ultimate salvation depends not on their performance but on Jesus's. It is no wonder such an understanding produces thankful hearts, godly lives, and hands and feet busy for the kingdom of God.

Union with Christ Means Belonging to Christ

Believers Belong to Christ

Faith union with Christ impacts tremendously the Christian life. It not only gives believers a new identity but also entails belonging to Christ. In at least ten passages Paul speaks of believers as belonging to Christ:

> . . . for the sake of his name among all the nations, including you who are called *to belong to Jesus Christ*. (Rom. 1:5–6)

> You also have died to the law through the body of Christ, so that *you may belong to another*, to him who has been raised from the dead. (7:4)

> Anyone who does not have the Spirit of Christ *does not belong to him*. (8:9)

> If we live, we live to the Lord, and if we die, we die to the Lord. So then, whether we live or whether we die, *we are the Lord's*. (14:8)

> Let no one boast in men. For all things are yours, whether Paul or Apollos or Cephas or the world or life or death or the present or the future—all are yours, and *you are Christ's*, and Christ is God's. (1 Cor. 3:21–23)

> If the foot should say, "Because I am not a hand, *I do not belong to the body*," that would not make it any less a part of the body. And if the ear should say, "Because I am not an eye, *I do not belong to the body*," that would not make it any less a part of the body. (12:15–16)

> . . . Christ the firstfruits, then at his coming *those who belong to Christ*. (15:23)

> Look at what is before your eyes. If anyone is confident that he is Christ's, let him remind himself that just as he is Christ's, so also are we. (2 Cor. 10:7)

> *Those who belong to Christ Jesus* have crucified the flesh with its passions and desires. (Gal. 5:24)

> Not that I have already obtained this or am already perfect, but I press on to make it my own, because *Christ Jesus has made me his own*. (Phil. 3:12)

Belonging to Christ is a product of union with Christ. As a result of being spiritually united to the Son of God, we are his and belong to him. Paul teaches that belonging to Christ is necessary for salvation: "Anyone who does not have the Spirit of Christ does not belong to him" (Rom. 8:9). Those who do not have the Spirit are not Christ's, and that in turn indicates that they are not joined to him in salvation. When Paul defends his apostolic ministry, he asserts that he and the other apostles belong to Christ (2 Cor. 10:7); that is, they are Christians.

Richard Longenecker correctly argues that those belonging to Christ are "equivalent to 'those in Christ Jesus'":

> The substantival use of the plural article οἱ ("those") coupled with the possessive genitive phrase τοῦ Χριστοῦ Ἰησοῦ ("of Christ Jesus," or "who belong to Christ Jesus") is equivalent to "those in Christ Jesus," as the parallel use of Χριστοῦ ("of Christ") at [Gal.] 3:29 with ἐν Χριστῷ Ἰησοῦ ("in Christ Jesus") at 3:26 and 28 indicates.[15]

The apostle teaches that effectual calling results in belonging to Jesus (Rom. 1:6). Paul implies that union with Christ in his death means that believers have died to the power of the law (7:4); they are no longer enslaved to its commands. Instead, they obey God's law willingly from hearts overflowing with love toward Christ who saved them. What is the result of our death to the law through union with Christ? We belong to the risen one, who first died for us.

Paul uses belonging as a synonym for "Christians" or "believers": raised from the dead are "Christ the firstfruits, then at his coming those who belong to Christ" (1 Cor. 15:23). The apostle describes this belonging: "Those who belong to Christ Jesus have crucified the flesh with its passions and desires" (Gal. 5:24). That is, faith union with Christ in his crucifixion necessarily involves belonging to Christ. You cannot have one without the other. Union means belonging, and belonging means union.

Christ who died and arose for us claims us as his own and lays claim to our lives. Belonging to Christ our Lord, then, is all-encompassing; it includes our life and death. We are his and therefore should live for him and other believers and not selfishly for ourselves (Rom. 14:7–8). Paul strives to attain to the resurrection of the dead. He presses on to make it his own "because Christ Jesus has made" Paul "his own" (Phil. 3:12).

---

[15] Richard N. Longenecker, *Galatians*, Word Biblical Commentary (Nashville: Thomas Nelson, 1990), 264.

Furthermore, union and its corollary, belonging to him, rule out dividing into factions that pit Christian against Christian. Such foolish behavior reflects a forgetting of our identity in Christ. We are his, and therefore everything belongs to us (1 Cor. 3:21–23).

As a result of our belonging to Jesus the Head of the body, the church, we belong to all those who also belong to Jesus as members of his body. This is the point of Paul's words about the foot thinking it does not belong to the human body because it is not a hand, or the ear thinking it does not belong to the body because it is not an eye (1 Cor. 12:15–16). Nonsense! Every member of the human body belongs to the body! And "so it is with Christ" (v. 12). All who have been united to Christ belong to him and to all others who belong to him. Again, we see that union is a principle of personal *and* shared salvation.

Believers Fellowship with Christ

As a result of the fact that union with Christ involves belonging to him, Christians have fellowship with Christ. Said differently, union with Christ brings communion with Christ. Before he begins his extensive criticism of the Corinthian church, Paul has encouraging words for them. After reminding them of God's spiritual gifts to them and of their security in Christ, he points to the wonderful outworking of God's faithfulness toward them. "God is faithful, by whom you were called into the fellowship of his Son, Jesus Christ our Lord" (1 Cor. 1:9). Salvation is not only an initial transaction; it is an ongoing relationship with God. Here effectual calling, God's successful summoning of his people to himself in the gospel, issues in fellowship with Christ. Viewed from this angle, the Christian life is a life of fellowship with Christ.

John says much the same thing. He testifies to having sensory knowledge of the fact that "Jesus Christ has come in the flesh" (1 John 4:2; cf. 1:1–3). Why? So that his readers may have fellowship with him and others who know Christ (1:3). Listen how he describes this fellowship: "Our fellowship is with the Father and with his Son, Jesus Christ" (v. 3). Because of the incarnation and atonement of the Son of God, anyone who "abides in him" has fellowship with him (1:3; 3:6). Abiding in Christ means continuing in a warm, ongoing attachment to him. It means continuing in his love by loving him who first loved us (John 15:9). And, of course, it involves having fellowship with and loving others united to Christ (1 John 1:3; 3:17–18; 4:7–8). R. Tudur Jones reminds us of this when he sums up the Puritans' view: "The presupposition of communion with God and with other Christians is union with Christ."[16]

Paul highlights believers' fellowship with Christ when he paints the beautiful metaphor of the church as Christ's beloved bride. This is the apostle's most intimate portrait of union with Christ: that of marriage and sexual union between husband and wife (1 Cor. 6:16). Believers are spiritually united to Christ in marriage: "He who is joined to the Lord becomes one spirit with him" (1 Cor. 6:17). God's grace abounds in the marriage metaphor. Christ prepares the marriage, takes the initiative, and sustains the relationship. His bride, the church, is the object of his affection from beginning to end. Christ loves his bride and gives himself up for her (Eph. 5:25). He cherishes her, lavishes attention upon her, and meets her every need (v. 29). All of this brings to light Christ's delightful grace shown to his bride. What can the church do in return but love and obey her loving, faithful Husband?

Believers Are Indwelt by the Holy Spirit

Belonging to Christ and having fellowship with him are inseparable from another key Pauline theme—that of indwelling. In at least sixteen texts Paul teaches that the Trinity makes his home in and with God's people as individuals and as the church. Paul usually ascribes indwelling to the Spirit, but does so six times to the Son (Rom. 8:10; 2 Cor. 13:5; Gal. 2:20; Eph. 3:17; Col. 1:27; 3:11), and twice to the Father (2 Cor. 6:16; Eph. 2:22). Christians, then, are indwelt by the Father, Son, and Holy Spirit.

Being united to Christ means being indwelt by the Holy Trinity! It is the indwelling of a holy God that makes a saint a saint (1 Cor. 6:19) and the church the church (Eph. 2:22). Marvelously, he dwells within every believer individually and dwells within believers corporately as they gather to worship him.

Scripture itself applies this truth in many helpful ways. Our hope for final salvation is secure, for "hope does not put us to shame, because God's love has been poured into our hearts through the Holy Spirit who has been given to us" (Rom. 5:5). All who have been joined to Christ will be raised unto eternal life, for "if the Spirit of him who raised Jesus from the dead dwells in you, he who raised Christ Jesus from the dead will also give life to your mortal bodies through his Spirit who dwells in you" (8:11).

God's people ought to pursue holiness with all their might, for, Paul says, "You are God's temple and . . . God's Spirit dwells in you" (1 Cor. 3:16). Particu-

---

[16] R. Tudur Jones, "Union with Christ: The Existential Nerve of Puritan Piety," *Tyndale Bulletin* 41 (1990): 187.

larly, we ought to cultivate sexual purity: "Do you not know your body is a temple of the Holy Spirit within you, whom you have from God? You are not your own, for you were bought with a price. So glorify God in your body" (6:19–20).

We need never doubt God's love for us, for "God has sent the Spirit of his Son into our hearts, crying, 'Abba! Father!'" (Gal. 4:6). And we need never doubt God's empowering presence, for Paul commands Timothy, "By the Holy Spirit who dwells within us, guard the good deposit entrusted to you" (2 Tim. 1:14).

Union with Christ Means Suffering and Glory

Faith union with Christ gives believers a new identity. From now on we are "in Christ." Union with Christ means we belong to him. He is ours and we are his. In addition, union with Christ means present suffering and future glory for all the children of God.

The Spirit of Christ within the Old Testament prophets "predicted the sufferings of Christ and the subsequent glories" (1 Pet. 1:11). Those predictions are fulfilled in Jesus's earthly life and crucifixion, and in his resurrection and return to the Father, respectively. We await the full revelation of his glory at his second coming. His people will also experience suffering and glory, especially suffering now and glory at his return. Why should this come as no surprise? Because our sharing Jesus's suffering and glory is a result of union with him. Even as we are joined to his death and suffering, we shall be joined to his resurrection and glory. Paul says as much: "The Spirit himself bears witness with our spirit that we are children of God, and if children, then heirs—heirs of God and fellow heirs with Christ, provided we suffer with him in order that we may also be glorified with him" (Rom. 8:16–17). Varying the emphasis in verse 17 helps us coax out three truths, with which we will end this chapter:

- Believers share in Christ's sufferings: ". . . provided *we suffer with him* in order that we may also be glorified with him."
- Believers persevere: ". . . *provided* we suffer with him *in order that* we may also be glorified with him."
- Believers will share in Christ's glory: ". . . provided we suffer with him in order that *we may also be glorified with him*."

Believers Share in Christ's Sufferings

Peter says two things that are not true of every believer: "I exhort the elders among you, as a fellow elder and a witness of the sufferings of Christ, as well as a partaker in the glory that is going to be revealed" (1 Pet. 5:1). None of us are witnesses of Jesus's crucifixion, as Peter was. And few of us are elders in the church, as Peter was. But all believers partake of Jesus's suffering and glory, for that is part and parcel of union with him in his death and resurrection.

Peter did not hide the fact that believers are called to suffering: "Resist him [Satan], firm in your faith, knowing that the same kinds of suffering are being experienced by your brotherhood throughout the world" (v. 9). The apostle follows these sobering words with very encouraging ones: "And after you have suffered a little while, the God of all grace, who has called you to his eternal glory in Christ, will himself restore, confirm, strengthen, and establish you" (v. 10). If God's people cling to him in faith, resist the Devil, and do God's will regardless of the present outcome, he will make them strong in the faith. And he will eventually bring them to "his eternal glory in Christ"—a bright prospect indeed!

Paul too contrasts Christians' present suffering with their future glory in Christ: "I consider that the sufferings of this present time are not worth comparing with the glory that is to be revealed to us" (Rom. 8:18). In another place he makes the same contrast and combines it with a contrast between the temporal and the eternal: "This light momentary affliction is preparing for us an eternal weight of glory beyond all comparison, as we look not to the things that are seen but to the things that are unseen. For the things that are seen are transient, but the things that are unseen are eternal" (2 Cor. 4:17–18).

Again this should not surprise us, for faith union with Christ means participating in Jesus's story. And a key element in that story is his crucifixion. Paul speaks difficult words concerning this:

> We have this treasure in jars of clay, to show that the surpassing power belongs to God and not to us. We are afflicted in every way, but not crushed; perplexed, but not driven to despair; persecuted, but not forsaken; struck down, but not destroyed; always carrying in the body the death of Jesus, so that the life of Jesus may also be manifested in our bodies. For we who live are always being given over to death for Jesus' sake, so that the life of Jesus also may be manifested in our mortal flesh. (2 Cor. 4:7–11)

There is much here for our faith. Paul and the other apostles suffered greatly for the gospel. Their "always carrying in the body the death of Jesus," their "always being given over to death for Jesus' sake," is what union with

Christ in his crucifixion entails. Thankfully, this also entails knowing God's "surpassing power" and giving him the glory, even as he works in us when we suffer. All of this is worthwhile because all who are united to Christ in his death are united to him also in his resurrection. That is why Paul says that even now he and the other apostles suffer "so that the life of Jesus may also be manifested in our bodies," and they risk death "so that the life of Jesus also may be manifested in our mortal flesh."

The fact that union with Christ in his death involves suffering for his people is axiomatic for Paul, so much so that he quotes it as part of a confession the church makes in worship:

The saying is trustworthy, for:

> If we have died with him, we will also live with him;
> if we endure, we will also reign with him. (2 Tim. 2:11–12)

The same fact also means a great deal to Paul personally, for it is a part of his life's goal, he says, "that I may know him and the power of his resurrection, and may share his sufferings, becoming like him in his death" (Phil. 3:10).

God strengthens his people when they suffer for Christ. And great reward lies ahead for all who will reign with him. But they must persevere to obtain the prize.

Believers Persevere

The writer to the Hebrews underlines the importance of his readers' (and all professed believers') continuing in their faith to the end:

We are his house if indeed we hold fast our confidence and our boasting in our hope. (3:6)

Since then we have a great high priest who has passed through the heavens, Jesus, the Son of God, let us hold fast our confession. (4:14)

We desire each one of you to show the same earnestness to have the full assurance of hope until the end, so that you may not be sluggish, but imitators of those who through faith and patience inherit the promises. (6:11–12)

You have need of endurance, so that when you have done the will of God you may receive what is promised. (10:36)

Therefore, since we are surrounded by so great a cloud of witnesses, let us also lay aside every weight, and sin which clings so closely, and let us run with endurance the race that is set before us. (12:1)

The writer to the Hebrews specifically correlates perseverance in faith and faith union with Christ: "We have come to share in Christ, if indeed we hold our original confidence firm to the end" (3:14). This saying is imbedded in a context of warning. Using Psalm 95, the author alerts his readers not to emulate the Israelites in the wilderness, who hardened their hearts, rebelled against the Lord, put him to the test, and went astray (Heb. 3:7–11). Next he applies the warning, "Take care, brothers, lest there be in any of you an evil, unbelieving heart, leading you to fall away from the living God" (v. 12). He urges readers to self-examination. His words—"lest there be in *any of you*"—show his concern for each person. They must beware lest they, professed Jewish Christians, imitate their ancestors. They must guard their hearts from sin and unbelief and not commit apostasy.

The corrective the writer offers to guard his readers from rebellion is mutual exhortation: "But exhort one another every day, as long as it is called 'today,' that none of you may be hardened by the deceitfulness of sin" (v. 13). Alone, each one is more prone to wander; mutual accountability fortifies them. Such encouragement safeguards professed believers from turning away from the living God.

In this context the writer teaches that we share in Christ's person and work: "We have come to share in Christ, if indeed we hold our original confidence firm to the end" (v. 14). As Hughes says, "Participation . . . in an inclusive and radical sense seems to be intended here."[17] That inclusive and radical sense means we partake of the Son of God and his saving benefits. This overlaps Paul's conception of believers' being "in Christ."[18]

The writer to the Hebrews, therefore, after warning and encouraging his readers, urges them and us to partake of the person of Christ and his saving benefits by persevering to the end in faith. Authentic union with Christ involves more than a profession of faith; it entails endurance, even in the difficult circumstances of the original audience of Hebrews. And true saving faith, which according to Hebrews perseveres to the end, joins believers to Christ so that they "come to share in" him.

---

[17] Philip E. Hughes, *A Commentary on the Epistle to the Hebrews* (Grand Rapids: Eerdmans, 1977), 150.
[18] Peter T. O'Brien, *The Letter to the Hebrews*, The Pillar New Testament Commentary (Grand Rapids: Eerdmans, 2010), 150.

This truth plays an important role in Hebrews and should do the same for us today. The original readers needed encouragement to persevere in trying circumstances. The writer provides this encouragement at key places, even in the midst of strong warnings (see 6:9 and 10:39). Hebrews 3:14 also provides significant encouragement. To those considering dropping out of the race because of temptations and sin's hardening effects, the writer gives this admonition: "We have come to share in Christ, if indeed we hold our original confidence firm to the end." Christ's church around the world needs to hear these same words today.

Peter also exhorts believers to persevere amid difficulties:

> Even if you should suffer for righteousness' sake, you will be blessed. Have no fear of them, nor be troubled, but in your hearts honor Christ the Lord as holy, always being prepared to make a defense to anyone who asks you for a reason for the hope that is in you; yet do it with gentleness and respect, having a good conscience, so that, when you are slandered, those who revile your good behavior in Christ may be put to shame. (1 Pet. 3:14–16)

Peter urges Christians to continue in faith and godliness, even when falsely accused of evil. They must be ready to share their faith gently and respectfully with inquirers (3:15). In addition, they are to live admirable lives before those who do not know the Lord so that, says Peter, "those who revile your good behavior in Christ may be put to shame" (v. 16). Their "good behavior in Christ" speaks of holy conduct that stems from their union with Christ. Peter's use of "in Christ" language implies where the power for this God-honoring living comes from—the living Christ, residing within his people.

In his second epistle Peter also promotes perseverance, desiring that his readers, through God's "precious and very great promises, . . . become partakers of the divine nature" (2 Pet. 1:4). We must not misconstrue Peter's words. They do not blur the distinction between Creator and creature. Peter does not mean that we become God or a part of God. Instead, to "become partakers of the divine nature" speaks of believers' sharing in God's moral "excellence" (v. 3). Peter's next words corroborate this understanding, for they tell of "having escaped from the corruption that is in the world because of sinful desire" (v. 4). Participating in God's nature means escaping from the world's corruption. God wills for his people to share in Christ's moral qualities. Although these moral qualities will be perfected only at Christ's return, already through the indwelling Spirit believers bear a moral resemblance to God to a degree.

Union with Christ in his death involves suffering in the Christian life. This necessarily involves perseverance if we are to make it to the end.[19] It is eminently worth it, for the end is glorious indeed.

Believers Will Share in Christ's Glory

All who sincerely trust Christ as Lord and Savior are united to him in salvation. Along with other blessings, they are joined to him in his death and resurrection. This involves, as surely as we were crucified with him, sharing in his sufferings now, as we have seen. It also involves, as surely as we were raised with him, sharing in his glory when he returns, as we will now see in the writings of Paul, Peter, and John.

We will briefly revisit a few texts we have already examined. Paul promises future glory for those who suffer with Christ now: believers are God's children, and "if children, then heirs—heirs of God and fellow heirs with Christ, provided we suffer with him in order that we may also be glorified with him" (Rom. 8:17). This involves "life after death" and more, even the "glory of the final consummation," as Cranfield asserts.[20]

Peter does the same near the end of his first epistle: "After you have suffered... God... who has called you to his eternal glory in Christ, will himself restore, confirm, strengthen, and establish you" (1 Pet. 5:10). Christ suffered before entering into his glory, and Christians follow him. "The God of all grace" will enable suffering believers to persevere to the end, where they will receive "eternal glory" in the resurrection. God has called overcomers "to his eternal glory *in Christ*" (v. 10). Best is pithy when he says, "It is only because of God's activity in and through Christ that they can be called to be members of his people and eventually participate in his glory."[21]

John rejoices in the triumph of those who have Christ in them: "Little children, you are from God and have overcome them, for he who is in you is greater than he who is in the world" (1 John 4:4). There is spiritual warfare: the "spirit of the antichrist" energizes false prophets to deny the Son's incarnation (vv. 1–3). John's readers are not to fear, however, because their almighty Victor has overpowered their foe. Consequently, John says, "You... have overcome them, for he who is in you is greater than he who is in the world" (v. 4). John's

---

[19] For a defense of the perseverance of the saints and a treatment of Scripture's warning passages, see Robert A. Peterson, *Our Secure Salvation: Preservation and Apostasy*, Explorations in Biblical Theology (Phillipsburg, NJ: P&R, 2009).

[20] C. E. B. Cranfield, *The Epistle to the Romans*, International Critical Commentary (Edinburgh, UK: T&T Clark, 1975), 408.

[21] Ernest Best, *1 Peter*, The New Century Bible Commentary (Grand Rapids: Eerdmans, 1974), 176.

readers are not to trust themselves. Instead, their victory is assured because of Christ's death, resurrection, and indwelling presence. Christ is stronger than Satan and Antichrist and has overcome them. Moreover, this conquering Christ indwells his people, promising them ultimate victory. So Yarbrough says, "His powerful presence guarantees his followers' arrival at the destination to which he beckons them."[22]

The first chapter of the Bible's last book also testifies to the ultimate triumph of God's people in Christ. There John introduces himself as his readers' "brother and partner [συγκοινωνός] in the tribulation and the kingdom and the patient endurance that are *in Jesus*" (Rev. 1:9). At first blush "kingdom" does not seem to fit with "tribulation" and "patient endurance." However, if we note John's reference to union with Christ, it fits well. Ladd regards John's teaching that hardships are experienced "in Jesus" as parallel to Paul's "in Christ," "signifying the believer's spiritual union with his Lord."[23]

We are joined to Christ in his crucifixion and consequently experience trials that require perseverance. We are joined to Christ in his resurrection, which involves membership in his kingdom now and forever. Jesus taught that to be his disciple means cross and crown for Jesus *and* the disciple. Here John demonstrates that he learned Jesus's lesson well. As a result, he refers to himself as one who shares (as a "partner") with all other believers in struggles and victories, both of which are "in Jesus." Swete is succinct: "The whole life of a Christian, whether he suffers or reigns or waits, is in union with the life of the Incarnate Son."[24]

Conclusion

Union with Christ is revealed in Scripture and yet transcends human understanding. It is a general term for the plan of salvation from eternity to eternity (from election to resurrection). It is also a specific term for the application of salvation, because actual union can occur only with actual people. It is both the umbrella over all the aspects of the application of salvation and the glue that holds them together.

The impact of union with Christ on the Christian life is enormous. Union constitutes Christian identity. Believers are "in Christ," intimately related to him in salvation. The faith union between Christ and Christians is brought

[22] Robert W. Yarbrough, *1–3 John*, Baker Exegetical Commentary on the New Testament (Grand Rapids: Baker Academic, 2008), 227.
[23] George E. Ladd, *A Commentary on the Revelation of John* (Grand Rapids: Eerdmans, 1972), 30.
[24] Henry Barclay Swete, *The Apocalypse of St. John* (London: Macmillan, 1911), 12.

about by the Holy Spirit and is comprehensive, vital, and permanent. Believers are corporately and individually joined to Christ. Astonishingly, they and the Father, Son, and Holy Spirit mutually indwell one another. By grace through faith they participate in Jesus's story from his crucifixion to his second coming, and only then will their identity be made fully known.

Union with Christ means belonging to Christ. The Holy Spirit's most important work in salvation is to unite us to Jesus Christ, the Mediator of the new covenant. As a result, he belongs to us and we to him forever. Because we belong to Christ, we have fellowship with him, akin to the intimate fellowship of wife and husband. We are Christ's bride and he loves us dearly. Consequently, we are indwelt by the holy Trinity, especially the Holy Spirit.

Union with Christ means present suffering and future glory. Because we are identified with him in his death, we share in his sufferings. We are saved by grace through faith and persevere in the same way—by grace through faith. God strengthens his people when they suffer, and they endure to the end. Mysteriously, his grace enables their perseverance, and they actively persevere themselves. As a result, authentic believers do not turn away from Christ totally and finally. Instead, they continue in the faith and ultimately will share in the glory of Christ's resurrection. As surely as they suffered with him, they will reign with him on the new earth forever. To God be the glory!

Bibliography

Articles and Essays

Achtemeier, P. Mark. "Union with Christ (Mystical Union)." In *Encyclopedia of the Reformed Faith*, edited by Donald K. McKim and David F. Wright, 379–80. Louisville: Westminster John Knox, 1992.

Baker, J. P. "Union with Christ." In *New Dictionary of Theology*, edited by Sinclair B. Ferguson, David F. Wright, and J. I. Packer, 2:697–99. Downers Grove, IL: InterVarsity, 1988.

Crump, David. "Re-examining the Johannine Trinity: Perichoresis or Deification?" *Scottish Journal of Theology* 59 (2006): 395–412.

Ferguson, Sinclair. "Christus Victor et Propitiator: The Death of Christ, Substitute and Conqueror." In *For the Fame of God's Name: Essays in Honor of John Piper*, edited by Sam Storms and Justin Taylor, 171–89. Wheaton, IL: Crossway, 2010.

Gaffin, Richard B., Jr. "Union with Christ: Some Biblical and Theological Reflections." In *Always Reforming: Explorations in Systematic Theology*, edited by A. T. B. McGowan, 271–88. Downers Grove, IL: IVP Academic, 2006.

Hart, Trevor. "Humankind in Christ and Christ in Humankind: Salvation as Participation in Our Substitute in the Theology of John Calvin." *Scottish Journal of Theology* 42 (1989): 67–84.

Johnson, Dennis E. "Jesus against the Idols: The Use of Isaianic Servant Songs in the Missiology of Acts." *Westminster Theological Journal* 52 (1990): 343–53.

Jones, R. Tudur. "Union with Christ: The Existential Nerve of Puritan Piety." *Tyndale Bulletin* 41 (1990): 186–208.

Liefeld, Walter L. "Theological Motifs in the Transfiguration Narrative." In *New Dimensions in New Testament Study*, edited by Richard N. Longenecker and Merrill C. Tenney, 162–79. Grand Rapids: Zondervan, 1974.

Moessner, David P. "'The Christ Must Suffer': New Light on the Jesus–Peter, Stephen, Paul Parallels in Luke-Acts," *Novum Testamentum* 28 (1986): 220–56.

Rightmire, R. David. "Union with Christ." In *Evangelical Dictionary of Biblical Theology*, edited by Walter A. Elwell, 789–92. Grand Rapids: Baker, 1996.

Seifrid, Mark A. "In Christ." In *Dictionary of Paul and His Letters*, edited by Gerald F. Hawthorne, Ralph P. Martin, and Daniel G. Reid, 433–36. Downers Grove, IL: InterVarsity, 1993.

Tipton, Lane G. "Union with Christ and Justification." In *Justified in Christ: God's Plan for Us in Justification*, edited by K. Scott Oliphint, 23–49. Fearn, Ross-shire, UK: Mentor, 2007.

Commentaries

Achtemeier, Paul J. *1 Peter*. Hermeneia. Minneapolis: Fortress, 1996.

Attridge, Harold W. *A Commentary on the Epistle to the Hebrews*. Hermeneia. Philadelphia: Fortress, 1989.

Baker, William. *1 Corinthians*. Cornerstone Biblical Commentary. Carol Stream, IL: Tyndale House, 2009.

Barnett, Paul. *The Second Epistle to the Corinthians*. The New International Commentary on the New Testament. Grand Rapids: Eerdmans, 1997.

Barrett, C. K. *A Commentary on the First Epistle to the Corinthians*. Harper's New Testament Commentaries. Peabody, MA: Hendrickson, 1993.

———. *The Gospel according to St. John*. 2nd ed. Philadelphia: Westminster, 1978.

Bauckham, Richard J. *Jude, 2 Peter*. Word Biblical Commentary. Waco, TX: Word, 1983.

Beale, G. K. *The Book of Revelation*. New International Greek Testament Commentary. Grand Rapids: Eerdmans, 1999.

Beasley-Murray, George R. *John*. Word Biblical Commentary. Waco, TX: Word, 1987.

———. *Revelation*. The New Century Bible Commentary. Grand Rapids: Eerdmans, 1974.

Best, Ernest. *A Commentary on the First and Second Epistles to the Thessalonians*. Harper's New Testament Commentaries. New York: Harper and Row, 1972.

———. *Ephesians*. International Critical Commentary. Edinburgh, UK: T&T Clark, 2004.

———. *1 Peter*. The New Century Bible Commentary. 1971. Reprint, Grand Rapids: Eerdmans, 1977.

Bock, Darrell L. *Luke 1:1–9:50*. Baker Exegetical Commentary on the New Testament. Grand Rapids: Baker Academic, 1994.

Boxall, Ian. *The Revelation of Saint John*. Black's New Testament Commentary. Peabody, MA: Hendrickson, 2006.

Brown, Raymond E. *The Epistles of John*. Anchor Bible. Garden City, NY: Doubleday, 1982.

———. *The Gospel according to John: I–XII*. Anchor Bible. Garden City, NY: Doubleday, 1966.

———. *The Gospel according to John: XIII–XXI*. Anchor Bible. Garden City, NY: Doubleday, 1970.

Bruce, F. F. *Commentary on the Book of the Acts*. The New International Commentary on the New Testament. Grand Rapids: Eerdmans, 1954.

———. *The Epistles to the Colossians, to Philemon, and to the Ephesians*. The New International Commentary on the New Testament. Grand Rapids: Eerdmans, 1984.

———. *The Epistle to the Galatians*. New International Greek Testament Commentary. Grand Rapids: Eerdmans, 1982.

———. *1 & 2 Thessalonians*. Word Biblical Commentary. Waco, TX: Word, 1982.

Carson, D. A. *The Gospel according to John*. The Pillar New Testament Commentary. Grand Rapids: Eerdmans, 1991.

———. *Matthew*. The Expositor's Bible Commentary. Grand Rapids: Zondervan, 1984.

Ciampa, Roy E., and Brian S. Rosner. *The First Letter to the Corinthians*. The Pillar New Testament Commentary. Grand Rapids: Eerdmans, 2010.

Collins, C. John. *Genesis 1–4: A Linguistic, Literary, and Theological Commentary*. Phillipsburg, NJ: P&R, 2006.

Collins, Raymond F. *First Corinthians*. Sacra Pagina. Collegeville, MN: Liturgical Press, 1999.

Cranfield, C. E. B. *The Epistle to the Romans*. International Critical Commentary. Edinburgh, UK: T&T Clark, 1975.

Davids, Peter H. *The First Epistle of Peter*. The New International Commentary on the New Testament. Grand Rapids: Eerdmans, 1990.

———. *The Letters of 2 Peter and Jude*. The Pillar New Testament Commentary. Grand Rapids: Eerdmans, 2006.

Dodd, C. H. *The Interpretation of the Fourth Gospel*. Cambridge, UK: Cambridge University Press, 1953.

Dunn, James D. G. *Romans 1–8*. Word Biblical Commentary. Dallas: Word, 1988.

Ellingworth, Paul. *The Epistle to the Hebrews*. New International Greek Testament Commentary. Grand Rapids: Eerdmans, 1993.

Fee, Gordon D. *The First and Second Letters to the Thessalonians*. The New International Commentary on the New Testament. Grand Rapids: Eerdmans, 2009.

———. *The First Epistle to the Corinthians*. The New International Commentary on the New Testament. Grand Rapids: Eerdmans, 1987.

Garland, David E. *1 Corinthians*. Baker Exegetical Commentary on the New Testament. Grand Rapids: Baker Academic, 2003.

Green, Gene L. *The Letters to the Thessalonians*. The Pillar New Testament Commentary. Grand Rapids: Eerdmans, 2002.

Grudem, Wayne. *1 Peter*. Tyndale New Testament Commentaries. Grand Rapids: Eerdmans, 1988.

Guthrie, Donald. *The Pastoral Epistles*. Tyndale New Testament Commentaries. 2nd ed. Leicester, UK: Inter-Varsity, 1990.

Harris, Murray J. *The Second Epistle to the Corinthians*. New International Greek Testament Commentary. Grand Rapids: Eerdmans, 2005.

Hawthorne, Gerald F. *Philippians*. Word Biblical Commentary. Waco, TX: Word, 1983.

Hoehner, Harold W. *Ephesians: An Exegetical Commentary*. Grand Rapids: Baker Academic, 2002.

Hughes, Philip E. *The Book of the Revelation*. The Pillar New Testament Commentary. Grand Rapids: Eerdmans, 1990.

———. *A Commentary on the Epistle to the Hebrews*. Grand Rapids: Eerdmans, 1977.

———. *The Second Epistle to the Corinthians*. The New International Commentary on the New Testament. Grand Rapids: Eerdmans, 1962.

Keener, Craig S. *Acts: An Exegetical Commentary*. Grand Rapids: Baker Academic, 2012.

Kelly, J. N. D. *A Commentary on the Epistles of Peter and of Jude*. Black's New Testament Commentary. Grand Rapids: Baker, 1969.

Knight, George W. *The Pastoral Epistles*. New International Greek Testament Commentary. Grand Rapids: Eerdmans, 1992.

Köstenberger, Andreas J. *John*, Baker Exegetical Commentary on the New Testament. Grand Rapids: Baker Academic, 2004.

Ladd, George Eldon. *A Commentary on the Revelation of John*. Grand Rapids: Eerdmans, 1972.

Lane, William L. *Hebrews 9–13*. Word Biblical Commentary. Dallas: Word, 1991.

Lincoln, Andrew T. *Ephesians*. Word Biblical Commentary. Dallas: Word, 1990.

Longenecker, Richard N. *Galatians*. Word Biblical Commentary. Nashville: Thomas Nelson, 1990.

Lucas, Richard C., and Christopher Green. *The Message of 2 Peter and Jude*. The Bible Speaks Today. Leicester, UK: Inter-Varsity, 1995.

Marshall, I. Howard. *The Epistles of John*. The New International Commentary on the New Testament. Grand Rapids: Eerdmans, 1978.

Michaels, J. Ramsey. *1 Peter*. Word Biblical Commentary. Waco, TX: Word, 1988.

Moffatt, James. *A Critical and Exegetical Commentary on the Epistle to the Hebrews*. New York: Scribner's, 1924.

Montefiore, Hugh. *A Commentary on the Epistle to the Hebrews*. Harper's New Testament Commentaries. New York: Harper, 1964.

Moo, Douglas J. *The Epistle to the Romans*. The New International Commentary on the New Testament. Grand Rapids: Eerdmans, 1996.

———. *The Letters to the Colossians and to Philemon*. The Pillar New Testament Commentary. Grand Rapids: Eerdmans, 2008.

———. *2 Peter, Jude*. NIV Application Commentary. Grand Rapids: Zondervan, 1996.

Morris, Leon. *The Epistles of Paul to the Thessalonians*. Tyndale New Testament Commentaries. Rev. ed. Leicester, UK: Inter-Varsity, 1984.

———. *The First and Second Epistles to the Thessalonians*. Rev. ed. The New International Commentary on the New Testament. Grand Rapids: Eerdmans, 1991.

———. *The Gospel according to John*. The New International Commentary on the New Testament. Grand Rapids: Eerdmans, 1971.

Mounce, Robert H. *The Book of Revelation*. The New International Commentary on the New Testament. Grand Rapids: Eerdmans, 1977.

Mounce, William D. *Pastoral Epistles*. Word Biblical Commentary. Nashville: Thomas Nelson, 2000.

O'Brien, Peter T. *Colossians, Philemon*. Word Biblical Commentary. Waco, TX: Word, 1982.

———. *The Letter to the Ephesians*. The Pillar New Testament Commentary. Grand Rapids: Eerdmans, 1999.

———. *The Letter to the Hebrews*. The Pillar New Testament Commentary. Grand Rapids: Eerdmans, 2010.

Peterson, David G. *The Acts of the Apostles*. The Pillar New Testament Commentary. Grand Rapids: Eerdmans, 2009.

Richard, Earl J. *First and Second Thessalonians*. Sacra Pagina. Collegeville, MN: Liturgical Press, 1995.

Schnackenburg, Rudolf. *The Johannine Epistles: A Commentary*. Translated by Reginald and Ilse Fuller. New York: Crossroad, 1992.

Schreiner, Thomas R. *1, 2 Peter, Jude*. New American Commentary. Nashville: Broadman and Holman, 2003.

———. *Galatians*. Zondervan Exegetical Commentary on the New Testament. Grand Rapids: Zondervan, 2010.

———. *Romans*. Baker Exegetical Commentary on the New Testament. Grand Rapids: Baker Academic, 1998.

Shogren, Gary S. *1 & 2 Thessalonians*. Zondervan Exegetical Commentary on the New Testament. Grand Rapids: Zondervan, 2012.

Sidebottom, E. M. *James, Jude, 2 Peter*. The New Century Bible Commentary. Grand Rapids: Eerdmans, 1967.

Sklar, Jay. *Leviticus*. Tyndale Old Testament Commentaries. Downers Grove, IL: IVP Academic, 2013.

Smalley, Stephen S. *1, 2, 3, John*. Word Biblical Commentary. Waco, TX: Word, 1984.

Swete, Henry Barclay. *The Apocalypse of St. John*. 3rd ed. London: Macmillan, 1911.

Thielman, Frank. *Ephesians*. Baker Exegetical Commentary on the New Testament. Grand Rapids: Baker Academic, 2010.

Thiselton, Anthony C. *The First Epistle to the Corinthians*. New International Greek Testament Commentary. Grand Rapids: Eerdmans, 2000.

Towner, Philip H. *The Letters to Timothy and Titus*. The New International Commentary on the New Testament. Grand Rapids: Eerdmans, 2006.

Witherington, Ben. *Conflict and Community in Corinth: A Socio-Rhetorical Commentary on 1 and 2 Corinthians*. Grand Rapids: Eerdmans, 1995.

Yarbrough, Robert W. *1–3 John*. Baker Exegetical Commentary on the New Testament. Grand Rapids: Baker Academic, 2008.

Other Books

Allen, R. Michael. *Justification and the Gospel: Understanding the Contexts and Controversies*. Grand Rapids: Baker Academic, 2013.

Barber, Dan C., and Robert A. Peterson. *Life Everlasting: The Unfolding Story of Heaven*. Explorations in Biblical Theology. Phillipsburg, NJ: P&R, 2012.

Bauckham, Richard J. *Jesus and the God of Israel*. Grand Rapids: Eerdmans, 2008.

Bayer, Hans F. *A Theology of Mark: The Dynamic between Christology and Authentic Discipleship*. Explorations in Biblical Theology. Phillipsburg, NJ: P&R, 2012.

Beilby, James K., and Paul Rhodes Eddy, eds. *Justification: Five Views*. Downers Grove, IL: IVP Academic, 2011.

Billings, J. Todd. *Union with Christ: Reframing Theology and Ministry for the Church*. Grand Rapids: Baker Academic, 2011.

Bird, Michael F. *Evangelical Theology: A Biblical and Systematic Introduction*. Grand Rapids: Zondervan, 2013.

———. *The Saving Righteousness of God: Studies on Paul, Justification and the New Perspective*. Milton Keynes, UK: Paternoster, 2006.

Burger, Hans. *Being in Christ: A Biblical and Systematic Investigation in a Reformed Perspective*. Eugene, OR: Wipf and Stock, 2009.

Calvin, John. *Institutes of the Christian Religion*. Edited by John T. McNeill. Translated by Ford Lewis Battles. 2 vols. Philadelphia: Westminster, 1960.

Campbell, Constantine R. *Paul and Union with Christ: An Exegetical and Theological Study*. Grand Rapids: Zondervan, 2012.

Cullmann, Oscar. *Salvation in History*. Translated by S. G. Sowers. New York: Harper and Row, 1967.

Dunn, James D. G. *The Theology of Paul the Apostle*. Grand Rapids: Eerdmans 1998.

Erickson, Millard J. *Christian Theology*. 2nd ed. Grand Rapids: Baker, 1998.

Evans, William B. *Imputation and Impartation: Union with Christ in American Reformed Theology*. Studies in Christian History and Thought. Eugene, OR: Wipf and Stock, 2009.

Fairbairn, Donald. *Life in the Trinity: An Introduction to Theology with the Help of the Church Fathers*. Downers Grove, IL: IVP Academic, 2008.

Fee, Gordon D. *Pauline Christology: An Exegetical-Theological Study*. Peabody, MA: Hendrickson, 2007.

Ferguson, Sinclair. *The Holy Spirit*. Contours of Christian Theology. Downers Grove, IL: InterVarsity, 1996.

Frame, John M. *The Doctrine of God*. A Theology of Lordship. Phillipsburg, NJ: P&R, 2002.

Gaffin, Richard B., Jr. *By Faith, Not by Sight: Paul and the Order of Salvation*. 2nd ed. Phillipsburg, NJ: P&R, 2013.

———. *Resurrection and Redemption: A Study in Paul's Soteriology*. 2nd ed. Phillipsburg, NJ: P&R, 1987.

Gathercole, Simon J. *The Pre-existent Son: Recovering the Christologies of Matthew, Mark, and Luke*. Grand Rapids: Eerdmans, 2006.

Gifford, James D., Jr. *Perichoretic Salvation: The Believer's Union with Christ as a Third Type of Perichoresis*. Eugene, OR: Wipf and Stock, 2011.

Goulder, M. D. *Type and History in Acts*. London: SPCK, 1964.

Green, Joel B., and Mark D. Baker. *Recovering the Scandal of the Cross: Atonement in the New Testament and Contemporary Contexts*. Downers Grove, IL: InterVarsity, 2000.

Hoekema, Anthony A. *Created in God's Image*. Grand Rapids: Eerdmans, 1986.

———. *Saved by Grace*. Grand Rapids: Eerdmans, 1989.

Horton, Michael S. *Covenant and Salvation: Union with Christ*. Louisville: Westminster John Knox, 2007.

Hughes, Philip E. *The True Image: The Origin and Destiny of Man in Christ*. Grand Rapids: Eerdmans, 1989.

Husbands, Mark, and Daniel J. Trier. *Justification: What's at Stake in the Current Debates?* Downers Grove, IL: InterVarsity, 2004.

Johnson, Dennis E. *The Message of Acts in the History of Redemption.* Phillipsburg, NJ: P&R, 1997.

Johnson, Marcus Peter. *One with Christ: An Evangelical Theology of Salvation.* Wheaton, IL: Crossway, 2013.

Kelly, J. N. D. *Early Christian Doctrines.* Rev. ed. San Francisco: Harper and Row, 1978.

Kim, Seyoon. *The Origin of Paul's Gospel.* Grand Rapids: Eerdmans, 1981.

Köstenberger, Andreas J. *A Theology of John's Gospel and Letters: The Word, the Christ, the Son of God.* Biblical Theology of the New Testament. Grand Rapids: Zondervan, 2009.

Letham, Robert. *Union with Christ: In Scripture, History, and Theology.* Phillipsburg, NJ: P&R, 2011.

Macaskill, Grant. *Union with Christ in the New Testament.* Oxford: Oxford University Press, 2013.

Machen, J. Gresham. *The Origin of Paul's Religion.* New York: Macmillan, 1921.

Macleod, Donald. *The Person of Christ.* Contours of Christian Theology. Downers Grove, IL: InterVarsity, 1998.

McCready, Douglas. *He Came Down from Heaven: The Preexistence of Christ and the Christian Faith.* Downers Grove, IL: InterVarsity, 2005.

Morgan, Christopher W., and Robert A. Peterson, eds. *The Deity of Christ.* Theology in Community. Wheaton, IL: Crossway, 2011.

———, eds. *Faith Comes by Hearing: A Response to Inclusivism.* Downers Grove, IL: InterVarsity, 2008.

———, eds. *Hell under Fire: Modern Scholarship Reinvents Eternal Punishment.* Grand Rapids: Zondervan, 2004.

Morris, Leon. *The Cross in the New Testament.* Grand Rapids: Eerdmans, 1965.

Muller, Richard A. *Dictionary of Latin and Greek Theological Terms: Drawn Principally from Protestant Scholastic Theology.* Grand Rapids: Baker, 1985.

Murray, John. *Redemption Accomplished and Applied.* Grand Rapids: Eerdmans, 1955.

Packer, J. I. *Keep in Step with the Spirit.* Grand Rapids: Revell, 1984.

Peterson, Robert A. *Adopted by God: From Wayward Sinners to Cherished Children.* Phillipsburg, NJ: P&R, 2001.

———. *Calvin and the Atonement*. Fearn, Ross-shire, UK: Mentor, 1999.

———. *Election and Free Will: God's Gracious Choice and Our Responsibility*. Explorations in Biblical Theology. Phillipsburg, NJ: P&R, 2007.

———. *Getting to Know John's Gospel: A Fresh Look at Its Main Ideas*. Phillipsburg, NJ: P&R, 1989.

———. *Our Secure Salvation: Preservation and Apostasy*. Explorations in Biblical Theology. Phillipsburg, NJ: P&R, 2009.

———. *Salvation Accomplished by the Son: The Work of Christ*. Wheaton, IL: Crossway, 2012.

Peterson, Robert A., and Michael D. Williams. *Why I Am Not an Arminian*. Downers Grove, IL: InterVarsity, 2004.

Pinnock, Clark H., ed. *Grace Unlimited*. Minneapolis: Bethany House, 1975.

Piper, John. *Counted Righteous in Christ: Should We Abandon the Imputation of Christ's Righteousness?* Wheaton, IL: Crossway, 2002.

Powers, Daniel G. *Salvation through Participation: An Examination of the Notion of the Believers' Corporate Unity with Christ in Early Christian Soteriology*. Leuven, Belgium: Peeters, 2001.

Quarles, Charles L. *A Theology of Matthew: Jesus Revealed as Deliverer, King, and Incarnate Creator*. Explorations in Biblical Theology. Phillipsburg, NJ: P&R, 2013.

Reymond, Robert L. *A New Systematic Theology of the Christian Faith*. Nashville: Thomas Nelson, 1998.

Ridderbos, Herman. *Paul: An Outline of His Theology*. Translated by John Richard de Witt. Grand Rapids: Eerdmans, 1975.

Schreiner, Thomas R. *New Testament Theology: Magnifying God in Christ*. Grand Rapids: Baker Academic, 2008.

Schweitzer, Albert. *The Mysticism of Paul the Apostle*. London: A & C Black, 1931.

Smedes, Lewis B. *All Things Made New: A Theology of Man's Union with Christ*. Grand Rapids: Eerdmans, 1970. Reprint, Eugene, OR: Wipf and Stock, 1998.

———. *Union with Christ: A Biblical View of the New Life in Jesus Christ*. Rev. ed. Grand Rapids: Eerdmans, 1983.

Starr, J. M. *Sharers in Divine Nature: 2 Peter 1:4 in Its Hellenistic Context*. Coniectanea Biblica New Testament. Stockholm: Almqvist & Wiksell, 2000.

Tiessen, Terrance L. *Who Can Be Saved? Reassessing Salvation in Christ and World Religions*. Downers Grove, IL: InterVarsity, 2004.

Vickers, Brian. *Jesus' Blood* and *Righteousness: Paul's Theology of Imputation.* Wheaton, IL: Crossway, 2006.

Vos, Geerhardus. *The Pauline Eschatology.* Grand Rapids: Eerdmans, 1953.

Wallace, Daniel B. *Greek Grammar beyond the Basics: An Exegetical Syntax of the New Testament.* Grand Rapids: Zondervan, 1996.

Walls, Jerry L., and Joseph R. Dongell. *Why I Am Not a Calvinist.* Downers Grove, IL: InterVarsity, 2004.

Waltke, Bruce K. *Genesis: A Commentary.* Grand Rapids: Zondervan, 2001.

Wells, David F. *The Person of Christ.* Westchester, IL: Crossway, 1984.

Westerholm, Stephen. *Perspectives Old and New on Paul: The "Lutheran" Paul and His Critics.* Grand Rapids: Eerdmans 2004.

Wright, N. T. *Justification: God's Plan and Paul's Vision.* Downers Grove, IL: IVP Academic, 2009.

General Index

abiding, 57, 64, 65–66, 71, 249–52, 253, 254, 257, 259, 260–63, 376–81, 420
Abraham
 blessing of, 27, 122, 413
 as covenant mediator, 26–27, 37
Achtemeier, Paul J., 241, 314–15
Achtemeier, P. Mark, 348
actual union, 278, 365, 366, 372, 412, 428
Adam
 brought death into the world, 105–6
 and Christ, 77
 as covenant mediator, 26
 covenant with, 25
 disobedience of, 26, 282–83, 362
adoption, 83, 122, 123, 127, 198, 292, 332–35, 342, 400
adultery, 116
afflictions, 108–9
age to come, 352
allegorical interpretation, 19
all things, united in Christ, 290–91, 384
already and not yet, 136, 205, 228, 230, 294, 329, 353, 387, 390
antichrist, 250, 255, 260, 427–28
antinomianism, 79
Apelles, 88
apostasy, 65
apostles, 310–11
apostolic tradition, 156
application of salvation, 295, 305, 348, 365, 372, 411, 412
Aquila, 107
Archippus, 165–66
Arminians, 276–77
armor of God, 143, 191, 194–95, 384–85
asceticism, 160–63, 201, 244, 343

assurance, 249
atoning sacrifice, 354
Attridge, Harold, 235
Augustine, 70, 394
Aulén, Gustav, 364–65

Babylon, 266–67, 270, 293
Baker, J. P., 405
Baker, Mark D., 331
Baker, William, 321
baptism, 44–45, 48
 as circumcision, 159, 401
 and Holy Spirit, 321–22
 as incorporation into Christ, 122–23, 333
 instituted by Christ, 395
 Paul on, 400–402
 and union with Christ, 80, 101, 159, 210–11, 222
Barnett, Paul, 93, 112
Barrett, C. K., 91, 107
Bauckham, Richard J., 244–45, 246, 308–9, 351
Bavinck, Herman, 13, 279
Bayer, Hans, 39
Beale, G. K., 268–69, 270
Beasley-Murray, George R., 60, 65, 265, 266, 269, 271
Belleville, Linda, 325
belonging to Jesus Christ, 74, 82, 83, 86, 94, 115, 418–20, 429
Best, Ernest, 239, 241, 243, 247, 427
Billings, J. Todd, 13–14, 409
Bird, Michael, 329, 330
blood of Christ, 128, 132
 in Lord's Supper, 100, 102, 403–5

incarnation, 24, 38, 56, 57, 203, 230, 255,
256, 258, 282, 284–87, 288, 294,
350–51, 359, 361, 386
"in Christ," 41, 185–95
as association, 187, 193, 382
broad and narrow senses of, 186
as caused by person and work of Christ,
187
as Christian, 383
church as, 381–85
and eternal life, 175–76
in 1 John, 259–60, 262
as instrumental, 111, 113, 186–87, 193,
382
in John, 250
and justification, 120–21, 190
as locative for realm of Christ, 149, 176,
188, 193, 265, 266, 383
as manner in which believers do things,
382
Paul on, 73–74, 81, 84, 87
as periphrasis for believers, 119, 145–46,
152, 153, 165, 169, 188
in Peter, 241–43, 247
as relationship between believers and
Christ, 186, 414–15
as salvation, 75, 127, 177, 192
as union with Christ, 128, 269
inclusivism, 370–71
incorporation, 20, 24–29, 32, 36–38, 41,
133–34, 215–16, 410
in rite of baptism, 41, 44–45
indicative and imperative, 252
individualism, 214, 384, 389
indwelling, 68–69, 230–33. *See also* mutual
indwelling
as union with Christ, 75–76, 199
infants in Christ, 92
inheritance, 128–29, 342, 413
"in the Father and the Son," 195–97, 415–16
"in the flesh," 322–23
"in the Lord"
believers' actions as, 148
as locative, 151
as locative to indicate realm or domain,
143
as periphrasis for believers, 144
as under influence, 181
"in the Spirit," 322–23
intimacy, of union with Christ, 220–21, 391

invincible grace, 366–71, 372
irresistible grace, 366
Israel
as God's "son," 28n6
as kingdom of priests, 27
rebellion in the wilderness, 234
as treasured possession, 27

Jesus Christ
ascension of, 131–32, 138, 199, 288, 360,
361, 386
as bridegroom, 35–36, 39, 141, 267
circumcision of, 158–59, 200
conception of, 312–13
crucifixion of, 112
death and resurrection of, 33, 38, 80–81,
118, 183, 197, 205, 359, 361, 386–87
death of, 313–14
deity of, 258, 285, 351–54
earthly ministry of, 313
emotions of, 355–56
exaltation of, 109, 351
as fullness of deity embodied, 157–58,
192, 195, 229–30, 385, 390
as Great High Priest, 351
as Head of church, 130, 141, 142, 154,
160–61, 209–10, 420
humanity of, 285, 354–58
intercession of, 360, 361, 387
as living stone, 238–40, 246, 374
lordship of, 151
love of, 137
made perfect, 356–57
as Mediator, 24, 25, 36–38, 39, 76, 78, 89
mutual abiding with believers in love,
65–66
as object of faith, 188, 365–71, 383
in Old Testament, 19–20
person of, 348–58
power of, 129–30
preexistence of, 349–50
as reconciler, 133
resurrection of, 105, 112, 154, 239, 302,
314–16
return of, 163–64, 170, 202, 203, 204, 293,
360, 361, 384, 387
reveals the Father, 72
as second Adam, 26, 77–78, 105–6, 130,
133, 351, 362

obedience, 66, 73, 249, 254
obligation, and abiding, 261–62, 379–80
O'Brien, Peter T., 128, 130, 131, 132, 142, 155, 159, 210, 212, 216, 225–27, 236, 291, 314, 341, 343–44
O'Donovan, Oliver, 13
Old Testament
 foreshadows union with Christ, 19–32
 predictions of the Spirit, 311–12
 prefigures work of Christ, 54
Onesimus, 180–81
ordinances. *See* sacraments
original sin, 76–77
orphans, 63
Owen, John, 13

pagan worship, 99–100
parents, 165
partakers of the divine nature, 244–46, 248
participation, in the story of Christ, 20, 29–31, 32, 38, 41, 46, 47–48, 147, 163, 192, 194, 197–206, 235–37, 265, 343, 385–87, 410, 417–18
 in baptism, 401
 discipleship as, 39
 in Lord's Supper, 403
Pastoral Epistles, 174–79
Paul
 apostleship of, 99, 116–17
 on baptism, 400–402
 conversion of, 43–44, 48
 on Holy Spirit, 301–8
 on "in Christ," 73–74
 journey to Jerusalem, 46
 as prisoner, 177
 on sacraments, 398–400
 on union with Christ, 15
penal substitution, 122
Pentecost, 30, 31, 41–42, 48, 204, 288–89, 316–18, 360, 361
perichoresis, 14, 55, 59, 61–62, 67, 69, 377
persecution, 48, 169, 179
perseverance, 176–77, 179, 198, 424–28
Persis, 88
Philip, 51, 60–62
Phoebe, 87–88, 382–83
Piper, John, 331
Platonism, 244
pluralism, 370

Powers, Daniel G., 331
prayer, 299
predestination, 127
present age, 352
preservation, 337–41
Priscilla, 107
progressive sanctification, 83, 169, 205, 336, 387, 417
propitiation, 362
prostitution, 95–97, 98, 388
providence, 353
Puritans, 420–21
purity, 116
putting off/putting on, 140, 164
putting on Christ, 86, 122–23, 221–24, 333, 401

Quarles, Charles, 35

reconciliation, 291, 327, 361, 413
re-creation, 362
redemption, 75, 91–92, 98, 128, 190, 361
"refresh my heart," 182
regeneration, 31, 62, 324–26, 368
Reimer, David J., 31n7
rejoicing, 148, 151
rest, 266
resurrection, 105, 106, 118, 171, 197, 198, 202, 292
 power of, 150, 200
 and union with Christ, 177–78
revelation, second coming as, 164, 204, 293, 417
Reymond, Robert L., 330
riches in glory, 152, 155
Ridderbos, Herman, 85, 210, 213, 226, 390, 414
righteousness of Christ, 78, 91, 114, 149, 189, 200, 327
Rightmire, R. David, 384
Roman triumphal march, 111, 160
rooted and built up in Christ, 157
Rosner, Brian S., 90–91, 96, 100, 102, 103, 106, 189, 214, 217, 321, 405

sacraments, 394–400
sacrifice, 362
saints, 89, 126
salvation, 90–92, 353–54, 413

Scripture Index

Also Available from Robert A. Peterson

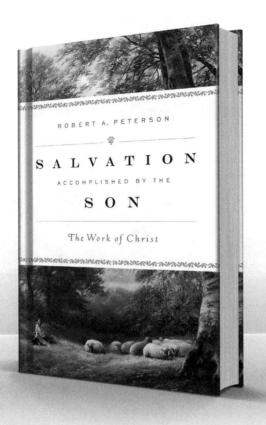

"Peterson conducts a full-orbed tour of christology, particularly highlighting the often neglected role of Christ's resurrection in our salvation. He writes with a pastor's heart, as is evident in the biblical fidelity and remarkable clarity that mark this work."

THOMAS R. SCHREINER, James Buchanan Harrison Professor of New Testament Interpretation, The Southern Baptist Theological Seminary

"A refreshing and insightful study, which is much needed at the present time and deserves to be widely read."

GERALD BRAY, Research Professor of Divinity, Beeson Divinity School, Samford University

"Systematic theology at its very best. This is the book to which, after Scripture itself, I would first turn to explore any question about Jesus's incarnation, atonement, or resurrection."

JOHN M. FRAME, J. D. Trimble Chair of Systematic Theology and Philosophy, Reformed Theological Seminary, Orlando

For more information, visit crossway.org.

THEOLOGY IN COMMUNITY

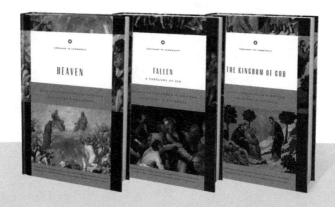

FIRST-RATE EVANGELICAL SCHOLARS
take a multidisciplinary approach
to key Christian doctrines

Edited by CHRISTOPHER W. MORGAN
and ROBERT A. PETERSON

BOOKS IN THIS SERIES INCLUDE:

For more information visit www.crossway.org.